MENTAL CAPACITY ACT 2005

Related titles by Law Society Publishing

Civil Partnership: Law and Practice
Andrea Woelke
1 85328 973 6

Elderly Client Handbook (3rd Edition)
General Editors: Caroline Bielanska and Martin Terrell
Consultant Editor: Gordon R. Ashton
1 85328 872 1

Probate Practitioner's Handbook (4th Edition)
General Editor: Lesley King
1 85328 831 4

Trust Practitioner's Handbook
Gill Steel with contributions by Robert Mowbray and Charles Christian
1 85328 945 0

Will Draftsman's Handbook (8th Edition)
Robin Riddett
1 85328 826 8

Titles from Law Society Publishing can be ordered from all good legal bookshops or direct from our distributors, Marston Book Services (tel. 01235 465656 or email law.society@marston.co.uk). For further information or a catalogue, e-mail our editorial and marketing office at publishing@lawsociety.org.uk.

MENTAL CAPACITY ACT 2005

A Guide to the New Law

Nicola Greaney, Fenella Morris and Beverley Taylor

The Law Society

ISBN 10: 1–85328–903–5

ISBN 13: 978–1–85328–903–3

Published in 2005 by the Law Society
113 Chancery Lane, London WC2A 1PL

Typeset by J&L Composition, Filey, North Yorkshire
Printed by Antony Rowe Ltd, Chippenham, Wiltshire

CONTENTS

Appendices   114

ABBREVIATIONS

ANH	artificial nutrition and hydration
BMA	British Medical Association
DCA	Department for Constitutional Affairs
DoH	Department of Health
DPA 1998	Data Protection Act 1998
ECHR	European Convention on Human Rights
EPA	Enduring Power of Attorney
EPAA 1985	Enduring Power of Attorney Act 1985
HRA 1998	Human Rights Act 1998
IMCA	Independent Mental Capacity Advocate
LPA	Lasting Power of Attorney
MHA 1983	Mental Health Act 1983
PCT	primary care trust
PVS	persistent vegetative state
Scottish Act	Adults with Incapacity (Scotland) Act 2000

FOREWORD

For too long the law relating to mental capacity has been the product of piece-meal and unsystematic development. As the codification of a number of common law principles, together with an extension of certain rights and responsibilities for those unable to make decisions for themselves, the Mental Capacity Act 2005 is a welcome development, long overdue.

While the Act is not unduly long, some of the concepts and principles it introduces to the statute book require a practical explanation. This new guide, broadly set out in the same order as the provisions of the Act, takes those new concepts and principles and provides the analysis required. Appended to the guide is a useful set of resources including the Act itself, its accompanying Explanatory Notes and a copy of the draft Code of Practice (yet to be finalised) which provides extremely helpful guidance, together with examples, for those tasked with caring and making decisions for persons who lack capacity.

As the newly appointed President of the Court of Protection, responsible for resolution of the issues arising under the Act, including matters relating to property, financial affairs and personal welfare, I shall be sure to keep a copy of this guide close at hand and I commend it to the legal profession at large.

Sir Mark Potter
President of the Family Division and Head of Family Justice
October 2005

TABLE OF CASES

TABLE OF STATUTES

TABLE OF SECONDARY AND EUROPEAN LEGISLATION

Statutory Instruments

Treaties and Conventions

Directives

1 INTRODUCTION

1.1 BACKGROUND TO THE MENTAL CAPACITY ACT 2005

The Mental Capacity Act 2005 (the Act) is the culmination of a 15-year-long consultation process. In 1989 the Law Commission started a six-year consultation period on all aspects of mental incapacity. This culminated in 1995 with the publication of its Report and Draft Bill *Mental Incapacity*[1] which set out detailed recommendations for the introduction of comprehensive legislation for making decisions on behalf of people who lack capacity. The Report recognised that:

> . . . in this area, the law as it now stands is unsystematic and full of glaring gaps. It does not rest on clear or modern foundations of principle. It has failed to keep up with social and demographic changes. It has also failed to keep up with developments in our understanding of the rights and needs of those with mental disability.[2]

The government responded in 1997 with a Green Paper, *Who Decides?*[3], seeking views on the Commission's proposals for reform. The government published the Policy Statement *Making Decisions*[4] in 1999. *Making Decisions* confirmed the government's commitment to legislation on issues relating to mental incapacity and set out the areas intended to be covered in future legislation.

The government published a Draft Mental Incapacity Bill in June 2003. The Bill was subject to pre-legislative scrutiny by a Committee of both Houses.[5] The Committee concluded:

> On the whole, we endorse the principles and general direction of the draft Bill . . . We believe that there is a clear need for the Bill and our report, whilst critical, should be read accordingly . . . Those it is intended to help have waited long enough.

It made substantial recommendations for improving the Draft Bill. The government published its response in February 2004 which included a commitment to rename the bill the Mental Capacity Bill, to 'emphasise its focus on enablement'.[6]

The Mental Capacity Bill was published on 17 June 2004. In accordance with the Joint Committee's recommendations the Bill now included a set of key principles to frame the Bill (at 43–4), the removal of the power for deputies to refuse consent to life-sustaining treatment (at 184), clearer safeguards regarding advanced decisions to refuse treatment (at 205–9), provisions on research (at 288–91) with strict safeguards and additional reassurance regarding euthanasia (at 204).

1 Law Com No. 231, 1995.
2 Ibid., p. 1.
3 *Who Decides? Making Decisions on behalf of Mentally Incapacitated Adults*, Cm. 3903, 1997.
4 *Making Decisions*, Cm. 4465, 1999.
5 Report of the Joint Committee on the Draft Mental Incapacity Bill, vol. 1 HL Paper 189–1, HC 1083–1.
6 Parliamentary Under-Secretary of State for Constitutional Affairs, Mr David Lammy MP. House of Commons Hansard Debate, 11 October 2004: col. 22.

1.2 IMPLEMENTATION

The Mental Capacity Bill received Royal Assent in April 2005. The provisions of the Act are to be implemented in April 2007. The Department for Constitutional Affairs (DCA) and the Department of Health (DoH) have in addition to the Draft Code of Practice issued helpful Explanatory Notes relating to the Act (see Appendix 2 of this book). The Notes do not form part of the Act and have not been endorsed by Parliament but are stated to be 'in order to assist the reader in understanding the Act' and are to be 'read in conjunction with the Act'.

The DCA and the DoH have a very strict timetable towards implementation of the Act in April 2007. At the time of writing, the DoH had issued a consultation paper on the Independent Mental Capacity Advocate (IMCA) Service. The consultation period ended on 30 September 2005. Consulting on the design of the Office of the Public Guardian, the Court of Protection and Lasting Powers of Attorney is due to take place towards the end of 2005 with a view to preparing the processes, regulations, forms and training, and updating the Draft Code of Practice, in April 2006.

1.3 AIM AND PURPOSE OF THE ACT

Lord Filkin in a letter to the Joint Committee stated that the aim of the Bill was to:

> maximise the capacity of those who lack or may lack capacity to make certain decisions for themselves, protect vulnerable adults with mental incapacity issues from abuse and neglect, and, provide clarity to families, informal carers and professionals as to when they may act or make decisions themselves.[1]

In order to achieve this aim the Act provides a comprehensive statutory framework for assisting those lacking capacity to make decisions for themselves, wherever possible, and allows for decisions to be taken properly on their behalf and in their best interests when they lack capacity. It rests on well-established common law principles of 'best interests' and the presumption of capacity. The Act seeks to strike a delicate balance between respect for individual autonomy and the need to protect the vulnerable.[2]

The Act will affect a large range of people. It is estimated that over 700,000 people in the UK currently suffer from dementia, and this is projected to rise to around 840,000 by 2010. Around 145,000 adults in England have severe and profound learning disabilities and at least 1.2 million have a mild to moderate disability. In Wales over 12,000 people were registered as having a learning disability in 2001. It is estimated that at some point in their lives approximately 1 per cent of the UK population will suffer from schizophrenia, 1 per cent will be subject to manic depression and 5 per cent will have serious or clinical depression.[3] In addition, many people suffer serious brain injury. Many of these people are likely to lack capacity to make some or all decisions for themselves and decisions will have to be made for them.

The main purpose of the Act is stated to be to:

> clarify and reform obscure common law provisions which govern the ways in which people can and should deal with people who lack decision-making capacity, supplemented by new and reformed statutory schemes for advanced decision making and court-based resolution of disputes or difficulties.[4]

The Act is in three parts. Part 1 sets out a number of key principles, contains provisions defining 'persons who lack capacity', sets out a statutory checklist to be used in ascertaining their best interests and establishes statutory protection for 'acts done in connection with the care or treatment' of persons who lack capacity. Part 1 also establishes a new statutory scheme for powers of attorney which can extend to personal welfare and health care matters and which survive the incapacity of the donor, known as 'lasting powers of attorney' (LPAs). Part 1 sets out the jurisdiction of the new Court of Protection to make declarations, orders and directions in relation to persons who lack capacity, and provides that the court may also appoint substitute decision makers, 'deputies' for them. It also sets out rules about making an advanced decision to refuse medical treatment and for participation in research, and sets up a new independent consultee service for particularly vulnerable people. It provides for Codes of Practice to give guidance about the legislation and creates a new offence of neglect or ill-treatment.

Part 2 of the Act deals with the setting up of the new Court of Protection, and establishes a new statutory official, the Public Guardian, and provides for Court of Protection Visitors.

Part 3 of the Act contains technical and consequential provisions.

---

1 Report of the Joint Committee on the Draft Mental Incapacity Bill, vol. 1 HL Paper 189–1, HC 1083–1, at 34.
2 Ibid.
3 News Release DCA 22 April 2004.
4 Draft Mental Capacity Bill Commentary and Explanatory Notes.

1.4   DECISIONS EXCLUDED FROM THE OPERATION OF THE ACT

The Act expressly does not govern 'family relationships' decisions (s.27(1)) and questions about the voting rights of incapable persons (s.29) whether taken by the court, a deputy or an attorney under an LPA.

The excluded 'family relationships' decisions are laid down by s.27(1) of the Act:

(a) consent to marriage or civil partnership;
(b) consent to sexual relations;
(c) consent to divorce on the grounds of two years' separation;
(d) consent to dissolution of marriage on the grounds of two years' separation;
(e) consent to a child being placed for adoption;
(f) consent to the making of an adoption order;[1]
(g) discharging parental responsibilities in relation to matters not concerning the child's property;
(h) giving consent under the Human Fertilisation and Embryology Act 1990.

The approach to the question of whether a person has capacity to marry was recently considered by the court in the case of *Sheffield City Council* v. *E and S* [2005] Fam 326. Munby J held that the test was capacity to understand the nature of the marriage contract and not the implications of a particular marriage. Its law-fulness depended entirely on consent and, if a person lacked capacity, no one could consent on his or her behalf. Nor could the doctrine of necessity apply. A similar analysis would surely apply to the other 'family relationships' decisions referred to above.

---

1 The Explanatory Notes provide that the rules as to dispensing of consent under the adoption legislation will apply (para. 93).

1.5   MINORS

The Act governs decision making for people who lack capacity who are aged 16 or over, and in respect of the property and affairs of younger children if the court considers it likely that the person concerned will still lack capacity to make the relevant decision when he or she reaches 18 years of age (s.18(3)).

There is an overlap between the jurisdiction of the courts which deal with family proceedings under the Children Act 1989 and the jurisdiction of the Court of Protection under the Act. Section 21 of the Act gives the Lord Chancellor powers to make transfer of proceeding orders so that a case may be transferred to the court most suitable to deal with the matter.

1.6 DATA PROTECTION AND CONFIDENTIALITY

Difficulties frequently arise over the access to personal data of incapable persons, particularly when it is sought by persons seeking to make a decision on their behalf.

Access to personal data is regulated under:

- the Data Protection Act 1998 (DPA 1998);
- the common law duty of confidence; and
- the professional codes of conduct on confidentiality.

Both the common law and the professional codes are based on the common law requirement for consent to be given to disclosure of personal information by the person to whom it relates.

A person making a decision on behalf of someone who lacks capacity to make that decision and to consent to disclosure of personal information, will need to have access to personal information and may be required to disclose personal information about that person. Medical professionals and various public authorities are sometimes reluctant to disclose information about a patient to a third party who is not acting under formal powers without the patient's consent. Currently, if such a difficulty persists the Court of Protection will issue a limited authority for the purposes of obtaining information. The Court may continue this practice once the Act is in force.

A person making a disclosure must be assured that they are acting lawfully and that the disclosure is justified (see para. 13.12 of the Draft Code of Practice). Full guidance is contained in chapter 13 of the Draft Code of Practice (paras. 13.13–13.27) which can be found at Appendix 3 of this book.

1.7 SCOTLAND

The Adults with Incapacity (Scotland) Act 2000 (the Scottish Act) was one of the first Acts of the Scottish Parliament. The Scottish Act to some extent mirrors the provisions of the England and Wales Act, but is also importantly different. Key similarities and differences will be highlighted in the relevant chapters.

The Scottish Act has been implemented in stages. The Scottish Executive has commissioned surveys to find out how the Scottish Act is working in practice and what impact it is having on those whom it affects.

1.8 INTERNATIONAL PROTECTION OF ADULTS

The provisions for the international protection of adults in the private international law of England and Wales are contained in Schedule 3 to the Act. The Act gives effect in England and Wales to the Convention on the International Protection of Adults.[1] The aims of the Convention are to:

■   provide for the protection in international situations of adults, who by reason of impairment or insufficiency of their personal faculties, are not in a
position to defend their interests;
■   establish rules on jurisdiction, applicable law, and international recognition
and enforcement of protective measures which are to be respected by all
states.

The Schedule is divided into six parts. Part 1 deals with definitions and other preliminary matters. Part 2 sets out the jurisdiction of the 'competent authority'; the
Court of Protection is the competent authority for England and Wales. Part 3
makes provision as to which law applies in various situations. Part 4 provides for
the recognition and enforcement of protective measures taken in other countries.
Part 5 deals with co-operation between the appropriate authorities in England
and Wales and authorities in other Convention countries. Part 6 deals with general matters. For a fuller overview of the provisions of the Schedule see paras.
169–84 of the Explanatory Notes which can be found at Appendix 2 of this book.

Scotland is as yet the only country that has ratified the Convention, which must
be ratified by three countries before it will come into force. The provisions of
Schedule 3 are compatible with the provisions contained in the Scottish Act. Once
the Act is in force, Schedule 3 will provide private international law rules to govern jurisdictional issues between England and Wales, and Scotland *irrespective of
whether the Convention is in force.*

1 The Convention was signed in the Hague on 13 January 2000, Cm. 5881
www.hcch.net/e/conventions/text35e.html

1.9   THE MENTAL HEALTH ACT 1983 AND THE MENTAL
HEALTH BILL 2004

The Mental Health Act 1983 (MHA 1983) currently governs the detention, care
and treatment of those with a mental disorder. The Mental Capacity Act 2005
provides that if a person is detained under the MHA 1983 his treatment for that
mental disorder, or his giving consent for that treatment, must be dealt with
under the MHA 1983 and not the 2005 Act (s.28). This is intended to ensure that
there may be no conflict in relation to treatment of incapable patients who are
also detained under the MHA 1983, and the provisions of the 2005 Act: all the
safeguards under the MHA 1983 are retained.[1]

However, the government has accepted the need to replace the MHA 1983 with
new mental health legislation[2] since 1998. It has also accepted that new legislation is needed to meet its obligations under the European Convention on Human
Rights (ECHR).[3] Following on from a Green and a White Paper and a draft consultation Bill in 2002, the government published a further Draft Mental Health
Bill for pre-legislative scrutiny in September 2004. The Joint Committee published its report on the Bill in March 2005.[4] The government responded to the
Report of the Joint Committee in July 2005.[5] The government has accepted in full

or in part over half the 107 recommendations of the Joint Committee. At the time of writing the government is redrafting the Bill to take account of changes to be made following consideration of the Committee's report and plans to introduce the Mental Health Bill into Parliament in the autumn of 2005.

The Bill sets out a framework for determining when and how treatment for mental disorder may be provided under formal powers. In a change from the MHA 1983, the Bill introduces a single definition of mental disorder. Having a mental disorder is the first of a list of conditions which must be met before formal powers may be used. The Bill also aims to:

- provide new support for patients – such as making a new specialist independent mental health advocacy service available to the patient;
- strengthen safeguards – defining when a person can be treated without his or her consent, and what a person's rights are in such a case;
- ensure that patients receive appropriate treatment – for example, treatment under formal powers may be provided in the community as well as in hospital;
- increase choice for patients under compulsion.

A detailed consideration of the provisions of the Mental Health Bill is outside the scope of this book.

The Bill replaces most of the MHA 1983 with the exception of Part VII which currently regulates the management of the property and affairs of mentally disordered people and the powers and jurisdiction of the Court of Protection.

Once the Act comes into force the jurisdiction, powers and duties of the Court of Protection will no longer be dealt with by Part VII of the MHA 1983. They will be replaced by the provisions of the Act which establishes a new Court of Protection, which is a superior court of record, and creates a new public official, the Public Guardian (see **Chapter 12**). The new Court of Protection will have jurisdiction to deal with the health, welfare and the financial affairs of those who lack capacity.

Considerable concern has been expressed about the relationship between the Draft Mental Health Bill and the Act.[6] There is an obvious need for there to be clarity about the interface between the Act and the Draft Mental Health Bill. The two pieces of legislation aim to serve very different purposes, but could affect the same people.[7] The government has undertaken to clarify the relationship between the two pieces of legislation and to include guidance in the respective Codes of Practice.[8]

---

1   Explanatory Notes at para. 94.
2   Expert Committee. *Review of the Mental Health Act 1983*, 1999, App. A.
3   There have been a number of declarations of incompatibility made with the 1983 Act.
4   HL Paper 79–1, HC 95–1.
5   Cm. 6624.
6   The Law Society in its written evidence to the Joint Committee on the Draft Mental Health Bill in October 2004 stated that it 'believes that the relationship between the two

Bills is so complex that, in many cases, it would be practically impossible to work out when one Act should be used and the other should not'.

7   The decision in *HL* v. *United Kingdom* Application no. 45580/09 5 October 2004 has created further confusion about the interface between the Bill and the Act.

8   Government response to the report of the Joint Committee on the Draft Mental Health Bill 2004, Recommendation 27.

1.10   THE CODE OF PRACTICE

The Code is expected to play a key role in the interpretation of the Act and its implementation. Very often, as this text demonstrates, the Code is the principal guide to the legislation. The Joint Committee specifically recommended that the Act should not be introduced to Parliament until it could be considered alongside a Draft Code.[1] Its importance to the Committee was reinforced by the fact that many of its recommendations related to matters which it considered should be covered in the Code such as the duty of care of attorneys and deputies,[2] the standards of conduct of decision makers[3] and the requirements to be fulfilled upon an assessment of capacity.[4]

However, the Draft Code was described by David Lammy MP at the House of Commons Committee Stage as 'a work in progress'[5] although it was intended that it would be published 'in good time before the Bill is implemented'.[6] At the time of writing, the Code, despite its vital role, remains in draft and it is expected that its final format may be very different from the current draft.[7] It is to be hoped that it does not take as long as the Code of Practice issued under the MHA 1983 which was not published until 1990. The uncertainty about the content of the Code is intensified because it is anticipated that it will be reviewed after the first year and revised regularly, 'perhaps several times a year',[8] thereafter.

The Act imposes a duty on the Lord Chancellor to prepare and issue a Code of Practice governing a very wide range of issues (s.42(1)). This list, which was already lengthy, was expanded by Parliament from the initial proposal in the Bill. The Joint Committee also recommended that family members and carers be strongly encouraged to follow the Code.[9]

1.10.1   The duty to have regard to the Code

Section 42(4) of the Act imposes a duty on a person to 'have regard to any relevant code if he is acting in relation to a person who lacks capacity' and is doing so in one of the ways listed. Section 42(5) provides that a court or tribunal conducting any criminal or civil proceedings may find the Code or a failure to comply with it a relevant matter to be taken into account in its adjudication. The Draft Code itself provides that persons who are under a duty to 'have regard to' it must be able to demonstrate that they are familiar with the relevant part of it, and if they depart from it they will be expected to give reasons why (para. 1.9).

The question of what 'having regard to' the Code might mean is a difficult one. In the closely analogous Code issued under the MHA 1983, although there is no parallel requirement to 'have regard to' it under s.118 of that Act, the Court of Appeal held that persons carrying out functions under the Act which engage individual human rights should comply with it unless they have good reason to depart from it in an individual case or in the case of a group of individuals with the same identifiable characteristic (*R (on the application of Munjaz)* v. *Mersey Care NHS Trust* [2004] QB 395, at paras. 74 and 76). This appears to reflect the interpretation proposed in the Draft Code of Practice itself. Certainly, many of the issues with which it is concerned engage individual rights. Further, this interpretation is supported by contrast with the Scottish Act which provides for a Code but imposes no obligation to have regard to it.

The decision of the Court of Appeal in *Munjaz*, however, has recently been considered by the House of Lords on the appeal of the hospital and Secretary of State for Health and judgment is awaited. It may be that the House of Lords does not uphold the Court of Appeal's interpretation and adopts that put forward by the hospital and Secretary of State in that case, namely, that the Code should be taken into account by decision makers but no more, and there is no duty to give reasons for any departure from it. If so, the status of the Code under the Act may by analogy be down-graded. Alternatively, a different status will attach to the Codes issued under two closely related pieces of legislation.

1   Preface to the Draft Code of Practice.
2   Paragraph 154.
3   Paragraph 98.
4   Paragraph 245.
5   Hansard, HC Committee Stage, 19 October 2004.
6   David Lammy MP, Hansard, HC Committee Stage, 4 November 2004, col. 379.
7   Preface to the Draft Code of Practice.
8   David Lammy MP, Hansard, HC Committee Stage, 4 November 2004, col. 378.
9   At para. 232.

1.11   EUTHANASIA AND ASSISTED SUICIDE

Throughout the passage of the Bill and during debates, a great deal of parliamentary time and column inches in the press were taken up discussing whether key clauses in the Bill would authorise 'euthanasia by omission', 'suicidally motivated advanced directives' and 'euthanasia by the back door'.

Concerns were expressed that:

- Allowing people to make advance refusal of life-sustaining treatments, in particular the refusal of artificial nutrition and hydration (ANH), would legalise euthanasia by omission.
- A doctor who complies with a patient's contemporaneous or advanced refusal of treatment, by withholding or withdrawing treatment, may be committing euthanasia or a mercy killing or assisting a suicide.

- Attorneys, deputies or those providing care and treatment for a person may seek to harm that person at the end of his or her life.

The common law is clear that the refusal of medical treatment by a competent adult that results in death is not suicide. A competent adult is entitled to refuse any medical treatment even if the treatment is life-sustaining.[1] In *Airedale NHS Trust v. Bland*[2], Lord Goff stated:

> I wish to add that in cases of this kind, there is no question of the patient having committed suicide, nor therefore of the doctor having aided or abetted him in doing so. It is simply that the patient has, as he is entitled to do so, declined to consent to treatment which might or would have the effect of prolonging his life, and the doctor in accordance with his duty, complied with the patient's wishes.

The law is also clear that a doctor who complies with a patient's contemporaneous or advance refusal of treatment, by withholding or withdrawing treatment, is not committing euthanasia or mercy killing or assisting a suicide.

> . . . the law draws a crucial distinction between cases in which doctors decide not to provide, or to continue to provide, for his patient treatment or care which could or might prolong his life and those which he decides, for example by administering a lethal drug, actively to bring his patient's life to an end.[3]

The government resisted all attempts to include a clause in the Bill stating that the Bill did not permit euthanasia. Instead s.62 (then cl.58) was added which provides:

> For the avoidance of doubt, it is hereby declared that nothing in this Act is to be taken to affect the law relating to murder or manslaughter of the operation of section 2 of the Suicide Act 1961.

The final debates on the Lords' amendments to the Bill have made it clear that this provision is unlikely to resolve the ethical arguments surrounding the issue.

Specific safeguards have been included in the Act concerning the withdrawal or withholding of life-sustaining treatment:

- Advanced Decisions: Provision for a patient to make an advanced decision regarding treatment in ss.24–26 of the Act (see **Chapter 7**) will not apply to life-sustaining treatment unless the person has specified that it should (s.25(5)) and that it complies with the additional formalities set out in s.25(6) of the Act.
- Lasting Powers of Attorney (LPA): The donee of an LPA cannot make a healthcare decision relating to life-sustaining treatment unless he or she is expressly authorised to do so (s.11(8)(a)) (see **Chapter 4**).
- Acts in Connection with Care or Treatment: If there is any doubt whether the life-sustaining treatment is in the best interests of the patient, s.6(7) allows treatment to be given whilst a decision is sought from the court (see **Chapter 5**).

- Independent Mental Capacity Advocates (IMCA): The Act creates a new service, to help particularly vulnerable people who lack capacity and have no family or friends when decisions are being made by NHS bodies or local authorities about serious medical treatment or where they should live (see **Chapter 9**).
- Best Interests: Section 4(5) sets out in statutory form the current common law position that the person making a decision on behalf of a person about treatment that is necessary to sustain life must not be motivated by a desire to bring about the person's death.
- Deputies may not refuse consent to the carrying out or continuation of life-sustaining treatment (s.20(5)).

The Draft Code of Practice provides at paras. 5.21–5.24 instances when serious healthcare and treatment decisions are likely be referred to the Court of Protection for a decision.

---

1 *St George's Healthcare NHS Trust* v. *S* [1998] 3 All ER 673 (CA); *Re B (Adult: Refusal of Medical Treatment)* [2002] EWHC 429 (Fam); (2002) BMLR 149 (Butler-Sloss P).
2 *Airedale NHS Trust* v. *Bland* [1993] 1 All ER 821, at 869.
3 Ibid., at 869.

1.12   COMPATIBILITY WITH THE ECHR

Although the Act has been certified by Parliament as compatible with the ECHR, it is likely that human rights issues will arise in its implementation and in litigation.

The following Articles are potentially engaged by issues arising under the Act:

- 2 (the right to life);
- 3 (prohibition of torture);
- 5 (right to liberty and security);
- 6 (right to a fair trial);
- 8 (right to respect for private and family life);
- 9 (freedom of thought, conscience and religion);
- 14 (prohibition on discrimination); and
- Article 1 of the First Protocol (protection of property).

Inevitably, these Articles will be invoked in decision making and litigation under the Act. Certainly, the case law which developed the common law which the Act is intended to enshrine frequently considered the impact of the ECHR. However, no case in this area apart from *HL* v. *United Kingdom* (Appn. No. 45598/99) (2005), 81 BMLR 131 had a different conclusion because of the impact of the ECHR.

Careful consideration to the human rights consequences of the Act was given by the Joint Parliamentary Select Committee on Human Rights 23rd Report 2003–2004, and 15th Report 2004–2005. The Explanatory Notes set out the way in which the Act is considered to fulfill the requirements of the ECHR (paras.

10–16). There is no specific discussion, however, of the impact of the ECHR in the Draft Code of Practice.

1.13   THE *BOURNEWOOD* GAP

This is considered by some to be the most significant human rights issue facing persons who lack capacity, but it is not addressed by the Act. The gap exists because of a lack of procedural safeguards for incapable persons who are detained or otherwise suffer a restriction on their liberty but who are not subject to the MHA 1983. While the Act does not close the gap, the government is currently consulting on other statutory measures to fill it (see below), although they may depend upon the principles laid down by the Act and involve the new Court of Protection.

1.13.1   The nature of the gap

In *R* v. *Bournewood Community and Mental Health NHS Trust ex p. L* [1999] 1 AC 458 the House of Lords considered the case of an incapable person who was admitted to hospital and treated there but not detained under the MHA 1983. A majority of the House of Lords held that L was not detained in hospital because he was on an unlocked ward and did not attempt to leave, although there was evidence that if he had attempted to leave he would have been detained. It was further held, Lord Steyn dissenting, that the arrangements for L's care and treatment were governed by the doctrine of necessity and were lawful being in his best interests.

The European Court considered the case and gave judgment on 5 October 2004 (*HL* v. *United Kingdom*). It specifically considered the common law governing the care and treatment of persons found to be incapable, the guidance contained in the Code of Practice issued under the MHA 1983 and the then proposed Mental Capacity Bill. It nevertheless found that the applicant, and potentially others like him, had been detained in hospital in breach of the requirements of Art. 5(1) and (4) of the ECHR which provides:

> (1) Everyone has the right to liberty and security of person. No one shall be deprived of his liberty save in the following cases and in accordance with a procedure prescribed by law . . .
> (e) the lawful detention . . . of persons of unsound mind
>
> . . .
> (4) Everyone who is deprived of his liberty by arrest or detention shall be entitled to take proceedings by which the lawfulness of his detention shall be decided speedily by a court and his release ordered if the detention is not lawful.

The European Court held that the applicant had suffered an unlawful interference with his liberty because of the 'complete and effective control over his care and movements' by the health care professionals (para. 91) and the fact that the common law doctrine of necessity did not afford an adequate legal framework to avoid arbitrariness in his treatment (paras. 119–22). Further, judicial review and habeas corpus proceedings, determined as they were at the relevant time on a super-*Wednesbury* basis, did not afford an adequate review of the detention (para. 140). Since no case was put forward in which the inherent jurisdiction had been invoked to determine the lawfulness of such a detention, the Court was unable to adjudicate upon whether such an application might be sufficient (paras. 141–2).

Since the judgment, questions have arisen as to what deprivation of liberty or restraint might mean in this context. Some have suggested that it might include 'control' through medication such as sedation, or cover people who are unable to gain egress from a placement under their own volition because of their condition or because of the care regime where they are accommodated.

1.13.2   The approach in the Act

The Joint Parliamentary Select Committee on Human Rights reported on the Mental Capacity Bill in its 15th report in 2004–2005. It was concerned that the Bill failed to close the Bournewood gap in the light of its earlier observations in its 23rd report in 2003–2004 and the judgment of the European Court in *HL* v. *United Kingdom*.[1] Parliament was unmoved and the Act was passed without closing the gap.

In ss. 6, 11 and 20 the Act deals with the 'restraint' and restrictions on the 'liberty' of incapable persons (see **Chapters 5** and **6**). In summary:

- an individual, including an attorney or deputy, may restrain or interfere with the liberty of a person only if:
  - the person lacks, or the attorney or deputy or other person reasonably believes that he lacks, capacity in relation to the matter in question;
  - the attorney or deputy or other person believes it is reasonably necessary to do so in order to prevent harm to the person;
  - the restraint is a proportionate response to the likelihood of harm and the seriousness of that harm;
  - in the case of a deputy, the restraint is within the scope of the authority conferred on him;
- such restraint or interference with liberty will not be lawful if it amounts to an interference with the person's liberty in breach of Art. 5 of the ECHR.

Thus the Act effectively preserves the statutory or procedural gap where any act amounts to a breach of Art. 5 of the ECHR. Difficult questions are likely to arise if legislation is not enacted to close the gap by the time the Act comes into force including:

- the identification in practice of 'restraint' or 'interference with liberty' which reaches the Art. 5 threshold and is therefore not covered by the Act;
- the scope of the authority conferred on a deputy;
- the type of 'harm' which might justify restraint, e.g. damage to property or finances.

It should be noted that the Code of Practice issued under the MHA 1983 provides that an incapable person who is subject to restraint should be considered for an assessment for admission under the MHA 1983 (para. 19.8). It therefore seems to be the case that the 2005 Act should not be utilised to justify repeated or prolonged restraint without consideration of the statutory alternatives, although no reference is made to this in the Draft Code of Practice.

1.13.3   Future proposals

Following the judgment of the European Court the DoH issued interim guidance, and then a consultation document.

The interim guidance (*Advice on the Decision of the European Court of Human Rights in the Case of HL v. UK (The Bournewood Case)* dated 10 December 2004, Gateway Reference 4269 – Appendix 5 of this book) suggests that certain steps are taken by NHS bodies and local authorities to avoid a breach of Art. 5 of the ECHR in the care of incapable persons. In summary, the guidance provides that where an incapable person is deprived of his liberty, or is at risk of it, in the course of his care or treatment then:

- consideration should be given to alternatives in order to avoid situations in which professionals may be said to be taking 'full and effective control' over the person: the principle of the least restrictive alternative should be applied;
- detention under the MHA 1983 should not be used where the statutory criteria are not fulfilled or to be 'on the safe side';
- if such control is taken, decisions should be taken in a structured way including a professional assessment of capacity;
- there should be effective, documented care planning including the documented involvement of family, friends, carers and others interested in the person's welfare;
- appropriate information should be given to the person and his family, friends and carers;
- steps should be taken to retain contact between the person and his family, friends and carers unless exceptionally it is not in his best interests;
- the assessment of capacity and care plan should be regularly reviewed, with an independent element if possible, particularly where there are no involved family members, friends or carers.

In March 2005 the DoH issued the *Bournewood Consultation Paper: The approach to be taken in response to the judgment of the European Court of Human Rights in the Bournewood Case*. It stated that it wished to implement 'safeguards' for incapable persons not subject to mental health legislation as soon as possible, and expected to come to its policy conclusions by September 2005. It estimated that around 50,000 persons would be affected by the proposals. It suggested that an approach entitled 'protective care' should be adopted which comprises a new system of admission procedures, reviews of detention and appeals for incapable persons in accordance with the principles contained in the Mental Capacity Act 2005. The procedures would be utilised where:

- a person needs to be detained in order that care and treatment can be provided to him in his best interests; and
- a public authority is involved in arranging the placement.

Consideration is being given to whether the new Court of Protection might be the appropriate body to oversee these procedures.

---

1   Paragraphs 2.34ff.

2 THE PRINCIPLES

2.1 BACKGROUND TO REFORM

The Joint Committee in its Report of 28 November 2003 recommended that in order to achieve the Bill's stated aim it was essential that a statement of fundamental principles on which the Bill is based be inserted as an initial point of reference; this would give invaluable guidance to the courts, as well as helping non-lawyers to weigh up difficult decisions.

The Joint Committee[1] suggested five principles similar to those set out in s.1 of the Scottish Act. It was noted by the Joint Committee, however, that the Scottish Act was designed to run in conjunction with the common law, whereas the Draft Bill was designed to codify existing common law practice in statute.

The government ultimately accepted the recommendation and inserted a new cl.1 in the Bill, now s.1 of the Act.

---

1 Recommendations 4 and 5 of Joint Committee on the Draft Mental Incapacity Bill, HL Paper 189–1.

2.2 KEY PRINCIPLES

Section 1 sets out the key principles which underpin the Act. The Act is designed to codify the existing common law practice in statute. It is here that the existing case law may most assist the court in interpreting the Act.

Section 1(1)

Applies the key principles to the Act.

Section 1(2)

The presumption of capacity:

> A person must be assumed to have capacity unless it is established that he lacks capacity.

The ethical principle that every person has a right to self-determination and to have their autonomy respected is reflected in the common law presumption that every adult is competent to make his or her own decisions[1] – unless it can be shown that the person lacks capacity to make that particular decision. Section 3 of the Act (see **para. 3.2**) sets out the test for assessing whether a person is able to make a particular decision. The test is issue specific,[2] i.e. can this person, make this decision, now?

Section 2(3) of Act (see **para. 3.2.1**) introduces what the Explanatory Notes call 'a principle of equal consideration' in relation to determining a person's capacity. It ensures that those assessing a person's capacity do not make unjustified assumptions about their capacity based on prejudices and preconceptions relating to a person's age, condition, appearance or behaviour.

However, consideration ought also to be given to the conclusion reached by Dame Elizabeth Butler-Sloss (Butler-Sloss LJ as she then was) in the seminal case of *Re MB (Medical Treatment)*[3] that:

> . . . the graver the consequences of the decision, the commensurately greater the level of competence is required to take the decision.

(See also para. 3.37 of the Draft Code of Practice.)

Section 1(3)

Maximising decision making capacity:

> A person is not to be treated as unable to make a decision unless all practicable steps to help him to do so have been taken without success.

Again, in order to assist a person to make autonomous decisions, the Act requires all practical steps be taken to support a person to arrive at his or her own decision. A person should be supported and enabled to make as many decisions for him or herself as possible. The stated aim of this provision is to ensure that 'people who make decisions for themselves, but may need help and support to do so, are not automatically labelled as incapable of making these decisions and therefore subjected to unnecessary interventions'.[4] The Draft Code of Practice suggests that such help and support may include using specific communication strategies such as involving an expert to help him express his views and choosing the best time and location.

Section 1(4)

Unwise decisions:

> A person is not to be treated as unable to make a decision merely because he makes an unwise decision.

Again, in *Re MB*, Butler-Sloss LJ made it clear that:

> A competent woman, who has capacity to decide, may, for religious reasons, other reasons, for rational or irrational reasons or for no reason at all, choose not to have medical intervention . . .

The Act makes it clear that in determining the criteria of competence the guiding principle is respect for autonomy; that the Act should be enabling rather than restricting. Each person has his or her own values, beliefs, preferences and attitudes to risk, which ought to be respected. However, those assessing capacity must be aware of circumstances when the person has a misconception of reality such as to render that person unable to make that decision.

A key concern of stakeholders was whether the functional approach, which deals only with specific-issue incapacity, would sufficiently protect those with general incapacity. The Master of the Court of Protection, Master Lush, giving evidence to the Joint Committee, gave examples of the potential for people with on-going incapacity to make a series of judgments or decisions that may have disastrous consequences. In those circumstances, under the current law the Court of Protection may appoint a receiver. The Joint Committee recommended that consideration be given to recognising the issue of 'general incapacity' in the Draft Bill in a way that would not 'undermine the primacy of the functional approach'.

In response the government stated that it was committed to the functional approach, but agreed to provide guidance as to how this might work in order to provide people with adequate protection (see para. 3.22 of the Draft Code).

Section 1(5)

Best interests:

> An act done, or decision made, under this Act for or on behalf of a person who lacks capacity must be done, or made, in his best interests.

Since the decision of the House of Lords in the leading case of *Re F (Mental Patient: Sterilisation)* [1990] 2 AC 1, HL, the courts have recognised the necessity to act and make decisions for another person when the person lacks capacity to make decisions for him or herself and that such decisions and acts should be in that person's 'best interests'.

At common law, a best interests determination can only be made once it has been shown that a person lacks capacity to make the decision him or herself. The Family Division of the High Court, exercising its inherent jurisdiction has developed the concept of best interests, to include not only 'medical best interests' but also a wide range of ethical, social, moral, emotional and welfare considerations.[5]

> In deciding what is best for the disabled patient the judge must have regard to the patient's welfare as the paramount consideration. That embraces issues far wider

than the medical. Indeed it would be undesirable and probably impossible to set bounds to what is relevant to a welfare determination.[6]

The court has extended the jurisdiction to making decisions in relation to an incompetent adult's welfare as well as medical treatment.

> The court has jurisdiction to grant whatever relief in declaratory form is necessary to safeguard and promote the incapable adult's welfare and interests.[7]

Thorpe LJ in *Re A Male Sterilisation*[8] suggested that an evaluation of best interests could be facilitated by the use of a balance sheet:

> there can be no doubt in my mind that the evaluation of best interests is akin to a welfare appraisal . . . it seems to me that the first instance judge with the responsibility to make an evaluation of the best interests of a claimant lacking capacity should draw up a balance sheet. The first entry should be of any factor or factors of actual benefit. . . . Then on the other sheet the judge should write any counterbalancing dis-benefits to the applicant. . . . Then the judge should enter on each sheet the potential gains and losses in each instance making some estimate of the extent of the possibility that the gain or loss might accrue. At the end of that exercise the judge should be better placed to strike a balance between the sum of the certain and possible gains against the sum of the certain and possible losses. Obviously, only if the account is in relatively significant credit will the judge conclude that the application is likely to advance the best interests of the claimant.

Presently, in order for the Family Division of the High Court to exercise its jurisdiction the court has to be satisfied:

- that there is a 'serious justiciable issue';[9] and
- that the case falls within the confines of private law and that there is not an element of public law;[10] and
- that the governing consideration is the best interests of the incompetent adult.[11]

The Court of Appeal in *Burke* v. *General Medical Council*[12] rejected Munby J's suggestion at first instance that in the context of life-prolonging treatment the touchstone of 'best interests' is the 'intolerability' of continued life and stated that:

> We do not think it is possible to attempt to define what is in the best interests of a patient by a single test, applicable in all circumstances.

Section 1(5) now enshrines the best interests principle in statute as the principle that must guide all actions done for, or decisions made on behalf of, someone lacking capacity. Section 4 of the Act sets out statutory guidance, and a checklist of factors, that must be taken into account when assessing a person's best interests (see **Chapter 3** for a more detailed consideration).

Section 4(5) makes it clear that where the best interests determination relates to life-sustaining treatment, the person considering whether the treatment is in the best interests of the person concerned must not be motivated by a desire to bring about his death. (For a full discussion see **Chapter 3**.)

In any case, where there is a doubt or dispute about whether a particular act or decision is in the patient's best interests, the new Court of Protection will have jurisdiction to resolve the doubt or dispute.

Section 1(6)

Least restrictive alternative:

> Before the act is done, or the decision is made, regard must be had to whether the purpose for which it is needed can be as effectively achieved in a way that is less restrictive of the person's rights and freedom of action.

In order to safeguard and protect the rights and freedoms of people lacking capacity it is necessary to consider first, whether the act or decision needs to be done or taken at all, and then if the act or decision is necessary, the least restrictive way of carrying out the action or decision in their best interests.

Again, the decision maker must achieve a delicate balance between respecting a person's autonomy (e.g. allowing them to experience day-to-day risks without placing them in danger) and providing the person with adequate protection. This places a considerable burden on those owing a duty of care to the incapacitated person who may find themselves liable in negligence, or the tort of conversion or subject to the criminal law if their judgment proves wrong (see s.5(3) and later at **Chapter 5**).

1   *Re T (Adult: Refusal of Treatment)* [1992] 3 WLR 782; *Re B (Adult: Refusal of Medical Treatment)* [2002] 2 All ER 449.

2   *Masterman-Lister* v. *Jewell* Joined Cases: *Masterman-Lister* v. *Brutton & Co* [2002] EWCA Civ 1889.

3   [1997] 2 FLR 426, CA.

4   Paragraph 2.10 of the Draft Code of Practice.

5   *Re A Male Sterilisation* [2001] FLR 549 per Thorpe LJ.

6   *Re S (Adult Patient: Sterilisation: Patient's Best Interests)* [2001] Fam 15 per Thorpe LJ, at p. 30E.

7   *Re S (Adult Patient) (Inherent Jurisdiction: Family Life)* [2002] EWHC 2278 (Fam), [2003] 1 FLR 292.

8   Supra. at p.560E.

9   *Re S (Hospital Patient: Court's Jurisdiction) (No.1)* [1996] Fam 1 and *Re F (Adult: Court's Jurisdiction)* [2001] Fam 38.

10   *A (A Patient)* v. *A Health Authority* Joined Cases *Re J (A Child) (Choice of Forum)*, *R(S)* v. *Secretary of State for the Home Department* [2002] EWHC 18; [2002] Fam 213.

11   *Sheffield City Council* v. *S(1) DS(2)* [2002] EWHC 2278 (Fam).

12   [2005] EWCA Civ 1003 per Lord Phillips MR at p. 63. See also *Wyatt & Anor* v. *Portsmouth Hospital NHS & Anor* [2005] EWCA Civ 1181 per Wall LJ at p.84.

3 THE 'PRELIMINARIES'

3.1 BACKGROUND

Having established the 'principles' which are to govern the operation of the Act in s.1, these sections lay down a series of tests in relation to the key concepts of the Act – incapacity and best interests. The provisions follow closely the original recommendations of the Law Commission which in turn reflected to a great extent the then common law.[1] First, the test of capacity has both a diagnostic and a functional element. Secondly, a further provision is added to cover persons who are unable to communicate the decisions they might otherwise be found capable of making. Thirdly, the test to be adopted when making decisions on behalf of those persons found to be incapable – the best interests test – is both borrowed from the common law, and built upon and amended. Underpinning the whole scheme is a commitment to involving the person in the decision as much as possible. Before being found to be incapable, efforts should be made to 'enhance' his capacity. If he is found to be incapable, his wishes and feelings should nevertheless be taken into account, although they cannot be determinative of the decision.

Although the Act emphasises the importance of an assessment of capacity, it does not require that the assessment is carried out by a doctor or other professional before a decision is taken upon a person's behalf in every case, and sometimes a lay person's assessment will be sufficient. The Draft Code of Practice gives guidance as to when a professional assessment is likely to be required (paras. 3.29–3.39).

---

1 *Mental Incapacity* Law Com. No. 231, February 1995.

3.2 'DIAGNOSTIC TEST' OF CAPACITY

Section 2(1) provides that, for the purposes of the Act:

> . . . a person lacks capacity in relation to a matter if at the material time he is unable to make a decision for himself in relation to the matter because of an impairment of, or a disturbance in the functioning of, the mind or brain.

The 'diagnostic test' under s.2(1) has the following two elements:

(a) Capacity is to be assessed in relation to a particular decision at a particular time.

This part of the test emphasises the principle that there must be a 'time-specific and decision-specific approach to determining capacity'.[1] It derives directly from the common law principle expressed most clearly in *Masterman-Lister* v. *Brutton and Co* [2002] EWCA Civ 1889, [2003] 3 All ER 167. In that case the court held that a lack of capacity in respect of one matter did not automatically mean a lack of capacity in relation to another, and in particular the fact that the claimant required a litigation friend did not automatically mean he was under a disability for the purposes of limitation periods in litigation.

(b) Incapacity must derive from an impairment or disturbance of the person's mind or brain.

This 'diagnostic' element is designed to cover a wide range of conditions including 'psychiatric illness, learning disability, dementia, brain damage or even a toxic confusional state'[2] and 'people who are affected by the symptoms of alcohol or drug mis-use, delirium'.[3] The test reflects the common law position that incapacity may derive from an 'impairment or disturbance of mental functioning' of an organic cause, e.g. brain injury or non-organic cause, e.g. personality disorder (*R (Brady)* v. *Collins and Ashworth Hospital Authority* [2000] Lloyd's Rep Med 355[4]) or phobia (*Re MB (Medical Treatment)* [1997] 2 FLR 426.

The impairment or disturbance which causes the incapacity may be permanent or temporary (s.2(2)). Again this reflects the common law position, typically arising where loss of capacity is temporary, e.g. caused by the effects of a particular short-lived illness or medical procedure (*Re T (Adult: Refusal of Treatment)* [1993] Fam 95). The Draft Code of Practice specifically addresses the difficult situation of fluctuating capacity (paras. 3.23–3.24).

3.2.1   The need to avoid assumptions and discrimination

A lack of capacity may not be established merely by reference to:

■   a person's age or appearance; or
■   a condition of his or an aspect of his behaviour which lead others to make unjustified assumptions about his capacity (s.2(3)).

This provision was added at the 3rd reading in the House of Lords.[5] It was intended to 'reinforce the belief . . . that no-one should be assumed to lack capacity, excluded from decision-making, or discriminated against or given substandard care and treatment simply, for example, as a result of disability'. The key principle is that the fact of mental disorder should not automatically imply incapacity.

3.2.2   Lack of capacity decided on the balance of probabilities

The question of whether a person lacks capacity within the meaning of the Act must be decided on the balance of probabilities (s.2(4)).

3.2.3   Minors

The powers conferred under the Act in respect of persons found or believed to be incapable may only be exercised in respect of persons aged under 16 (s.2(5)). Thus a conflict between the provisions of this Act and the Children Act 1989 is avoided: a mentally impaired child should, if possible, be dealt with under that legislation, subject to the exceptions identified later in the Act (s.18(3) and s.21 – see para. 1.5).

1   David Lammy MP, Hansard, HC Committee Stage, 19 October 2004.
2   Explanatory Notes at para. 22.
3   Draft Code of Practice at para. 3.7.
4   It should be noted that this was a controversial decision, Maurice Kay J being satisfied that 'whilst Mr Brady had the intellectual capacity to appreciate the risks of his food refusal and the possible consequences, his ability to "weigh the information" was impaired by the emotions and perceptions he had at the time, these being engendered by the move and his reaction to it . . . Although he weighs facts, his set of scales are not calibrated properly in a whole range of things'.
5   Hansard, 15 March 2005, col. 1318.

3.3   'FUNCTIONAL TEST' OF CAPACITY

Section 3 of the Act lays down the 'functional test' for determining capacity. It provides as follows:

a person is unable to make a decision for himself if he is unable –

(a) to understand the information relevant to the decision,
(b) to retain that information,
(c) to use or weigh that information as part of the process of making the decisions, or
(d) to communicate his decision (whether by talking, using sign language or any other means).

The test follows very closely, on the recommendation of the Law Commission,[1] the common law test of capacity laid down by the Court of Appeal in *Re MB (Medical Treatment)* above. Butler-Sloss LJ, as she then was, in giving the judgment of the court held at 553–4:

A person lacks capacity if some impairment or disturbance of mental functioning renders the person unable to make a decision whether to consent to or to refuse treatment. That inability to make a decision will occur when:

(a)   the patient is unable to comprehend and retain the information which is
material to the decision, especially as to the likely consequences of having or
not having the treatment in question; or

(b)   the patient is unable to use the information and weigh it in the balance as part
of the process of arriving at a decision.[2]

The new Act adds a further element at s.3(1)(d) to cover the residual class of persons who cannot communicate their decisions, such as those suffering from a 'locked-in syndrome'. If such a person cannot communicate at all, e.g. not even by blinking, then they may be treated as incapable under the Act (Explanatory Notes, at para. 27).

3.3.1   The enhancement of capacity

A person is not to be regarded as unable to understand the information relevant to a decision if he is able to understand an explanation of it given to him in a way that is appropriate to his circumstances (simple language, visual aids or any other means) (s.3(2)). This provision focuses on a key recommendation of the Law Commission: that a person's capacity should be enhanced as far as possible. This particular amendment was added at the House of Commons' Committee Stage in order that 'no one should be labelled incapable merely because insufficient efforts have been made to help him understand and communicate'.[3] It reflects an issue that arose in cases under the common law where it was sometimes said on behalf of the apparently incapable person that insufficient efforts appropriate to his understanding had been made to enable him to acquire the necessary capacity to make a particular decision, e.g. E (by her litigation friend the Official Solicitor) v. Channel Four [2005] EWHC 1144 (Fam).

The Draft Code of Practice makes extensive suggestions as to the steps that might be taken to enhance a person's capacity (paras. 3.17–3.20) including:

- providing all the relevant information;
- providing the information in a format the person can understand;
- using cognitive aids such as pictures;
- choosing the best time and location;
- delaying the decision until a more appropriate time, or an improvement in the person's condition;
- using an advocate.

These suggestions should be considered alongside those given to doctors in the joint publication of the British Medical Association and the Law Society, Assessment of Mental Capacity: Guidance for Doctors and Lawyers at paras. 2.3 and 14.7.

The fact that a person is able to retain the information relevant to the decision for a short period only does not prevent him from being regarded as able to make the decision.

3.3.2 The significance of the consequences of the decision under consideration

The information relevant to a decision includes information about the reasonably foreseeable consequences of:

(a) deciding one way or another;
(b) failing to make the decision (s.3(4)).

Again, this provision in the Act derives from the common law *Re MB* test set out above – the key information upon which the person must decide relates to the consequences of his decision.

---

1 Law Com. 231, para. 3.23.
2 This formulation built upon that adopted in the case of *Re C (Adult: Refusal of Medical Treatment)* [1994] 1 All ER 819 which emphasised the need for a link between the impairment or disturbance of functioning and the inability to take the decision concerned.
3 Hansard, HC, 14 December 2004, col. 1632.

3.4 INCAPABLE PERSON'S BEST INTERESTS

3.4.1 Background to this section

The Law Commission in its report was in no doubt that this principle, long-established in the common law (see **para. 2.2**), should govern decision making on behalf of incapable persons. The issue was what criteria should be devised for the assessing of best interests. The Law Commission's initial proposed list of four factors[1] has grown into the 11 sub-sections of s.4 of the Act.

The best interests test laid down by s.4 'underpins the [Act] and expands on the principle set out in [s.1(5) of the Act] . . . It is the fundamental principle that governs everything that is done for a person who lacks capacity'.[2] The best interests test was preferred over an assessment of 'benefit' to the incapable person for the following reasons:

> . . . although the concept of benefit would place the focus firmly on the person concerned, it might not allow for a consideration of other relevant factors, such as those affecting carers. Let me give an example. Someone caring for their mother or young child might want to arrange for them to go into a care home for a few weeks in order to give the carer a rest, and they might want the care home to provide the respite care that all of us have heard carers in our community talking about. There is a hospice not far from any constituency where people experience that. That situation would be to the benefit of the carer and the mother or partner. It might not be to the direct benefit of the person who lacks capacity, but it would certainly be in their best interest, as it would better for the carer to have had that respite care. That encapsulates why 'best interests' is an all-embracing concept. 'Benefit' is narrower and more prescriptive. That is why the Joint Committee ruled out that test.'[3]

The test has both objective and subjective elements. Clause 4 of the Bill was amended at the House of Commons Committee Stage in order 'to make clear that the test of best interests should be objective' as well as taking into account subjective considerations such as the individual's wishes and feelings and 'all the factors that a reasonable person would consider relevant'.[4]

3.4.2   The need to avoid assumptions or discrimination

In a provision mirroring s.2(3) (see **para. 3.2.1**), s.4(1) provides that:

> In determining for the purposes of this Act what is in a person's best interests, the person making the determination must not take it merely on the basis of –
>
> (a) the person's age or appearance, or
> (b) a condition of his, or an aspect of his behaviour, which might lead others to make unjustified assumptions about what might be in his best interests.

The best interests test is intended to protect against any kind of discrimination, including disability discrimination.[5]

3.4.3   The method of determining best interests

The method of decision making as to best interests laid down by the Act applies to the court, an attorney or donee of a Lasting Power of Attorney (LPA), or an informal decision maker (s.4(8) and (9)). It is also extended to decisions made by an attorney when he reasonably believes a person to lack capacity although in fact the person does not (s.4(8) and Explanatory Notes at para. 34). Where the decision is taken by an informal decision maker, he will have complied sufficiently with the requirements of the section if, having gone through the specified steps, he 'reasonably believes that what he does or decides is in the best interests of the person concerned' (s.4(9)). The test of 'reasonable belief' is objective (Explanatory Notes, at para. 35).

The Act requires that best interests are determined by:

(a) considering all the relevant circumstances, which are defined as those of which the decision maker is aware, and which it would be reasonable to regard as relevant (s.4(11)); and
(b) taking the steps set out in the succeeding subsections (s.4(2)).

The steps are intended as a checklist not a definition nor an exhaustive list of factors: the assessment of best interests always depends on the facts of the case (Draft Code of Practice, at para. 4.9). The question of what is a 'relevant circumstance' is addressed in the Draft Code of Practice giving useful examples in both the health and financial sphere (paras. 4.10–4.11).

First, the decision maker must consider whether it is likely that the person will at some time have capacity in relation to the matter and, if so, when (s.4(3)). This provision allows for the possibility that the decision may be put off until the person has capacity to take it.[6] The Draft Code of Practice gives useful guidance on this issue at paras. 4.14–4.16.

Secondly, the decision maker must, so far as reasonably practicable, permit and encourage the person to participate, or to improve his ability to participate, as fully as possible in any act done for him and any decision affecting him (s.4(4)). The purpose of the inclusion of the words 'so far as reasonably practicable' is to allow for situations, either urgent or not, in which it would not be appropriate or in a person's best interests to delay acting for those steps to be taken.[7] Otherwise, the person should be involved to the 'fullest possible extent' (Draft Code of Practice at para. 4.17). Regard should also be had to the guidance issued jointly by the Law Society and BMA on the assessment of capacity, op. cit., at pp. 17 and 159.

Thirdly, the decision maker must consider, so far as it reasonably ascertainable:

(a) the person's past and present wishes and feelings (including any written statement made by him when he had capacity);
(b) the beliefs and values that would be likely to influence his decision if he had capacity; and
(c) the other factors that he would be likely to consider if he were able to do so (s.4(6)).

The first of these factors may require particular work. Often an advocate can assist a person to express his feelings (Draft Code of Practice, at para. 4.19). It is often useful to keep a note of spontaneous expressions of wishes and feelings, rather than relying only upon formal assessments and interviews which are often artificial. It is important, however, that this material does not lead decision makers into confusing a person's wishes, feelings or past values with what is in his best interests given his lack of capacity (Draft Code of Practice, at para. 4.21).

Fourthly, the decision maker must, if it is practicable and appropriate to consult them, take into account the views of:

(a) anyone named by the person as someone to be consulted on the matter in question or on matters of that kind;
(b) anyone engaged in caring for the person or interested in his welfare;
(c) any donee of an LPA granted by the person;
(d) any deputy appointed by the court for the person;

as to what would be in the person's best interests (s.4(7)).

It is worth noting that this subsection does not expressly refer to the person's relatives rather than a 'carer' or 'person interested in his welfare'. It is not the fact of blood relationship which is determinative of the interest, and it is more than possible that an absent blood relation would not fall within the statutory category.

Although relatives are likely to have a significant role in some cases, there is no guarantee that they are the best arbiters of a person's best interests. Moreover, there is no common law presumption in favour of an adult child's residence or contact with his parents either at common law (Re D-R (Adult: Contact) [1999]

1 FLR 1161, CA) or under Art. 8 of the ECHR. This approach was adopted and expanded by Munby J in *Re S (Adult Patient) (Inherent Jurisdiction: Family Life)* [2002] EWHC 2278 (Fam), [2003] 1 FLR 292. His Lordship held that an individual's right to private life under Art. 8 may require his separation from members of his family. However, where a person has resided with his family all his life, then there is an evidential burden on those who wish to accommodate the person elsewhere.

In difficult cases, the Draft Code of Practice gives guidance to determining an incapable person's best interests (paras. 4.30–4.35).

3.4.4   The interests of third parties

At common law, considerable difficulty has arisen in cases where powerful interests of third parties are engaged by the decision in issue. For example, in *Re Y (Mental Patient) (Bone Marrow Donation)* [1997] 2 WLR 556 the court was asked to declare that it was lawful to harvest bone marrow from an incapable person in order to treat her sister's lymphoma. Connell J held that it was lawful because 'it is to the benefit of the [incapable person] that she should act as donor to her sister, because in this way her positive relationship with her sister is most likely to be prolonged. Further, if the transplant occurs, this is likely to improve the [incapable person's] relationship with her mother who in her heart clearly wishes it to take place and also to improve her relationship with [her sister] who will be eternally grateful to her'. Whether this was the correct approach or not, when the court next considered a similar matter, it 'left open' the question of whether a third party's interests should also be considered (*R-B (A Patient)* v. *The Official Solicitor* sub nom *Re A (Mental Patient: Sterilisation)* (2000) Lloyd's Rep Med 87). The foetus of a pregnant, incapable woman does not have an independent set of interest to be weighed against the woman's (*St. George's Healthcare NHS Trust* v. *S* [1998] 3 All ER 673.

3.4.5   Life-sustaining treatment

Where the determination relates to life-sustaining treatment, the decision maker must not, in considering whether the treatment is in the best interests of the person concerned, be motivated by a desire to bring about his death (s.4(5)). 'Life-sustaining treatment' is defined as 'treatment which in the view of a person providing health care for the person concerned is necessary to sustain life' (s.4(10)). The Explanatory Notes explain this part of the Act as follows:

> This means that whatever a decision-maker personally feels about, or wants for, the person concerned this must not affect his assessment of whether a particular treatment is in the person's best interests . . . It does not mean that doctors are under an obligation to provide, or to continue to provide, life-sustaining treatment where that treatment is not in the bests interests of the person (para. 31).

Thus the protracted ethical debates which accompanied the passage of the Bill through Parliament are dealt with in a few words.

1 The ascertainable past and present wishes and feelings of the person concerned and the factors the person would consider if able to do so; the need to permit and encourage the person to participate or improve his or her ability to participate as fully as possible in anything done for and any decision making affecting him or her; the views of other people whom it is appropriate and practical to consult about the person's wishes and feelings and what would be in his or her best interests; and whether the purpose for which any action or decision is required can be as effectively achieved in a manner less restrictive of the person's freedom of action.
2 David Lammy MP, Hansard, HC Committee Stage, 19 October 2004.
3 Ibid.
4 Hansard, HC, 14 December 2004, col. 1631 and David Lammy MP, HC Committee Stage, 21 October 2004.
5 David Lammy MP, Hansard, HC Committee Stage, 19 October 2004
6 Explanatory Notes at para. 28.
7 David Lammy MP, Hansard, HC Committee Stage, 21 October 2004, col. 092.

4 LASTING POWERS OF ATTORNEY

4.1 BACKGROUND

4.1.1 EPAs

A power of attorney involves the grant of a legal power by the donor to another person, the donee or attorney, to act on the donor's behalf. Prior to the introduction of enduring powers of attorney by the Enduring Powers of Attorney Act 1985 (EPAA 1985), powers of attorney only had effect while the donor had capacity and were automatically revoked upon incapacity of the donor. The EPAA 1985 introduced a particular type of power of attorney, the Enduring Power of Attorney (EPA) which permitted the attorney to continue to act on the donor's behalf in relation to property and financial affairs after the donor lacked capacity to act on his or her own behalf.

4.1.2 Differences between EPAs and LPAs

The Act introduces a new type of power of attorney, the Lasting Power of Attorney (LPA). LPAs replace EPAs as the type of power of attorney which can operate after a person ceases to have capacity. An important difference between LPAs and EPAs is that LPAs can authorise the attorney to make decisions on the donor's behalf in respect of welfare matters as well as matters related to property and financial affairs. Accordingly, the power to make decisions about medical treatment, residence and contact with other persons can be given to an attorney. Welfare LPAs can only be used once a donor has lost capacity.

Further, it is important to note that an LPA must be registered before it is valid and therefore before any powers conferred by it can be exercised. This contrasts with the situation in respect of EPAs which do not require registration until the donee believes the donor is or is becoming mentally incapable (s.4(1) and (2) of the EPAA 1985). The LPA must be registered with the Public Guardian. The practical effect will be that the Public Guardian will know about all LPAs in use. This is not the situation with EPAs because many have not been registered (either because the donor has capacity or there has been a failure to comply with the registration requirements by the donee).

4.1.3   Abuse

There was much debate in both Houses of Parliament in relation to concerns about abuse of LPAs by donees and conflicts of interest. Evidence presented to the Joint Committee indicated that financial abuse occurred in approximately 10–20 per cent of cases involving EPAs (para. 138 of Joint Committee report on the Draft Mental Capacity Bill). But all proposals for more rigorous controls (in addition to the requirement to register which is discussed below) to prevent abuse such as routine monitoring of LPAs by the Public Guardian were resisted on the basis that respect has be accorded to the individual's autonomy to choose the person he or she wishes to act and for the state to respect that choice and place the responsibility on the donor to make a good choice. The appointment must after all be made when the donor has capacity (see in particular the debates in the House of Lords at the Committee Stage on 8 February 2005 at col. 761).

4.2   DEFINITION OF LPAs

Section 9(1) of the Act defines an LPA as a power of attorney under which the donor (P) confers on the donor or donees (D) authority to make decisions about all or any of the following matters:

- P's personal welfare or specified matters concerning P's personal welfare;
- P's property and affairs or specified matters concerning P's property and affairs.

This also includes authority to make decisions in circumstances where P no longer has capacity.

The following points should be noted:

- P can confer power on more than one attorney. This could involve P choosing to have separate attorneys for welfare and property matters. P could also choose to have different attorneys in respect of specific financial or property matters.
- P can confer general powers on an attorney to make welfare and/or financial and property decisions or specify specific matters in respect of which an attorney has powers.
- In order to be a valid LPA, the instrument must include authority to make decisions once P loses capacity. Otherwise, it is simply an ordinary power of attorney. Further, no authority can be conferred to make welfare decisions prior to P losing capacity in respect of this matter (see discussion of s.11(7) at **para. 4.4.1**).

4.2.1   Different attorneys

P might choose different individuals to act as attorneys in respect of welfare and property and financial matters so as to avoid any conflicts arising (e.g. whether P should go into an expensive residential home when this would have a substantial impact on the size of P's savings and investments).

However, there is no obligation under the Act to choose separate persons. It is a matter for each donor to decide which individual/s should be conferred with which powers.

The Draft Code of Practice states that the Office of the Public Guardian will produce detailed guidance, in due course, on explaining the procedures involved in making an LPA and important issues to consider when making an LPA (chapter 6, p. 54).

4.3   VALIDITY REQUIREMENTS OF AN LPA

Sections 9 and 10 of Schedule 1 to the Act contain the requirements for the creation of a valid LPA. Unless these requirements are complied with, the LPA confers no authority (s.9(3)).

The validity requirements can be divided into three categories:

- The use of a particular form and registration.
- Appointment of the donees in compliance with s.10.
- That the donor has reached the age of 18 at the time of execution of the instrument and has capacity to execute the instrument.

4.3.1   Form and registration

The instrument must be in the prescribed form and be registered in accordance with Schedule 1 to the Act. Further, it must confer authority to make general or specific decisions about welfare and/or property and financial affairs and include authority to make decisions when P no longer has capacity (s.9(2)(b) and 9(1)).

The formality requirements set down in Schedule 1 will be supplemented by regulations which will contain further details in respect of the particular requirements of the prescribed form and other matters. Where the word 'prescribed' is used below, it relates to matters which will be prescribed by regulations where further information is not currently available because regulations have yet to be made. The requirements set out in Schedule 1 include the following.

Requirements of the instrument (Part 1 of Schedule 1)

An instrument creating an LPA must be in a prescribed form and have a specific content, in particular:

- Prescribed information about the purpose of the instrument and the effect of an LPA.
- Statement by the donor stating that he has read the prescribed information

and intends the instrument to confer power to make decisions when he no longer has capacity.

- Statement by the donor naming persons he wishes to be notified of any application to register (who cannot be donees under the instrument) or stating that he does not wish any persons to be notified.
- Statement by the donee that he has read the prescribed information and understands the duties imposed on an LPA under ss. 1(the principles) and 4 (best interests).
- A certificate (in the prescribed form containing the prescribed information) by a person of a prescribed description (who cannot be a donee under the instrument) that in his opinion at the time when the donor executes the instrument the donor understands the purpose and scope of the instrument, no fraud or undue pressure is being used and there is nothing else to prevent an LPA being created. It is not yet clear which persons will be prescribed. This is a new requirement introduced by the Act to address a problem with the current system. There is no requirement at present that the person witnessing a donor's signature should be specially qualified and this has created difficulties and led to litigation in many cases where a donor's capacity is later disputed. Regulations may also provide that two such certificates are required where the donor states that he does not want anyone to be notified of an application to register. This is an additional safeguard to prevent fraud. It was stated in the House of Lords on behalf of the government that it was considered this provided sufficient additional protection against fraud and specific provisions for monitoring by the Public Guardian on LPAs where no named persons are notified were not necessary nor justified (see Committee debates on 8 February 2005 at col. 761).

If an instrument fails to comply with the prescribed form, the Public Guardian is to treat it as sufficient to create an LPA if it differs in an immaterial respect. Otherwise, the Court of Protection may declare that an instrument is to be treated as a valid LPA if satisfied that the person executing the instrument intended to create an LPA.

Registration requirements (Part 2 of Schedule 1)

No powers in an LPA can be exercised until the instrument is registered. The application for registration is made to the Public Guardian. The procedure and requirements can be summarised as follows:

- The application must be in the prescribed form and contain prescribed information and attach the instrument and the fee for registration (the amount of the fees have not yet been determined – see further **para. 11.4.5**)
- It may be made by the donor or donee(s) to the Public Guardian.
- The person applying must notify the named persons in the instrument to inform them of the application to register.
- The Public Guardian must notify the donor or donee(s) (depending who makes the application) of the fact that an application has been received.

- The court will have the power to dispense with notification requirements upon application by the donor or donee(s) if satisfied they will serve no useful purpose.
- If the instrument received by the Public Guardian is flawed (because it is ineffective as an LPA or contains a provision making it inoperable as an LPA), he must not register it but refer the matter to the Court of Protection.
- The Court of Protection must then notify the Public Guardian that it has severed the offending provision (so that it can be registered) or direct the Public Guardian not to register it.
- The Public Guardian must not register an instrument if there is a deputy appointed by the Court whose powers would conflict with the attorney under the LPA unless directed to do so by the Court. (There is no obligation on the Public Guardian himself to refer the matter to the Court in these circumstances.)
- Objections can be made to registration to the Public Guardian within a prescribed period.
- If a donor objects to the registration by the donee, the Public Guardian must not register the instrument unless directed to do by the Court. The Court will only direct him to register the instrument if satisfied that the donor lacks capacity to object to registration.
- If a donee or named person objects to registration on the ground that the LPA has already been revoked (by bankruptcy of the donee or other circumstances set out in s.13(6)(a)–(d) of the Act), the Public Guardian will not register the LPA if satisfied that the ground is made out. If the person applying for registration disagrees with the decision not to register, he may apply to the Court who can direct the Public Guardian to register the instrument if satisfied that the ground is not established. There is provision for donees and named persons to make objections on other prescribed grounds to the Court (and the Public Guardian must not then register until directed to do so by the Court).

4.3.2   Appointment of donees

A donee must be an individual who has reached the age of 18 or a trust corporation (in respect of property and affairs LPAs which is defined in s.68(1) of the Trustee Act 1925 as the Public Trustee or a corporation either appointed by the court in a particular case to be a trustee or entitled by rules made under s.4(3) of the Public Trustee Act 1906 to act as a custodian trustee). An individual is therefore required to make welfare decisions (s.10(1)).

A person who is bankrupt may not act as a donee in respect of property and affairs (s.10(2)). But such a person is not prevented from being a donee in respect of welfare.

These provisions mirror those in respect of deputies (see **para. 6.6**).

More than one donee

When there is more than one donee, the instrument creating the LPA can appoint them to act jointly or severally or jointly in respect of some matters and severally in respect of others (s.10(4)). Jointly means that both attorneys must act together in any act carried out under the LPA (e.g. both must sign cheques). Jointly and severally means that the attorneys can act separately from one another (e.g. the signature of one attorney on the cheque is enough).

In the absence of specification in the instrument about this, donees are assumed to be appointed to act jointly (s.10(5)). However, care should be taken when specifying how attorneys are to act. The Court of Appeal has held in a case about an EPA that where three attorneys were appointed to act jointly 'save that any two of the attorneys may sign', that the instrument could not operate as an EPA (*Re E* [2000] 3 WLR 1974). It is likely that the same approach would be adopted in respect of an LPA because the fall back provision in s.10(5) only applies when no specification has been made.

If they are appointed to act jointly or severally, a failure by one donee to satisfy the formality requirements as regards execution of the instrument or failure to meet the requirements about age or non-bankruptcy does not prevent the instrument having effect in respect of other donees (s.10(7)).

Successive donees

An instrument creating an LPA cannot give the donee the power to appoint his or her own successor. The power to appoint a donee is personal to the donor and any instrument conferring a power of substitution on the donee will not be a valid LPA (ss.10(8), 9(3)). But the instrument can itself appoint a person to replace a donee or any donee in the event that a donee's power is automatically revoked in accordance with s.13(6) of the Act (namely, upon the occurrence of disclaimer of the appointment by the donee), death/bankruptcy/winding up of the donee (if a property and financial affairs LPA), dissolution or annulment of a marriage or civil partnership between the donor and donee or lack of capacity of the donee (discussed further at **para. 4.8.2**).

4.3.3   Age and capacity of donor

Under s.9(2)(c) of the Act, the donor must be aged 18 at the time of execution of the instrument.

The donor must have capacity to execute the instrument. The Draft Code of Practice does not contain any guidance on the assessment of capacity of a person to execute an LPA. The presumption of capacity will apply so that the burden will be on a person objecting to registration to establish lack of capacity.

This is an area which has been considered in case law in respect of EPAs and it seems unlikely that the test will change substantially in respect of LPAs. The leading case is the Court of Appeal's decision in *Re W* (*Enduring Power of Attorney*) [2001] 2 WLR 957 which endorsed the four-stage test that the donor should understand:

(1) the scope of the authority;
(2) the terms of the power (i.e. do anything which the donor could have done);
(3) that the authority will continue upon incapacity of the donor;
(4) that the power will be irrevocable when a person becomes incapable without the intervention of the Court
     (although it should be noted that the particular phrasing of the test in *Re W* reflected the fact that the EPA related only to financial matters, but it can be summarised as stated here so as to make it of general application).

It is to be noted that Schedule 1 to the Act requires certification only to the effect that the donor understands the purpose of the instrument and the scope of the authority conferred under it (para. 2(1)(e)) which sets out the test of capacity in a simpler form than in *Re W*.

4.4   CONTENT OF LPAs

As stated above, LPAs can cover property and financial affairs and welfare matters. Property and financial affairs LPAs (financial LPAs) can be used both before and after the donor loses capacity. When donees of LPAs exercise their powers, they must comply with all the provisions in the Act and, in particular, the principles set out in s.1 and they must always act in the best interests of the donor (in accordance with s.4) (s.9(4)) (see **para. 3.4**). (The express reference to the general principles in Part 1 was added to the Bill at the report stage in the House of Lords (HL Bill 48.) (This is discussed further below at **para. 4.7**.)

Further, all powers are subject to any conditions or restrictions specified in the instrument granting the LPA (s.9(4)(b)). In this way the donor is able to regulate exactly what powers he or she wishes to grant to the donee.

4.4.1   Welfare LPAs

Donors are able to make a general welfare LPA which permits a donee to act in respect of all matters concerning welfare or to list specific matters in respect of which the donee has authority.

Welfare LPAs can only be used once the donor has lost capacity or the donee reasonably believes that he has lost capacity (s.11(7)(a) of the Act).

There is no list in the Act of the types of decisions which welfare donees can be authorised to take, although the list of powers which the Court has (although only a sample list of those powers) in respect of welfare matters (in s.17) is instructive. The Draft Code of Practice also provides a sample list of powers which a welfare donee could be authorised to take by an LPA (at para.6.7). Welfare powers include:

- decisions on where a donor should live;
- deciding what contact, if any, P is to have with specified persons;
- giving or refusing consent to medical examination and/or treatment (including the continuation of treatment);
- giving a direction that a person responsible for P's health care allow a different person to take over that responsibility;
- arranging for the donor to access medical, dental or optical treatment;
- applying for and having access to confidential documents and personal information relating to the donor held by any organisation such as medical records or personal files held by social services authorities.

A general LPA will permit a donee to make all of the sorts of decisions listed above. However, it is open to the donor to specify or exclude specific powers. Certain powers have to be specified in the instrument in order for the donee to be able to exercise them (see **para. 4.5.4**).

4.4.2   Financial LPAs

Financial LPAs can include powers to be exercised:

- while a donor retains capacity and to continue after the donor loses capacity;
- only once a donor loses capacity.

Donors can make a general financial LPA covering all matters relating to their property and affairs or grant powers in specific areas to the donee.

There is no list in the Act of powers included in financial LPAs. However, the list provided in respect of the Court of Protection's powers in respect of financial matters is a useful guide save that certain restrictions are placed on the powers that can be exercised by donees of financial LPAs (s.18). Further, there is a list of the types of powers that can be granted and exercised in the Draft Code of Practice (at para.6.13).

The Draft Code of Practice lists the types of powers that can be granted under a financial LPA as including:

- buying or selling property;
- opening, closing or operating any bank, building society or other account containing the donor's funds;
- giving access to financial information to others concerning the donor;
- claiming, receiving and using on the donor's behalf all benefits, pensions, allowances, rebates etc. to which the donor may be entitled (unless another person has already been appointed to do this and all wanted this arrangement to continue);
- receiving any income, inheritance or other entitlement of the donor;
- dealing with the donor's tax affairs;
- paying the donor's mortgage, rent and/or household expenses;

- making appropriate arrangements to insure, maintain and repair the donor's property;
- investing the donor's savings in interest bearing accounts, bonds, stocks and shares or any other form of investment;
- making gifts on behalf of the donor (but subject to restrictions – see **para. 4.6**);
- paying for private medical care and/or residential care or nursing home fees;
- using the donor's income or capital to purchase a vehicle or any aids, adaptations or equipment required by the donor where these are not provided free of charge;
- borrowing money on behalf of the donor and repaying interest and capacity on any loan taken out by the donor or donee on his/her behalf;
- making a provision for any person for whom the donor might be expected to provide if he did not lack capacity, such as a spouse or dependent children.

4.5   RESTRICTIONS ON LPAs

The restrictions on LPAs are contained in s.11 of the Act.

4.5.1   General restrictions

These restrictions apply to financial LPAs and welfare LPAs.

4.5.2   Restraint

The principal restriction upon donees of LPAs relates to the use of restraint. This is discussed in more detail in **Chapter 5** at **para. 5.3.1** and those paragraphs should be referred to for more detailed analysis of the use of restraint.

An attorney may restrain the donee of a power only if three conditions are satisfied (s.11(1)):

- P lacks or the donee reasonably believes that P lacks capacity in relation to the matter (s.11(2));
- the donee reasonably believes that it is necessary to do the act to prevent harm to P (s.11(3));
- the act is a proportionate response to the likelihood of P suffering harm and the seriousness of that harm (s.11(4)).

Further, the donee must be satisfied that it is in P's best interests to restrain him. This requirement arises from the fact that a donee's authority is subject to the provisions of the Act generally and, in particular, the best interests provisions in s.4 (s.9(4)(a)).

Restraint is defined as (s.11(5)):

■ the use or threat of use of force to secure the doing of an act which P resists;
■ the restriction of P's liberty of movement whether or not P resists.

A donee is not authorised to deprive P of his liberty within the meaning of Art.5(1) of the ECHR (s.11(6)).

4.5.3   Restrictions imposed by the instrument

A donee will be subject to any restrictions and conditions which are contained in the instrument (s.9(4)(b)).

4.5.4   Specific restrictions on welfare LPAs

The specific restrictions on welfare LPAs are as follows:

■ The powers cannot be exercised except where P lacks capacity or the donee reasonably believes P lacks capacity (s.11(7)). Reasonable belief is an objective test and the donee will need to show reasonable grounds for believing that P lacks capacity. This particular restriction ensures that P's autonomy to make decisions about matters most personal to him or her is preserved.
■ The welfare powers are subject to advance decisions about treatment made by P (s.11(7)(b)). Advance decisions are discussed in **Chapter 7**. This restriction ensures proper respect for the wishes of P. If P had made an advance decision about a particular medical treatment, that decision takes priority as opposed to a decision by the donee of an LPA made in P's best interests.
■ There is no general power to give or refuse consent to the carrying out or continuation of life-sustaining treatment unless the instrument contains express provision to that effect and that power will be subject to any conditions or restrictions laid down by the instrument (although there is a general power to give or refuse consent to the carrying out or continuation of other types of medical treatment) (s.11(7)(c) and (8)). The need for an express grant of a power in respect of decisions concerning life-sustaining treatment reflects the fundamental importance of such a power. While the donor may be happy for a donee to make all other types of welfare decisions, he or she may not be content for the donee to have authority to decide matters of life and death. A donor may choose instead to make an advance directive (which would take precedence in any event over the exercise of power by a donee under an LPA) or prefer to leave this type of decision to medical professionals.

4.6   SCOPE OF FINANCIAL LPAs: GIFTS

4.6.1   Background

The EPAA 1985 imposed restrictions on gifts that a donee of an EPA could make. Section 3(5) of the EPAA 1985 provided that an attorney could make gifts on behalf of charities or persons 'related to or connected with the donor'. In respect of gifts, they had to be of 'a seasonal nature or at a time, or on an anniversary, of a birth or marriage' implying that it was a gift given on a regular basis as opposed to one-off gifts on customary occasions (save for the specific occasions of weddings and births which were expressly mentioned).

There was also a provision that the size of the gift should not be unreasonable having regard to all the circumstances and, in particular, the size of the donor's estate.

4.6.2   Position under the Act

Although the provisions relating to gifts in the Act are largely the same, the wording has been changed to permit gifts being made on customary but one-off occasions such as baptism or graduation.

A donee may make gifts (s.12(2)):

- on customary occasions to persons (including himself) who are related to or connected with the donor if the value of the gift is not unreasonable having regard to all the circumstances and, in particular, the size of the donor's estate;
- to any charity to whom the donor made or might have been expected to make gifts if the value of the gift is not unreasonable having regard to all the circumstances and, in particular, the size of the donor's estate.

4.6.3   Customary occasion

This is defined as:

- the occasion or anniversary of a birth, a marriage or formation of a civil partnership; or
- any other occasion on which presents are customarily given within families or among friends or associates.

This definition, therefore, includes the occasion and anniversary of a civil partnership as well as marriage.

Further, in contrast with the definition in the EPAA 1985, there is a broader definition of other occasions when gifts may be made. The requirement is that gifts must be given customarily on that occasion but it does not need to be a regularly occurring event (e.g. a graduation, retirement, housewarming).

4.6.4   Reasonableness of size

The test is the same as that under the EPAA 1985. It will depend on all the circumstances. The donee has to apply his own judgment. In general, it can be said that gifts ought to be made from surplus income or not significant with respect to the size of the donor's estate.

4.6.5   Other restrictions in the instrument

The donor may also include specific restrictions and conditions on the donee's powers to make a gift which must be adhered to by the donee (s.12(4)).

4.6.6   Application to the Court of Protection

If the proposed gift is not covered by s.12(2) or if the donee is in doubt, he can apply to the Court of Protection which has the power to authorise the making of gifts which are not within s.12(2) (s. 23(4)).

4.7   DUTIES ON ATTORNEYS

4.7.1   Background

The Act does not materially alter the general duties imposed on attorneys of LPAs from the duties that are imposed on attorneys of EPAs.

An authority conferred by an LPA does not oblige a donee to act but authorises a donee to act if he wishes to do so. Once a donee starts to act, he or she will assume a number of duties and responsibilities which are imposed by the Act and the common law including a duty of care and fiduciary duties. The attorney acts as the donor's agent and has all the duties and obligations of an agent.[1] As an agent, an attorney owes the same duties to his principal as does a deputy (who also acts as an agent see (s.19(6) and discussion at **para. 6.6.1**). If the donee fails to comply, this could result in his removal as attorney. Alternatively, he or she could be liable for civil or criminal offences.

Donees are in a position of trust so there is always the potential for abuse. The main protection against abuse is the donor selecting a suitable donee. However, that will not always be an adequate safeguard against abuse. One change from the EPA scheme is that LPAs must be registered before they can be used. It is envisaged that the new registration requirements will assist in combating abuse. Concerns about abuse of powers by donees can be reported to the Office of the Public Guardian who can direct a Court of Protection Visitor to visit a donee or donor to investigate and report to the Public Guardian (s.58(1)(d)). The Public Guardian could then report to the Court and the Court of Protection could decide to revoke the instrument (s.22(3) which is discussed further below).

4.7.2   Duties on the attorney of an LPA

Duty to act in accordance with the principles of the Act and in the donor's best interests

When donees of LPAs exercise their powers, they must comply with all the provisions in the Act and, in particular, the principles set out in s.1 and they must always act in the best interests of the donor (in accordance with s.4) (s.9(4)). This means, for example, that the donee must (see **Chapter 3** for detailed discussion of ss.1 and 4):

- not treat the donor as unable to make a decision unless all practicable steps have been taken to help him to do so without success (s.1(3));
- not treat the donor as incapable merely because he makes an unwise decision (s.1(4));
- make decisions or take actions in accordance with the best interests of a person who lacks capacity (s.1(5));
- in coming to a view as to the donor's best interests, consider whether the person is likely to obtain capacity in the future, permit and encourage the donor to participate as fully as possible in the decision, consider the donor's past and present wishes and feelings and beliefs and consult where appropriate with friends and relatives with an interest in P's welfare (s.4).

Duty to act within the scope of the LPA

A donee must act within the actual scope of the powers set out in the LPA including any specific conditions and restrictions laid down by the donor (s.9(4)(b)). If the donee considers that additional powers are needed to act, he or she must make an application to the Court of Protection (see **para. 4.10.3**).

However, as an agent an attorney will have implied authority to do what is necessary for or incidental to the effective execution of express authority. This is not a matter addressed in the Draft Code of Practice or the Explanatory Notes.

Duty to comply with directions of the Court of Protection

The Court of Protection has wide powers under ss.22 and 23 of the Act to determine questions and give directions as to the meaning and effect of an LPA. The Court can also require donees to provide accounts, reports or records, require the donee to supply information or produce documents or things in the possession of the donee, give directions for remuneration of the donee and relieve the donee wholly or partly from any liability incurred for breach of his or her duties as donee. Donees must comply with any orders or directions of the Court.

Not to disclaim without notifying the donor and the Court

The precise requirements of a disclaimer will be set out in regulations.

Duty to keep accounts

A financial donee must keep up-to-date accounts of his or her dealings and transactions on the donor's behalf. The Draft Code of Practice states that where a lay person, such as a family member, is acting as donee, and the donor's affairs are fairly straightforward, all that will be required is a record of income, major items or regular items of expenditure and details of the donor's bank accounts (para.6.29). However, more will be required when the attorney is acting as a professional attorney or the financial affairs are complicated.

Duty to preserve the separate character of the donor's property

Donees should keep donor's money separate from his or her own. A possible exception stated in the Draft Code is where the donee is a husband or wife and the couple have always had a joint bank account.

Duty of care

A donee owes the donor a duty of care in carrying out his or her functions as attorney, commensurate with any skills he has or holds himself out as having. A higher standard of care will be expected of a professional attorney who receives remuneration for acting.

Duty not to delegate

It is a principle of the law of agency that an agent cannot delegate his or her authority. The donee is the agent of the donor. It is only in respect of tasks which the donor would not expect the donee to carry out personally which can be delegated. Any wider powers of delegation will need to be expressly set out in the instrument.

Duty not to take advantage of his position

The donee is a fiduciary and must not profit from his or her position. Donees must avoid any conflicts between their responsibilities towards the donor and their own interests. They must be guided by the principles of the Act and the duty to act in the donor's best interests. If a donee is concerned about a conflict of interest, he or she can apply to the Court for directions as to how to operate the LPA or for approval of a gift (s.23(2) and (4)).

Duty of good faith

A donee must act honestly and in good faith.

Duty of confidentiality

A donee has a duty to keep the donor's affairs confidential unless the donor has consented to disclosure or there is some other good reason for disclosing personal or financial information which overrides the duty such as the public interest.

---

1   See *Bowstead on Agency* 17th edn (Sweet & Maxwell, 2001) for more detailed discussions of the duty of an agent.

4.8   REVOCATION OF AN LPA

4.8.1   Background

The revocation provisions in the EPAA 1985 are broadly similar to those in the Act. However, it is no longer necessary for the Court to confirm revocation by the donor as was necessary under the EPAA 1985 (in respect of instruments which had been registered) (ss.7(1)(a), 8(3) of the EPAA 1985). The Court previously had to confirm that the donor had done what was necessary to effect an express revocation and that the donor had capacity to revoke. The difference with EPAs is that a donor would already be incapable or becoming incapable otherwise the instrument would not be registered at all. Confirmation by the Court is no longer required (s.13(2) of the Act). However, the Court has the power to declare whether the instrument has in fact been revoked by the donor if an application to it is made (s.22(2)(b)). Under the EPAA 1985, it was the Court which had the responsibility for cancelling the registration of an instrument in circumstances where it had been revoked (s.8(4)). That is now the remit of the Public Guardian (see Part 3 of Schedule 1 to the Act).

4.8.2   Position under the Mental Capacity Act 2005

The revocation provisions apply when the donor has executed an instrument with a view to creating an LPA or when an LPA has been registered. It should also be noted that the Court of Protection has additional powers of revocation in situations of fraud, undue pressure, contravention of authority or acts contrary to a donor's best interests (see **para. 4.10.2**).

The situations where the appointment power will be revoked under s.13 are as follows:

Matters affecting the donor:

■   the donor revokes the power when he has capacity to do so (s.13(2));
■   the donor's bankruptcy revokes the power in respect of property and affairs (s.13(3)). But the power is merely suspended if an interim bankruptcy order is made for the duration of the order (s.13(4)).

Matters affecting the donee:

■   the disclaimer by the donee of his power (in accordance with the requirements to be set down by the Lord Chancellor for disclaimer in regulations) (s.13(5), (6)(a));
■   the death of a donee (s.13(5), (6)(b));
■   the bankruptcy of a donee in respect of financial powers but not welfare powers (save that if an interim bankruptcy restrictions order is made, the financial powers will only be suspended for the duration of that order) (s.13(5), (6)(b), (8), (9));

- the dissolution or annulment of a marriage or civil partnership between the donor or donee unless the instrument expressly provides that it does not have that effect (s.13(6)(c), (11));
- the lack of capacity of the donee (s.13(6)(d)).

If the donee has been replaced under the instrument or there remains one or more other donee(s) appointed to act jointly and severally, the effect of these events will be only to terminate the appointment of the donee but not to revoke the power itself (s.13(6), (7)).

Following revocation of the instrument, the Public Guardian must cancel the registration of an instrument as an LPA when it has been revoked as a result of the donor's bankruptcy or on the occurrence of an event affecting the donee as provided for in s.13(6)(a)–(d) (listed above) or when directed by the Court of Protection to cancel the instrument (Part 3 of Schedule 1).

4.8.3   Concerns

There is no mechanism in the Act for the Public Guardian being informed of acts or circumstances giving rise to revocation of the LPA (except when the Court of Protection directs him to cancel registration). Unless the Public Guardian is made so aware, he will not be in a position to cancel the registration of the instrument and the register will include LPAs that have in fact been revoked pursuant to the provisions of s.13 of the Act.

4.9   PROTECTION IF NO POWER CREATED OR REVOKED

4.9.1   Background

Protection is afforded by the EPAA 1985 to provide protection to the attorney under an EPA and any person dealing with him in good faith (s.9 of the EPAA 1985). These provisions are broadly mirrored in the Act (s.14).

4.9.2   Scope of the protection

The protection provided by the Act is in circumstances:

- where the LPA instrument was registered under Schedule 1 (see registration provisions discussed above) but an LPA was not created, regardless of whether or not the registration has been cancelled;
- where the power has been revoked.

4.9.3   No power created

Donees (s.14(2))

A donee exercising powers when no LPA was ever created, does not incur liability to the donor or others unless:

- he knows an LPA was not created; or
- is aware of circumstances which would have terminated his authority to act even if an LPA had been created.

The test is one of actual knowledge or awareness and not an objective test as to whether the donee ought reasonably to have known.

Other persons (s.14(3))

Transactions between a donee and other person (in circumstances where no LPA was ever created) which are in favour of that person (and not the donee) are valid unless that person, at the time of the transaction:

- knew an LPA was not created; or
- was aware of circumstances which would have terminated the donee's authority to act even if an LPA had been created.

Further, s.14(4) of the Act provides that there is a presumption of validity in a transaction between a donee and another person where the interest of the purchaser (i.e. a third party) depends on the transaction being valid under s.14(3), if the transaction was completed within 12 months of the instrument being registered or the third party makes a statutory declaration within three months after completion of the purchase stating that he had no reason to doubt the donee's authority to dispose of the property at the time of purchase.

4.9.4   Power revoked

Section 5 of the Powers of Attorney Act 1971 (the 1971 Act) applies to provide protection to the donee and third parties where the LPA is revoked. The donee is protected if at the time he did not know of the revocation (or of an event which has the effect of revoking the power, e.g. death of the donor) (s.5(1), (5) of the 1971 Act). A transaction between the donee and a third party is valid in favour of the third party if the third party did not know of the revocation (or of an event which has the effect of revoking the power) (s.5(2), (5) of the 1971 Act). The same presumption of validity in respect of disposals of property applies (s.5(4) of the 1971 Act).

Section 14(5) of the Act provides that the protection afforded by s.5 of the 1971 Act also applies in situations where an LPA covers welfare as well as property and affairs and it is only the donee's powers in respect of property and affairs which have come to an end, e.g. as a result of bankruptcy of the donee.

4.10   POWERS OF THE COURT IN RESPECT OF LPAs

4.10.1   Background

The powers of the Court in respect of LPAs are broadly similar to the powers contained in the EPAA 1985.

4.10.2   Powers in relation to validity of LPA

The Court can determine any question relating to whether the requirements for the creation of an LPA have been met or whether the power has been revoked or come to an end (s.22(2)).

Further, the Court can direct that an instrument is not registered or revoke the instrument or LPA (where the donor does not have capacity to do so) where it is satisfied:

- that fraud or undue pressure was put on the donor to create an LPA; or
- that the donee is behaving or proposing to behave so as to contravene his authority or contrary to the donor's best interests (s.14(3), (4)).

4.10.3   Powers in relation to the operation of LPAs

This provision allows the Court to decide questions about the meaning or effect of LPAs (s.23(1)). Further, the Court has power to give directions to donees or give consent or authorisation on behalf of the donor where the donor lacks capacity to do so (s.23(2), (3)). The directions that the Court may give when the donor lacks capacity include directions in respect of:

- rendering accounts and reports and associated records;
- requiring the provision of information by the donee or produce documents or other things in his possession as donee;
- remuneration or expenses of the donee;
- relieving the donee wholly or partly from any liability which he has incurred in breach of his duties as donee.

The Court can also authorise the making of gifts which are not covered by s.12(2) (s.23(4)).

4.11   ARRANGEMENTS FOR EPAs

4.11.1   Background

The Act repeals the EPAA 1985 (s.66 of the Act). It will not be possible to execute an EPA once the Act is in force. However, many EPAs will have been executed prior to the coming into force of the Act. It was expressly stated in Parliament that it would be unfair to deprive those who had executed EPAs of using them once the Act comes into force. Further, given that registration of EPAs occurs only when the donor loses or is believed to be losing capacity, practically it would not be possible to contact all those who have executed EPAs in order to arrange for an LPA to be executed instead (if the donor still had capacity) (see Hansard in the Committee Stage in the House of Lords at col. 783). Of course donors may decide to destroy the EPA and create an LPA.

4.11.2   Arrangements for EPAs

The Act makes transitional provisions for EPAs. Essentially, the EPAA 1985 is reproduced in Schedule 5 in its entirety save that minor amendments are made to take account of changes in the Court of Protection and the role of the new Public Guardian.

Part 2 of Schedule 5 also contains transitional provisions relating to EPAs in respect of procedural matters. Provision is made for pending applications and appeals under the EPAA 1985 to be treated as proceedings brought under Schedule 4 to the Act in so far as that is possible.

5 ACTS IN CONNECTION WITH CARE OR TREATMENT

5.1 BACKGROUND

5.1.1 The problem

Many everyday actions involve touching a person or interfering with their property. At common law, touching someone without their consent can amount to the tort of battery or the crime of assault. Interfering with someone's property, without their consent, may amount to the crime of theft or the tort of conversion. The need for consent is the legal reflection of the ethical principle of respect for autonomy.

Carers of people lacking capacity, whether family members or professionals, are faced every day with having to carry out actions for people who are unable to do them for themselves and who are unable to consent to others doing those actions for them. These actions may range from simple acts like washing and dressing, buying food or paying gas or electricity bills, to moving a person from their own home to a care or nursing home, or carrying out an operation to preserve or enhance a person's life.

The courts have long accepted that any physically invasive medical treatment or procedure, however trivial, is unlawful unless authorised by consent or other lawful authority.[1] When a person lacks capacity to give consent the common law doctrine of necessity may provide lawful authority for the action:

> ... not only (1) must there be a necessity to act when it is not practicable to communicate with the assisted person, but also (2) the action taken must be such as a reasonable person would in all the circumstances take, acting in the best interests of the assisted person.[2]

5.1.2 The common law solution

The uncertainty surrounding which actions are lawful without a valid consent, particularly when there have been doubts or disputes about a person's best interests, has led to a number of high profile and costly cases. These cases are heard in the Family Division of the High Court and are determined under the Court's inherent jurisdiction. The use of this jurisdiction for granting declaratory relief in respect of incapacitated adults is relatively new, starting with the case of *Re F*[3] in 1990 and has continued to be developed by the High Court to cover new situations.

The claimant in such a case is usually the relevant local authority or NHS Trust or primary care trust (PCT), which seeks declarations as to the incapacity of the person concerned and the lawfulness of the proposed action.[4] The purpose of bringing proceedings for a declaration is to protect both the patient and the doctors and to reassure the patient's family and the public that what is proposed to be done is lawful.

Is there a legal requirement to bring cases to court?

There is a currently some confusion about when cases should be brought before the court. Certain acts are considered to be so serious that each case should be brought before the court. They are the proposed withdrawal of artificial nutrition and hydration (ANH) from a person in a permanent vegetative state (PVS) and the-non therapeutic sterilisation of a person lacking capacity to consent. In all other cases of doubt or dispute over capacity and/or best interests:

> Good practice may require medical practitioners to seek such a declaration where the legality of the proposed treatment is in doubt. This is not, however, something that they are required to do as a matter of law.[5]

Munby J at first instance in *Burke*, when considering the decision of the European Court in *Glass v. UK* [2004] 1 FLR 1019, held that the advent of the Human Rights Act 1998 (HRA 1998) has converted what had previously only been a 'matter of good practice' into a 'matter of legal requirement'. The Court of Appeal rejected this suggestion.[6] However, the court cited without comment at para. 74 the observations of Coleridge J in *D v. NHS Trust (Medical Treatment: Consent: Termination)* [2003] EWHC 2793; [2004] 1 FLR 1110 at p.31.

> The advent of the Human Rights Act 1998 has enhanced the responsibility of the court to protect the welfare of these patients and, in particular, to protect the patient's right to respect for her private and family life under Art 8(1) of the European Convention for the Protection of Human Rights and Fundamental Freedoms 1950.

Current procedure

The claimant issues an application under Part 8 of the Civil Procedure Rules 1998 in the Family Division of the High Court.[7] The Official Solicitor is usually appointed by the Court to act as litigation friend of the person under a disability. The Court has power to make interim and final declarations and injunctions. In an appropriate case the Court can make a prospective declaration to cover the happening of a future event.[8] The Court also has power to declare that some specified person, in relation to specified matters, is effectively a surrogate decision maker for the incapable adult.[9]

Declarations are generally only a 'snapshot in time' and do not provide continuing authority to act in a particular way if new circumstances arise. A declaration cannot make lawful that which without a declaration would be unlawful or make unlawful that which without a declaration would be lawful. Such transitory outcomes may leave both the incapacitated person and those caring for the person in a vulnerable position.

5.1.3   The solution under the Mental Incapacity Bill

The Draft Bill of June 2003 provided for a 'general authority' to act on behalf of a person who lacked capacity. The provision had been intended to clarify the common law principle of necessity and to make lawful many day-to-day decisions made on behalf of people without capacity. There was, however, widespread misunderstanding of the concept and purpose of the 'general authority' and it was criticised in the report of the Joint Committee. The government agreed that 'the term "general authority" created false and unhelpful impressions'[10] and it agreed to change it.

The Mental Capacity Bill of 17 June 2005 contained a new cl.5, entitled 'acts in connection with care or treatment'. This clause survived without amendment to become s.5 of the Act.

5.1.4   The solution under the Act

The purpose of s.5 of the Act is to 'allow carers and healthcare professionals who have a responsibility to care for a person who lacks capacity to be able to carry out that caring obligation without incurring liability'.[11]

It is anticipated, however, that even after the Act comes into force serious healthcare and treatment decisions will still have to come before the new Court of Protection for a decision. Paragraphs 5.23 and 5.24 of the Draft Code of Practice anticipate the making of a Practice Direction by the new President of the Court of Protection confirming that it will be necessary to refer both withdrawal of ANH from PVS patients and non-therapeutic sterilisations to the court for a declaration. Other cases that are likely to need a court decision are those involving ethical dilemmas, or irresolvable disputes between professionals and family members.

Section 51(2)(e) of the Act provides that the court may appoint the Official Solicitor to represent the person in such proceedings (see **Chapter 11** for a further discussion of the new Court of Protection).

However, much of the detail has been left to the Code of Practice and guidance. The government has acknowledged that it will be important for the Act to be accompanied by appropriate training for professionals, and for substantial information to be provided for informal carers who will be affected by the Act's provisions. It is envisaged that the guidance and training will complement the Code of Practice. It is vitally important, particularly in relation to serious treatment and care decisions, that the Code of Practice is finalised and the training and guidance in place by the time that the Act comes into force. Only then will the law, as implemented, properly safeguard the interests of informal and professional carers as well as some of the most vulnerable members of society.

 1   *Re F (Mental Patient: Sterilisation)* [1990] 2 AC 1; *Re T (Adult: Refusal of Treatment)* [1993] Fam 95; *Re MB* [1997] 8 Med LR 217, CA.
 2   In *re F (Mental Patient: Sterilisation)* [1990] 2 AC 1, 75–76 per Lord Goff of Chieveley.
 3   Supra.
 4   *St George's Healthcare NHS Trust* v. *S* [1999] Fam 26.
 5   *Burke* v. *GMC and Others* [2005] EWCA 1003 (Fam) per Lord Phillips MR, at para 80; [2005] All ER (D) 445. See also, Coleridge J at paras. 32, 34 and 36 of *D* v. *NHS Trust (Medical Treatment: Consent: Termination)* [2003] EWHC 2793 (Fam), [2004] 1 FLR 1110 for a full discussion regarding termination of pregnancy.
 6   Ibid., at para 74.
 7   See *Practice Note (Official Solicitor Declaratory Proceedings: Medical and Welfare Decisions for Adults who Lack Capacity)* [2001] 2 FLR 158.
 8   *Re S (Adult Patient) (Inherent Jurisdiction: Family Life)* [2002] EWHC 2278 (Fam), [2003] 1 FLR 292. See also *Wyatt & Anor* v. *Portsmouth Hospital NHS & Anor* [2005] EWCA Civ 1181 per Wall LJ at paras 117 and 118.
 9   Supra.
10   *Government Response to Recommendation 30 of the Scrutiny Committee's Report on the Draft Mental Incapacity Bill*, February 2004.
11   Paragraph 5.8 of the Draft Code.

5.2   SECTION 5 ACTS

5.2.1   Section 5 applies to provide protection from liability to 'a person who does acts in connection with care or treatment'

'A person'

The Act does not define 'a person'. The section therefore refers to any person carrying out such an act and may relate to a number of people at any given time. The current Draft Code of Practice makes it clear that:

- there is no question of one person having a statutory power which excludes all others;
- the provisions do not confer any special powers on anyone to make substitute decisions or to give substitute consent.

'Acts in connection with care or treatment'

The Act does not define 'care' or 'treatment', other than to state at s.64(1) that ' "treatment" includes a diagnostic or other procedure'. The category is therefore left intentionally wide and the words should be given their ordinary meaning. Personal care could include washing, dressing, shopping or assisting in clearing a person's house after they have moved into residential care. Health care and treatment could include medical and dental treatment, nursing care, taking blood or acupuncture.

As a rule of thumb, it is necessary to comply with s.5 requirements if consent would normally be required from a person of full capacity to the carrying out of a particular act (s.5(2)).

5.2.2   Conditions a person must fulfil

'Taken reasonable steps to establish that the person lacks capacity in relation to the matter in question': s.5(1)(a)

Reasonable steps must be taken to ascertain whether a person has capacity in relation to the particular decision (see **Chapter 3**). The principles relating to assessment of capacity are set out in ss.2 and 3 of the Act. The key principles apply and all practical steps must be taken to assist the person to make his or her own decision.

'Reasonably believes that the person lacks capacity, and that it is in the best interests of that person for the act to be done: s.5(1)(b)

Provided the person has reasonable grounds of believing that the person lacks capacity, the person must then consider whether there are reasonable grounds for believing that it is in the incapacitated person's best interests for the act to be done (see **Chapter 3**), taking into account all the circumstances, the best interests checklist and the key principles.

As the Draft Code points out at para. 5.12 'carers acting informally are not expected to be experts in assessing capacity, but they must be able to show that they have reasonable grounds for believing the person lacks capacity in relation to the particular matter, at that particular time'. Such a person will be protected from liability provided that 's/he can point to the grounds which justified a reasonable belief of lack of capacity'. Informal carers, relying on a reasonable belief that the act was in the best interests of the person, will also be protected from liability if they can show that it was reasonable in all the circumstances for them to have done the particular act.

Where professionals are involved their professional skill will be taken into account in determining whether they took reasonable steps to determine lack of capacity (see para. 5.14 of the Draft Code) and best interests.

5.2.3   No protection from civil or criminal liability resulting from negligent acts

The Act makes it clear that s.5 does not provide a defence to negligent acts. Consent does not provide a defence to the tort of negligence. A surgeon may obtain a patient's consent to an operation but if he then performs that operation negligently he can still be sued in the tort of negligence. If the patient then dies as a result of the surgeon's gross negligence the surgeon may then be charged with the manslaughter of the patient.

5.2.4   Effect of an advanced decision to refuse treatment

An advanced directive is an exercise of a person's autonomy once he has lost capacity to make a decision him or herself. If a person has made a valid and applicable advanced directive this takes priority over s.5 (see ss.24–26 of the Act and **Chapter** 7 for further details about advanced decisions).

Provided the healthcare professional is satisfied that the advanced directive exists, is valid and applicable to the circumstances, he must act in accordance with the advanced directive even if he believes that in doing so he will not be acting in the patient's best interests. Section 5 is not applicable in these circumstances.

5.3   LIMITATION ON SECTION 5 ACTS

5.3.1   Background

The limitations provided in s.6 of the Act restrict the immunity from liability granted by s.5 in respect of acts carried out by persons in connection with care and treatment of an incapable person.

Of particular concern in both Houses of Parliament was the reliance that could be placed on s.5 in cases where it was proposed to use force or interfere with a person's liberty in order to bring about a particular act. There was a desire to restrict the circumstances when force or the threat of force could be used. Further, given that the purpose of s.5 is to reduce the number of occasions when carers or other people will not feel it necessary to go to court in order to obtain a declaration that a particular act is in a person's best interests, it was obviously of importance to make it as clear as possible when the use of or threat of force would be sanctioned.

There was debate in both Houses of Parliament about a potential conflict between s.5 and Art.5 of the ECHR if the effect of s.5 was that an incapable person could be deprived of his liberty. This concern was raised by the Joint Committee of Human Rights (see 4th Report and 23rd Report of the Joint Committee of Human Rights). It was for that reason that an amendment was introduced at the Report Stage in the House of Lords to include the provision in s.6(5) that restraint does not include a deprivation of liberty within the meaning of Art.5(1) of the Convention (see Hansard 17 March 2005, col. 1468 and HL Bill 48). Although this amendment has made it clear that deprivations of liberty are not sanctioned under s.5, identifying what amounts to a deprivation of liberty is not so straightforward. The European Court of Human Rights in the *Bournewood Case* (*HL* v. *United Kingdom* Case No. 45508/99, 81 BMLR 131) stated at para. 89 of the judgment that: 'The distinction between a deprivation of, and restriction upon, liberty is merely one of degree or intensity and not nature or substance' (see **para.** 1.13 for further discussion).

5.3.2   Restraint

There is no general protection from liability under the Act in respect of acts intended to restrain a person lacking capacity. The Draft Code of Practice emphasises that:

> no protection is offered to people who use or threaten violence in order to carry out any action in connection with the care or treatment of a person lacking capacity or to force that person to comply with the carer's actions. However, there may be limited circumstances when the use of some form of restraint or physical intervention may be permitted in order to protect the person from harm (para. 5.25).

The Code of Practice to the MHA 1983 provides that when restraint is used on a person (whether in an emergency or as part of a treatment plan) consideration should be given as to whether formal detention under the MHA 1983 is appropriate, particularly if the restraint occurred on a repeated basis (at para. 19.8). The provisions on restraint in the Act do not refer to this issue but carers and others ought to be aware that if restraint is being used on a repeated basis, consideration should be given by the appropriate professionals as to whether formal detention under the MHA 1983 is required.

Definition of restraint

Section 6(4) provides that someone restrains a person if: (1) he uses or threatens to use force to secure the doing of an act which the person lacking capacity resists; or (2) restricts that person's liberty of movement whether or not that person resists.

It is important to note that it is the threat of force as well as the use of actual force which is covered. Secondly, compliance by the person lacking capacity is irrelevant if the act involves a restriction of that person's liberty of movement. Holding a person down or locking a person in a room would both involve restrictions of liberty of movement.

Further, the Draft Code of Practice expressly refers to chemical restraint as being covered by the definition which includes, for example, a person being given sleeping pills in order to sedate them and restrict their liberty of movement (at para. 5.28).

The restriction on the use of restraint applies to financial decisions as well as welfare decisions. However, it seems far less likely that an act of restraint would be justified in the context of a financial decision. The Draft Code of Practice does not discuss restraint in the context of financial decisions. However, since the purpose of an act of restraint must be to prevent 'harm' this could include financial harm (see example at para. 5.31 of the Draft Code about a person who is running up huge debts). On the other hand, it seems unlikely that a financial donee or deputy would need to use acts of restraint against the incapable person to protect his finances because, if a financial LPA or other order under the Act is in place, there is power to act on the incapable person's behalf.

Conditions justifying the use of restraint

Section 5 provides a general immunity in respect of acts of care and treatment where a person has taken reasonable steps to establish that the person lacking capacity does indeed lack capacity and also reasonably believes that that person lacks capacity in relation to the matter and that it is in that person's best interests for the act to be done.

It is not enough to comply with these provisions in respect of acts involving restraint because they are not generally permitted by the Act. Two further conditions must both be satisfied in order for carers and others to obtain protection from liability which are:

- the person acting must reasonably believe that it is necessary to do the act in order to prevent harm to the person lacking capacity (s.6(2)); and
- the act is a proportionate response to the likelihood of the person lacking capacity suffering harm and the seriousness of the harm (s.6(3)).

Necessity

The Act requires reasonable belief in the necessity of acting. This is an objective test. The onus is on the decision maker to identify reasons which provide objective justification for the belief that the act is necessary in order to avert harm.

The purpose of the act must be to avert harm. The Act does not sanction restraint when the purpose is simply to enable a carer or someone else to do something more quickly or easily. The reference is simply to 'harm'. There is no requirement of a risk of serious harm (although the degree of harm is relevant to the proportionality of the response). Further, there is no definition of what constitutes 'harm'. The difficulties of defining what constitutes harm in a particular situation has meant that no such definition is available. The obvious types of harm covered would be mental or physical injury. But there is no reason why the definition of harm is so restricted. Harm to a person's financial situation is also capable of falling into the definition of harm. This is supported by the Draft Code of Practice which includes as an example a person with bi-polar affect disorder running up huge debts through spending money excessively when in a manic phase (at para. 5.31). However, clearly the type of harm is relevant to the issues of necessity and proportionality. In many cases it will be possible to avert some or all of the risk by taking measures which do not amount to the use or threat of force or restraint of liberty. If not, a proportionate response will be required.

Proportionality

The concept of proportionality is now fairly familiar following the entry into force of the HRA 1998. Section 6(3) of the Act requires that an act of restraint is proportionate to the likelihood of the person lacking capacity suffering harm and the seriousness of that harm. What this means in practice is that the means of restraint should be commensurate with the desired outcome. The minimum degree of force for the shortest time possible should be used. The more likely and more serious the risk of harm, the greater the degree of force that will be justified. An example provided in the Draft Code of Practice (at para. 5.33) is that of a man with learning difficulties who gets distressed in his college class and will sometimes hit the wall in frustration. Staff do not want to stop him attending the class because he enjoys it and do not want to sit a support worker next to him in class because he gets upset and they regard it as inappropriately invasive for the support worker actively to restrain him. Instead, they decide to provide him with a restrictive hand cuff for a few weeks while they work with him to find other ways to manage his emotions.

5.3.3   Deprivation of liberty

Section 6(5) expressly provides that the definition of restraint in the Act does not cover acts which amount to deprivations of liberty for the purpose of Art. 5(1) of the ECHR. This subsection was included in the Mental Capacity Bill at the Report Stage (HL Bill 48), the Joint Parliamentary Select Committee on Human Rights in its 15th report 2004–2005 being concerned that the proposed Bill might lead to deprivations of liberty which were not compatible with Art. 5 of the ECHR or involuntary placement of an incapable person in a psychiatric hospital (paras. 4.6–4.9).

As stated above, whether something amounts to a deprivation of liberty is a matter of degree or intensity and not nature or substance (see *HL* v. *United Kingdom* Case No. 45508/99). Detention in a hospital against a person's will is something that would amount to a deprivation of liberty. Further, following the European Court's decision in *HL* v. *United Kingdom*, detention of a compliant patient can also amount to a deprivation of liberty, for example, when a person is subject to continuous supervision and control and is not free to leave the hospital (see para. 91 of the judgment). Similarly, if a person is held down for a significant period of time, this could also amount to a deprivation of liberty as opposed to an act of restraint.

5.3.4   Effect on formal decision-making powers

Where formal powers already exist for making decisions on a person's behalf under an existing LPA (see **Chapter 4**) or by a deputy appointed by the Court (see **Chapter 6**), these decision-making powers take priority (s.6(6)). However, it is only if a donee of an LPA or a deputy has authority to make decisions in respect of the particular matter in question. An LPA, the deputy or the Court of Protection is able to provide consent on behalf of the person so it is not necessary for a carer or other person to act without consent in reliance on the s.5 immunity. This avoids acts being done which conflict with the decision of an LPA (who has been chosen by the person lacking capacity to make decisions on his behalf) or that of the deputy appointed by the Court to make this decision.

However, there is a fall-back provision which permits healthcare or other care staff to take action to provide life-sustaining treatment or acts reasonably necessary to prevent a serious deterioration in the condition of the person lacking capacity while the Court is approached for a decision to be made (s.6(7)). This addresses the situation where care staff are of the view than an LPA or deputy is not acting outside the scope of their authority or not in the best interests of the patient and want to seek guidance from the Court about this.

5.4   PAYMENT FOR NECESSARY GOODS AND SERVICES

5.4.1   Background

The general position at common law is that a contract is voidable if entered into by a person who lacks capacity and the other contracting party knows or ought to have known (i.e. constructive knowledge) of the other's incapacity. The Sale of Goods Act 1979, s.3 created an exception to this rule in respect of 'necessaries', i.e. goods which are necessary in a person's life . The effect of s.7 of the Act is to consolidate the law in this area and to provide a comprehensive definition of 'necessaries'.

An amendment proposed to this provision at the Committee Stage in the House of Lords was to change the underlying common law position that contracts are voidable if it is established that the other contracting party knew or ought to have known of the other person's incapacity. It was proposed (by Lord Goodhart (see Hansard 27 January 2005, at col. 1396)) that an amendment should be introduced to bring the law in England and Wales into line with that in Scotland where there is no requirement that the other contracting party knew or ought to have known of the incapacity. The proposal was stated to address the situation where unfair advantage is taken of persons who lack capacity. The proposed amendment was resisted on the basis that the current law enables persons who lack capacity to ensure that they can obtain the goods and services to enable them to live independently. Traders can supply necessaries in the knowledge that they will be able to recoup a reasonable price. There was concern that businesses would be reluctant to do business with incapacitated persons if all contracts could be set aside. Further, it was considered that other legislative initiatives such as the Consumer Credit Bill and the Unfair Commercial Practices Directive will address the position of unfairness in commercial relationships as they affect incapacitated persons (see Baroness Ashton of Upholland, Hansard 27 January 2005, at cols. 1388–1410). Baroness Ashton committed the government at the Committee Stage in the House of Lords to carrying out further research into the current law and the nature of the problems facing persons who lack capacity in commercial transactions (see Hansard 27 January 2005, at col. 1471).

5.4.2 The definition of necessary

The definition in s.7(2) of the Act is that necessary means suitable to a person's condition in life and to his actual requirements at the time when the goods or services are supplied.

5.4.3 Condition in life

The Draft Code of Practice states that condition in life is to be interpreted as the person's place in society rather than any physical or mental condition (at para. 5.36). The reference to condition in life appears to be aimed at ascertaining the types of goods or services which can be said to be necessary for a particular individual. It seeks to ensure that a person is able to maintain a similar standard of living and way of life to that experienced prior to losing capacity. If a uniform definition of necessary in respect of goods and services were adopted, this would have the effect of introducing a lowest common denominator. So a person who has always bought expensive clothes and food ought to be able to continue to buy these as necessary goods.

5.4.4 Actual requirements at the time of supply

This requires that there is an actual need for the goods or services at the time of supply. There will be no actual requirement at the time of supply if the person already has an existing stock which is sufficient or has no need for the goods/services at all. The example given by the Draft Code of Practice (at para. 5.36) is that evening clothes for a person moving into a residential home would not be necessary goods if the person was comfortable in and preferred to wear casual clothing. The position might be different if the person was used to dressing for dinner at home and would be distressed at not continuing to do this. Although, if the person had some evening clothes already which were in a reasonable condition, there may be no actual requirement for new clothes. In extreme cases, it will not be difficult to ascertain whether something is or is not necessary goods or services (e.g. supplying gardening tools to a person without a garden). In more subtle situations, there is unlikely to be a clear line defining whether goods or services are necessary because the test necessarily involves a considerable subjective element when deciding whether something is necessary with regard to a person's condition in life.

5.4.5 The obligation to pay a reasonable price

Section 7(1) of the Act imposes an obligation on a person who lacks capacity to pay a reasonable price in respect of necessary goods or services. The legal responsibility for making payment rests on the person who lacks capacity even if he or she lacks capacity to contract for the goods or services. In so far as a dispute arose about what constitutes a reasonable price which could not be resolved between the parties, it would be ultimately a matter which the county court or High Court (depending on the value of the claim) would have to adjudicate upon. The ascertainment of a reasonable price would not be for the Court of Protection whose jurisdiction is concerned with making decisions on behalf of or appointing deputies to make decisions on behalf of persons who lack capacity.

5.5   EXPENDITURE

5.5.1   Background

Section 8 of the Act operates with s.5 to enable a carer or other person who arranges for goods or services to be supplied to a person lacking capacity (P) also to make arrangements for payment in respect of those goods or services.

Expenditure is made lawful under s.8 in respect of acts to which s.5 applies, so this requires that the goods or services are supplied in connection with care and treatment and ordered by the decision maker with the reasonable belief that the person lacking capacity does indeed lack capacity and the supply of the goods/services is in the best interests of that person.

Section 8 permits a carer to use the money of the person lacking capacity to pay directly for the goods or services or to pay on that person's behalf and to be reimbursed by that person.

5.5.2   Use of P's money

Section 8(1) permits a carer or other person to pledge credit to the person lacking capacity and use money in that person's possession to pay for goods or services contracted for by the carer or other person on that person's behalf. The money has to be in that person's possession. Hence, this provision does not authorise a carer to access that person's bank account or other investments to obtain the necessary money. The specific authority of an LPA, a deputyship or a single order of the Court of Protection would usually be required to access a bank account or other savings.

5.5.3   Reimbursement

Section 8(2) authorises the decision maker to reimburse himself from money in the possession of the person lacking capacity if he has paid for the goods or services supplied on behalf of that person. This provision also permits the decision maker to be 'otherwise indemnified by [the person lacking capacity]'. It is not clear what is thereby permitted. The only example provided in the Draft Code of Practice is that the person lacking capacity could give an 'IOU' to the decision maker pending specific authority being obtained to access a bank account (at para. 5.37). It is unlikely that this provision would be given a wide interpretation by the courts so as to allow, for example, the person lacking capacity to give the decision maker an item of his or her property so as to compensate the decision maker for his expenditure. The Draft Code of Practice states that this section does not authorise the decision maker to sell property belonging to the person lacking capacity in order to secure funds. Unless the person lacking capacity has money in his or her possession sufficient to meet the debt, carers and others persons should apply to the Court or to request the sum from an LPA or deputy (when one is appointed to deal with property and affairs). Otherwise a carer or other person puts himself at risk of not complying with ss.5 and 8 and acting unlawfully.

5.5.4   Formal powers

Section 8(3) provides that the provisions in s.8 do not affect any formal powers held by others to control P's money or spend money on P's behalf. Formal powers in this respect could be held by an LPA or by a deputy appointed by the Court. Informal powers under ss.5 and 8 in respect of P's money or property cannot, therefore, be used by carers or others to conflict with formal powers held by attorneys or deputies.

6 POWERS OF THE COURT OF PROTECTION TO MAKE DECLARATIONS AND APPOINT DEPUTIES

6.1 BACKGROUND

This part of the Act contains the core jurisdiction of the Court.[1] It is intended to provide a forum of last resort for difficult cases or complex decisions.[2] It empowers the Court to make decisions on behalf of incapable persons, or to confer a power to make those decisions upon a new statutory creature – the deputy. The Act frames within a statutory structure the existing common law powers exercised under the inherent jurisdiction of the Court and extends them to include the making of declarations about general 'matters' rather than only specific decisions, and the conferring of authority on a deputy to make a specific decision or decisions about certain matters on behalf of the incapable person.

There is a presumption in favour of the Court making specific orders and declarations in respect of decisions rather than the appointment of a deputy, which is intended to be a 'de minimis' power.[3] Further, there are a number of substantial restrictions on a deputy's functions, and his powers may be varied or revoked by the Court.

These narrowly circumscribed powers should be contrasted with the broad ones granted under the Scottish Act.

---

1 Explanatory Notes at para. 65. It is proposed that there will be further Official Guidance and information in Rules of the Court, Regulations and Practice Directions – Draft Code of Practice at para. 7.1.
2 Draft Code of Practice, at para. 7.3.
3 Hansard, HC, 11 October 2004, col. 29

6.2 COURT'S POWER TO MAKE DECLARATIONS

The Court may, by s.15(1) of the Act, make three types of declaration in relation to an incapable person:

(a) whether a person has or lacks capacity to make a decision specified in the declaration;[1]

(b) whether a person has or lacks capacity to make decisions on such matters as are described in the declaration;

(c) the lawfulness or otherwise of any act done or yet to be done in relation to the person.

6.2.1   Declarations as to capacity or incapacity

It is anticipated that the need for a declaration as to capacity will be relatively rare, but the Draft Code of Practice gives examples of cases such as professionals disagreeing about an individual's capacity to make a specific, important decision or a wide-ranging dispute between family members about whether an elderly person has capacity to make an LPA (para. 7.10).

6.2.2   Declarations as to the lawfulness of an act

The specific power in s.15(1)(c) of the Act is expected to be invoked in relation to serious medical treatment cases, including those which are currently referred to the Family Division. They include cases concerning patients in a persistent vegetative state, non-therapeutic sterilisation, ethical dilemmas or cases where there are irresolvable conflicts between professionals and family members.[2] It is also expected to be invoked in cases concerning specific issues such as the existence or applicability of an advance directive, a major dispute about where a person should live, prohibition on contact, or one-off financial decisions such as sale of a valuable item or making a will.[3]

This distinction between declarations as to capacity to make specific decisions[4] and declarations as to what is lawful, being in the best interests of a patient,[5] reflects the common law practice which preceded the Act of making separate declarations as to lack of capacity in respect of the decision concerned and as to the lawfulness of the act proposed. The making of a declaration of lack of capacity to make decisions about 'matters' more generally was not usually exercised under the common law. It emerges in the new Act together with the new power to appoint a deputy to take over the decision-making function in relation to 'matters' generally rather than just a specific decision.

6.2.3   Acts and omissions

As well as allowing the Court to make declarations as to both the present and future (s.15(1)(c)), it is expressly provided that an 'act' in the context of s.15(1)(c) of the Act includes both an omission and a course of conduct (s.15(2)).

---

1 For the definition of capacity and the methods to be adopted when assessing capacity see **Chapter** 3.

2 Draft Code of Practice, at paras. 7.13–7.15.

3 Draft Code of Practice, at paras. 7.16–7.17.

4 For the grounds upon which such a declaration may be made, see ss.1, 2 and 3 of the Act.

5 For the grounds upon which such a declaration may be made, see ss.1 and 4 of the
   Act.

6.3   COURT'S POWER TO MAKE DECISIONS AND APPOINT
          DEPUTIES

The Court may, by s.16(2) of the Act, either:

(a) make a decision or decisions on behalf of an incapable person or appoint a
     deputy to make a specific decision; or
(b) make decisions about 'matters' identified by the Court.

The latter course should only be adopted where the former is not appropriate, for
example where there is a need for on-going rather than one-off decision making.[1]

6.3.1   The type of decisions covered by the Court's powers

The Court's powers may be exercised if the person concerned lacks capacity in
relation to two types of decision:

(a) those concerning personal welfare (previously dealt with under the common
     law inherent jurisdiction of the Family Division of the High Court); and
(b) those concerning their property and affairs (previously dealt with under Part
     VII of the MHA 1983 by the Court of Protection and the Public Guardianship
     Office by the appointment of a receiver or the making of a short order)
     (s.16(1)).

Thus both types of decision making are brought under one statutory scheme by
the new Act.

6.3.2   The principles to be applied by the court

The Court when making decisions or appointing a deputy must act in accordance
with the other provisions of the Act, and in particular the principles of s.1 of the
Act and the method of determining a person's best interests laid down by s.4 of
the Act (s.16(3)) – see **para 3.4**.

The Court must also, however, when exercising its powers under this Part of the
Act, have regard to the following key principles:

(a) a decision by the court is to be preferred to the appointment of a deputy to
     make a decision; and
(b) the powers conferred on a deputy should be as limited in scope and duration
     as is reasonably practicable in the circumstances (s.16(4)).

6.3.3   The other powers of the Court

If the Court decides to make an order making a decision upon the person's behalf it may:

(a) make further orders or directions as it considers necessary or expedient for giving effect to or otherwise in connection with the order or appointment (s.16(5));

(b) vary or discharge the order (s.16(7)).

This provision acknowledges the difficulty faced by courts making orders under the common law where they only have a 'snapshot' of the individual's capacity and interests at the time of the order (see **para. 3.4**). It ameliorates the problem by expressly allowing for the matter to return to court on a wide range of grounds.

If the Court does decide to appoint a deputy it may:

(a) make further orders or directions, or confer on the deputy such powers or impose on him such duties as it considers necessary or expedient for giving effect to or otherwise in connection with the order or appointment (s.16(5));

(b) revoke his appointment or vary the powers conferred on him if it is satisfied that:

  (i) he has behaved or is behaving in a way that contravenes the authority conferred on him or is not in the person's best interests; or

  (ii) proposes to behave in a way that would contravene that authority or would not be in the person's best interests (s.16(8)).

This provision was added in order to bring the Court's powers in relation to deputies and attorneys into line (see **para. 4.8**).

The Court has a general 'own motion' power to make orders or give directions in a person's best interests even though no application is before it (s.16(6)).

---

1   Draft Code of Practice, at para. 7.22.

6.4   SECTION 16 COURT POWERS: PERSONAL WELFARE

Section 17 of the Act sets out a list of personal welfare issues which the jurisdiction, whether in relation to the making of declarations or orders or the appointment of deputies, is intended to cover. It includes where the person is to live, what contact, if any, he is to have with specific persons, the prohibition of contact with specific persons, giving or refusing consent for treatment and giving a direction that responsibility for health care is transferred to another person. The list of issues reflects those which have typically been decided under the common law, although not all of them, given the wide range of the common law jurisdiction which covers all 'serious justiciable issues'.[1] The list, however, is intended to be indicative rather than exhaustive,[2] and the court's jurisdiction may even go beyond the old common law parameters.

The extent of a deputy's decision-making powers in relation to personal welfare is not extended by this section past the limits laid down in s.20 of the Act set out below (s.17(2)). It is expected that a deputy will be appointed to take personal welfare decisions in only the most extreme cases, and the Court will usually seek to make a single order in respect of a decision rather than confer an on-going power on a deputy (s.17(2)).

1   In *Re S (Hospital Patient: Court's Jurisdiction) (No.1)* [1996] Fam 1 at 18.
2   Explanatory Notes at paras. 70 and 71.

6.5   SECTION 16 COURT POWERS: PROPERTY AND AFFAIRS

The aspects of a person's property and affairs upon which the Court or a deputy may decide are listed at s.18(1) of and Schedule 2 to the Act. They include the acquisition, control and management of property, gifts or other dispositions, carrying on of professions, trades or business, carrying out of contracts, discharge of debts, executions of wills, exercise of the powers under trusts and the conduct of legal proceedings. In essence, they are the old Court of Protection powers.

The extent of a deputy's decision-making powers in relation to property and affairs is not extended by this section past the limits laid down in s.20 of the Act set out below (s.18(6)).

Although generally the powers under the Act may not be exercised until the person concerned has reached the age of 16 (s.2(5)), powers in relation to that person's property and affairs may be exercised if the Court considers it likely that the person will still lack capacity to make decisions in respect of that matter when he reaches the age of 18. This allows the Court to become involved in long-term planning without artificial cut-off points not in a person's best interests. It is easy to imagine how this power might be exercised in relation to an award of damages made consequent upon a brain injury to a teenager.

6.6   APPOINTMENT OF A DEPUTY BY THE COURT

A person may be appointed a deputy if he:

(a) is aged 18 or over, or, in relation to a person's property and affairs, a trust corporation (s.19(1));
(b) consents to the appointment (s.19(3)).

In deciding whether to appoint a deputy, and who, the Court will consider whether the proposed deputy is reliable and trustworthy and has an appropriate level of skill and competence to carry out the necessary tasks. The decision will be influenced by the type of issue to be decided by the deputy.[1] It is expected that a deputy will be someone known to the person.[2]

The Court may appoint two or more deputies to act jointly, jointly or severally or jointly in respect of some matters and joint and severally in respect of others (s.19(4)). The Draft Code of Practice explains how these arrangements might operate (para. 7.30).

These provisions mirror those made in respect of attorneys appointed under an LPA (see **Chapter 4**)

The Court may also appoint a successor to a deputy, for example, when a person who is involved in the life of the incapable person is likely to become ill or die within a short time.[3]

6.6.1   Agency

Crucially, s.19(6) of the Act provides that a deputy will be treated as an agent of the person who lacks capacity. The Explanatory Notes state that the law of agency is specifically engaged here (para. 73). For a more detailed treatment of the law see *Bowstead and Reynolds on Agency*, 17th edn 2001, but the following issues should be borne in mind:

■ an agent has an implied authority to do what is necessary for or incidental to effective execution of express authority; so it appears that a deputy will have such implied authority in respect of those powers expressly conferred on him by the Court although this issue does not appear to have been addressed in the Draft Code of Practice or the Explanatory Notes;

■ an agent is under a fiduciary duty to his principal and should not take advantage of his position;

■ an agent is under a duty to use due care and skill in performing his duties;

■ an agent may not delegate his authority.

(See also **para. 4.7.2**)

Once a deputy is appointed then:

(a) he is entitled to be reimbursed out of the person's property for his reasonable expenses in discharging his functions and, if the Court so directs, for remuneration for discharge of his functions (s.19(7));

(b) the Court may confer on him a power to take possession or control of any part of the person's property or to exercise a range of powers in respect of it including investment (s.19(8));

(c) he may be required to give the Public Guardian security for the discharge of his functions and to submit reports to him (s.19(9)).[4]

---

1 Draft Code of Practice, at para. 7.23.
2 David Lammy MP, Hansard, HC Committee Stage, 26 October 2004, col. 195.
3 Section 19(6) of the Act and Draft Code of Practice, at para. 7.31.
4 It is intended that the Court should decide upon what matters a deputy should report in each case (David Lammy MP, HC Committee Stage, 26 October 2004, col. 189).

6.7   RESTRICTIONS ON DEPUTIES

A deputy's powers are significantly limited by the Act which makes clear that he does not assume a complete or general decision-making power in respect of a person.

First, a deputy does not have power to make a decision on behalf of a person if he knows or has reasonable grounds to believe that the person has capacity (s.20(1)). This provision covers the situation of fluctuating capacity, where a person may sometimes have capacity to make decisions and sometimes not.[1] The provision emphasises that the appointment of a deputy is not a final act.

If the person has capacity in relation to a particular issue, including one in respect of which the deputy has been given a particular power because of the person's incapacity at the relevant time, the deputy may not make a decision in relation to that issue if the person regains capacity, even on a temporary basis. While the intention of the provision is clear, and the motive laudable, it may be a brave deputy who declines to exercise his power on the grounds that he has formed the view that the person has capacity when a court has declared that he lacks it in order to appoint the deputy in the first place. A prudent deputy may wish to confirm his view with a professional assessment.

Secondly, although a deputy may be given a power to make decisions about 'matters' generally identified by the Court in a declaration or order, his powers cannot extend to prohibiting a named individual from having contact or allowing a different person to take over responsibility for the person's healthcare (s.20(2)). These provisions reflect the fundamental Parliamentary intention that a deputy 'cannot do more than the person could do if he or she had capacity'.[2] It remains the case that the most important decisions will be decided by the Court and not hived off to deputies.

Thirdly, a deputy may not be given powers with respect to the execution of a person's will, the settlement of his property or the exercise of any power vested in the person under a trust (s.20(3)).

Fourthly, a deputy may not be given power to make a decision inconsistent with a decision made by the donee of an LPA (s.20(4)). The Explanatory Notes emphasise that a deputy may not 'trump' an attorney chosen by the donor at a time when he had capacity (para. 77). If there is concern about an attorney the court must use its statutory powers under ss.22 and 23 of the Act rather than appoint a deputy. It is easy to imagine circumstances in which the views of attorneys and deputies divide and the Act here provides a mechanism for the resolution of such issues.

Fifthly, a deputy may not refuse consent to the carrying out of continuation of life-saving treatment in relation to the person (s.20(5)). The original clause in the Bill provided that a deputy might not refuse consent 'unless the court has conferred on the deputy express authority to that effect . . . in exceptional circumstances'. The provision was removed in the light of widespread anxieties and consequent Parliamentary debate about the unintended introduction of euthanasia and assisted suicide by the Act.

Sixthly, a deputy must exercise powers in accordance with the guiding principles of the Act contained in s.1 and the method of determining best interests in s.4 (see **para. 3.4**). Discussion is likely to continue as to how a lay person appointed as a deputy should be expected to apply the s.4 framework to the various decisions he may have to make when granted a general power to make decisions as to 'matters' rather than a specific issue.

These restrictions also mirror those imposed on an attorney appointed under an LPA (see **para. 4.5**).

6.7.1   A deputy may not 'restrain' a person

A deputy may not do an act that is intended to restrain the person unless four conditions are satisfied (s.20(7)):

(a) in doing the act, the deputy is acting within the scope of an authority expressly conferred on him by the Court (s.20(8));
(b) the person lacks or the deputy reasonably believes that he lacks capacity in relation to the matter in question (s.20(9));
(c) the deputy reasonably believes that it is necessary to do the act in order to prevent harm to the person (s.20(1));
(d) the act is a proportionate response to:

  (i) the likelihood of the person suffering harm; or
  (ii) the seriousness of that harm (s.20(11)).

The meaning and effect of these requirements is considered under the heading of the parallel prohibitions on attorneys or any other person restraining incapable persons (see **paras. 1.13** and **5.3.2**).

The concept of 'restraint' is defined by s.20(12) of the Act. A deputy restrains a person if he:

(a) uses, or threatens to use, force to secure the doing of an act which the person resists; or
(b) restricts the person's liberty of movement whether or not he resists.

This also mirrors the definition contained in s.6(4) of the Act in relation to restraint by attorneys or others. Its meaning and effect is discussed at **para. 5.3.2**.

The Act further provides, at s.20(13), that a deputy does more than merely restrain P if he deprives P of his liberty within the meaning of Art. 5(1) of the ECHR (see **paras. 1.13** and **5.3.2**).

---

1   See the guidance in the Draft Code of Practice, at paras. 3.23–3.24.
2   David Lammy MP, Hansard, HC Committee Stage, 26 October 2004, col. 191.

6.8   TRANSFER OF PROCEEDINGS

The difficulties in deciding upon the appropriate forum for disputes concerning 16- and 17-year-olds who may also be incapable once they become adults at the age of 18 is anticipated by s.21 of the Act. The section provides that the Lord Chancellor may make provision for the transfer of proceedings relating to a person aged under 18 from the Court of Protection to a court having jurisdiction under the Children Act 1989 or vice versa. The Explanatory Notes state that the powers under s.21 of the Act may be utilised to transfer proceedings to the court most suitable to deal with the issues. For example, if the parents of a 17-year-old with profound learning difficulties are in dispute about residence or contact then it may be more appropriate for the Court of Protection to deal with the case since an order made under the Children Act 1989 would expire on the child's eighteenth birthday (para. 79).

7 ADVANCED DECISIONS TO REFUSE TREATMENT

7.1 BACKGROUND

At common law advanced directives, known as 'living wills', are given legal effect provided that they meet the elements necessary for validity as set out in *Re T*[1] and *HE* v. *NHS Trust A and AE* [2003] EWHC 1017 (Fam), [2003] 2 FLR 408. The constituent elements of a valid advanced refusal of treatment at common law are that the patient:

■ is competent at the time the decision was made;
■ is free from undue influence;
■ is sufficiently informed; and
■ intends the refusal to apply to the circumstances that subsequently arise.

However, an advanced decision requiring a certain specific form of treatment or treatments (as opposed to refusing treatment) which the doctor considers to be clinically unnecessary, futile or inappropriate, is not binding on the doctor. This was recently confirmed by the Court of Appeal in R (*on the application of Burke*) v. *GMC* [2005] EWCA 1003 Civ at 55.

The common law, however, was felt to be unclear and poorly understood. The Law Commission's Report No. 231 *Mental Incapacity*, February 1995, recommended the need for specific statutory provision for those cases where the patient has decided in advance to refuse some particular form of treatment.

The Report also noted that 'there is a clear distinction to be drawn between the legal effect of an *advance expression of views and preferences* on the one hand and an *advance decision* on the other'. The Report similarly made a distinction between an advanced decision *in favour* of a particular treatment and a decision *against* such treatment.

The Report went on further to propose that the court should not have power to override a valid and applicable anticipatory decision in the exercise of its 'best interests' jurisdiction. Resort should only be had to the Court where a decision is required over the validity of the refusal or its applicability. The Report recommended that if such a decision was required from the courts, the refusal should not preclude those treating the patient from taking any steps necessary to prevent the death or a serious deterioration of the maker of the advance refusal. This has found statutory expression in s.26 (5) of the Act.

The government accepted the need to place advanced directives within a statutory framework so that their legal status and the safeguards governing them would be clearly stated. The Draft Mental Incapacity Bill followed the recommendations of the Law Commission's Report. The pre-legislative Joint Committee supported the need for the Bill to make provision for the making of advanced decisions to refuse treatment. The provisions relating to advanced directives are now contained in ss.24–26 of the Act.

However, the Joint Committee expressed great concern about the possible connections between the Draft Bill and euthanasia and it suggested that an additional clause be added to the Bill to provide additional assurance. The government responded by inserting a new cl.58 in the Bill, which made it clear that 'nothing in this Act is to be taken to affect the law relating to murder or manslaughter or the operation of section 2 of the Suicide Act 1961'.

Despite the addition of cl.58, the debates in both Houses and in the press during the passage of the Bill were dominated by discussions of 'euthanasia by omission' and 'suicidally motivated advanced directives'. In the event the clause survived without change as s.62 of the Act.

---

1   *Re T (Adult: Refusal of Medical Treatment)* [2004] EWHC 1279 (Fam).

7.2   ADVANCED DECISIONS TO REFUSE TREATMENT: GENERAL

An advanced decision as defined in s.25(1) of the Act is a special type of advance statement that represents an actual decision to refuse treatment, even though it was made at an earlier date. The effect of a valid advanced decision will be to enable that decision to be carried out even though at a point in the future that person no longer has the capacity to give or refuse consent to that treatment. The terms 'advanced directive' and 'living wills' are now subsumed into the new statutory term 'advanced decision'.

7.2.1   Characteristics of an advanced decision to refuse treatment for the purposes of the Act

- The decision must be made by a person who is aged 18 or over.
- At the time it was made, the person had capacity to make the decision (see **Chapter 3**).
- It must specify the treatment that is to be refused (s.24(1)(a)). It can be expressed in medical language or layman's terms, as long as it is clear what is meant (s.24(2)).
- It may set out the circumstances in which the refusal will apply (s.24(1)(a)).

It will only apply when the person lacks capacity to consent to the specified treatment (s.24(1)(b)).

7.2.2 Withdrawal or alteration of an advanced decision to refuse treatment

■ A person may withdraw or change an advanced decision if he has the capacity to do so (s.24(3)).
■ A withdrawal, or partial withdrawal need not be in writing, and can be by any means (s.24(4)).
■ An alteration to an advanced decision need not be in writing unless it applies to an advanced decision refusing life-sustaining treatment, in which case s.25(5) applies (see below).

7.3 VALIDITY AND APPLICABILITY OF ADVANCED DECISIONS

The consequences of complying with an advanced decision to refuse treatment for both the person making the advanced decision and his or her family and the professionals are serious. Section 25 provides two important safeguards in relation to an advanced decision to refuse treatment, i.e. that at the material time the decision is both *valid* and *applicable*.

7.3.1 Validity

A valid advanced decision must comply with the requirements of s.24.

In addition, an advanced decision would be invalid if:

■ the maker has withdrawn the decision while he or she still has capacity to do so (s.25(2)(a));
■ the maker subsequently made an LPA giving a donee the authority to consent or refuse consent to the treatment specified in the advanced decision (s.25(2)(b));
■ the person has acted in a way that it is clearly inconsistent with the advanced decision remaining his fixed decision (s.25(2)(c)).

7.3.2 Applicability

The advanced decision will not apply if:

■ the maker still has capacity to make his or her own decisions at the time of the proposed treatment (s.24(3));
■ the proposed treatment is not treatment specified in the advanced decision (s.24(4)(a));

- the circumstances are different from those set out in the advance decision (s.24(4)(b)); or
- there are reasonable grounds for believing that circumstances have now arisen which were not anticipated by the person when making the advance decision and which would have affected their advance decision had the maker anticipated them at the time.

In relation to the last three bullet points, consideration will have to be given to the length of time that has passed since the advanced decision was made, the change in the maker's personal circumstances and any developments in treatment or therapies for the maker's medical condition.

7.3.3   Advanced decisions relating to life-sustaining treatment

Additional safeguards have been added where the person intends the advanced decision to apply to the refusal of life-sustaining treatment:

- the advanced decision must contain a statement by the maker confirming that the decision is to apply to that treatment even if life is at risk (s.25(5)(a)); and
- it must be in writing (s.25(6)(a)); and
- it must be signed by the maker or by another person in the maker's presence and by the maker's direction (s.25(6)(b)); and
- the signature must be properly witnessed (s.25(6)(c)–(d)).

7.4   FORMALITIES

Apart from the above requirements relating to advanced decisions regarding life-sustaining treatment, there are no specified formats for advanced decisions. To meet the statutory requirements, they must exist, be valid and apply to the treatment under consideration.

Advanced decisions can be made orally or in writing. The Draft Code of Practice contains helpful suggestions about what may be included in a written advanced directive and how both written and oral advanced directives should be recorded.[1]

---

1   See paras. 18.15–18.17 of the Draft Code of Practice.

7.5   EFFECT OF A VALID AND APPLICABLE ADVANCED DIRECTIVE

A valid and applicable advanced directive will be as effective as a contemporaneous refusal of consent by a person with capacity to make the decision.[1] The treatment provider is obliged to carry out the maker's advanced decision (s.26(1)). The treatment cannot lawfully then be given. If treatment is given, nonetheless, those treating the maker may face both civil and criminal liability.

Section 26(2) and (3) clarify the position for the treatment provider. The treatment provider may continue or start treating without incurring liability, provided that he is satisfied at that time that the patient has not made a valid and applicable advanced refusal of treatment. Conversely, the treatment provider may withhold or withdraw treatment from the patient without incurring liability if he has reasonable grounds for believing that there exists a valid and applicable advanced directive.

A valid and applicable advanced directive takes precedence over a consent made by a donee acting under a welfare LPA made before the advance decision was made, or a consent given by a court-appointed deputy.

Once the treatment providers are satisfied that an advanced decision is effective, the provisions of s.5 (consideration of the incapacitated person's best interests) do not apply.

---

1   See *Re T* and *HE* above.

7.6   ROLE OF THE COURT OF PROTECTION IN RELATION TO AN ADVANCED DECISION

The Court of Protection will only have power to make declarations as to the existence, validity and applicability of the advanced decision in relation to the treatment under consideration. The Court will have no power to override an effective advanced decision.

If, however, there is a doubt as to the existence, or a dispute as to the validity or applicability of an advanced decision, the doctors may take action to prevent the death of or deterioration in the condition of the person concerned while the matter is resolved by the Court (s.26(5)).

7.7   STEPS THAT CAN BE TAKEN BY HEALTH CARE PROFESSIONALS TO COMPLY WITH THE ACT

7.7.1   Ascertain if an advanced decision exists

If a health professional has reasonable grounds to believe that an advanced decision may exist, then he or she should, if possible, make reasonable efforts to find out what that decision was. It is suggested in the Draft Code at para. 8.33, that reasonable efforts might include having discussions with the patient's relatives, contacting the patient's GP and looking through the patient's clinical or nursing records.

7.7.2   Validity and applicability

Once the health professional satisfies him or herself that the advanced decision exists, then consideration needs to be given to whether it complies with s.21 of the Act, whether it is valid and applicable to the treatment proposed.

Again, the Draft Code of Practice suggests at para. 8.35, that particular care needs to be given to whether the advance decision is applicable in the circumstances which have now arisen. Particular care should be given to considering how long ago the advanced decision was made, and any change of circumstances.

7.7.3   Emergencies

Unless a doctor is satisfied that a valid and applicable advanced decision exists, he may legally treat the patient. Treatment should not be delayed in order to search for an advanced decision if there is no clear indication that one exists.

If a doubt arises as to the existence of an advanced decision, the matter may be referred to the court for a decision and s.26(5) applies.

7.8   ADVANCED DECISIONS AND ADVANCED STATEMENTS

There is a clear legal distinction between an advanced decision which complies with s.24, that it exists, is valid and applicable and is binding on those treating the patient, and a more general advanced statement dealing with a person's wishes and feelings about how they wish to be cared for and treated in the future.

A general advanced statement will be taken into account by those determining a person's best interests in accordance with s.4(6)(a) of the Act, as an expression of past wishes and feelings once that person has lost capacity to make a particular decision. An advanced statement will, however, be one of only a number of considerations to be taken into account when assessing a person's best interests (see for example, the recent case of W Healthcare NHS Trust v. H and Others [2004] EWCA Civ 1324, [2005] 1 WLR 834).[1] The Court of Appeal held that H's statement, remembered by her family, that she 'wouldn't want to be kept alive by machines' was not a valid advanced directive because she could not at the time of making the statement have anticipated that if the statement was complied with, her death would be as a result of dehydration and starvation. The court concluded that it was in her best interests for the PEG feeding tube to be reinserted.[2]

---

1   H suffered from the end stages of multiple sclerosis, she was sensate, but totally dependent on others. Her PEG feeding tube had become dislodged and the family did not wish it to be replaced. Those treating H applied for a declaration that it was lawful for the PEG tube to be reinserted.
2   See also HE v. NHS Trust A and AE [2003] EWHC 1017 (Fam), [2003] 2 FLR 408.

8 RESEARCH

8.1 BACKGROUND

Since 1991, research has been carried out under the Medical Research Council's guidelines. The Law Commission in its Report *Mental Incapacity* in 1995 complained about and called for improvements to the 'lack of clarity around research'. It also considered that non-therapeutic research on mentally incapacitated adults was unlawful.[1] Nevertheless, the Law Commission supported the use of mentally incapacitated adults in clinical trials and proposed the introduction of safeguards.

The Draft Mental Incapacity Bill did not make provision for incapacitated adults to take part in research. The Royal College of Psychiatrists gave evidence to the Joint Committee considering the Mental Incapacity Bill that legislation was needed because 'the common law does not strictly provide such authority, as it cannot be argued that research is necessarily in the incapacitated person's best interests'.

Evidence to the Joint Committee included that the Bill would deny patients without capacity the possibility of benefit if they were unable to participate in research. At the same time, concerns were expressed that unregulated research could well lead to opportunities for abuse. The Joint Committee concluded that 'a clause should be included in the Bill to enable strictly controlled medical research to explore the causes and consequences of mental incapacity and to develop effective treatment for such conditions'. The Joint Committee then suggested that key principles governing research should be added to the Bill and covered in the Code of Practice.

The recommendations were largely accepted by the government and became cls. 30–33 of the Bill. During the passage of the Bill, a number of amendments were made to address the concerns of the Medical Research Council, the Wellcome Trust and members of the House of Lords. These amendments included additional safeguards and provisions for people who have capacity at the beginning of a research project but then go on to lose capacity.

Regulatory provision has already been made for some clinical trials under the Medicines for Human Use (Clinical Trials) Regulations 2004, SI 2004/1031 which came into force on 1 May 2004 and gave effect to Directive 2001/20/EC.[2] Trials which are governed by clinical trials regulations are excluded from the Act because protection is already provided by those regulations (s.30(3) and (5)). In contrast, the Act introduces a legal framework for research in general.

1 Paragraph 6.29.
2 The Directive provides: 'Persons who are incapable of giving legal consent should be given special protection . . . in cases such as persons with dementia, psychiatric patients, etc . . . the written consent of the person's legal representative, given in coop-eration with the treating doctor, is necessary before participation in any such trial'.

8.2   RESEARCH

The stated aim of the Act and the Code of Practice in relation to research is 'to establish the right balance between the need for research to bring benefit or information and the need for protection against exploitation and abuse'.

The Act applies to intrusive research which would require consent if the person involved was capable of giving consent. A researcher who complies with all the requirements of ss.30–34 will have lawful authority for his actions.

8.2.1   Hierarchy of safeguards

Baroness Andrews during the second day of the Report Stage of the Bill in the House of Lords set out a hierarchy of safeguards that are contained in the Act:

- research must entail negligible risk;
- anything done must not interfere with the person's freedom and privacy;
- it must not be unduly invasive or restrictive;
- consultation must take place with the person's carers or a nominated person;
- there must be an assessment of whether the research itself is burdensome;
- the people concerned must be listened to and respected if they show any distress or objection;
- the whole process must be validated and reviewed by a research ethics committee.

Sections 30–33 allow 'intrusive research' to be lawfully carried out on a person who lacks capacity provided that the research project is carried out by:

- an appropriate body; and
- in accordance with the conditions set down in ss.32 and 33 of the Act.

8.2.2   'Appropriate body' and 'appropriate authority'

Section 30(4) defines an 'appropriate body'. The appropriate authority, defined in s.30(6) as the Secretary of State in relation to research in England and the National Assembly for Wales in relation to research in Wales, must specify an appropriate body for approving research projects, such as a Research Ethics Committee.

8.2.3   Requirements for approval

Section 31 defines the bounds of what kind of research can be approved involving people who lack capacity to consent.

Section 31(1) provides that the research must be connected with an impairing condition which affects the person participating in the research or with the treatment of the condition.

'Impairing condition' is defined in s.31(3) and means one that is, or may be, attributable to or causes or contributes to the impairment of or disturbance in the functioning of the person's mind or brain.

Section 31(4) requires that there are reasonable grounds for believing that there is no alternative to the involvement of the person in the research, and it could not be carried out as effectively if only people who have capacity to consent take part.

Section 31(5) states that the research must meet one of two requirements:

- it must have potential to benefit the subject of the research without imposing a burden that is disproportionate to the benefit; or
- it must intend to provide knowledge relevant to the causes, treatment or care of people affected by the same or similar conditions.

The anticipated benefits and risks of research are dealt with in s.31(5) and (6). There are two alternatives:

- research that will benefit the person without imposing a disproportionate burden;
- research intended to provide knowledge of the cases of the person's condition and its treatment of the care of people who have the same or similar condition. Further safeguards are added in respect of this alternative; there must be reasonable grounds for believing that the risk to the person is negligible and the research must not interfere with the person's freedom of action or privacy in a significant way or be unduly invasive or restrictive (s.31(6)).

8.3   ADDITIONAL SAFEGUARDS

8.3.1   Consulting carers

The person conducting the research, before taking any steps to involve a person in approved research, must take all reasonable steps to identify a person who is close to the person[1] and who is prepared to be consulted about the person's involvement in research (s.32(2)). This person must *not* be someone acting in a professional capacity or for payment, such as a carer. A donee under an LPA or a deputy can be a person consulted under s.32 (s.32(7)).

If the researcher cannot find such a person, then the researcher must nominate a person independent of the research in accordance with guidance issued by the appropriate authority (s.32(3)).[2]

Section 32(4) requires the researcher to provide the person consulted with information about the research and asks that person to:

- provide advice as to whether the incapable person should take part in the research; and
- indicate what in his opinion the incapable person's wishes and feelings about taking part in the project would be likely to be if the person had capacity in relation to the matter.

This latter requirement is at odds with the current common law,[3] which looks at best interests rather than substituted judgment and does not sit happily with the rest of the provisions of the Act. Section 32(5) further provides that if the person consulted advises the researcher that in his opinion the person's wishes and feelings would be likely to lead him to decline to take part in the project then the researcher must ensure the person does not take part in the project, or if already underway, is withdrawn from the research. It is particularly difficult to envisage how this provision will work in practice if the person concerned has always lacked capacity.

Section 32(6) requires treatment to be continued even if the person is withdrawn from research if there is a significant health risk to the person if the treatment was discontinued.

Section 32(8)–(10) provides additional safeguards in an emergency when it is not practical to consult within the meaning of the Act.

8.3.2   Additional safeguards once research has begun

The researcher is asked to respect any signs of resistance from the person where the person 'appears to object (whether by showing signs of resistance or otherwise)', and not to involve the person in any research that would be contrary to any valid and applicable advanced decision or any other form of statement made and not subsequently withdrawn (s.33(2)).

Although it is not clear from the subsection, one assumes that the Act refers to a statement that was made when the person still had capacity to make his or her own decisions. It is not clear why here such a statement is binding on the researchers and not merely a matter to be taken into account (in accordance with s.4(6)(a)) in a best interest assessment (see **Chapter 3**).

It is, however, clearly stated in s.33(3) that the interests of the person must be assumed to outweigh those of science and society.

The person must be withdrawn from the project without delay if he indicates that he wishes to be withdrawn from it or if the researcher has reasonable ground for believing that any of the requirements for approval of the project as set out in s.31(2)–(7) are no longer met.

8.3.3   Loss of capacity during the research project and transitional provisions

This section was a late government amendment to the Act. It provides for a transitional regulation-making power to cover research that starts before s.30 comes into force and which involves people who had capacity when the research project started, but lose capacity before the end of the project. It enables ongoing and essential research to continue and is particularly important for long-term projects.

It is intended by the government that the regulations will include safeguards similar to those already set out in ss.31–33 of the Act (s.34(4)). These regulations, made by the Secretary of State, will be subject to the affirmative procedure in Parliament (s.65(2)(a)).

1 It is intended that the Secretary of State will issue guidance on who will satisfy the requirements of the Act.
2 The government has indicated that it intends to ensure that healthcare providers that host clinical research make arrangements, through the chief executive, to identify a panel of people who could be available to act as a nominated legal representative.
3 Although it accords with Schedule 1, Part 5, para. 12 of the Medicines for Human Use (Clinical Trials) Regulations 2004, SI 2004/1031 'Informed consent given by a legal representative to an incapacitated adult in a clinical trial shall represent that person's presumed will'.

9 INDEPENDENT MENTAL CAPACITY ADVOCATE SERVICE

9.1 BACKGROUND

Access to advocacy services has been one of the more problematic issues throughout the passage of the Act. The government, while recognising the value of independent advocacy services to people with capacity problems, made it clear from the outset that it did not wish to provide for general advocacy. The Draft Mental Incapacity Bill therefore contained no provision for independent advocacy.

Subsequently, very real concerns were expressed in relation to the 'unbefriended'. These are particularly vulnerable adults without capacity who have lost contact with family or friends, or whose relatives have passed away and have no one to represent and support them when decisions are being taken about serious medical treatment or significant changes of residence. The government responded by introducing into the Mental Capacity Bill the 'independent consultee' who was to advise NHS bodies and local authorities on a person's best interests.

Further concern was expressed during the deliberations of the House of Commons Standing Committee by Mr Paul Burstow (Liberal Democrat MP for Sutton and Cheam), about the confusion surrounding the role of the independent consultee. He noted a 'conflation between advocacy and the independent appointee type of function' in the provisions of the Bill.

The government was well aware of the difficulties and made it clear that the provisions relating to the independent consultee were a 'work in progress' and that the government needed time to develop its thinking and to consult widely.

Baroness Ashton of Upholland on the second day of the Report Stage of the Bill in the House of Lords,[1] when moving amendments to the Bill stated that 'it was always our intention that the role of the IMCA is to support the individual by making representations about their wishes, feelings, beliefs and values, at the same time as bringing to the attention of the decision maker all factors that are relevant to the decision. The IMCA can also challenge the decision maker on behalf of the person if appropriate'.

The amendments removed references contained in the Draft Bill to 'independent consultees' giving advice about the person's 'best interests', and changed the name from independent consultee to 'independent mental capacity advocate (IMCA)' to reflect the new thinking that the role of the IMCA was to support and represent the person. The provisions are contained in ss.35–41 of the Act.

The DoH has issued a consultation paper on the Independent Mental Capacity Advocate Service. The consultation period ended on 30 September 2005. At the time of writing, the government has yet to clarify the exact role of the IMCA. Much of the detail about how the IMCA system will operate is not contained in the Act but will be defined and brought about by regulations made under the Act.

---

1 At col. 1524.

9.2 APPOINTMENT OF IMCA

Section 35(1) places a duty upon the 'appropriate authority' to make 'such arrangements as it considers reasonable' for the provision of a new IMCA Service. The 'appropriate authority' for England is the Secretary of State and, in relation to Wales, the National Assembly for Wales (s.35(7)).

Section 35(2) and (3) provide for the appropriate authority to make regulations as to the appointment and conditions of appointment of IMCAs. The Explanatory Notes comment that this provision will ensure that an individual will need to meet common standards in order to be approved as an IMCA.

Section 35(4) importantly provides that the IMCA should be as far as possible independent of the person making the decision concerned. Subsection 35(5) provides for payment of the IMCA.

In order to properly represent and support the person concerned, s.35(6) provides that the IMCA may:

- interview the person concerned in private (s.35(6)(a)); and
- examine and take copies of health records, social services and care homes records (s.35(6)(b)(i)–(iii)).

9.3 FUNCTIONS OF IMCA

Section 36(1) provides for the appropriate authority to make regulations setting out the functions of the IMCAs.

Section 36(2) provides for the regulations to set out the steps that the IMCA is required to take in order to carry out these functions. These steps should ensure that the IMCA:

- provides support to enable the person to participate as fully as possible in the decision (s.36(2)(a));
- obtains and evaluates the relevant information (s.36(2)(b));

- ascertains and represents the person's wishes, feelings, beliefs and values (s.36(2)(c)). It is worth noting that the curious wording of the subsection introduces the possibility of the IMCA substituting his or her own judgment for that of the person, particularly if that person has always lacked capacity and has never been able to express his or her own wishes and feelings;
- finds out about available options (s.36(2)(d)); and
- seeks further medical opinions if necessary (s.36(2)(e)). Provision does not appear to have been made in the projected costs of the IMCA Service for the cost of these further opinions.

Section 36(3) provides that the regulations may also set out the circumstances in which the IMCA may challenge the decision maker or provide assistance for the purpose of challenging any relevant decision. The DoH is consulting extensively on this provision. The government notes in its consultation document at paras. 19 and 20 that:

> the government does not regard the new IMCA Service as a replacement or substitute for independent advocacy as it is commonly understood . . . Many people take the view that the conventional independent advocacy role is to represent the person's wishes and feelings, but not to influence the decision itself. The role of the IMCA goes further than this, it includes not only representing and supporting the person but also bringing to the attention of the decision maker all factors that are relevant to the person's best interests; and challenging the decision, where necessary.

The role of the IMCA can therefore be divided into two parts:

- the 'traditional' advocate role, supporting and representing a person's wishes and feelings so that they will be fully taken into account by the decision maker; and
- the 'new' role of challenging and providing assistance for challenging the decision makers when the person has no one else to do so on their behalf. The IMCA would in effect take on the role of an informal carer, relative or friend, challenging decisions on a person's behalf.

The DoH in the Consultation Paper questions whether the IMCA should be able to bring simple cases before the Court without the need for legal representation. It is relatively easy to envisage how the second role might be carried out using the relevant complaints procedures of the public authority concerned. However, it is less clear how the role should develop if the IMCA's submissions are not accepted by the public authority concerned and all the available internal mechanisms for resolving disputes have been exhausted. It is essential that the Code of Practice clarifies the boundaries of the role of the IMCA. The IMCA's role should not surplant the need for expert legal representation and advice.

There are a number of troubling aspects to the proposal that the IMCA should be able to bring simple cases before the Court without the need for legal representation:

- it blurs the role of IMCA and the litigation friend;
- it blurs the existing distinction between decision-making capacity and litigation capacity;
- it is unclear what is meant by 'a simple case' where doubts remain as to capacity and/or best interests, or where despite everyone's best efforts a dispute is unresolved;
- the current proposals for funding the IMCA Service would be inadequate.

The IMCA should be involved, in appropriate cases, at the stage where a decision is to be taken by a public authority. In the event that the public authority does not accept the IMCA's submissions and an area of doubt or dispute remains that cannot be resolved through the appropriate dispute procedures, the matter should be brought before the Court of Protection by the NHS Trust, or PCT or local authority for resolution at the earliest opportunity.

It is the view of the authors that the person concerned should be a party to the proceedings as a matter of course and be represented by a litigation friend (or by his or her own legal representative if capacity is in issue) in the normal way.

It is difficult to envisage, because of the lack of detail, how the current proposals will work in practice and how the role of the IMCA will 'fit in' with the role of a litigation friend representing the person in proceedings before the Court of Protection. The regulations and rules will need to clarify the role of the IMCA, the party status of the incapable person and the role of the litigation friend.

At present, it is of concern that there are no firm proposals for making funding available for the representation of eligible parties in proceedings before the Court of Protection.

9.4   PROVISION OF SERIOUS MEDICAL TREATMENT BY NHS BODY

Section 37(1) applies where 'serious medical treatment' is to be provided or arranged by the NHS for a person who lacks capacity, and there is no one with whom the decision maker can consult in determining what would be in the person's best interests. An IMCA is to be instructed if there is no one from the list in s.40 (a person nominated by the person, an attorney under an LPA, a deputy or a donee of an EPA) or a non-professional carer or friend whom it is appropriate to consult.

9.4.1   'Serious medical treatment'

Section 37(6) provides a general definition of what constitutes 'serious medical treatment'. It means:

> . . . treatment which involves providing, withholding or withdrawing treatment of a kind prescribed by regulations made by the appropriate authority.

The government is currently consulting on what constitutes 'serious medical treatment'. It has identified three options:

1. a list of specific treatments; or
2. a focus on the characteristics of the decision to be taken (e.g. where the treatment would be irreversible, or where the risks and benefits are finely balanced); or
3. a combination of the above two options.

At present there are only two types of serious medical treatment decisions which must be referred to court: the withdrawal of treatment from a person in PVS and non-therapeutic sterilisations. The government intends, either by regulation or by the Code of Practice, to ensure that these types of treatment will continue to be referred to the Court together with cases involving experimental or untested forms of treatment.[1] It will be inappropriate for an IMCA to be appointed in such cases.

There are other serious medical treatment cases, i.e. those in which an application to the Court of Protection is not anticipated, where it may be appropriate to appoint an IMCA.

The IMCA will represent and support the person in accordance with the regulations made under s.36. Section 37(5) provides that the NHS body must take into account any submissions made or information given by the IMCA when arriving at its decision.

Subsection (2) provides that where the person's treatment is regulated by Part 4 of the 1983 Act, then the IMCA need not be instructed under s.37(3). Provision is made in s.37(4) for urgent treatment and s.37(7) makes provision for regulations which will define the particular 'NHS bodies' which will become subject to the duties.

Where, however, a dispute remains unresolved or the legality of a proposed treatment is in doubt because of doubts over the person's capacity or what is in the person's best interests, then good practice may require the cases to be referred to the court for a decision. At this point the person concerned should be represented in any proceedings by a litigation friend.

---

1   *Simms* v. *Simms* sub nom *A* v. *A* *(A Child)* [2002] EWHC 2734, [2003] Fam 83.

9.5   PROVISION OF ACCOMMODATION BY NHS BODY

Section 38 applies if an NHS body proposes to provide or arrange long-stay accommodation in a hospital or care home, or to move a person between such accommodations. Subsections (6) and (7) define the types of care homes and hospitals which are covered by this section.

An IMCA must be instructed where such accommodation is proposed and the person concerned lacks capacity to agree to the arrangements and there is no one with whom the decision maker can consult in determining what would be in that person's best interests. Any information or submissions from the IMCA must be taken into account by the NHS body.

Section 38(9) provides that this section only applies if such accommodation is provided for more than 28 days in hospital or more than eight weeks in a care home; or where a shorter term is later extended into the applicable period (s.38(4)).

Section 38 does not apply where the person concerned is to be accommodated as a result of an obligation imposed on him under the 1983 Act (s.38(2)). Subsection (3) makes provision in relation to urgent placements.

Subsection (8) provides that regulations will also define which particular NHS bodies will become subject to the duties under this section.

The NHS responsibilities for community care services are complex and the IMCA may need specialist advice to represent the incapable person and to challenge decisions on the person's behalf. Ultimately, if a decision is taken by the NHS authority that is contrary to the IMCA's submissions, then judicial review proceedings may need to be brought on behalf of the incapable person. In these circumstances the IMCA should refer the matter to a solicitor for consideration. The solicitor may then approach the Official Solicitor, who may, if he considers it appropriate, bring proceedings in the Administrative Court on behalf of the incapable person.

9.6   PROVISION OF ACCOMMODATION BY LOCAL AUTHORITY

Section 39 applies to long-stay (eight weeks or more) accommodation arranged by the local authority or a change in such accommodation. It applies to residential accommodation provided in accordance with s.21 or s.29 of the National Assistance Act 1948, or s.117 of the 1983 Act, as a result of a decision taken by the local authority under s.47 of the National Health Service and Care in the Community Act 1990 (s.39(2)).

'Residential accommodation' can mean accommodation in a care home, a nursing home, ordinary and sheltered housing, housing association or other registered housing, or in private sector housing provided by a local authority or in hostel accommodation (see para. 121 of Explanatory Notes).

The provisions mirror the provisions made in relation to accommodation by an NHS body. The IMCA is to be instructed where a person lacks capacity to make decisions about where he or she should live and there is no one with whom the decision maker can consult when determining what would be in that person's best interests. Any information or submissions from the IMCA must be taken into account by the local authority (s.39(6)).

It is interesting to consider what role the IMCA may have once a social services authority has assessed an incapable person as eligible for accommodation under the National Assistance Act 1948, s.21. The local authority is then obliged to make arrangements for accommodation in a care home for that person in a place of his or her choice provided certain conditions are satisfied.[1] If the person is incapable of making the choice the guidance provides that the local authority should act on the preferences and wishes of the person's carers unless exceptionally that would be against the best interests of the resident. It seems that an IMCA should be treated as a 'carer' for the purposes of this provision.

Section 39(3) provides that the section does not apply where the person concerned is accommodated as a result of an obligation imposed on him under the 1983 Act. Subsection (4) makes provision for urgent accommodation.

Subsection (5) ensures that an IMCA is provided for a person whose residence was initially intended to be less than eight weeks, but is then extended.

Again, if a decision is taken by the local authority which does not accord with the IMCA's submissions the IMCA may wish to refer the matter to a solicitor to consider challenging the decision by way of judicial review in the Administrative Court on the person's behalf. In such a case, it may be appropriate for the Official Solicitor to be asked to consider representing the person as his or her litigation friend in the absence of another suitable individual.

---

1   National Assistance Act 1948 (Choice of Accommodation) Directions 1992 (as amended).

9.7   EXCEPTIONS

Section 40 provides that the NHS body or local authority concerned does not have to instruct an IMCA for a person who lacks capacity in accordance with ss.37(3), 38(3) and (4) and 39(4) and (5) if there is:

- a person chosen in advance; or
- an attorney under an LPA or EPA; or
- a deputy (s.40 (a)–(d)).

The exceptions contained in s.40(b)–(d) may undermine the purpose of the IMCA Service, which is to safeguard vulnerable people who are facing important decisions about treatment and residence. Section 40 removes the duty on the appropriate authorities to appoint an IMCA for an incapacitated person even if the attorney under an LPA has only been given authority to make financial decisions on behalf of a person, or the Court has only authorised the deputy to deal with a person's property and business affairs. The Court-appointed deputy may have been appointed from a list of panel deputies and he or she may have no personal knowledge of the person concerned.

It will be open to the appropriate authorities to appoint an IMCA even if a person set out in s.40(b)–(d) has been appointed or chosen on behalf of the person, although there will be no duty upon the appropriate authority to do so.

9.8   POWER TO ADJUST THE ROLE OF THE IMCA

Both the scope of the IMCA Service and the obligations to make arrangements imposed by s.35 may be extended or altered by regulations made by the Secretary of State in England or, in Wales, the National Assembly for Wales.

10 ILL-TREATMENT OR NEGLECT

10.1 BACKGROUND

The current law criminalises certain conduct against mentally disordered persons. The Sexual Offences Act 2003 creates a number of offences 'against persons with a mental disorder impeding choice' which prohibits sexual activity with or in the presence of those with a mental disorder impeding choice as well as the incitement, procuring, threatening or use of deception to bring about such acts (Sexual Offences Act 2003, ss.30–37). The MHA 1983 creates three offences of ill-treatment or neglect of mentally disordered persons by:

1. employees or managers of hospitals and care homes in respect of mentally disordered persons who are in-patients or out-patients;
2. a guardian or some other person with care and custody of a mentally disordered person in the community; and
3. any person in respect of a patient who is subject to supervised discharge (s.127).

It is a prerequisite of all the offences under the MHA 1983 that the person has a mental disorder within the meaning of s.1.

Further, there is guidance from the DoH and the Home Office about the procedures that local authorities should adopt to monitor and respond to adult abuse.[1] This does not contain any new powers but is concerned with the process local authorities should follow and also provides clarification of the roles of different agencies, i.e. the police and NHS bodies.

The Mental Capacity Bill contains a new criminal offence of ill-treatment or neglect by an attorney, deputy or carer of a person who lacks capacity. This broadens the current protection against ill-treatment and neglect contained in the MHA 1983 because it is not necessary to show that the person has a mental disorder as defined by the MHA 1983 but only that the person lacks capacity.

The Joint Committee on the Draft Mental Incapacity Bill recommended that the Bill should go further by granting statutory authorities greater powers of investigation and intervention in cases of alleged physical, sexual or financial abuse of persons lacking capacity.[2] That recommendation was rejected by the government on the basis that the *No Secrets*[3] adult protection guidance requires councils to liaise with other public bodies and agencies to adopt a joint strategy and procedure for handling incidents. Also, the government relied on the fact that the Public Guardian has powers to cooperate with other agencies (see Cm. 6121).

The Joint Committee also recommended in its Report (at para. 272) that the new criminal offence be extended to include the misappropriation of property and financial assets of the person lacking capacity, but this was rejected by the government on the basis that it is already covered by the current law of theft (Cm. 6121).

1   *No Secrets: Guidance on Developing and Implementing Multi-agency Policies and Procedures to Protect Vulnerable Adults from Abuse* (2000).
2   *Joint Committee on the Draft Mental Incapacity Bill Report*, para. 73.
3   Guidance on developing multi-agency policies and procedures to protect vulnerable adults from abuse (March 2000). Many local authorities have now set up Adult Protection Committees in response to this guidance.

10.2   POSITION UNDER THE MENTAL CAPACITY ACT 2005

10.2.1   Persons liable

The offence of ill-treatment or neglect applies to three categories of person (all known as 'D'):

■   a person who has the care of a person ('P') who lacks capacity or whom D reasonably believes lacks capacity (this includes professional carers as well as non-professionals such as relatives);
■   the donee of an LPA or an EPA created by P;
■   a deputy appointed by the court for P.

10.2.2   D is guilty of an offence if he ill-treats or wilfully neglects P

There is no definition of ill-treatment or wilful neglect in the Act.

However, there is case law in respect of the MHA 1983 offences of ill-treatment or neglect of mentally disordered persons which provides guidance.[1] The Court of Appeal has held that ill-treatment and wilful neglect under the MHA 1983 ought not to be equated and that they should appear as separate counts in an indictment (*R v. Newington* (1990) 91 Cr App R 247). This applies equally to the offence of ill-treatment or wilful neglect under the Act.

Ill-treatment

In *R v. Newington*, the Court of Appeal gave guidance on the requirements of the offence of ill-treatment in the context of the offence of ill-treatment of a mentally disordered person under s.127 of the MHA 1983. It is necessary for the prosecution to prove:

1. deliberate conduct by the accused which can properly be described as ill-treatment irrespective of whether or not it damaged or threatened to damage the victim's health; and
2. a guilty mind: either an appreciation by the accused that he or she was inexcusably ill-treating a person or recklessness as to whether he or she was inexcusably acting in this way.

The Court did not accept that violence would always amount to ill-treatment because violence necessarily used for the control of a patient would not amount to ill-treatment.

Wilful neglect

The leading case on wilful neglect is *R* v. *Sheppard* [1981] AC 394, HL. The primary meaning of the word 'wilful' is deliberate. As a matter of general principle, recklessness is also covered (see Lord Keith, at 418). Neglect is an objective state which is not defined by the Act. Neglect could consist of an omission.

10.2.3   Penalties

The offence is triable either way and the penalties are:

■   on summary conviction, a maximum prison term of 12 months and/or a fine not exceeding the statutory maximum;
■   on conviction on indictment, a maximum prison term of five years and/or a fine.

The penalties are more severe than those imposed by the offences of ill-treatment and neglect under the MHA 1983.

---

1   For more detailed discussion, refer to Richard Jones *Mental Health Act Manual* 9th edn and *Blackstones Criminal Practice 2005*.

11 THE COURT OF PROTECTION

11.1 BACKGROUND

The jurisdiction of the current Court of Protection is entirely statutory and derives from Part VII of the MHA 1983 and the EPAA 1985.[1] It is an office of the Supreme Court. Its jurisdiction is restricted to matters relating to the property and affairs of a patient within its jurisdiction. It has no jurisdiction over matters relating to the patient's welfare such as residence, medical treatment or contact between the patient and other persons.

---

1 Both are repealed by the Act (s.66).

11.2 POSITION UNDER THE MENTAL CAPACITY ACT 2005

11.2.1 Changes introduced

The Act introduces important changes in respect of the Court of Protection affecting its jurisdiction and powers. First, it is made a superior court of record with all the powers of the High Court. Secondly, its jurisdiction is no longer restricted to matters concerning the property and affairs of a person who lacks capacity but also covers the person's personal welfare. Thirdly, there is no longer any provision for the appointment of receivers. Receivers have been replaced by deputies under the Act. The Court is responsible for the appointment of deputies.

It is intended that the new Court of Protection will have a comprehensive jurisdiction in relation to welfare and financial matters and that it will not be necessary to invoke the inherent jurisdiction of the High Court to address these issues (as was the case under the old system in respect of welfare matters) (see Draft Code of Practice at para. 7.4).

The particular powers of the Court of Protection are explained in other chapters of this book (see **Chapters 4, 6 and 7**).

11.2.2   Forum of last resort

It is intended that the new Court of Protection will act as a judicial forum of last resort for addressing particularly complex decisions or difficult disputes (see Draft Code of Practice at para. 7.3 and Chapter 10). It is hoped that otherwise carers and other persons will rely on s.5 of the Act or that alternative informal dispute resolution mechanisms such as mediation or complaint procedures will be used (Draft Code of Practice, para. 10.31). The Draft Code of Practice (at paras. 5.23–5.24) states that it is anticipated that a Practice Direction will be issued confirming that it is necessary to refer to the Court withdrawal of ANH from PVS patients and non-therapeutic sterilisations. The Draft Code of Practice (at para. 10.32) gives examples of situations where an application to the court should be made which include:

- where it is unclear whether proposed serious and/or invasive medical treatment is likely to be in a person's best interests;
- where formal authority is required to deal with one-off important financial decisions but there is no need for ongoing financial powers;
- where it is necessary to make a will or amend an existing will on behalf of a person lacking testamentary capacity.

Where there is a dispute over capacity, it is difficult to see how that could be resolved informally. Also, in cases where there are intractable disputes between family members and professionals, informal resolution methods may not be effective. In practice, it seems unlikely that there will be far fewer applications made to the new Court of Protection under the Act than are currently brought in the Court of Protection or the Family Division of the High Court.

11.2.3   Practice and procedure

It is not possible at this stage to address in any detail the practical day-to-day procedure and workings of the new Court of Protection because these are not dealt with in the Act and have been left to subordinate legislation. Neither does the Draft Code of Practice assist on this point.

11.2.4   Repeals

Part VII of the MHA 1983 and the EPAA 1985 are repealed by the Act, although transitional provisions are in place for existing receivers and the EPAA 1985 is re-enacted in Schedule 4 to the Act with amendments (see discussion at **para. 4.11**).

11.3   THE COURT: JURISDICTION AND POWERS

11.3.1   The Court of Protection

Superior court of record (s.45(1))

The Court of Protection has hitherto existed only as an office of the Supreme Court and not as a separate court. The Court of Protection is now made a court of record which means that records of its proceedings which are preserved in its archives are called records and will be conclusive evidence of that recorded in them (*R v. Tyrone Justices* [1917] 2 IR 437).

Further, it is made a superior court which means that no matter is deemed to be beyond its jurisdiction unless expressly shown to be so. An objection to the jurisdiction of a superior court must show that another court has jurisdiction so as to show that the exercise of the general jurisdiction of a superior court is unnecessary.

The office of the Supreme Court called the Court of Protection ceases to exist.

Official seal (s.45(2))

The Court of Protection will have its own official seal. This is consistent with it being a separate court.

Sitting (s.45(3))

The Court of Protection may sit anywhere in England or Wales. The current Court of Protection sits only in London and Preston.

Registries (s.45(4), (5))

The Court of Protection will have a central office and registry as designated by the Lord Chancellor. However, it will also have a regional presence. Additional registries (being High Court district registries or county courts) will be designated by the Lord Chancellor.

11.3.2   Judges of the Court of Protection

Nomination of judges (s.46(1), (2))

Judges in the Court of Protection must be nominated by the Lord Chancellor or someone acting on his behalf. Those who can be nominated are listed in s.46(2) and are the President of the Family Division, the Vice-Chancellor, a puisne judge of the High Court, a circuit judge or a district judge.

Senior appointments (s.46(3), (4))

The Lord Chancellor must appoint one of the senior nominated judges to be the President of the Court of Protection and another to be the Vice-President. The Lord Chancellor must appoint a circuit judge or district judge to be the Senior Judge of the Court of Protection with such administrative functions as are directed.

11.3.3   General powers and effect of orders

Background

The current Court of Protection derives all its powers from the MHA 1983 and the EPAA 1985. The MHA 1983 provides that a judge exercising powers under Part VII of the MHA 1983 has the same powers as the High Court in respect of securing the attendance of witnesses and examining documents, and that acts or omissions occurring in the proceedings before the Court of Protection can be punished in the same way as a contempt of court although there is no power to commit for contempt of court (MHA 1983, s.104(1), (2)).

Same powers, rights, privileges and authority of the High Court (s.47(1))

The new Court of Protection's jurisdiction is expanded so that it is the same as that of the High Court. The High Court's powers derive from the Supreme Court Act 1981 as well as a variety of other statutes and the common law. The new Court of Protection has, therefore, powers to fine or imprison for contempt of court, to grant injunctions, to summons witnesses and order the production of documents, to secure and preserve evidence and has enforcement powers.

Section 204 of the Law of Property Act 1925 (s.47(2))

This provision making orders of the High Court conclusive in favour of purchasers applies to the Court of Protection.

Office copies of orders (s.47(3))

Office copies of orders or directions issued by the Court and sealed with the official seal are admissible in legal proceeding without further proof.

11.3.4   Interim orders and directions

Background

The current Court of Protection has power to make interim orders in respect of a patient's property and affairs when immediate provision is necessary (Court of Protection Rules 2001, SI 2001/824, r.42).

In respect of welfare matters, the High Court when exercising its inherent jurisdiction has made interim declarations and/or injunctions.

The difficulty that arose in both situations at an interim stage was providing the Court with the necessary evidence that a person was a patient or lacked capacity. This arose particularly in situations where health or social care professionals could not obtain access to a person's home in order to carry out an assessment of capacity.

Position under the Mental Capacity Act 2005

The Court will make an interim order or give directions in respect of a matter if it is satisfied that:

- There is reason to believe that a person lacks capacity in relation to the matter (s.48(a)). The Explanatory Notes to the Act state that this allows the Court to make interim orders even if evidence as to lack of capacity is not yet available. This refers to the current requirement that the Court be provided with medical evidence establishing that a person lacks capacity. However, clearly some evidence from carers or others concerned with a person's care will have to be presented to the Court setting out the facts and matters relied upon as the basis for the belief that a person lacks capacity.
- The matter is one to which its powers extend. The powers of the Court of Protection are discussed in **Chapters 4, 6** and **7**.
- It is in the incapable person's best interests to make the order, or give the directions without delay. This incorporates the best interests test at the interim stage. For discussion of the principles of best interests, see **Chapter 3**.

11.3.5   Power to call for reports

Background

A judge in the current Court of Protection has power to order a Lord Chancellor's Visitor (who has been asked by the Court to visit the patient for the purpose of investigating a matter related to property and affairs) to make such report to the Court as the judge may direct (MHA 1983, s.103(4)).

Position under the Mental Capacity Act 2005

The Court of Protection's power to call for reports has been expanded.

A question relating to the incapable person (s.49(1))

The Court's power to call for reports applies when it is considering a question relating to the incapable person. In practice, this is likely to apply in most cases.

Persons who can be asked to report (s.49(2), (3))

The Court can require the Public Guardian (see discussion of the Public Guardian and his role in **Chapter 12**), a Court of Protection Visitor (see further discussion on the role and functions of visitors at **para. 11.5**), a local authority or NHS body to report to it.

Scope of the report (s.49(4), (5))

The Court may direct that the report deals with specific matters. Further, Court of Protection Rules may specify matters which must be dealt with in such a report unless the Court directs otherwise.

Report in writing or orally (s.49(6))

The Court may direct that the report be in writing or be given orally. This provides the Court the greatest flexibility. In cases of urgency, an oral report will have the advantage of speed.

Disclosure of reports

No provision is made in the Act about disclosure of reports. The position under s.103(8) of the MHA 1983 is that a report is only disclosed to the judge and persons authorised by the judge. Baroness Andrews on behalf of the government confirmed in the House of Lords at the Committee Stage (debate of 8 February 2005) that the current practice in respect of disclosure would continue under the Act and that the express consent of the judge would be required for disclosure to third parties. This is a sensible provision because disclosure to a third party, such as an attorney of an LPA, may not be appropriate if he is suspected of abuse. Presumably, this matter will be addressed in the new procedural rules.

Access to records (s.49(7))

The Public Guardian and a Court of Protection Visitor may examine and take copies at all reasonable times of any health records, social services records or registered care home records so far as those records relate to the incapable person.

A local authority or health body will already have access to the relevant records for the purpose of preparing their reports to the court.

Interview with the incapable person (s.49(8))

The Public Guardian and a Court of Protection Visitor may interview the incapable person in private for the purpose of reporting to the court when a report has been ordered by the court. A Lord Chancellor's Visitor previously had power to interview a patient (MHA 1983, s.103(5)).

Medical examination (s.49(9))

A Court of Protection Visitor who is a Special Visitor (i.e. medical professional appointed by the Lord Chancellor) ordered by the court to report on the incapable person, may carry out a medical, psychiatric or psychological examination of the incapable person in private, if the Court directs that he may do so.

Under the MHA 1983, a Medical Visitor (the previous term for Special Visitor) had a general power to examine the patient in private and there was no requirement for an express direction by the court (MHA 1983, s.103(6)).

11.4   PRACTICE AND PROCEDURE

11.4.1   Applications to the Court of Protection

Background

The position with the current Court of Protection is that there is a general rule that applications may be made by any person interested (r.6(b) of Court of Protection Rules 2001). However, stricter rules are applied for particular types of application (e.g. applications for the settlement or gift of a patient's property or for the execution of a statutory will under s.96 of the MHA 1983).

Position under the Mental Capacity Act 2005

The Act introduces a general rule for all applications. Certain types of applicant can apply to the Court of Protection as of right. All other applicants require permission from the court to apply.

No permission required (s.50(1))

The following applicants do not require permission from the Court to bring an application:

■   a person who lacks or is alleged to lack capacity (or if that person is not yet 18, anyone with parental responsibility[1] for him);
■   the donor or donee of an LPA to which the application relates (the application to the Court must, therefore, relate to the LPA);
■   a deputy for a person to whom the application relates;
■   a person named in an existing order of the Court, if the application relates to the order.

Permission required (s.50(3))

Apart from the exceptions listed above, permission from the Court will be required to bring an application. In deciding whether to grant permission, the Court must have regard to the following factors:

- the applicant's connection with the person to whom the application relates;
- the reasons for the application;
- the benefit to the person to whom the application relates of a proposed order or directions; and
- whether the benefit can be achieved in any other way.

These factors seek to ensure that any proposed application will promote the interests of the person concerned, rather than causing unnecessary distress or difficulty for him (see para. 136 of the Explanatory Notes).

Presently, permission is not required for an application in relation to a person's health and welfare. It may be that the requirement of permission in the Act will introduce an unnecessary and undesirable delay and additional costs into the process.

As to who should make an application, the Draft Code of Practice states that when the dispute relates to the provision of medical treatment, the NHS Trust or other body responsible for a person's care should make the application. A local authority wishing to intervene in personal welfare issues should make the application. Further, the person lacking capacity should be made a party to the proceedings and that the Court may appoint the Official Solicitor to act for the person lacking capacity (at para. 7.5).

Subject to Court of Protection Rules and declarations relating to private international law (s.50(2))

The Court of Protection Rules can provide that permission is not required for other types of application.

No permission is required for an application to the Court for certain declarations relating to private international law (s.20(2) of and Schedule 3 to the Act).

11.4.2   Court of Protection Rules

Background

The Court of Protection's practice is currently regulated by the Court of Protection Rules 2001 (the 2001 Rules) and the Court of Protection (Enduring Power of Attorney Rules) 2001, SI 2001/825. The emphasis in the current rules is on informality of procedure where this is possible. For example, applications can be made by letter or on the general form of application (r.7 of the 2001 Rules).

Position under the Mental Capacity Act 2005

The Lord Chancellor may make rules of court (s.51(1))

The Lord Chancellor is charged with making the specialist practice and procedure rules for the Court of Protection which will be known as the Court of Protection Rules.

Matters to be covered by the Court of Protection Rules (s.51(2))

A non-exhaustive list is set out of the matters that may be covered by the Rules. This includes provisions relating to the manner and form in which proceedings are to be commenced, persons to be notified and made party to the proceedings, provision for the Official Solicitor to act on behalf of an incapable person, enabling the jurisdiction of the Court to be exercised by officers and staff of the Court, enabling an application to be disposed of without a hearing, enabling all or part of the proceedings to be in private.

It is not clear to what extent, if at all, the general practice and procedure will change in the Court of Protection. This is not an issue which was given much attention in the Houses of Parliament during the debates on the Mental Capacity Bill. On that basis, it seems unlikely that there will be much change in the general practice and procedure of the Court with regard to financial matters. The position in relation to health and welfare cases is more uncertain.

Directions (s.51(3))

The Court of Protection Rules can provide that provision is to be made about a matter in directions (see further discussion of Practice Directions at **para. 11.4.3**). The Explanatory Notes state that it is the intention to make rules accompanied by Practice Directions on the model of the Civil Procedure Rules 1998. Most parts of the Civil Procedure Rules are accompanied by Practice Directions which are of considerable assistance in interpreting the rules.

Different provision for different areas (s.51(4))

This permits the Rules to make different provision for different geographical areas.

11.4.3   Practice directions

Background

Practice Directions have been used in the current Court of Protection and the Family Division of the High Court to offer assistance and guidance to litigants and to support the rules of the court.

Position under the Mental Capacity Act 2005

The use of Practice Directions will continue under the Act. The implication is that greater use may be made of them because express provision is made in the Act to use directions instead of rules. The Explanatory Notes also state that the model of the Civil Procedure Rules is to be followed which make extensive use of Practice Directions (para. 138).

Directions by the President (s.52(1))

The President of the Court of Protection may give directions as to practice and procedure with the approval of the Lord Chancellor.

Directions by others (s.52(2))

Other persons (e.g. the Vice-President) may give directions with the approval of the President and the Lord Chancellor.

Guidance as to law or legal appointments (s.52(3))

The President can give directions containing such guidance without the approval of the Lord Chancellor.

11.4.4   Rights of appeal

Background

In the current Court of Protection, the Court has the power to review its decision when there has been no attendance at the hearing. Appeals from the decision of a Master are made to a nominated judge of the Court and do not require permission. Appeals from a judge lie to the Court of Appeal. The Court has the power to review its decisions made in the absence of any parties.

Position under the Mental Capacity Act 2005

No provision is made for a power to review decisions made in the absence of any parties.

Appeal to the Court of Appeal (s.53(1))

The general position is that an appeal lies to the Court of Appeal.

Appeal to higher judge of the Court of Protection (s.53(2), (3))

The Court of Protection Rules may make provision for appeals made by lower level judges (or officers or staff exercising functions) of the Court of Protection to be heard by higher judges in the Court of Protection. This deals with the fact that decisions in the Court of Protection can be made at different levels.

What constitutes a higher judge will depend on the level of decision maker, e.g. a higher judge in relation to a district judge is a circuit judge (s.53(3)(b)).

Permission (s.53(4))

The Court of Protection Rules may make provision as to when permission to appeal is required, who can grant permission and the criteria for granting permission.

Further, provision may be made that in cases where a higher judge makes a decision on appeal, no appeal to the Court lies unless the appeal would raise an important point of principle or there is some other compelling reason for the Court of Appeal to hear it. This mirrors the '2nd appeal' test in rule 52.13 of the Civil Procedure Rules 1998.

11.4.5   Fees

Background

The position under the 2001 Rules is that the Court has power to remit or postpone payment of fees when payment of the whole or part would cause hardship to the patient or his dependants or there are exceptional circumstances (r.83(1)). The Court waives or reduces fees in these circumstances.

Position under the Mental Capacity Act 2005

Fees are prescribed by the Lord Chancellor with the consent of the Treasury (s.54(1)).

Orders may make provision about scales and rates of fees as well as (s.54(2)):

- exemptions from and reduction in fees;
- remission of fees in whole or in part.

It was stated on behalf of the government during debates on the Mental Capacity Bill in both Houses of Parliament that people with low incomes and few assets would be exempt from paying fees.[2]

Consultation by the Lord Chancellor (s.54(3))

The Lord Chancellor is under a duty to consult the President, Vice-President and Senior Judge of the Court of Protection before making orders about fees.

Information about fees (s.54(4))

The Lord Chancellor is under an obligation to take steps that are reasonably practicable to bring information about fees to the attention of those likely to pay them. This reflects the provisions made about other court fees in s.92 of the Courts Act 2003.

Recovery of fees (s.54(5))

Fees payable can be recovered as civil debt.

11.4.6   Costs

Background

Costs in the current Court of Protection are at the discretion of the Court (r.84 of the 2001 Rules). The Court may order costs to be charged on or paid out of the patient's estate or for costs to be paid by any party. Costs are assessed and sometimes fixed costs are available. If costs are assessed, this is undertaken by the Supreme Court Costs Office applying Parts 43, 44, 47 and 48 of the CPR subject to amendment. The principles governing the payment of costs are set out in the decision of *Re Cathcart* [1892] 1 Ch 549 which states that costs do not automatically follow the event. Public funding from the Legal Services Commission is not available at present for Court of Protection proceedings.

Position under the Mental Capacity Act 2005

The Act seeks to put the Court of Protection in the same position as other civil courts in respect of its costs rules (see Explanatory Notes at para. 141). A new power is introduced permitting the Court to make wasted costs orders.

Costs of and incidental to all proceedings in the court are at its discretion (s.55(1))

This mirrors the previous rule. This rule is subject to the Court of Protection Rules so different provision could be made for particular proceedings.

The Court of Protection rules may make provisions regulating costs including the prescription of scales of costs to be paid to legal or other representatives (s.55(2))

It is envisaged that the Court will have powers to control the level of fees payable to representatives.

Full power to determine by whom and to what extent the costs are to be paid (s.55(3))

As with other courts, the Court of Protection has full power to determine who pays costs and how much is to be paid.

Wasted costs (s.55(4), (5), (6))

The Court has power to disallow wasted costs or to order legal or other representatives to meet such wasted costs.

This provision provides the Court with more draconian powers in respect of costs than were previously available. For further guidance on the principles applicable in wasted costs applications, see *Civil Procedure* vol. 1 (Sweet & Maxwell, 2005), at paras. 48.7.3–48.7.20).

Wasted costs are defined in s.55(6) as costs incurred as the result of improper, unreasonable or negligent acts or omissions of a party's representative (legal or other) or any employee of a representative or which in light of such an act or omission, it considers it unreasonable to expect the party to pay.

Public funding

Public funding will be available from the Legal Services Commission for people who lack capacity in the form of Legal Help and, where necessary, Legal Representation at the Court of Protection. The means and merits test will apply. The Draft Code of Practice states that Legal Representation will only be available for the most serious cases, that is cases heard previously by the High Court and primarily those concerning the personal liberty or medical treatment of a person who lacks capacity. It is proposed that a direction will be issued to the Legal Services Commission to ensure that Legal Representation is available for serious cases that meet the specified criteria (see paras. 10.34–10.37 of the Draft Code of Practice). For further information on public funding, visit the Legal Services Commission website (**www.legalservices.gov.uk**).

11.4.7   Fees and costs: supplementary

Background

Section 106(5) of the MHA 1983 contains provisions for rules to make supplementary rules about fees and costs.

Position under the Mental Capacity Act 2005

This contains similar provisions to s.106(5) of MHA 1983.

This section provides that the Court of Protection Rules may make provision for the way in which, and funds from which, fees and costs are to be paid, for charging fees and costs upon the estate of the person in respect of whom the proceedings relate, for the payment of fees and costs within a specified time of the death of a person to whom the proceedings relate or at the conclusion of the proceedings.

---

1   Which has the same meaning as in the Children Act 1989 (s.50(4)).
2   See Hansard, Committee in Commons 28 October 2004, at col. 398, Committee in Lords 8 February 2005, at col. 754.

11.5   COURT OF PROTECTION VISITORS

11.5.1   Background

The MHA 1983 provides for the appointment by the Lord Chancellor of persons known as Lord Chancellor's Visitors who are either Medical Visitors (registered medical practitioners with special knowledge and experience of mental disorder), Legal Visitors (with legal qualifications) or General Visitors (with neither medical nor legal qualifications) (MHA 1983, s.102). A judge of the Court of Protection can order that a Lord Chancellor's Visitor visit a patient for the purpose of investigating any matter relating to the patient's capacity to manage and administer his property and affairs or related to the exercise of any functions by the judge under Part VII of the MHA 1983 (MHA 1983, s.103(2)).

11.5.2   Position under the Mental Capacity Act 2005

The position under the Act is broadly the same as that under Part VII of the MHA 1983 save that Lord Chancellor's Visitors are now renamed Court of Protection Visitors. Visitors who are medically qualified are known as Special Visitors. Other visitors are known as General Visitors. No special provision is made for Legal Visitors under the Act.

Appointment by the Lord Chancellor (s.61(1), (4))

The Lord Chancellor will appoint persons to the panel for Special Visitors and General Visitors. The Lord Chancellor will determine the terms and conditions of their appointment and their remuneration and allowances.

Special Visitors (s.61(2))

The necessary qualifications to be a Special Visitor are that a person:

■   is a registered medical practitioner or appears to the Lord Chancellor to have other suitable qualifications and training; and
■   appears to the Lord Chancellor to have a special knowledge and experience in cases of impairment of or disturbance in the functioning of the mind and brain. This requirement refers to the definition of incapacity in s.2 of the Act.

General Visitors (s.61(3))

No qualifications are specified in respect of General Visitors, although the Act specifies that a General Visitor does not require medical qualifications.

Functions of Court of Protection Visitors

Court of Protection Visitors are appointed to carry out visits and produce reports as directed by the Court of Protection (s.49(2)) or the Public Guardian (s.58(1)(d)) in respect of persons who lack capacity (see further commentary on these sections at **para. 12.3.2**).

Access to records and interview (s.61(5), (6))

A Court of Protection Visitor has power to examine and take copies of relevant health, social services or care records which relate to a person who lacks capacity.

A Court of Protection Visitor can also interview the person that lacks capacity in private.

These powers are broadly similar to those held by the Public Guardian (s.58(5), (6)).

11.6   EXISTING RECEIVERS

An important part of the current Court's work is the appointment and supervision of receivers who act as agents for the patient in respect of his property and affairs. The Court itself (through its Chief Executive) acts as receiver of last resort when no other receiver is available, although to a very limited extent in more recent times.

Schedule 5 sets out transitional arrangements arising from the repeal of Part VII of the MHA 1983. Part 1 of Schedule 5 sets out provisions applying to receivers appointed under Part VII of the MHA 1983.

Receivers treated as deputies

Persons appointed as receivers under the MHA 1983 will be treated under the Act as though they are deputies appointed by the Court of Protection. They will retain the functions given to them as receivers.

The Court of Protection has powers to end their appointment as deputies (Schedule 5, para. 1(3), (5)).

12 THE PUBLIC GUARDIAN

12.1 BACKGROUND

There is no equivalent of the Public Guardian in the current regime. The Public Guardianship Office carries out only the administrative functions arising from the Court of Protection's jurisdiction including overseeing and supporting the activities of receivers and managing the financial affairs of patients when no one else was willing to act as receiver. The Public Guardian has an expanded remit and a greater regulatory role. Concerns were expressed about the amount of abuse by attorneys and others which had gone unchecked as well as the quality of the work carried out by the Public Guardianship Office.[1] The creation of the new Office of the Public Guardian with an expanded remit is one of the methods adopted to combat these problems.

1 See Hansard, Lord Kingsland at Committee Stage in the Lords 8 February 2005, at col. 765.

12.2 POSITION UNDER THE MENTAL CAPACITY ACT 2005

This section provides for the appointment of a new public official, the Public Guardian, who has a range of functions contributing to the protection of persons who lack capacity (functions discussed at **para. 12.3**).

The Public Guardian (s.57(2))

The Public Guardian will be appointed by the Lord Chancellor.

Officers and staff (s.58(3), (4), (5))

These will be provided to the Public Guardian by the Lord Chancellor. The Lord Chancellor will also enter into contracts for the provision of officers, staff or services as he thinks are necessary to discharge properly the functions of the Public Guardian. The Public Guardian can authorise his officers to perform functions on his behalf.

12.3   FUNCTIONS OF THE PUBLIC GUARDIAN

12.3.1   Background

Baroness Andrews on behalf of the government in the House of Lords at the Committee Stage stated that the Public Guardian has regulatory functions which fall into three main areas: (1) the registration body for LPAs; (2) the supervision of deputies appointed by the Court; (3) investigative functions.[1]

12.3.2   Functions of the Public Guardian

The Act provides that the Public Guardian has the following functions.

Establishing and maintaining a register of LPAs (s.58(1)(a))

The application and procedure for registration and the role of the Public Guardian is discussed in **Chapter 4** on LPAs. The Public Guardian has to ensure that the application complies with the statutory requirements.

LPAs cannot be used until they have been registered so the Public Guardian will have a comprehensive register of all LPAs in operation. This differs from the current position in respect of EPAs (see **Chapter 4** for further discussion).

The Public Guardian is also responsible for cancelling the registration of an instrument as an LPA (see Part 3 of Schedule 1 to the Act) and for making notes of alterations to registered LPAs (e.g. that the power has been revoked or suspended – see Part 4 of Schedule 1 to the Act).

The government resisted proposed amendments to the Mental Capacity Bill which would have required the Public Guardian to be responsible for the regular supervision of attorneys of LPAs, primarily on the basis that this would undermine respect for the autonomy of the individual who chose that particular attorney to act on his or her behalf. However, the Public Guardian can investigate cases of suspected abuse upon the issue being brought to his attention (see further below).

Establishing and maintaining a register of orders appointing deputies (s.58(1)(b))

The Public Guardian has a full list of all those appointed by the Court to act as deputies. This is necessary for it to carry out its supervisory functions in respect of deputies (see below).

Supervising deputies appointed by the Court (s.58(1)(c))

Appointment of a deputy is by the Court and is made at the time when a person lacks capacity. There are more stringent safeguards in place for supervision of deputies than for attorneys of LPAs to protect persons who lack capacity from abuse.

The particular procedure and methods that will be adopted by the Public Guardian in order to supervise deputies are not set out in the Act. The Draft Code of Practice provides that the major focus of protection will be at the application stage. The Office of the Public Guardian will carry out a risk assessment to determine the level of future supervision and the amount and type of checks that need to be carried out on the deputy at that stage. The checks will be proportionate to the risk presented so that, for example, it would not normally be necessary to carry out criminal record checks on a local authority official who is appointed to act as a deputy (see para. 9.14 of the Draft Code of Practice).

Further, s.58(2) provides that this function can be carried out in cooperation with other persons who have functions in relation to the care and treatment of P (e.g. health bodies or local authorities).

Directing visits by Court of Protection Visitors (s.58(1)(d))

The Public Guardian has power to direct Court of Protection Visitors (see definition and discussion in **Chapter 11**, at **para. 11.5**) to visit:

- a donee of an LPA;
- a deputy appointed by the court;
- P (the donor of the LPA or for whom the deputy is appointed)

and report to the Public Guardian on such matters as directed.

The power to direct such visits previously only lay with the Court of Protection itself (MHA 1983, s.103). However, the Court of Protection has wider powers to call for reports than the Public Guardian (See **Chapter 11**, at **para. 11.3.5**).

Receiving security which the court requires a person to give for the discharge of his functions (s.59(1)(e))

The exercise of this power is going to be set out in more detail in regulations (see para. 144 of the Explanatory Notes).

Receiving reports from donees of LPAs and deputies appointed by the court (s.58(1)(f))

A donor of an LPA or the Court of Protection in respect of deputies can require that reports are provided to the Public Guardian by the donee of the LPA or the deputy respectively.

Reporting to the court on such matters relating to these proceedings as the court requires (s.59(1)(g))

The Court of Protection has power to call for a report from the Public Guardian (s.49(2)).

Dealing with representations including complaints about the way in which a donee or a deputy is exercising its powers (s.58(1)(h))

Any person may make representations or complaints to the Public Guardian about the way in which a donee of an LPA or a deputy is exercising his functions. The Public Guardian can carry out investigations.

Section 58(2) provides that these functions can be carried out in cooperation with other agencies. The Draft Code of Practice provides that, in some circumstances, the Public Guardian will not be the most appropriate person to investigate. It states that the Public Guardian may himself carry out investigations where there are allegations of financial abuse, although where the suggestion is that a criminal offence has been committed, the matter should be referred to the police. In respect of personal welfare, the Public Guardian should refer the matter to the appropriate health or social care agency (see para. 9.16).

When the Public Guardian makes such a referral, he will remain informed of the action taken by the other agency and will make sure that the Court has all the information it needs in order to take the necessary sanctions against the attorney or deputy (para. 9.16 of the Draft Code of Practice).

Publishing in any manner the Public Guardian thinks appropriate, any information he thinks appropriate about the discharge of his functions (s.58(1)(i))

This provision affords the Public Guardian a wide discretion as to how and what information to make available about the discharge of his functions.

Cooperation with others (s.58(2))

The Public Guardian may discharge his functions in respect of supervision of deputies and dealing with representations and complaints by cooperating with other persons concerned with the person who lacks capacity's care and treatment. It is intended that the Public Guardian will work closely with organisations such as local authorities and NHS bodies (see Explanatory Notes at para. 146). This is discussed further above.

Regulations (s.58(3), (4), (5))

The Lord Chancellor may make regulations:

- conferring other functions on the Public Guardian;
- providing more detail as to how the Public Guardian will exercise certain functions, in particular in respect of receiving Court-ordered security, matters concerning the fees of the Public Guardian and the making of reports to the Public Guardian.

Access to records and interview (s.58(5), (6))

The Public Guardian has power to examine and take copies of relevant health, social services or care records and to interview the donor of an LPA or person in respect of whom a deputy is appointed. This is to enable the Public Guardian to carry out his functions.

The Public Guardian has similar rights when reporting to the Court of Protection (s.49(7), (8)). Court of Protection Visitors have similar rights (s.61(5) and (6) – see discussion below).

---

1   See Hansard, 8 February 2005, at col. 770.

12.4   PUBLIC GUARDIAN BOARD

Section 59 provides for a body, the Public Guardian Board, which supervises the work of the Public Guardian.

The functions of the Public Guardian Board are to:

- scrutinise and review the way in which the Public Guardian discharges his functions; and
- make such recommendations to the Lord Chancellor as it thinks appropriate (s.59(2)).

Consideration of recommendations by the Lord Chancellor (s.59(3))

The Lord Chancellor must give due consideration to recommendations of the Public Guardian Board when discharging his functions in respect of the Public Guardian, e.g. in providing officers and staff to the Public Guardian or making regulations in respect of the Public Guardian's functions.

Membership of the Public Guardian Board

Members will be appointed by the Lord Chancellor (s.59(4)). There must be at least one member who is a judge of the Court of Protection and at least four members who appear to the Lord Chancellor to have appropriate knowledge or experience of the Public Guardian's work (s.59(5)).

Regulations by the Lord Chancellor (s.59(6))

The Lord Chancellor has power to make provision in regulations about appointment of members and the running of the Public Guardian Board.

Payments to members (s.59(8))

The Lord Chancellor has power to determine what payments are to be made to members of the Board by way of reimbursement of expenses, allowances and remuneration.

Annual report to the Lord Chancellor (s.59(9))

The Board must report annually to the Lord Chancellor about the discharge of its functions.

12.5   ANNUAL REPORT OF THE PUBLIC GUARDIAN BOARD

The Public Guardian Board must report annually to the Lord Chancellor about the discharge of its functions and the Lord Chancellor must lay a copy of that report before Parliament within one month of receiving it.

This is the mechanism for ensuring that the work of the Public Guardian Board is subject to scrutiny.

Appendix 1
MENTAL CAPACITY ACT 2005

CONTENTS

PART 1   PERSONS WHO LACK CAPACITY

PART 2   THE COURT OF PROTECTION AND THE PUBLIC GUARDIAN

PART 3   MISCELLANEOUS AND GENERAL

An Act to make new provision relating to persons who lack capacity; to establish a superior court of record called the Court of Protection in place of the office of the Supreme Court called by that name; to make provision in connection with the Convention on the International Protection of Adults signed at the Hague on 13th January 2000; and for connected purposes.

[7th April 2005]

BE IT ENACTED by the Queen's most Excellent Majesty, by and with the advice and consent of the Lords Spiritual and Temporal, and Commons, in this present Parliament assembled, and by the authority of the same, as follows: –

PART 1   PERSONS WHO LACK CAPACITY

The principles

1 The principles

(1) The following principles apply for the purposes of this Act.

(2) A person must be assumed to have capacity unless it is established that he lacks capacity.

(3) A person is not to be treated as unable to make a decision unless all practicable steps to help him to do so have been taken without success.

(4) A person is not to be treated as unable to make a decision merely because he makes an unwise decision.

(5) An act done, or decision made, under this Act for or on behalf of a person who lacks capacity must be done, or made, in his best interests.

(6) Before the act is done, or the decision is made, regard must be had to whether the purpose for which it is needed can be as effectively achieved in a way that is less restrictive of the person's rights and freedom of action.

Preliminary

2 People who lack capacity

(1) For the purposes of this Act, a person lacks capacity in relation to a matter if at the material time he is unable to make a decision for himself in relation to the matter because of an impairment of, or a disturbance in the functioning of, the mind or brain.

(2) It does not matter whether the impairment or disturbance is permanent or temporary.

(3) A lack of capacity cannot be established merely by reference to –

    (a) a person's age or appearance, or

    (b) a condition of his, or an aspect of his behaviour, which might lead others to make unjustified assumptions about his capacity.

(4) In proceedings under this Act or any other enactment, any question whether a person lacks capacity within the meaning of this Act must be decided on the balance of probabilities.

(5) No power which a person ('D') may exercise under this Act –

(a) in relation to a person who lacks capacity, or
(b) where D reasonably thinks that a person lacks capacity,

is exercisable in relation to a person under 16.

(6) Subsection (5) is subject to section 18(3).

3 Inability to make decisions

(1) For the purposes of section 2, a person is unable to make a decision for himself if he is unable –

(a) to understand the information relevant to the decision,
(b) to retain that information,
(c) to use or weigh that information as part of the process of making the decision, or
(d) to communicate his decision (whether by talking, using sign language or any other means).

(2) A person is not to be regarded as unable to understand the information relevant to a decision if he is able to understand an explanation of it given to him in a way that is appropriate to his circumstances (using simple language, visual aids or any other means).

(3) The fact that a person is able to retain the information relevant to a decision for a short period only does not prevent him from being regarded as able to make the decision.

(4) The information relevant to a decision includes information about the reasonably foreseeable consequences of –

(a) deciding one way or another, or
(b) failing to make the decision.

4 Best interests

(1) In determining for the purposes of this Act what is in a person's best interests, the person making the determination must not make it merely on the basis of –

(a) the person's age or appearance, or
(b) a condition of his, or an aspect of his behaviour, which might lead others to make unjustified assumptions about what might be in his best interests.

(2) The person making the determination must consider all the relevant circumstances and, in particular, take the following steps.

(3) He must consider –

(a) whether it is likely that the person will at some time have capacity in relation to the matter in question, and
(b) if it appears likely that he will, when that is likely to be.

(4) He must, so far as reasonably practicable, permit and encourage the person to participate, or to improve his ability to participate, as fully as possible in any act done for him and any decision affecting him.

(5) Where the determination relates to life-sustaining treatment he must not, in considering whether the treatment is in the best interests of the person concerned, be motivated by a desire to bring about his death.

(6) He must consider, so far as is reasonably ascertainable –

(a) the person's past and present wishes and feelings (and, in particular, any relevant written statement made by him when he had capacity),
(b) the beliefs and values that would be likely to influence his decision if he had capacity, and
(c) the other factors that he would be likely to consider if he were able to do so.

(7) He must take into account, if it is practicable and appropriate to consult them, the views of –

(a) anyone named by the person as someone to be consulted on the matter in question or on matters of that kind,

(b) anyone engaged in caring for the person or interested in his welfare,

(c) any donee of a lasting power of attorney granted by the person, and

(d) any deputy appointed for the person by the court,

as to what would be in the person's best interests and, in particular, as to the matters mentioned in subsection (6).

(8) The duties imposed by subsections (1) to (7) also apply in relation to the exercise of any powers which –

(a) are exercisable under a lasting power of attorney, or

(b) are exercisable by a person under this Act where he reasonably believes that another person lacks capacity.

(9) In the case of an act done, or a decision made, by a person other than the court, there is sufficient compliance with this section if (having complied with the requirements of subsections (1) to (7)) he reasonably believes that what he does or decides is in the best interests of the person concerned.

(10) 'Life-sustaining treatment' means treatment which in the view of a person providing health care for the person concerned is necessary to sustain life.

(11) 'Relevant circumstances' are those –

(a) of which the person making the determination is aware, and

(b) which it would be reasonable to regard as relevant.

5 Acts in connection with care or treatment

(1) If a person ('D') does an act in connection with the care or treatment of another person ('P'), the act is one to which this section applies if –

(a) before doing the act, D takes reasonable steps to establish whether P lacks capacity in relation to the matter in question, and

(b) when doing the act, D reasonably believes –

(i) that P lacks capacity in relation to the matter, and

(ii) that it will be in P's best interests for the act to be done.

(2) D does not incur any liability in relation to the act that he would not have incurred if P –

(a) had had capacity to consent in relation to the matter, and

(b) had consented to D's doing the act.

(3) Nothing in this section excludes a person's civil liability for loss or damage, or his criminal liability, resulting from his negligence in doing the act.

(4) Nothing in this section affects the operation of sections 24 to 26 (advance decisions to refuse treatment).

6 Section 5 acts: limitations

(1) If D does an act that is intended to restrain P, it is not an act to which section 5 applies unless two further conditions are satisfied.

(2) The first condition is that D reasonably believes that it is necessary to do the act in order to prevent harm to P.

(3) The second is that the act is a proportionate response to –

(a) the likelihood of P's suffering harm, and

(b) the seriousness of that harm.

(4) For the purposes of this section D restrains P if he –

   (a) uses, or threatens to use, force to secure the doing of an act which P resists, or
   (b) restricts P's liberty of movement, whether or not P resists.

(5) But D does more than merely restrain P if he deprives P of his liberty within the meaning of Article 5(1) of the Human Rights Convention (whether or not D is a public authority).

(6) Section 5 does not authorise a person to do an act which conflicts with a decision made, within the scope of his authority and in accordance with this Part, by –

   (a) a donee of a lasting power of attorney granted by P, or
   (b) a deputy appointed for P by the court.

(7) But nothing in subsection (6) stops a person –

   (a) providing life-sustaining treatment, or
   (b) doing any act which he reasonably believes to be necessary to prevent a serious deterioration in P's condition,

   while a decision as respects any relevant issue is sought from the court.

7 Payment for necessary goods and services

(1) If necessary goods or services are supplied to a person who lacks capacity to contract for the supply, he must pay a reasonable price for them.

(2) 'Necessary' means suitable to a person's condition in life and to his actual requirements at the time when the goods or services are supplied.

8 Expenditure

(1) If an act to which section 5 applies involves expenditure, it is lawful for D –

   (a) to pledge P's credit for the purpose of the expenditure, and
   (b) to apply money in P's possession for meeting the expenditure.

(2) If the expenditure is borne for P by D, it is lawful for D –

   (a) to reimburse himself out of money in P's possession, or
   (b) to be otherwise indemnified by P.

(3) Subsections (1) and (2) do not affect any power under which (apart from those subsections) a person –

   (a) has lawful control of P's money or other property, and
   (b) has power to spend money for P's benefit.

Lasting powers of attorney

9 Lasting powers of attorney

(1) A lasting power of attorney is a power of attorney under which the donor ('P') confers on the donee (or donees) authority to make decisions about all or any of the following –

   (a) P's personal welfare or specified matters concerning P's personal welfare, and
   (b) P's property and affairs or specified matters concerning P's property and affairs, and which includes authority to make such decisions in circumstances where P no longer has capacity.

(2) A lasting power of attorney is not created unless –

   (a) section 10 is complied with,
   (b) an instrument conferring authority of the kind mentioned in subsection (1) is made and registered in accordance with Schedule 1, and

(c) at the time when P executes the instrument, P has reached 18 and has capacity to execute it.

(3) An instrument which –

(a) purports to create a lasting power of attorney, but

(b) does not comply with this section, section 10 or Schedule 1, confers no authority.

(4) The authority conferred by a lasting power of attorney is subject to –

(a) the provisions of this Act and, in particular, sections 1 (the principles) and 4 (best interests), and

(b) any conditions or restrictions specified in the instrument.

10 Appointment of donees

(1) A donee of a lasting power of attorney must be –

(a) an individual who has reached 18, or

(b) if the power relates only to P's property and affairs, either such an individual or a trust corporation.

(2) An individual who is bankrupt may not be appointed as donee of a lasting power of attorney in relation to P's property and affairs.

(3) Subsections (4) to (7) apply in relation to an instrument under which two or more persons are to act as donees of a lasting power of attorney.

(4) The instrument may appoint them to act –

(a) jointly,

(b) jointly and severally, or

(c) jointly in respect of some matters and jointly and severally in respect of others.

(5) To the extent to which it does not specify whether they are to act jointly or jointly and severally, the instrument is to be assumed to appoint them to act jointly.

(6) If they are to act jointly, a failure, as respects one of them, to comply with the requirements of subsection (1) or (2) or Part 1 or 2 of Schedule 1 prevents a lasting power of attorney from being created.

(7) If they are to act jointly and severally, a failure, as respects one of them, to comply with the requirements of subsection (1) or (2) or Part 1 or 2 of Schedule 1 –

(a) prevents the appointment taking effect in his case, but

(b) does not prevent a lasting power of attorney from being created in the case of the other or others.

(8) An instrument used to create a lasting power of attorney –

(a) cannot give the donee (or, if more than one, any of them) power to appoint a substitute or successor, but

(b) may itself appoint a person to replace the donee (or, if more than one, any of them) on the occurrence of an event mentioned in section 13(6)(a) to (d) which has the effect of terminating the donee's appointment.

11 Lasting powers of attorney: restrictions

(1) A lasting power of attorney does not authorise the donee (or, if more than one, any of them) to do an act that is intended to restrain P, unless three conditions are satisfied.

(2) The first condition is that P lacks, or the donee reasonably believes that P lacks, capacity in relation to the matter in question.

(3) The second is that the donee reasonably believes that it is necessary to do the act in order to prevent harm to P.

(4) The third is that the act is a proportionate response to –

(a) the likelihood of P's suffering harm, and

(b) the seriousness of that harm.

(5) For the purposes of this section, the donee restrains P if he –

    (a) uses, or threatens to use, force to secure the doing of an act which P resists, or

    (b) restricts P's liberty of movement, whether or not P resists, or if he authorises another person to do any of those things.

(6) But the donee does more than merely restrain P if he deprives P of his liberty within the meaning of Article 5(1) of the Human Rights Convention.

(7) Where a lasting power of attorney authorises the donee (or, if more than one, any of them) to make decisions about P's personal welfare, the authority –

    (a) does not extend to making such decisions in circumstances other than those where P lacks, or the donee reasonably believes that P lacks, capacity,

    (b) is subject to sections 24 to 26 (advance decisions to refuse treatment), and

    (c) extends to giving or refusing consent to the carrying out or continuation of a treatment by a person providing health care for P.

(8) But subsection (7)(c) –

    (a) does not authorise the giving or refusing of consent to the carrying out or continuation of life-sustaining treatment, unless the instrument contains express provision to that effect, and

    (b) is subject to any conditions or restrictions in the instrument.

12 Scope of lasting powers of attorney: gifts

(1) Where a lasting power of attorney confers authority to make decisions about P's property and affairs, it does not authorise a donee (or, if more than one, any of them) to dispose of the donor's property by making gifts except to the extent permitted by subsection (2).

(2) The donee may make gifts –

    (a) on customary occasions to persons (including himself) who are related to or connected with the donor, or

    (b) to any charity to whom the donor made or might have been expected to make gifts,

if the value of each such gift is not unreasonable having regard to all the circumstances and, in particular, the size of the donor's estate.

(3) 'Customary occasion' means –

    (a) the occasion or anniversary of a birth, a marriage or the formation of a civil partnership, or

    (b) any other occasion on which presents are customarily given within families or among friends or associates.

(4) Subsection (2) is subject to any conditions or restrictions in the instrument.

13 Revocation of lasting powers of attorney etc.

(1) This section applies if –

    (a) P has executed an instrument with a view to creating a lasting power of attorney, or

    (b) a lasting power of attorney is registered as having been conferred by P,

and in this section references to revoking the power include revoking the instrument.

(2) P may, at any time when he has capacity to do so, revoke the power.

(3) P's bankruptcy revokes the power so far as it relates to P's property and affairs.

(4) But where P is bankrupt merely because an interim bankruptcy restrictions order has effect in respect of him, the power is suspended, so far as it relates to P's property and affairs, for so long as the order has effect.

(5) The occurrence in relation to a donee of an event mentioned in subsection (6) –

    (a) terminates his appointment, and

    (b) except in the cases given in subsection (7), revokes the power.

(6) The events are –

    (a) the disclaimer of the appointment by the donee in accordance with such require-ments as may be prescribed for the purposes of this section in regulations made by the Lord Chancellor,

    (b) subject to subsections (8) and (9), the death or bankruptcy of the donee or, if the donee is a trust corporation, its winding-up or dissolution,

    (c) subject to subsection (11), the dissolution or annulment of a marriage or civil partnership between the donor and the donee,

    (d) the lack of capacity of the donee.

(7) The cases are –

    (a) the donee is replaced under the terms of the instrument,

    (b) he is one of two or more persons appointed to act as donees jointly and severally in respect of any matter and, after the event, there is at least one remaining donee.

(8) The bankruptcy of a donee does not terminate his appointment, or revoke the power, in so far as his authority relates to P's personal welfare.

(9) Where the donee is bankrupt merely because an interim bankruptcy restrictions order has effect in respect of him, his appointment and the power are suspended, so far as they relate to P's property and affairs, for so long as the order has effect.

(10) Where the donee is one of two or more appointed to act jointly and severally under the power in respect of any matter, the reference in subsection (9) to the suspension of the power is to its suspension in so far as it relates to that donee.

(11) The dissolution or annulment of a marriage or civil partnership does not terminate the appointment of a donee, or revoke the power, if the instrument provided that it was not to do so.

14 Protection of donee and others if no power created or power revoked

(1) Subsections (2) and (3) apply if –

    (a) an instrument has been registered under Schedule 1 as a lasting power of attorney, but

    (b) a lasting power of attorney was not created,

    whether or not the registration has been cancelled at the time of the act or transaction in question.

(2) A donee who acts in purported exercise of the power does not incur any liability (to P or any other person) because of the non-existence of the power unless at the time of acting he –

    (a) knows that a lasting power of attorney was not created, or

    (b) is aware of circumstances which, if a lasting power of attorney had been created, would have terminated his authority to act as a donee.

(3) Any transaction between the donee and another person is, in favour of that person, as valid as if the power had been in existence, unless at the time of the transaction that person has knowledge of a matter referred to in subsection (2).

(4) If the interest of a purchaser depends on whether a transaction between the donee and the other person was valid by virtue of subsection (3), it is conclusively presumed in favour of the purchaser that the transaction was valid if –

    (a) the transaction was completed within 12 months of the date on which the instrument was registered, or

    (b) the other person makes a statutory declaration, before or within 3 months after the completion of the purchase, that he had no reason at the time of the transaction to doubt that the donee had authority to dispose of the property which was the subject of the transaction.

(5) In its application to a lasting power of attorney which relates to matters in addition to P's property and affairs, section 5 of the Powers of Attorney Act 1971 (c. 27) (protection where power is revoked) has effect as if references to revocation included the cessation of the power in relation to P's property and affairs.

(6) Where two or more donees are appointed under a lasting power of attorney, this section applies as if references to the donee were to all or any of them.

General powers of the court and appointment of deputies

15 Power to make declarations

(1) The court may make declarations as to –

  (a) whether a person has or lacks capacity to make a decision specified in the declaration;

  (b) whether a person has or lacks capacity to make decisions on such matters as are described in the declaration;

  (c) the lawfulness or otherwise of any act done, or yet to be done, in relation to that person.

(2) 'Act' includes an omission and a course of conduct.

16 Powers to make decisions and appoint deputies: general

(1) This section applies if a person ('P') lacks capacity in relation to a matter or matters concerning –

  (a) P's personal welfare, or

  (b) P's property and affairs.

(2) The court may –

  (a) by making an order, make the decision or decisions on P's behalf in relation to the matter or matters, or

  (b) appoint a person (a 'deputy') to make decisions on P's behalf in relation to the matter or matters.

(3) The powers of the court under this section are subject to the provisions of this Act and, in particular, to sections 1 (the principles) and 4 (best interests).

(4) When deciding whether it is in P's best interests to appoint a deputy, the court must have regard (in addition to the matters mentioned in section 4) to the principles that –

  (a) a decision by the court is to be preferred to the appointment of a deputy to make a decision, and

  (b) the powers conferred on a deputy should be as limited in scope and duration as is reasonably practicable in the circumstances.

(5) The court may make such further orders or give such directions, and confer on a deputy such powers or impose on him such duties, as it thinks necessary or expedient for giving effect to, or otherwise in connection with, an order or appointment made by it under subsection (2).

(6) Without prejudice to section 4, the court may make the order, give the directions or make the appointment on such terms as it considers are in P's best interests, even though no application is before the court for an order, directions or an appointment on those terms.

(7) An order of the court may be varied or discharged by a subsequent order.

(8) The court may, in particular, revoke the appointment of a deputy or vary the powers conferred on him if it is satisfied that the deputy –

(a) has behaved, or is behaving, in a way that contravenes the authority conferred on him by the court or is not in P's best interests, or

(b) proposes to behave in a way that would contravene that authority or would not be in P's best interests.

17 Section 16 powers: personal welfare

(1) The powers under section 16 as respects P's personal welfare extend in particular to –

(a) deciding where P is to live;

(b) deciding what contact, if any, P is to have with any specified persons;

(c) making an order prohibiting a named person from having contact with P;

(d) giving or refusing consent to the carrying out or continuation of a treatment by a person providing health care for P;

(e) giving a direction that a person responsible for P's health care allow a different person to take over that responsibility.

(2) Subsection (1) is subject to section 20 (restrictions on deputies).

18 Section 16 powers: property and affairs

(1) The powers under section 16 as respects P's property and affairs extend in particular to –

(a) the control and management of P's property;

(b) the sale, exchange, charging, gift or other disposition of P's property;

(c) the acquisition of property in P's name or on P's behalf;

(d) the carrying on, on P's behalf, of any profession, trade or business;

(e) the taking of a decision which will have the effect of dissolving a partnership of which P is a member;

(f) the carrying out of any contract entered into by P;

(g) the discharge of P's debts and of any of P's obligations, whether legally enforceable or not;

(h) the settlement of any of P's property, whether for P's benefit or for the benefit of others;

(i) the execution for P of a will;

(j) the exercise of any power (including a power to consent) vested in P whether beneficially or as trustee or otherwise;

(k) the conduct of legal proceedings in P's name or on P's behalf.

(2) No will may be made under subsection (1)(i) at a time when P has not reached 18.

(3) The powers under section 16 as respects any other matter relating to P's property and affairs may be exercised even though P has not reached 16, if the court considers it likely that P will still lack capacity to make decisions in respect of that matter when he reaches 18.

(4) Schedule 2 supplements the provisions of this section.

(5) Section 16(7) (variation and discharge of court orders) is subject to paragraph 6 of Schedule 2.

(6) Subsection (1) is subject to section 20 (restrictions on deputies).

19 Appointment of deputies

(1) A deputy appointed by the court must be –

(a) an individual who has reached 18, or

(b) as respects powers in relation to property and affairs, an individual who has reached 18 or a trust corporation.

(2) The court may appoint an individual by appointing the holder for the time being of a specified office or position.

(3) A person may not be appointed as a deputy without his consent.

(4) The court may appoint two or more deputies to act –

    (a) jointly,

    (b) jointly and severally, or

    (c) jointly in respect of some matters and jointly and severally in respect of others.

(5) When appointing a deputy or deputies, the court may at the same time appoint one or more other persons to succeed the existing deputy or those deputies –

    (a) in such circumstances, or on the happening of such events, as may be specified by the court;

    (b) for such period as may be so specified.

(6) A deputy is to be treated as P's agent in relation to anything done or decided by him within the scope of his appointment and in accordance with this Part.

(7) The deputy is entitled –

    (a) to be reimbursed out of P's property for his reasonable expenses in discharging his functions, and

    (b) if the court so directs when appointing him, to remuneration out of P's property for discharging them.

(8) The court may confer on a deputy powers to –

    (a) take possession or control of all or any specified part of P's property;

    (b) exercise all or any specified powers in respect of it, including such powers of investment as the court may determine.

(9) The court may require a deputy –

    (a) to give to the Public Guardian such security as the court thinks fit for the due discharge of his functions, and

    (b) to submit to the Public Guardian such reports at such times or at such intervals as the court may direct.

20 Restrictions on deputies

(1) A deputy does not have power to make a decision on behalf of P in relation to a matter if he knows or has reasonable grounds for believing that P has capacity in relation to the matter.

(2) Nothing in section 16(5) or 17 permits a deputy to be given power –

    (a) to prohibit a named person from having contact with P;

    (b) to direct a person responsible for P's health care to allow a different person to take over that responsibility.

(3) A deputy may not be given powers with respect to –

    (a) the settlement of any of P's property, whether for P's benefit or for the benefit of others,

    (b) the execution for P of a will, or

    (c) the exercise of any power (including a power to consent) vested in P whether beneficially or as trustee or otherwise.

(4) A deputy may not be given power to make a decision on behalf of P which is inconsistent with a decision made, within the scope of his authority and in accordance with this Act, by the donee of a lasting power of attorney granted by P (or, if there is more than one donee, by any of them).

(5) A deputy may not refuse consent to the carrying out or continuation of life-sustaining treatment in relation to P.

(6) The authority conferred on a deputy is subject to the provisions of this Act and, in particular, sections 1 (the principles) and 4 (best interests).

(7) A deputy may not do an act that is intended to restrain P unless four conditions are satisfied.

(8) The first condition is that, in doing the act, the deputy is acting within the scope of an authority expressly conferred on him by the court.

(9) The second is that P lacks, or the deputy reasonably believes that P lacks, capacity in relation to the matter in question.

(10) The third is that the deputy reasonably believes that it is necessary to do the act in order to prevent harm to P.

(11) The fourth is that the act is a proportionate response to –

   (a) the likelihood of P's suffering harm, or
   (b) the seriousness of that harm.

(12) For the purposes of this section, a deputy restrains P if he –

   (a) uses, or threatens to use, force to secure the doing of an act which P resists, or
   (b) restricts P's liberty of movement, whether or not P resists,

   or if he authorises another person to do any of those things.

(13) But a deputy does more than merely restrain P if he deprives P of his liberty within the meaning of Article 5(1) of the Human Rights Convention (whether or not the deputy is a public authority).

21 Transfer of proceedings relating to people under 18

The Lord Chancellor may by order make provision as to the transfer of proceedings relating to a person under 18, in such circumstances as are specified in the order –

   (a) from the Court of Protection to a court having jurisdiction under the Children Act 1989 (c. 41), or
   (b) from a court having jurisdiction under that Act to the Court of Protection.

Powers of the court in relation to lasting powers of attorney

22 Powers of court in relation to validity of lasting powers of attorney

(1) This section and section 23 apply if –

   (a) a person ('P') has executed or purported to execute an instrument with a view to creating a lasting power of attorney, or
   (b) an instrument has been registered as a lasting power of attorney conferred by P.

(2) The court may determine any question relating to –

   (a) whether one or more of the requirements for the creation of a lasting power of attorney have been met;
   (b) whether the power has been revoked or has otherwise come to an end.

(3) Subsection (4) applies if the court is satisfied –

   (a) that fraud or undue pressure was used to induce P –

      (i)   to execute an instrument for the purpose of creating a lasting power of attorney, or
      (ii) to create a lasting power of attorney, or

   (b) that the donee (or, if more than one, any of them) of a lasting power of attorney –

      (i)   has behaved, or is behaving, in a way that contravenes his authority or is not in P's best interests, or
      (ii) proposes to behave in a way that would contravene his authority or would not be in P's best interests.

(4) The court may –

   (a) direct that an instrument purporting to create the lasting power of attorney is not to be registered, or
   (b) if P lacks capacity to do so, revoke the instrument or the lasting power of attorney.

(5) If there is more than one donee, the court may under subsection (4)(b) revoke the instrument or the lasting power of attorney so far as it relates to any of them.

(6) 'Donee' includes an intended donee.

23 Powers of court in relation to operation of lasting powers of attorney

(1) The court may determine any question as to the meaning or effect of a lasting power of attorney or an instrument purporting to create one.

(2) The court may –

    (a) give directions with respect to decisions –

        (i) which the donee of a lasting power of attorney has authority to make, and

        (ii) which P lacks capacity to make;

    (b) give any consent or authorisation to act which the donee would have to obtain from P if P had capacity to give it.

(3) The court may, if P lacks capacity to do so –

    (a) give directions to the donee with respect to the rendering by him of reports or accounts and the production of records kept by him for that purpose;

    (b) require the donee to supply information or produce documents or things in his possession as donee;

    (c) give directions with respect to the remuneration or expenses of the donee;

    (d) relieve the donee wholly or partly from any liability which he has or may have incurred on account of a breach of his duties as donee.

(4) The court may authorise the making of gifts which are not within section 12(2) (permitted gifts).

(5) Where two or more donees are appointed under a lasting power of attorney, this section applies as if references to the donee were to all or any of them.

Advance decisions to refuse treatment

24 Advance decisions to refuse treatment: general

(1) 'Advance decision' means a decision made by a person ('P'), after he has reached 18 and when he has capacity to do so, that if –

    (a) at a later time and in such circumstances as he may specify, a specified treatment is proposed to be carried out or continued by a person providing health care for him, and

    (b) at that time he lacks capacity to consent to the carrying out or continuation of the treatment,

the specified treatment is not to be carried out or continued.

(2) For the purposes of subsection (1)(a), a decision may be regarded as specifying a treatment or circumstances even though expressed in layman's terms.

(3) P may withdraw or alter an advance decision at any time when he has capacity to do so.

(4) A withdrawal (including a partial withdrawal) need not be in writing.

(5) An alteration of an advance decision need not be in writing (unless section 25(5) applies in relation to the decision resulting from the alteration).

25 Validity and applicability of advance decisions

(1) An advance decision does not affect the liability which a person may incur for carrying out or continuing a treatment in relation to P unless the decision is at the material time –

    (a) valid, and

    (b) applicable to the treatment.

(2) An advance decision is not valid if P –

    (a) has withdrawn the decision at a time when he had capacity to do so,

    (b) has, under a lasting power of attorney created after the advance decision was made, conferred authority on the donee (or, if more than one, any of them) to give or refuse consent to the treatment to which the advance decision relates, or

    (c) has done anything else clearly inconsistent with the advance decision remaining his fixed decision.

(3) An advance decision is not applicable to the treatment in question if at the material time P has capacity to give or refuse consent to it.

(4) An advance decision is not applicable to the treatment in question if –

    (a) that treatment is not the treatment specified in the advance decision,

    (b) any circumstances specified in the advance decision are absent, or

    (c) there are reasonable grounds for believing that circumstances exist which P did not anticipate at the time of the advance decision and which would have affected his decision had he anticipated them.

(5) An advance decision is not applicable to life-sustaining treatment unless –

    (a) the decision is verified by a statement by P to the effect that it is to apply to that treatment even if life is at risk, and

    (b) the decision and statement comply with subsection (6).

(6) A decision or statement complies with this subsection only if –

    (a) it is in writing,

    (b) it is signed by P or by another person in P's presence and by P's direction,

    (c) the signature is made or acknowledged by P in the presence of a witness, and

    (d) the witness signs it, or acknowledges his signature, in P's presence.

(7) The existence of any lasting power of attorney other than one of a description mentioned in subsection (2)(b) does not prevent the advance decision from being regarded as valid and applicable.

26 Effect of advance decisions

(1) If P has made an advance decision which is –

    (a) valid, and

    (b) applicable to a treatment,

the decision has effect as if he had made it, and had had capacity to make it, at the time when the question arises whether the treatment should be carried out or continued.

(2) A person does not incur liability for carrying out or continuing the treatment unless, at the time, he is satisfied that an advance decision exists which is valid and applicable to the treatment.

(3) A person does not incur liability for the consequences of withholding or withdrawing a treatment from P if, at the time, he reasonably believes that an advance decision exists which is valid and applicable to the treatment.

(4) The court may make a declaration as to whether an advance decision –

    (a) exists;

    (b) is valid;

    (c) is applicable to a treatment.

(5) Nothing in an apparent advance decision stops a person –

    (a) providing life-sustaining treatment, or

    (b) doing any act he reasonably believes to be necessary to prevent a serious deterioration in P's condition,

while a decision as respects any relevant issue is sought from the court.

Excluded decisions

27 Family relationships etc.

(1) Nothing in this Act permits a decision on any of the following matters to be made on behalf of a person –

    (a) consenting to marriage or a civil partnership,

    (b) consenting to have sexual relations,

    (c) consenting to a decree of divorce being granted on the basis of two years' separation,

    (d) consenting to a dissolution order being made in relation to a civil partnership on the basis of two years' separation,

    (e) consenting to a child's being placed for adoption by an adoption agency,

    (f) consenting to the making of an adoption order,

    (g) discharging parental responsibilities in matters not relating to a child's property,

    (h) giving a consent under the Human Fertilisation and Embryology Act 1990 (c. 37).

(2) 'Adoption order' means –

    (a) an adoption order within the meaning of the Adoption and Children Act 2002 (c. 38) (including a future adoption order), and

    (b) an order under section 84 of that Act (parental responsibility prior to adoption abroad).

28 Mental Health Act matters

(1) Nothing in this Act authorises anyone –

    (a) to give a patient medical treatment for mental disorder, or

    (b) to consent to a patient's being given medical treatment for mental disorder,

if, at the time when it is proposed to treat the patient, his treatment is regulated by Part 4 of the Mental Health Act.

(2) 'Medical treatment', 'mental disorder' and 'patient' have the same meaning as in that Act.

29 Voting rights

(1) Nothing in this Act permits a decision on voting at an election for any public office, or at a referendum, to be made on behalf of a person.

(2) 'Referendum' has the same meaning as in section 101 of the Political Parties, Elections and Referendums Act 2000 (c. 41).

Research

30 Research

(1) Intrusive research carried out on, or in relation to, a person who lacks capacity to consent to it is unlawful unless it is carried out –

    (a) as part of a research project which is for the time being approved by the appropriate body for the purposes of this Act in accordance with section 31, and

    (b) in accordance with sections 32 and 33.

(2) Research is intrusive if it is of a kind that would be unlawful if it was carried out –

    (a) on or in relation to a person who had capacity to consent to it, but

    (b) without his consent.

(3) A clinical trial which is subject to the provisions of clinical trials regulations is not to be treated as research for the purposes of this section.

(4) 'Appropriate body', in relation to a research project, means the person, committee

or other body specified in regulations made by the appropriate authority as the appropriate body in relation to a project of the kind in question.

(5) 'Clinical trials regulations' means –

    (a) the Medicines for Human Use (Clinical Trials) Regulations 2004 (SI 2004/1031) and any other regulations replacing those regulations or amending them, and

    (b) any other regulations relating to clinical trials and designated by the Secretary of State as clinical trials regulations for the purposes of this section.

(6) In this section, section 32 and section 34, 'appropriate authority' means –

    (a) in relation to the carrying out of research in England, the Secretary of State, and

    (b) in relation to the carrying out of research in Wales, the National Assembly for Wales.

31 Requirements for approval

(1) The appropriate body may not approve a research project for the purposes of this Act unless satisfied that the following requirements will be met in relation to research carried out as part of the project on, or in relation to, a person who lacks capacity to consent to taking part in the project ('P').

(2) The research must be connected with –

    (a) an impairing condition affecting P, or

    (b) its treatment.

(3) 'Impairing condition' means a condition which is (or may be) attributable to, or which causes or contributes to (or may cause or contribute to), the impairment of, or disturbance in the functioning of, the mind or brain.

(4) There must be reasonable grounds for believing that research of comparable effectiveness cannot be carried out if the project has to be confined to, or relate only to, persons who have capacity to consent to taking part in it.

(5) The research must –

    (a) have the potential to benefit P without imposing on P a burden that is disproportionate to the potential benefit to P, or

    (b) be intended to provide knowledge of the causes or treatment of, or of the care of persons affected by, the same or a similar condition.

(6) If the research falls within paragraph (b) of subsection (5) but not within paragraph (a), there must be reasonable grounds for believing –

    (a) that the risk to P from taking part in the project is likely to be negligible, and

    (b) that anything done to, or in relation to, P will not –

        (i)   interfere with P's freedom of action or privacy in a significant way, or

        (ii) be unduly invasive or restrictive.

(7) There must be reasonable arrangements in place for ensuring that the requirements of sections 32 and 33 will be met.

32 Consulting carers etc.

(1) This section applies if a person ('R') –

    (a) is conducting an approved research project, and

    (b) wishes to carry out research, as part of the project, on or in relation to a person ('P') who lacks capacity to consent to taking part in the project.

(2) R must take reasonable steps to identify a person who –

    (a) otherwise than in a professional capacity or for remuneration, is engaged in caring for P or is interested in P's welfare, and

    (b) is prepared to be consulted by R under this section.

(3) If R is unable to identify such a person he must, in accordance with guidance issued by the appropriate authority, nominate a person who –

    (a) is prepared to be consulted by R under this section, but

    (b) has no connection with the project.

(4) R must provide the person identified under subsection (2), or nominated under subsection (3), with information about the project and ask him –

    (a) for advice as to whether P should take part in the project, and

    (b) what, in his opinion, P's wishes and feelings about taking part in the project would be likely to be if P had capacity in relation to the matter.

(5) If, at any time, the person consulted advises R that in his opinion P's wishes and feelings would be likely to lead him to decline to take part in the project (or to wish to withdraw from it) if he had capacity in relation to the matter, R must ensure –

    (a) if P is not already taking part in the project, that he does not take part in it;

    (b) if P is taking part in the project, that he is withdrawn from it.

(6) But subsection (5)(b) does not require treatment that P has been receiving as part of the project to be discontinued if R has reasonable grounds for believing that there would be a significant risk to P's health if it were discontinued.

(7) The fact that a person is the donee of a lasting power of attorney given by P, or is P's deputy, does not prevent him from being the person consulted under this section.

(8) Subsection (9) applies if treatment is being, or is about to be, provided for P as a matter of urgency and R considers that, having regard to the nature of the research and of the particular circumstances of the case –

    (a) it is also necessary to take action for the purposes of the research as a matter of urgency, but

    (b) it is not reasonably practicable to consult under the previous provisions of this section.

(9) R may take the action if –

    (a) he has the agreement of a registered medical practitioner who is not involved in the organisation or conduct of the research project, or

    (b) where it is not reasonably practicable in the time available to obtain that agreement, he acts in accordance with a procedure approved by the appropriate body at the time when the research project was approved under section 31.

(10) But R may not continue to act in reliance on subsection (9) if he has reasonable grounds for believing that it is no longer necessary to take the action as a matter of urgency.

33 Additional safeguards

(1) This section applies in relation to a person who is taking part in an approved research project even though he lacks capacity to consent to taking part.

(2) Nothing may be done to, or in relation to, him in the course of the research –

    (a) to which he appears to object (whether by showing signs of resistance or otherwise) except where what is being done is intended to protect him from harm or to reduce or prevent pain or discomfort, or

    (b) which would be contrary to –

        (i)   an advance decision of his which has effect, or

        (ii) any other form of statement made by him and not subsequently withdrawn,

    of which R is aware.

(3) The interests of the person must be assumed to outweigh those of science and society.

(4) If he indicates (in any way) that he wishes to be withdrawn from the project he must be withdrawn without delay.

(5) P must be withdrawn from the project, without delay, if at any time the person

conducting the research has reasonable grounds for believing that one or more of the requirements set out in section 31(2) to (7) is no longer met in relation to research being carried out on, or in relation to, P.

(6) But neither subsection (4) nor subsection (5) requires treatment that P has been receiving as part of the project to be discontinued if R has reasonable grounds for believing that there would be a significant risk to P's health if it were discontinued.

34 Loss of capacity during research project

(1) This section applies where a person ('P') –

    (a) has consented to take part in a research project begun before the commencement of section 30, but

    (b) before the conclusion of the project, loses capacity to consent to continue to take part in it.

(2) The appropriate authority may by regulations provide that, despite P's loss of capacity, research of a prescribed kind may be carried out on, or in relation to, P if –

    (a) the project satisfies prescribed requirements,

    (b) any information or material relating to P which is used in the research is of a prescribed description and was obtained before P's loss of capacity, and

    (c) the person conducting the project takes in relation to P such steps as may be prescribed for the purpose of protecting him.

(3) The regulations may, in particular, –

    (a) make provision about when, for the purposes of the regulations, a project is to be treated as having begun;

    (b) include provision similar to any made by section 31, 32 or 33.

Independent mental capacity advocate service

35 Appointment of independent mental capacity advocates

(1) The appropriate authority must make such arrangements as it considers reasonable to enable persons ('independent mental capacity advocates') to be available to represent and support persons to whom acts or decisions proposed under sections 37, 38 and 39 relate.

(2) The appropriate authority may make regulations as to the appointment of independent mental capacity advocates.

(3) The regulations may, in particular, provide –

    (a) that a person may act as an independent mental capacity advocate only in such circumstances, or only subject to such conditions, as may be prescribed;

    (b) for the appointment of a person as an independent mental capacity advocate to be subject to approval in accordance with the regulations.

(4) In making arrangements under subsection (1), the appropriate authority must have regard to the principle that a person to whom a proposed act or decision relates should, so far as practicable, be represented and supported by a person who is independent of any person who will be responsible for the act or decision.

(5) The arrangements may include provision for payments to be made to, or in relation to, persons carrying out functions in accordance with the arrangements.

(6) For the purpose of enabling him to carry out his functions, an independent mental capacity advocate –

    (a) may interview in private the person whom he has been instructed to represent, and

    (b) may, at all reasonable times, examine and take copies of –

        (i) any health record,

(ii)   any record of, or held by, a local authority and compiled in connection with a social services function, and

(iii) any record held by a person registered under Part 2 of the Care Standards Act 2000 (c. 14),

which the person holding the record considers may be relevant to the independent mental capacity advocate's investigation.

(7) In this section, section 36 and section 37, 'the appropriate authority' means –

(a)   in relation to the provision of the services of independent mental capacity advocates in England, the Secretary of State, and

(b)   in relation to the provision of the services of independent mental capacity advocates in Wales, the National Assembly for Wales.

36 Functions of independent mental capacity advocates

(1) The appropriate authority may make regulations as to the functions of independent mental capacity advocates.

(2) The regulations may, in particular, make provision requiring an advocate to take such steps as may be prescribed for the purpose of –

(a)   providing support to the person whom he has been instructed to represent ('P') so that P may participate as fully as possible in any relevant decision;

(b)   obtaining and evaluating relevant information;

(c)   ascertaining what P's wishes and feelings would be likely to be, and the beliefs and values that would be likely to influence P, if he had capacity;

(d)   ascertaining what alternative courses of action are available in relation to P;

(e)   obtaining a further medical opinion where treatment is proposed and the advocate thinks that one should be obtained.

(3) The regulations may also make provision as to circumstances in which the advocate may challenge, or provide assistance for the purpose of challenging, any relevant decision.

37 Provision of serious medical treatment by NHS body

(1) This section applies if an NHS body –

(a)   is proposing to provide, or secure the provision of, serious medical treatment for a person ('P') who lacks capacity to consent to the treatment, and

(b)   is satisfied that there is no person, other than one engaged in providing care or treatment for P in a professional capacity or for remuneration, whom it would be appropriate to consult in determining what would be in P's best interests.

(2) But this section does not apply if P's treatment is regulated by Part 4 of the Mental Health Act.

(3) Before the treatment is provided, the NHS body must instruct an independent mental capacity advocate to represent P.

(4) If the treatment needs to be provided as a matter of urgency, it may be provided even though the NHS body has not been able to comply with subsection (3).

(5) The NHS body must, in providing or securing the provision of treatment for P, take into account any information given, or submissions made, by the independent mental capacity advocate.

(6) 'Serious medical treatment' means treatment which involves providing, withholding or withdrawing treatment of a kind prescribed by regulations made by the appropriate authority.

(7) 'NHS body' has such meaning as may be prescribed by regulations made for the purposes of this section by –

(a)   the Secretary of State, in relation to bodies in England, or

(b)   the National Assembly for Wales, in relation to bodies in Wales.

38 Provision of accommodation by NHS body

(1) This section applies if an NHS body proposes to make arrangements –

(a) for the provision of accommodation in a hospital or care home for a person ('P') who lacks capacity to agree to the arrangements, or

(b) for a change in P's accommodation to another hospital or care home,

and is satisfied that there is no person, other than one engaged in providing care or treatment for P in a professional capacity or for remuneration, whom it would be appropriate for it to consult in determining what would be in P's best interests.

(2) But this section does not apply if P is accommodated as a result of an obligation imposed on him under the Mental Health Act.

(3) Before making the arrangements, the NHS body must instruct an independent mental capacity advocate to represent P unless it is satisfied that –

(a) the accommodation is likely to be provided for a continuous period which is less than the applicable period, or

(b) the arrangements need to be made as a matter of urgency.

(4) If the NHS body –

(a) did not instruct an independent mental capacity advocate to represent P before making the arrangements because it was satisfied that subsection (3)(a) or (b) applied, but

(b) subsequently has reason to believe that the accommodation is likely to be provided for a continuous period –

(i) beginning with the day on which accommodation was first provided in accordance with the arrangements, and

(ii) ending on or after the expiry of the applicable period,

it must instruct an independent mental capacity advocate to represent P.

(5) The NHS body must, in deciding what arrangements to make for P, take into account any information given, or submissions made, by the independent mental capacity advocate.

(6) 'Care home' has the meaning given in section 3 of the Care Standards Act 2000 (c. 14).

(7) 'Hospital' means –

(a) a health service hospital as defined by section 128 of the National Health Service Act 1977 (c. 49), or

(b) an independent hospital as defined by section 2 of the Care Standards Act 2000.

(8) 'NHS body' has such meaning as may be prescribed by regulations made for the purposes of this section by –

(a) the Secretary of State, in relation to bodies in England, or

(b) the National Assembly for Wales, in relation to bodies in Wales.

(9) 'Applicable period' means –

(a) in relation to accommodation in a hospital, 28 days, and

(b) in relation to accommodation in a care home, 8 weeks.

39 Provision of accommodation by local authority

(1) This section applies if a local authority propose to make arrangements –

(a) for the provision of residential accommodation for a person ('P') who lacks capacity to agree to the arrangements, or

(b) for a change in P's residential accommodation,

and are satisfied that there is no person, other than one engaged in providing care or treatment for P in a professional capacity or for remuneration, whom it would be appropriate for them to consult in determining what would be in P's best interests.

(2) But this section applies only if the accommodation is to be provided in accordance with –

    (a) section 21 or 29 of the National Assistance Act 1948 (c. 29), or

    (b) section 117 of the Mental Health Act,

as the result of a decision taken by the local authority under section 47 of the National Health Service and Community Care Act 1990 (c. 19).

(3) This section does not apply if P is accommodated as a result of an obligation imposed on him under the Mental Health Act.

(4) Before making the arrangements, the local authority must instruct an independent mental capacity advocate to represent P unless they are satisfied that –

    (a) the accommodation is likely to be provided for a continuous period of less than 8 weeks, or

    (b) the arrangements need to be made as a matter of urgency.

(5) If the local authority –

    (a) did not instruct an independent mental capacity advocate to represent P before making the arrangements because they were satisfied that subsection (4)(a) or (b) applied, but

    (b) subsequently have reason to believe that the accommodation is likely to be provided for a continuous period that will end 8 weeks or more after the day on which accommodation was first provided in accordance with the arrangements,

they must instruct an independent mental capacity advocate to represent P.

(6) The local authority must, in deciding what arrangements to make for P, take into account any information given, or submissions made, by the independent mental capacity advocate.

40 Exceptions

Sections 37(3), 38(3) and (4) and 39(4) and (5) do not apply if there is –

    (a) a person nominated by P (in whatever manner) as a person to be consulted in matters affecting his interests,

    (b) a donee of a lasting power of attorney created by P,

    (c) a deputy appointed by the court for P, or

    (d) a donee of an enduring power of attorney (within the meaning of Schedule 4) created by P.

41 Power to adjust role of independent mental capacity advocate

(1) The appropriate authority may make regulations –

    (a) expanding the role of independent mental capacity advocates in relation to persons who lack capacity, and

    (b) adjusting the obligation to make arrangements imposed by section 35.

(2) The regulations may, in particular –

    (a) prescribe circumstances (different to those set out in sections 37, 38 and 39) in which an independent mental capacity advocate must, or circumstances in which one may, be instructed by a person of a prescribed description to represent a person who lacks capacity, and

    (b) include provision similar to any made by section 37, 38, 39 or 40.

(3) 'Appropriate authority' has the same meaning as in section 35.

Miscellaneous and supplementary

42 Codes of practice

(1) The Lord Chancellor must prepare and issue one or more codes of practice –

    (a) for the guidance of persons assessing whether a person has capacity in relation to any matter,

    (b) for the guidance of persons acting in connection with the care or treatment of another person (see section 5),

    (c) for the guidance of donees of lasting powers of attorney,

    (d) for the guidance of deputies appointed by the court,

    (e) for the guidance of persons carrying out research in reliance on any provision made by or under this Act (and otherwise with respect to sections 30 to 34),

    (f) for the guidance of independent mental capacity advocates,

    (g) with respect to the provisions of sections 24 to 26 (advance decisions and apparent advance decisions), and

    (h) with respect to such other matters concerned with this Act as he thinks fit.

(2) The Lord Chancellor may from time to time revise a code.

(3) The Lord Chancellor may delegate the preparation or revision of the whole or any part of a code so far as he considers expedient.

(4) It is the duty of a person to have regard to any relevant code if he is acting in relation to a person who lacks capacity and is doing so in one or more of the following ways –

    (a) as the donee of a lasting power of attorney,

    (b) as a deputy appointed by the court,

    (c) as a person carrying out research in reliance on any provision made by or under this Act (see sections 30 to 34),

    (d) as an independent mental capacity advocate,

    (e) in a professional capacity,

    (f) for remuneration.

(5) If it appears to a court or tribunal conducting any criminal or civil proceedings that –

    (a) a provision of a code, or

    (b) a failure to comply with a code,

is relevant to a question arising in the proceedings, the provision or failure must be taken into account in deciding the question.

(6) A code under subsection (1)(d) may contain separate guidance for deputies appointed by virtue of paragraph 1(2) of Schedule 5 (functions of deputy conferred on receiver appointed under the Mental Health Act).

(7) In this section and in section 43, 'code' means a code prepared or revised under this section.

43 Codes of practice: procedure

(1) Before preparing or revising a code, the Lord Chancellor must consult –

    (a) the National Assembly for Wales, and

    (b) such other persons as he considers appropriate.

(2) The Lord Chancellor may not issue a code unless –

    (a) a draft of the code has been laid by him before both Houses of Parliament, and

    (b) the 40 day period has elapsed without either House resolving not to approve the draft.

(3) The Lord Chancellor must arrange for any code that he has issued to be published in such a way as he considers appropriate for bringing it to the attention of persons likely to be concerned with its provisions.

(4) '40 day period', in relation to the draft of a proposed code, means –

(a) if the draft is laid before one House on a day later than the day on which it is laid before the other House, the period of 40 days beginning with the later of the two days;

(b) in any other case, the period of 40 days beginning with the day on which it is laid before each House.

(5) In calculating the period of 40 days, no account is to be taken of any period during which Parliament is dissolved or prorogued or during which both Houses are adjourned for more than 4 days.

44 Ill-treatment or neglect

(1) Subsection (2) applies if a person ('D') –

(a) has the care of a person ('P') who lacks, or whom D reasonably believes to lack, capacity,

(b) is the donee of a lasting power of attorney, or an enduring power of attorney (within the meaning of Schedule 4), created by P, or

(c) is a deputy appointed by the court for P.

(2) D is guilty of an offence if he ill-treats or wilfully neglects P.

(3) A person guilty of an offence under this section is liable –

(a) on summary conviction, to imprisonment for a term not exceeding 12 months or a fine not exceeding the statutory maximum or both;

(b) on conviction on indictment, to imprisonment for a term not exceeding 5 years or a fine or both.

PART 2   THE COURT OF PROTECTION AND THE PUBLIC GUARDIAN

The Court of Protection

45 The Court of Protection

(1) There is to be a superior court of record known as the Court of Protection.

(2) The court is to have an official seal.

(3) The court may sit at any place in England and Wales, on any day and at any time.

(4) The court is to have a central office and registry at a place appointed by the Lord Chancellor.

(5) The Lord Chancellor may designate as additional registries of the court any district registry of the High Court and any county court office.

(6) The office of the Supreme Court called the Court of Protection ceases to exist.

46 The judges of the Court of Protection

(1) Subject to Court of Protection Rules under section 51(2)(d), the jurisdiction of the court is exercisable by a judge nominated for that purpose by –

(a) the Lord Chancellor, or

(b) a person acting on the Lord Chancellor's behalf.

(2) To be nominated, a judge must be –

(a) the President of the Family Division,

(b) the Vice-Chancellor,

(c) a puisne judge of the High Court,

(d) a circuit judge, or

(e) a district judge.

(3) The Lord Chancellor must –

    (a)   appoint one of the judges nominated by virtue of subsection (2)(a) to (c) to be President of the Court of Protection, and

    (b)   appoint another of those judges to be Vice-President of the Court of Protection.

(4)   The Lord Chancellor must appoint one of the judges nominated by virtue of subsection (2)(d) or (e) to be Senior Judge of the Court of Protection, having such administrative functions in relation to the court as the Lord Chancellor may direct.

Supplementary powers

47 General powers and effect of orders etc.

(1)   The court has in connection with its jurisdiction the same powers, rights, privileges and authority as the High Court.

(2)   Section 204 of the Law of Property Act 1925 (c. 20) (orders of High Court conclusive in favour of purchasers) applies in relation to orders and directions of the court as it applies to orders of the High Court.

(3)   Office copies of orders made, directions given or other instruments issued by the court and sealed with its official seal are admissible in all legal proceedings as evidence of the originals without any further proof.

48 Interim orders and directions

The court may, pending the determination of an application to it in relation to a person ('P'), make an order or give directions in respect of any matter if –

    (a)   there is reason to believe that P lacks capacity in relation to the matter,

    (b)   the matter is one to which its powers under this Act extend, and

    (c)   it is in P's best interests to make the order, or give the directions, without delay.

49 Power to call for reports

(1)   This section applies where, in proceedings brought in respect of a person ('P') under Part 1, the court is considering a question relating to P.

(2)   The court may require a report to be made to it by the Public Guardian or by a Court of Protection Visitor.

(3)   The court may require a local authority, or an NHS body, to arrange for a report to be made –

    (a)   by one of its officers or employees, or

    (b)   by such other person (other than the Public Guardian or a Court of Protection Visitor) as the authority, or the NHS body, considers appropriate.

(4)   The report must deal with such matters relating to P as the court may direct.

(5)   Court of Protection Rules may specify matters which, unless the court directs otherwise, must also be dealt with in the report.

(6)   The report may be made in writing or orally, as the court may direct.

(7)   In complying with a requirement, the Public Guardian or a Court of Protection Visitor may, at all reasonable times, examine and take copies of –

    (a)   any health record,

    (b)   any record of, or held by, a local authority and compiled in connection with a social services function, and

    (c)   any record held by a person registered under Part 2 of the Care Standards Act 2000 (c. 14),

so far as the record relates to P.

(8)   If the Public Guardian or a Court of Protection Visitor is making a visit in the course of complying with a requirement, he may interview P in private.

(9)   If a Court of Protection Visitor who is a Special Visitor is making a visit in the course

of complying with a requirement, he may if the court so directs carry out in private a medical, psychiatric or psychological examination of P's capacity and condition.

(10) 'NHS body' has the meaning given in section 148 of the Health and Social Care (Community Health and Standards) Act 2003 (c. 43).

(11) 'Requirement' means a requirement imposed under subsection (2) or (3).

Practice and procedure

50 Applications to the Court of Protection

(1) No permission is required for an application to the court for the exercise of any of its powers under this Act –

    (a) by a person who lacks, or is alleged to lack, capacity,

    (b) if such a person has not reached 18, by anyone with parental responsibility for him,

    (c) by the donor or a donee of a lasting power of attorney to which the application relates,

    (d) by a deputy appointed by the court for a person to whom the application relates, or

    (e) by a person named in an existing order of the court, if the application relates to the order.

(2) But, subject to Court of Protection Rules and to paragraph 20(2) of Schedule 3 (declarations relating to private international law), permission is required for any other application to the court.

(3) In deciding whether to grant permission the court must, in particular, have regard to –

    (a) the applicant's connection with the person to whom the application relates,

    (b) the reasons for the application,

    (c) the benefit to the person to whom the application relates of a proposed order or directions, and

    (d) whether the benefit can be achieved in any other way.

(4) 'Parental responsibility' has the same meaning as in the Children Act 1989 (c. 41).

51 Court of Protection Rules

(1) The Lord Chancellor may make rules of court (to be called 'Court of Protection Rules') with respect to the practice and procedure of the court.

(2) Court of Protection Rules may, in particular, make provision –

    (a) as to the manner and form in which proceedings are to be commenced;

    (b) as to the persons entitled to be notified of, and be made parties to, the proceedings;

    (c) for the allocation, in such circumstances as may be specified, of any specified description of proceedings to a specified judge or to specified descriptions of judges;

    (d) for the exercise of the jurisdiction of the court, in such circumstances as may be specified, by its officers or other staff;

    (e) for enabling the court to appoint a suitable person (who may, with his consent, be the Official Solicitor) to act in the name of, or on behalf of, or to represent the person to whom the proceedings relate;

    (f) for enabling an application to the court to be disposed of without a hearing;

    (g) for enabling the court to proceed with, or with any part of, a hearing in the absence of the person to whom the proceedings relate;

    (h) for enabling or requiring the proceedings or any part of them to be conducted in private and for enabling the court to determine who is to be admitted when the court sits in private and to exclude specified persons when it sits in public;

   (i)   as to what may be received as evidence (whether or not admissible apart from the rules) and the manner in which it is to be presented;

   (j)   for the enforcement of orders made and directions given in the proceedings.

(3) Court of Protection Rules may, instead of providing for any matter, refer to provision made or to be made about that matter by directions.

(4) Court of Protection Rules may make different provision for different areas.

52 Practice directions

(1) The President of the Court of Protection may, with the concurrence of the Lord Chancellor, give directions as to the practice and procedure of the court.

(2) Directions as to the practice and procedure of the court may not be given by anyone other than the President of the Court of Protection without the approval of the President of the Court of Protection and the Lord Chancellor.

(3) Nothing in this section prevents the President of the Court of Protection, without the concurrence of the Lord Chancellor, giving directions which contain guidance as to law or making judicial decisions.

53 Rights of appeal

(1) Subject to the provisions of this section, an appeal lies to the Court of Appeal from any decision of the court.

(2) Court of Protection Rules may provide that where a decision of the court is made by –

   (a)   a person exercising the jurisdiction of the court by virtue of rules made under section 51(2)(d),

   (b)   a district judge, or

   (c)   a circuit judge,

   an appeal from that decision lies to a prescribed higher judge of the court and not to the Court of Appeal.

(3) For the purposes of this section the higher judges of the court are –

   (a)   in relation to a person mentioned in subsection (2)(a), a circuit judge or a district judge;

   (b)   in relation to a person mentioned in subsection (2)(b), a circuit judge;

   (c)   in relation to any person mentioned in subsection (2), one of the judges nominated by virtue of section 46(2)(a) to (c).

(4) Court of Protection Rules may make provision –

   (a)   that, in such cases as may be specified, an appeal from a decision of the court may not be made without permission;

   (b)   as to the person or persons entitled to grant permission to appeal;

   (c)   as to any requirements to be satisfied before permission is granted;

   (d)   that where a higher judge of the court makes a decision on an appeal, no appeal may be made to the Court of Appeal from that decision unless the Court of Appeal considers that –

      (i)   the appeal would raise an important point of principle or practice, or

      (ii)   there is some other compelling reason for the Court of Appeal to hear it;

   (e)   as to any considerations to be taken into account in relation to granting or refusing permission to appeal.

Fees and costs

54 Fees

(1) The Lord Chancellor may with the consent of the Treasury by order prescribe fees payable in respect of anything dealt with by the court.

(2) An order under this section may in particular contain provision as to –

    (a) scales or rates of fees;

    (b) exemptions from and reductions in fees;

    (c) remission of fees in whole or in part.

(3) Before making an order under this section, the Lord Chancellor must consult –

    (a) the President of the Court of Protection,

    (b) the Vice-President of the Court of Protection, and

    (c) the Senior Judge of the Court of Protection.

(4) The Lord Chancellor must take such steps as are reasonably practicable to bring information about fees to the attention of persons likely to have to pay them.

(5) Fees payable under this section are recoverable summarily as a civil debt.

55 Costs

(1) Subject to Court of Protection Rules, the costs of and incidental to all proceedings in the court are in its discretion.

(2) The rules may in particular make provision for regulating matters relating to the costs of those proceedings, including prescribing scales of costs to be paid to legal or other representatives.

(3) The court has full power to determine by whom and to what extent the costs are to be paid.

(4) The court may, in any proceedings –

    (a) disallow, or

    (b) order the legal or other representatives concerned to meet,

the whole of any wasted costs or such part of them as may be determined in accordance with the rules.

(5) 'Legal or other representative', in relation to a party to proceedings, means any person exercising a right of audience or right to conduct litigation on his behalf.

(6) 'Wasted costs' means any costs incurred by a party –

    (a) as a result of any improper, unreasonable or negligent act or omission on the part of any legal or other representative or any employee of such a representative, or

    (b) which, in the light of any such act or omission occurring after they were incurred, the court considers it is unreasonable to expect that party to pay.

56 Fees and costs: supplementary

(1) Court of Protection Rules may make provision –

    (a) as to the way in which, and funds from which, fees and costs are to be paid;

    (b) for charging fees and costs upon the estate of the person to whom the proceedings relate;

    (c) for the payment of fees and costs within a specified time of the death of the person to whom the proceedings relate or the conclusion of the proceedings.

(2) A charge on the estate of a person created by virtue of subsection (1)(b) does not cause any interest of the person in any property to fail or determine or to be prevented from recommencing.

The Public Guardian

57 The Public Guardian

(1) For the purposes of this Act, there is to be an officer, to be known as the Public Guardian.

(2) The Public Guardian is to be appointed by the Lord Chancellor.

(3) There is to be paid to the Public Guardian out of money provided by Parliament such salary as the Lord Chancellor may determine.

(4) The Lord Chancellor may, after consulting the Public Guardian –

   (a) provide him with such officers and staff, or

   (b) enter into such contracts with other persons for the provision (by them or their sub-contractors) of officers, staff or services,

   as the Lord Chancellor thinks necessary for the proper discharge of the Public Guardian's functions.

(5) Any functions of the Public Guardian may, to the extent authorised by him, be performed by any of his officers.

58 Functions of the Public Guardian

(1) The Public Guardian has the following functions –

   (a) establishing and maintaining a register of lasting powers of attorney,

   (b) establishing and maintaining a register of orders appointing deputies,

   (c) supervising deputies appointed by the court,

   (d) directing a Court of Protection Visitor to visit –

      (i) a donee of a lasting power of attorney,

      (ii) a deputy appointed by the court, or

      (iii) the person granting the power of attorney or for whom the deputy is appointed ('P'),

   and to make a report to the Public Guardian on such matters as he may direct,

   (e) receiving security which the court requires a person to give for the discharge of his functions,

   (f) receiving reports from donees of lasting powers of attorney and deputies appointed by the court,

   (g) reporting to the court on such matters relating to proceedings under this Act as the court requires,

   (h) dealing with representations (including complaints) about the way in which a donee of a lasting power of attorney or a deputy appointed by the court is exercising his powers,

   (i) publishing, in any manner the Public Guardian thinks appropriate, any information he thinks appropriate about the discharge of his functions.

(2) The functions conferred by subsection (1)(c) and (h) may be discharged in co-operation with any other person who has functions in relation to the care or treatment of P.

(3) The Lord Chancellor may by regulations make provision –

   (a) conferring on the Public Guardian other functions in connection with this Act;

   (b) in connection with the discharge by the Public Guardian of his functions.

(4) Regulations made under subsection (3)(b) may in particular make provision as to –

   (a) the giving of security by deputies appointed by the court and the enforcement and discharge of security so given;

   (b) the fees which may be charged by the Public Guardian;

   (c) the way in which, and funds from which, such fees are to be paid;

   (d) exemptions from and reductions in such fees;

   (e) remission of such fees in whole or in part;

   (f) the making of reports to the Public Guardian by deputies appointed by the court and others who are directed by the court to carry out any transaction for a person who lacks capacity.

(5) For the purpose of enabling him to carry out his functions, the Public Guardian may, at all reasonable times, examine and take copies of –

(a) any health record,

(b) any record of, or held by, a local authority and compiled in connection with a social services function, and

(c) any record held by a person registered under Part 2 of the Care Standards Act 2000 (c. 14),

so far as the record relates to P.

(6) The Public Guardian may also for that purpose interview P in private.

59 Public Guardian Board

(1) There is to be a body, to be known as the Public Guardian Board.

(2) The Board's duty is to scrutinise and review the way in which the Public Guardian discharges his functions and to make such recommendations to the Lord Chancellor about that matter as it thinks appropriate.

(3) The Lord Chancellor must, in discharging his functions under sections 57 and 58, give due consideration to recommendations made by the Board.

(4) The members of the Board are to be appointed by the Lord Chancellor.

(5) The Board must have –

(a) at least one member who is a judge of the court, and

(b) at least four members who are persons appearing to the Lord Chancellor to have appropriate knowledge or experience of the work of the Public Guardian.

(6) The Lord Chancellor may by regulations make provision as to –

(a) the appointment of members of the Board (and, in particular, the procedures to be followed in connection with appointments);

(b) the selection of one of the members to be the chairman;

(c) the term of office of the chairman and members;

(d) their resignation, suspension or removal;

(e) the procedure of the Board (including quorum);

(f) the validation of proceedings in the event of a vacancy among the members or a defect in the appointment of a member.

(7) Subject to any provision made in reliance on subsection (6)(c) or (d), a person is to hold and vacate office as a member of the Board in accordance with the terms of the instrument appointing him.

(8) The Lord Chancellor may make such payments to or in respect of members of the Board by way of reimbursement of expenses, allowances and remuneration as he may determine.

(9) The Board must make an annual report to the Lord Chancellor about the discharge of its functions.

60 Annual report

(1) The Public Guardian must make an annual report to the Lord Chancellor about the discharge of his functions.

(2) The Lord Chancellor must, within one month of receiving the report, lay a copy of it before Parliament.

Court of Protection Visitors

61 Court of Protection Visitors

(1) A Court of Protection Visitor is a person who is appointed by the Lord Chancellor to –

(a) a panel of Special Visitors, or

(b) a panel of General Visitors.

(2) A person is not qualified to be a Special Visitor unless he –

(a) is a registered medical practitioner or appears to the Lord Chancellor to have other suitable qualifications or training, and

(b) appears to the Lord Chancellor to have special knowledge of and experience in cases of impairment of or disturbance in the functioning of the mind or brain.

(3) A General Visitor need not have a medical qualification.

(4) A Court of Protection Visitor –

(a) may be appointed for such term and subject to such conditions, and

(b) may be paid such remuneration and allowances,

as the Lord Chancellor may determine.

(5) For the purpose of carrying out his functions under this Act in relation to a person who lacks capacity ('P'), a Court of Protection Visitor may, at all reasonable times, examine and take copies of –

(a) any health record,

(b) any record of, or held by, a local authority and compiled in connection with a social services function, and

(c) any record held by a person registered under Part 2 of the Care Standards Act 2000 (c. 14),

so far as the record relates to P.

(6) A Court of Protection Visitor may also for that purpose interview P in private.

PART 3   MISCELLANEOUS AND GENERAL

Declaratory provision

62 Scope of the Act

For the avoidance of doubt, it is hereby declared that nothing in this Act is to be taken to affect the law relating to murder or manslaughter or the operation of section 2 of the Suicide Act 1961 (c. 60) (assisting suicide).

Private international law

63 International protection of adults

Schedule 3 –

(a) gives effect in England and Wales to the Convention on the International Protection of Adults signed at the Hague on 13th January 2000 (Cm. 5881) (in so far as this Act does not otherwise do so), and

(b) makes related provision as to the private international law of England and Wales.

General

64 Interpretation

(1) In this Act –

'the 1985 Act' means the Enduring Powers of Attorney Act 1985 (c. 29),

'advance decision' has the meaning given in section 24(1),

'the court' means the Court of Protection established by section 45,

'Court of Protection Rules' has the meaning given in section 51(1),

'Court of Protection Visitor' has the meaning given in section 61,

'deputy' has the meaning given in section 16(2)(b),

'enactment' includes a provision of subordinate legislation (within the meaning of the Interpretation Act 1978 (c. 30)),

'health record' has the meaning given in section 68 of the Data Protection Act 1998 (c. 29) (as read with section 69 of that Act),

'the Human Rights Convention' has the same meaning as 'the Convention' in the Human Rights Act 1998 (c. 42),

'independent mental capacity advocate' has the meaning given in section 35(1),

'lasting power of attorney' has the meaning given in section 9,

'life-sustaining treatment' has the meaning given in section 4(10),

'local authority' means –

(a)   the council of a county in England in which there are no district councils,
(b)   the council of a district in England,
(c)   the council of a county or county borough in Wales,
(d)   the council of a London borough,
(e)   the Common Council of the City of London, or
(f)   the Council of the Isles of Scilly,

'Mental Health Act' means the Mental Health Act 1983 (c. 20),

'prescribed', in relation to regulations made under this Act, means prescribed by those regulations,

'property' includes any thing in action and any interest in real or personal property,

'public authority' has the same meaning as in the Human Rights Act 1998,

'Public Guardian' has the meaning given in section 57,

'purchaser' and 'purchase' have the meaning given in section 205(1) of the Law of Property Act 1925 (c. 20),

'social services function' has the meaning given in section 1A of the Local Authority Social Services Act 1970 (c. 42),

'treatment' includes a diagnostic or other procedure,

'trust corporation' has the meaning given in section 68(1) of the Trustee Act 1925 (c. 19), and

'will' includes codicil.

(2)   In this Act, references to making decisions, in relation to a donee of a lasting power of attorney or a deputy appointed by the court, include, where appropriate, acting on decisions made.

(3)   In this Act, references to the bankruptcy of an individual include a case where a bankruptcy restrictions order under the Insolvency Act 1986 (c. 45) has effect in respect of him.

(4)   'Bankruptcy restrictions order' includes an interim bankruptcy restrictions order.

65 Rules, regulations and orders

(1)   Any power to make rules, regulations or orders under this Act –

(a)   is exercisable by statutory instrument;
(b)   includes power to make supplementary, incidental, consequential, transitional or saving provision;
(c)   includes power to make different provision for different cases.

(2)   Any statutory instrument containing rules, regulations or orders made by the Lord Chancellor or the Secretary of State under this Act, other than –

(a)   regulations under section 34 (loss of capacity during research project),
(b)   regulations under section 41 (adjusting role of independent mental capacity advocacy service),
(c)   regulations under paragraph 32(1)(b) of Schedule 3 (private international law relating to the protection of adults),
(d)   an order of the kind mentioned in section 67(6) (consequential amendments of primary legislation), or

(e)   an order under section 68 (commencement),

is subject to annulment in pursuance of a resolution of either House of Parliament.

(3)   A statutory instrument containing an Order in Council under paragraph 31 of Schedule 3 (provision to give further effect to Hague Convention) is subject to annulment in pursuance of a resolution of either House of Parliament.

(4)   A statutory instrument containing regulations made by the Secretary of State under section 34 or 41 or by the Lord Chancellor under paragraph 32(1)(b) of Schedule 3 may not be made unless a draft has been laid before and approved by resolution of each House of Parliament.

66 Existing receivers and enduring powers of attorney etc.

(1)   The following provisions cease to have effect –

(a)   Part 7 of the Mental Health Act,

(b)   the Enduring Powers of Attorney Act 1985 (c. 29).

(2)   No enduring power of attorney within the meaning of the 1985 Act is to be created after the commencement of subsection (1)(b).

(3)   Schedule 4 has effect in place of the 1985 Act in relation to any enduring power of attorney created before the commencement of subsection (1)(b).

(4)   Schedule 5 contains transitional provisions and savings in relation to Part 7 of the Mental Health Act and the 1985 Act.

67 Minor and consequential amendments and repeals

(1)   Schedule 6 contains minor and consequential amendments.

(2)   Schedule 7 contains repeals.

(3)   The Lord Chancellor may by order make supplementary, incidental, consequential, transitional or saving provision for the purposes of, in consequence of, or for giving full effect to a provision of this Act.

(4)   An order under subsection (3) may, in particular –

(a)   provide for a provision of this Act which comes into force before another provision of this Act has come into force to have effect, until the other provision has come into force, with specified modifications;

(b)   amend, repeal or revoke an enactment, other than one contained in an Act or Measure passed in a Session after the one in which this Act is passed.

(5)   The amendments that may be made under subsection (4)(b) are in addition to those made by or under any other provision of this Act.

(6)   An order under subsection (3) which amends or repeals a provision of an Act or Measure may not be made unless a draft has been laid before and approved by resolution of each House of Parliament.

68 Commencement and extent

(1)   This Act, other than sections 30 to 41, comes into force in accordance with provision made by order by the Lord Chancellor.

(2)   Sections 30 to 41 come into force in accordance with provision made by order by –

(a)   the Secretary of State, in relation to England, and

(b)   the National Assembly for Wales, in relation to Wales.

(3)   An order under this section may appoint different days for different provisions and different purposes.

(4)   Subject to subsections (5) and (6), this Act extends to England and Wales only.

(5)   The following provisions extend to the United Kingdom –

(a)   paragraph 16(1) of Schedule 1 (evidence of instruments and of registration of lasting powers of attorney),

(b)   paragraph 15(3) of Schedule 4 (evidence of instruments and of registration of enduring powers of attorney).

(6)   Subject to any provision made in Schedule 6, the amendments and repeals made by Schedules 6 and 7 have the same extent as the enactments to which they relate.

69 Short title

This Act may be cited as the Mental Capacity Act 2005.

SCHEDULES

SCHEDULE 1   LASTING POWERS OF ATTORNEY: FORMALITIES

Section 9

PART 1   MAKING INSTRUMENTS

General requirements as to making instruments

1   (1)   An instrument is not made in accordance with this Schedule unless –

    (a)   it is in the prescribed form,

    (b)   it complies with paragraph 2, and

    (c)   any prescribed requirements in connection with its execution are satisfied.

  (2)   Regulations may make different provision according to whether –

    (a)   the instrument relates to personal welfare or to property and affairs (or to both);

    (b)   only one or more than one donee is to be appointed (and if more than one, whether jointly or jointly and severally).

  (3)   In this Schedule –

    (a)   'prescribed' means prescribed by regulations, and

    (b)   'regulations' means regulations made for the purposes of this Schedule by the Lord Chancellor.

Requirements as to content of instruments

2   (1)   The instrument must include –

    (a)   the prescribed information about the purpose of the instrument and the effect of a lasting power of attorney,

    (b)   a statement by the donor to the effect that he –

       (i)   has read the prescribed information or a prescribed part of it (or has had it read to him), and

      (ii)   intends the authority conferred under the instrument to include authority to make decisions on his behalf in circumstances where he no longer has capacity,

    (c)   a statement by the donor –

       (i)   naming a person or persons whom the donor wishes to be notified of any application for the registration of the instrument, or

      (ii)   stating that there are no persons whom he wishes to be notified of any such application,

    (d)   a statement by the donee (or, if more than one, each of them) to the effect that he –

       (i)   has read the prescribed information or a prescribed part of it (or has had it read to him), and

      (ii)   understands the duties imposed on a donee of a lasting power of attorney under sections 1 (the principles) and 4 (best interests), and

    (e)   a certificate by a person of a prescribed description that, in his opinion, at the time when the donor executes the instrument –

       (i)   the donor understands the purpose of the instrument and the scope of the authority conferred under it,

(ii)   no fraud or undue pressure is being used to induce the donor to create a lasting power of attorney, and

(iii)   there is nothing else which would prevent a lasting power of attorney from being created by the instrument.

(2) Regulations may –

(a)   prescribe a maximum number of named persons;

(b)   provide that, where the instrument includes a statement under sub-paragraph (1)(c)(ii), two persons of a prescribed description must each give a certificate under sub-paragraph (1)(e).

(3) The persons who may be named persons do not include a person who is appointed as donee under the instrument.

(4) In this Schedule, 'named person' means a person named under sub-paragraph (1)(c).

(5) A certificate under sub-paragraph (1)(e) –

(a)   must be made in the prescribed form, and

(b)   must include any prescribed information.

(6) The certificate may not be given by a person appointed as donee under the instrument.

Failure to comply with prescribed form

3   (1) If an instrument differs in an immaterial respect in form or mode of expression from the prescribed form, it is to be treated by the Public Guardian as sufficient in point of form and expression.

(2) The court may declare that an instrument which is not in the prescribed form is to be treated as if it were, if it is satisfied that the persons executing the instrument intended it to create a lasting power of attorney.

PART 2   REGISTRATION

Applications and procedure for registration

4   (1) An application to the Public Guardian for the registration of an instrument intended to create a lasting power of attorney –

(a)   must be made in the prescribed form, and

(b)   must include any prescribed information.

(2) The application may be made –

(a)   by the donor,

(b)   by the donee or donees, or

(c)   if the instrument appoints two or more donees to act jointly and severally in respect of any matter, by any of the donees.

(3) The application must be accompanied by –

(a)   the instrument, and

(b)   any fee provided for under section 58(4)(b).

(4) A person who, in an application for registration, makes a statement which he knows to be false in a material particular is guilty of an offence and is liable –

(a)   on summary conviction, to imprisonment for a term not exceeding 12 months or a fine not exceeding the statutory maximum or both;

(b)   on conviction on indictment, to imprisonment for a term not exceeding 2 years or a fine or both.

5   Subject to paragraphs 11 to 14, the Public Guardian must register the instrument as a lasting power of attorney at the end of the prescribed period.

Notification requirements

6   (1)   A donor about to make an application under paragraph 4(2)(a) must notify any named persons that he is about to do so.

(2)   The donee (or donees) about to make an application under paragraph 4(2)(b) or (c) must notify any named persons that he is (or they are) about to do so.

7   As soon as is practicable after receiving an application by the donor under paragraph 4(2)(a), the Public Guardian must notify the donee (or donees) that the application has been received.

8   (1)   As soon as is practicable after receiving an application by a donee (or donees) under paragraph 4(2)(b), the Public Guardian must notify the donor that the application has been received.

(2)   As soon as is practicable after receiving an application by a donee under paragraph 4(2)(c), the Public Guardian must notify –

(a)   the donor, and

(b)   the donee or donees who did not join in making the application,

that the application has been received.

9   (1)   A notice under paragraph 6 must be made in the prescribed form.

(2)   A notice under paragraph 6, 7 or 8 must include such information, if any, as may be prescribed.

Power to dispense with notification requirements

10   The court may –

(a)   on the application of the donor, dispense with the requirement to notify under paragraph 6(1), or

(b)   on the application of the donee or donees concerned, dispense with the requirement to notify under paragraph 6(2),

if satisfied that no useful purpose would be served by giving the notice.

Instrument not made properly or containing ineffective provision

11   (1)   If it appears to the Public Guardian that an instrument accompanying an application under paragraph 4 is not made in accordance with this Schedule, he must not register the instrument unless the court directs him to do so.

(2)   Sub-paragraph (3) applies if it appears to the Public Guardian that the instrument contains a provision which –

(a)   would be ineffective as part of a lasting power of attorney, or

(b)   would prevent the instrument from operating as a valid lasting power of attorney.

(3)   The Public Guardian –

(a)   must apply to the court for it to determine the matter under section 23(1), and

(b)   pending the determination by the court, must not register the instrument.

(4)   Sub-paragraph (5) applies if the court determines under section 23(1) (whether or not on an application by the Public Guardian) that the instrument contains a provision which –

(a)   would be ineffective as part of a lasting power of attorney, or

(b)   would prevent the instrument from operating as a valid lasting power of attorney.

(5)   The court must –

(a)   notify the Public Guardian that it has severed the provision, or

(b)   direct him not to register the instrument.

(6)   Where the court notifies the Public Guardian that it has severed a provision, he must register the instrument with a note to that effect attached to it.

Deputy already appointed

12   (1)   Sub-paragraph (2) applies if it appears to the Public Guardian that –

(a)   there is a deputy appointed by the court for the donor, and

(b)   the powers conferred on the deputy would, if the instrument were registered, to any extent conflict with the powers conferred on the attorney.

(2)   The Public Guardian must not register the instrument unless the court directs him to do so.

Objection by donee or named person

13   (1)   Sub-paragraph (2) applies if a donee or a named person –

(a)   receives a notice under paragraph 6, 7 or 8 of an application for the registration of an instrument, and

(b)   before the end of the prescribed period, gives notice to the Public Guardian of an objection to the registration on the ground that an event mentioned in section 13(3) or (6)(a) to (d) has occurred which has revoked the instrument.

(2)   If the Public Guardian is satisfied that the ground for making the objection is established, he must not register the instrument unless the court, on the application of the person applying for the registration –

(a)   is satisfied that the ground is not established, and

(b)   directs the Public Guardian to register the instrument.

(3)   Sub-paragraph (4) applies if a donee or a named person –

(a)   receives a notice under paragraph 6, 7 or 8 of an application for the registration of an instrument, and

(b)   before the end of the prescribed period –

(i)   makes an application to the court objecting to the registration on a prescribed ground, and

(ii)   notifies the Public Guardian of the application.

(4)   The Public Guardian must not register the instrument unless the court directs him to do so.

Objection by donor

14   (1)   This paragraph applies if the donor –

(a)   receives a notice under paragraph 8 of an application for the registration of an instrument, and

(b)   before the end of the prescribed period, gives notice to the Public Guardian of an objection to the registration.

(2) The Public Guardian must not register the instrument unless the court, on the application of the donee or, if more than one, any of them –

    (a) is satisfied that the donor lacks capacity to object to the registration, and

    (b) directs the Public Guardian to register the instrument.

Notification of registration

15 Where an instrument is registered under this Schedule, the Public Guardian must give notice of the fact in the prescribed form to –

    (a) the donor, and

    (b) the donee or, if more than one, each of them.

Evidence of registration

16 (1) A document purporting to be an office copy of an instrument registered under this Schedule is, in any part of the United Kingdom, evidence of –

    (a) the contents of the instrument, and

    (b) the fact that it has been registered.

(2) Sub-paragraph (1) is without prejudice to –

    (a) section 3 of the Powers of Attorney Act 1971 (c. 27) (proof by certified copy), and

    (b) any other method of proof authorised by law.

PART 3   CANCELLATION OF REGISTRATION AND NOTIFICATION OF SEVERANCE

17 (1) The Public Guardian must cancel the registration of an instrument as a lasting power of attorney on being satisfied that the power has been revoked –

    (a) as a result of the donor's bankruptcy, or

    (b) on the occurrence of an event mentioned in section 13(6)(a) to (d).

(2) If the Public Guardian cancels the registration of an instrument he must notify –

    (a) the donor, and

    (b) the donee or, if more than one, each of them.

18 The court must direct the Public Guardian to cancel the registration of an instrument as a lasting power of attorney if it –

    (a) determines under section 22(2)(a) that a requirement for creating the power was not met,

    (b) determines under section 22(2)(b) that the power has been revoked or has otherwise come to an end, or

    (c) revokes the power under section 22(4)(b) (fraud etc.).

19 (1) Sub-paragraph (2) applies if the court determines under section 23(1) that a lasting power of attorney contains a provision which –

    (a) is ineffective as part of a lasting power of attorney, or

    (b) prevents the instrument from operating as a valid lasting power of attorney.

(2) The court must –

    (a) notify the Public Guardian that it has severed the provision, or

    (b) direct him to cancel the registration of the instrument as a lasting power of attorney.

20   On the cancellation of the registration of an instrument, the instrument and any office copies of it must be delivered up to the Public Guardian to be cancelled.

PART 4   RECORDS OF ALTERATIONS IN REGISTERED POWERS

Partial revocation or suspension of power as a result of bankruptcy

21   If in the case of a registered instrument it appears to the Public Guardian that under section 13 a lasting power of attorney is revoked, or suspended, in relation to the donor's property and affairs (but not in relation to other matters), the Public Guardian must attach to the instrument a note to that effect.

Termination of appointment of donee which does not revoke power

22   If in the case of a registered instrument it appears to the Public Guardian that an event has occurred –

(a)   which has terminated the appointment of the donee, but
(b)   which has not revoked the instrument,

the Public Guardian must attach to the instrument a note to that effect.

Replacement of donee

23   If in the case of a registered instrument it appears to the Public Guardian that the donee has been replaced under the terms of the instrument the Public Guardian must attach to the instrument a note to that effect.

Severance of ineffective provisions

24   If in the case of a registered instrument the court notifies the Public Guardian under paragraph 19(2)(a) that it has severed a provision of the instrument, the Public Guardian must attach to it a note to that effect.

Notification of alterations

25   If the Public Guardian attaches a note to an instrument under paragraph 21, 22, 23 or 24 he must give notice of the note to the donee or donees of the power (or, as the case may be, to the other donee or donees of the power).

SCHEDULE 2   PROPERTY AND AFFAIRS: SUPPLEMENTARY PROVISIONS   Section 18(4)

Wills: general

1   Paragraphs 2 to 4 apply in relation to the execution of a will, by virtue of section 18, on behalf of P.

Provision that may be made in will

2 The will may make any provision (whether by disposing of property or exercising a power or otherwise) which could be made by a will executed by P if he had capacity to make it.

Wills: requirements relating to execution

3 (1) Sub-paragraph (2) applies if under section 16 the court makes an order or gives directions requiring or authorising a person ('the authorised person') to execute a will on behalf of P.

   (2) Any will executed in pursuance of the order or direction –

   (a) must state that it is signed by P acting by the authorised person,
   (b) must be signed by the authorised person with the name of P and his own name, in the presence of two or more witnesses present at the same time,
   (c) must be attested and subscribed by those witnesses in the presence of the authorised person, and
   (d) must be sealed with the official seal of the court.

Wills: effect of execution

4 (1) This paragraph applies where a will is executed in accordance with paragraph 3.

   (2) The Wills Act 1837 (c. 26) has effect in relation to the will as if it were signed by P by his own hand, except that –

   (a) section 9 of the 1837 Act (requirements as to signing and attestation) does not apply, and
   (b) in the subsequent provisions of the 1837 Act any reference to execution in the manner required by the previous provisions is to be read as a reference to execution in accordance with paragraph 3.

   (3) The will has the same effect for all purposes as if –

   (a) P had had the capacity to make a valid will, and
   (b) the will had been executed by him in the manner required by the 1837 Act.

   (4) But sub-paragraph (3) does not have effect in relation to the will –

   (a) in so far as it disposes of immovable property outside England and Wales, or
   (b) in so far as it relates to any other property or matter if, when the will is executed –

   (i) P is domiciled outside England and Wales, and
   (ii) the condition in sub-paragraph (5) is met.

   (5) The condition is that, under the law of P's domicile, any question of his testamentary capacity would fall to be determined in accordance with the law of a place outside England and Wales.

Vesting orders ancillary to settlement etc.

5 (1) If provision is made by virtue of section 18 for –

   (a) the settlement of any property of P, or
   (b) the exercise of a power vested in him of appointing trustees or retiring from a trust,

the court may also make as respects the property settled or the trust property such consequential vesting or other orders as the case may require.

(2) The power under sub-paragraph (1) includes, in the case of the exercise of such a power, any order which could have been made in such a case under Part 4 of the Trustee Act 1925 (c. 19).

Variation of settlements

6   (1) If a settlement has been made by virtue of section 18, the court may by order vary or revoke the settlement if –

    (a)   the settlement makes provision for its variation or revocation,

    (b)   the court is satisfied that a material fact was not disclosed when the settlement was made, or

    (c)   the court is satisfied that there has been a substantial change of circumstances.

(2) Any such order may give such consequential directions as the court thinks fit.

Vesting of stock in curator appointed outside England and Wales

7   (1) Sub-paragraph (2) applies if the court is satisfied –

    (a)   that under the law prevailing in a place outside England and Wales a person ('M') has been appointed to exercise powers in respect of the property or affairs of P on the ground (however formulated) that P lacks capacity to make decisions with respect to the management and administration of his property and affairs, and

    (b)   that, having regard to the nature of the appointment and to the circumstances of the case, it is expedient that the court should exercise its powers under this paragraph.

(2) The court may direct –

    (a)   any stocks standing in the name of P, or

    (b)   the right to receive dividends from the stocks,

to be transferred into M's name or otherwise dealt with as required by M, and may give such directions as the court thinks fit for dealing with accrued dividends from the stocks.

(3) 'Stocks' includes –

    (a)   shares, and

    (b)   any funds, annuity or security transferable in the books kept by any body corporate or unincorporated company or society or by an instrument of transfer either alone or accompanied by other formalities,

and 'dividends' is to be construed accordingly.

Preservation of interests in property disposed of on behalf of person lacking capacity

8   (1) Sub-paragraphs (2) and (3) apply if –

    (a)   P's property has been disposed of by virtue of section 18,

    (b)   under P's will or intestacy, or by a gift perfected or nomination taking effect on his death, any other person would have taken an interest in the property but for the disposal, and

    (c)   on P's death, any property belonging to P's estate represents the property disposed of.

(2) The person takes the same interest, if and so far as circumstances allow, in the property representing the property disposed of.

(3) If the property disposed of was real property, any property representing it is to be treated, so long as it remains part of P's estate, as if it were real property.

(4) The court may direct that, on a disposal of P's property –

(a) which is made by virtue of section 18, and

(b) which would apart from this paragraph result in the conversion of personal property into real property,

property representing the property disposed of is to be treated, so long as it remains P's property or forms part of P's estate, as if it were personal property.

(5) References in sub-paragraphs (1) to (4) to the disposal of property are to –

(a) the sale, exchange, charging of or other dealing (otherwise than by will) with property other than money;

(b) the removal of property from one place to another;

(c) the application of money in acquiring property;

(d) the transfer of money from one account to another;

and references to property representing property disposed of are to be construed accordingly and as including the result of successive disposals.

(6) The court may give such directions as appear to it necessary or expedient for the purpose of facilitating the operation of sub-paragraphs (1) to (3), including the carrying of money to a separate account and the transfer of property other than money.

9   (1) Sub-paragraph (2) applies if the court has ordered or directed the expenditure of money –

(a) for carrying out permanent improvements on any of P's property, or

(b) otherwise for the permanent benefit of any of P's property.

(2) The court may order that –

(a) the whole of the money expended or to be expended, or

(b) any part of it,

is to be a charge on the property either without interest or with interest at a specified rate.

(3) An order under sub-paragraph (2) may provide for excluding or restricting the operation of paragraph 8(1) to (3).

(4) A charge under sub-paragraph (2) may be made in favour of such person as may be just and, in particular, where the money charged is paid out of P's general estate, may be made in favour of a person as trustee for P.

(5) No charge under sub-paragraph (2) may confer any right of sale or foreclosure during P's lifetime.

Powers as patron of benefice

10   (1) Any functions which P has as patron of a benefice may be discharged only by a person ('R') appointed by the court.

(2) R must be an individual capable of appointment under section 8(1)(b) of the 1986 Measure (which provides for an individual able to make a declaration of communicant status, a clerk in Holy Orders, etc. to be appointed to discharge a registered patron's functions).

(3) The 1986 Measure applies to R as it applies to an individual appointed by the registered patron of the benefice under section 8(1)(b) or (3) of that Measure to discharge his functions as patron.

(4) 'The 1986 Measure' means the Patronage (Benefices) Measure 1986 (No. 3).

SCHEDULE 3   INTERNATIONAL PROTECTION OF ADULTS

Section 63

PART 1   PRELIMINARY

Introduction

1 This Part applies for the purposes of this Schedule.

The Convention

2 (1) 'Convention' means the Convention referred to in section 63.
   (2) 'Convention country' means a country in which the Convention is in force.
   (3) A reference to an Article or Chapter is to an Article or Chapter of the Convention.
   (4) An expression which appears in this Schedule and in the Convention is to be construed in accordance with the Convention.

Countries, territories and nationals

3 (1) 'Country' includes a territory which has its own system of law.
   (2) Where a country has more than one territory with its own system of law, a reference to the country, in relation to one of its nationals, is to the territory with which the national has the closer, or the closest, connection.

Adults with incapacity

4 'Adult' means a person who –

   (a)   as a result of an impairment or insufficiency of his personal faculties, cannot protect his interests, and
   (b)   has reached 16.

Protective measures

5 (1) 'Protective measure' means a measure directed to the protection of the person or property of an adult; and it may deal in particular with any of the following –

   (a)   the determination of incapacity and the institution of a protective regime,
   (b)   placing the adult under the protection of an appropriate authority,
   (c)   guardianship, curatorship or any corresponding system,
   (d)   the designation and functions of a person having charge of the adult's person or property, or representing or otherwise helping him,
   (e)   placing the adult in a place where protection can be provided,
   (f)   administering, conserving or disposing of the adult's property,
   (g)   authorising a specific intervention for the protection of the person or property of the adult.

   (2) Where a measure of like effect to a protective measure has been taken in relation to a person before he reaches 16, this Schedule applies to the measure in so far as it has effect in relation to him once he has reached 16.

Central Authority

6   (1)   Any function under the Convention of a Central Authority is exercisable in England and Wales by the Lord Chancellor.

     (2)   A communication may be sent to the Central Authority in relation to England and Wales by sending it to the Lord Chancellor.

PART 2   JURISDICTION OF COMPETENT AUTHORITY

Scope of jurisdiction

7   (1)   The court may exercise its functions under this Act (in so far as it cannot otherwise do so) in relation to –

           (a)   an adult habitually resident in England and Wales,

           (b)   an adult's property in England and Wales,

           (c)   an adult present in England and Wales or who has property there, if the matter is urgent, or

           (d)   an adult present in England and Wales, if a protective measure which is temporary and limited in its effect to England and Wales is proposed in relation to him.

     (2)   An adult present in England and Wales is to be treated for the purposes of this paragraph as habitually resident there if –

           (a)   his habitual residence cannot be ascertained,

           (b)   he is a refugee, or

           (c)   he has been displaced as a result of disturbance in the country of his habitual residence.

8   (1)   The court may also exercise its functions under this Act (in so far as it cannot otherwise do so) in relation to an adult if sub-paragraph (2) or (3) applies in relation to him.

     (2)   This sub-paragraph applies in relation to an adult if –

           (a)   he is a British citizen,

           (b)   he has a closer connection with England and Wales than with Scotland or Northern Ireland, and

           (c)   Article 7 has, in relation to the matter concerned, been complied with.

     (3)   This sub-paragraph applies in relation to an adult if the Lord Chancellor, having consulted such persons as he considers appropriate, agrees to a request under Article 8 in relation to the adult.

Exercise of jurisdiction

9   (1)   This paragraph applies where jurisdiction is exercisable under this Schedule in connection with a matter which involves a Convention country other than England and Wales.

     (2)   Any Article on which the jurisdiction is based applies in relation to the matter in so far as it involves the other country (and the court must, accordingly, comply with any duty conferred on it as a result).

     (3)   Article 12 also applies, so far as its provisions allow, in relation to the matter in so far as it involves the other country.

10   A reference in this Schedule to the exercise of jurisdiction under this Schedule is to the exercise of functions under this Act as a result of this Part of this Schedule.

PART 3   APPLICABLE LAW

Applicable law

11   In exercising jurisdiction under this Schedule, the court may, if it thinks that the matter has a substantial connection with a country other than England and Wales, apply the law of that other country.

12   Where a protective measure is taken in one country but implemented in another, the conditions of implementation are governed by the law of the other country.

Lasting powers of attorney, etc.

13   (1)   If the donor of a lasting power is habitually resident in England and Wales at the time of granting the power, the law applicable to the existence, extent, modification or extinction of the power is –

   (a)   the law of England and Wales, or
   (b)   if he specifies in writing the law of a connected country for the purpose, that law.

   (2)   If he is habitually resident in another country at that time, but England and Wales is a connected country, the law applicable in that respect is –

   (a)   the law of the other country, or
   (b)   if he specifies in writing the law of England and Wales for the purpose, that law.

   (3)   A country is connected, in relation to the donor, if it is a country –

   (a)   of which he is a national,
   (b)   in which he was habitually resident, or
   (c)   in which he has property.

   (4)   Where this paragraph applies as a result of sub-paragraph (3)(c), it applies only in relation to the property which the donor has in the connected country.

   (5)   The law applicable to the manner of the exercise of a lasting power is the law of the country where it is exercised.

   (6)   In this Part of this Schedule, 'lasting power' means –

   (a)   a lasting power of attorney (see section 9),
   (b)   an enduring power of attorney within the meaning of Schedule 4, or
   (c)   any other power of like effect.

14   (1)   Where a lasting power is not exercised in a manner sufficient to guarantee the protection of the person or property of the donor, the court, in exercising jurisdiction under this Schedule, may disapply or modify the power.

   (2)   Where, in accordance with this Part of this Schedule, the law applicable to the power is, in one or more respects, that of a country other than England and Wales, the court must, so far as possible, have regard to the law of the other country in that respect (or those respects).

15   Regulations may provide for Schedule 1 (lasting powers of attorney: formalities) to apply with modifications in relation to a lasting power which comes within paragraph 13(6)(c) above.

Protection of third parties

16   (1)   This paragraph applies where a person (a 'representative') in purported exercise of an authority to act on behalf of an adult enters into a transaction with a third party.

(2)   The validity of the transaction may not be questioned in proceedings, nor may the third party be held liable, merely because –

    (a)   where the representative and third party are in England and Wales when entering into the transaction, sub-paragraph (3) applies;

    (b)   where they are in another country at that time, sub-paragraph (4) applies.

(3)   This sub-paragraph applies if –

    (a)   the law applicable to the authority in one or more respects is, as a result of this Schedule, the law of a country other than England and Wales, and

    (b)   the representative is not entitled to exercise the authority in that respect (or those respects) under the law of that other country.

(4)   This sub-paragraph applies if –

    (a)   the law applicable to the authority in one or more respects is, as a result of this Part of this Schedule, the law of England and Wales, and

    (b)   the representative is not entitled to exercise the authority in that respect (or those respects) under that law.

(5)   This paragraph does not apply if the third party knew or ought to have known that the applicable law was –

    (a)   in a case within sub-paragraph (3), the law of the other country;

    (b)   in a case within sub-paragraph (4), the law of England and Wales.

Mandatory rules

17   Where the court is entitled to exercise jurisdiction under this Schedule, the mandatory provisions of the law of England and Wales apply, regardless of any system of law which would otherwise apply in relation to the matter.

Public policy

18   Nothing in this Part of this Schedule requires or enables the application in England and Wales of a provision of the law of another country if its application would be manifestly contrary to public policy.

PART 4   RECOGNITION AND ENFORCEMENT

Recognition

19   (1)   A protective measure taken in relation to an adult under the law of a country other than England and Wales is to be recognised in England and Wales if it was taken on the ground that the adult is habitually resident in the other country.

    (2)   A protective measure taken in relation to an adult under the law of a Convention country other than England and Wales is to be recognised in England and Wales if it was taken on a ground mentioned in Chapter 2 (jurisdiction).

    (3)   But the court may disapply this paragraph in relation to a measure if it thinks that –

        (a)   the case in which the measure was taken was not urgent,

        (b)   the adult was not given an opportunity to be heard, and

        (c)   that omission amounted to a breach of natural justice.

    (4)   It may also disapply this paragraph in relation to a measure if it thinks that –

        (a)   recognition of the measure would be manifestly contrary to public policy,

(b)   the measure would be inconsistent with a mandatory provision of the law of England and Wales, or

(c)   the measure is inconsistent with one subsequently taken, or recognised, in England and Wales in relation to the adult.

(5)   And the court may disapply this paragraph in relation to a measure taken under the law of a Convention country in a matter to which Article 33 applies, if the court thinks that that Article has not been complied with in connection with that matter.

20   (1)   An interested person may apply to the court for a declaration as to whether a protective measure taken under the law of a country other than England and Wales is to be recognised in England and Wales.

(2)   No permission is required for an application to the court under this paragraph.

21   For the purposes of paragraphs 19 and 20, any finding of fact relied on when the measure was taken is conclusive.

Enforcement

22   (1)   An interested person may apply to the court for a declaration as to whether a protective measure taken under the law of, and enforceable in, a country other than England and Wales is enforceable, or to be registered, in England and Wales in accordance with Court of Protection Rules.

(2)   The court must make the declaration if –

(a)   the measure comes within sub-paragraph (1) or (2) of paragraph 19, and

(b)   the paragraph is not disapplied in relation to it as a result of sub-paragraph (3), (4) or (5).

(3)   A measure to which a declaration under this paragraph relates is enforceable in England and Wales as if it were a measure of like effect taken by the court.

Measures taken in relation to those aged under 16

23   (1)   This paragraph applies where –

(a)   provision giving effect to, or otherwise deriving from, the Convention in a country other than England and Wales applies in relation to a person who has not reached 16, and

(b)   a measure is taken in relation to that person in reliance on that provision.

(2)   This Part of this Schedule applies in relation to that measure as it applies in relation to a protective measure taken in relation to an adult under the law of a Convention country other than England and Wales.

Supplementary

24   The court may not review the merits of a measure taken outside England and Wales except to establish whether the measure complies with this Schedule in so far as it is, as a result of this Schedule, required to do so.

25   Court of Protection Rules may make provision about an application under paragraph 20 or 22.

PART 5   CO-OPERATION

Proposal for cross-border placement

26 (1) This paragraph applies where a public authority proposes to place an adult in an establishment in a Convention country other than England and Wales.

(2) The public authority must consult an appropriate authority in that other country about the proposed placement and, for that purpose, must send it –

(a)   a report on the adult, and

(b)   a statement of its reasons for the proposed placement.

(3) If the appropriate authority in the other country opposes the proposed placement within a reasonable time, the public authority may not proceed with it.

27 A proposal received by a public authority under Article 33 in relation to an adult is to proceed unless the authority opposes it within a reasonable time.

Adult in danger etc.

28 (1) This paragraph applies if a public authority is told that an adult –

(a)   who is in serious danger, and

(b)   in relation to whom the public authority has taken, or is considering taking, protective measures,

is, or has become resident, in a Convention country other than England and Wales.

(2) The public authority must tell an appropriate authority in that other country about –

(a)   the danger, and

(b)   the measures taken or under consideration.

29 A public authority may not request from, or send to, an appropriate authority in a Convention country information in accordance with Chapter 5 (co-operation) in relation to an adult if it thinks that doing so –

(a)   would be likely to endanger the adult or his property, or

(b)   would amount to a serious threat to the liberty or life of a member of the adult's family.

PART 6   GENERAL

Certificates

30 A certificate given under Article 38 by an authority in a Convention country other than England and Wales is, unless the contrary is shown, proof of the matters contained in it.

Powers to make further provision as to private international law

31 Her Majesty may by Order in Council confer on the Lord Chancellor, the court or another public authority functions for enabling the Convention to be given effect in England and Wales.

32 (1) Regulations may make provision –

(a)   giving further effect to the Convention, or

(b)   otherwise about the private international law of England and Wales in relation to the protection of adults.

(2) The regulations may –
- (a) confer functions on the court or another public authority;
- (b) amend this Schedule;
- (c) provide for this Schedule to apply with specified modifications;
- (d) make provision about countries other than Convention countries.

Exceptions

33   Nothing in this Schedule applies, and no provision made under paragraph 32 is to apply, to any matter to which the Convention, as a result of Article 4, does not apply.

Regulations and orders

34   A reference in this Schedule to regulations or an order (other than an Order in Council) is to regulations or an order made for the purposes of this Schedule by the Lord Chancellor.

Commencement

35   The following provisions of this Schedule have effect only if the Convention is in force in accordance with Article 57 –
- (a) paragraph 8,
- (b) paragraph 9,
- (c) paragraph 19(2) and (5),
- (d) Part 5,
- (e) paragraph 30.

SCHEDULE 4   PROVISIONS APPLYING TO EXISTING ENDURING POWERS OF ATTORNEY   Section 66(3)

PART 1   ENDURING POWERS OF ATTORNEY

Enduring power of attorney to survive mental incapacity of donor

1   (1) Where an individual has created a power of attorney which is an enduring power within the meaning of this Schedule –

- (a) the power is not revoked by any subsequent mental incapacity of his,
- (b) upon such incapacity supervening, the donee of the power may not do anything under the authority of the power except as provided by sub-paragraph (2) unless or until the instrument creating the power is registered under paragraph 13, and
- (c) if and so long as paragraph (b) operates to suspend the donee's authority to act under the power, section 5 of the Powers of Attorney Act 1971 (c. 27) (protection of donee and third persons), so far as applicable, applies as if the power had been revoked by the donor's mental incapacity,

and, accordingly, section 1 of this Act does not apply.

(2) Despite sub-paragraph (1)(b), where the attorney has made an application for registration of the instrument then, until it is registered, the attorney may take action under the power –

     (a)   to maintain the donor or prevent loss to his estate, or

     (b)   to maintain himself or other persons in so far as paragraph 3(2) permits him to do so.

(3) Where the attorney purports to act as provided by sub-paragraph (2) then, in favour of a person who deals with him without knowledge that the attorney is acting otherwise than in accordance with sub-paragraph (2)(a) or (b), the transaction between them is as valid as if the attorney were acting in accordance with sub-paragraph (2)(a) or (b).

Characteristics of an enduring power of attorney

2   (1) Subject to sub-paragraphs (5) and (6) and paragraph 20, a power of attorney is an enduring power within the meaning of this Schedule if the instrument which creates the power –

     (a)   is in the prescribed form,

     (b)   was executed in the prescribed manner by the donor and the attorney, and

     (c)   incorporated at the time of execution by the donor the prescribed explanatory information.

(2) In this paragraph, 'prescribed' means prescribed by such of the following regulations as applied when the instrument was executed –

     (a)   the Enduring Powers of Attorney (Prescribed Form) Regulations 1986 (SI 1986/126),

     (b)   the Enduring Powers of Attorney (Prescribed Form) Regulations 1987 (SI 1987/1612),

     (c)   the Enduring Powers of Attorney (Prescribed Form) Regulations 1990 (SI 1990/1376),

     (d)   the Enduring Powers of Attorney (Welsh Language Prescribed Form) Regulations 2000 (SI 2000/289).

(3) An instrument in the prescribed form purporting to have been executed in the prescribed manner is to be taken, in the absence of evidence to the contrary, to be a document which incorporated at the time of execution by the donor the prescribed explanatory information.

(4) If an instrument differs in an immaterial respect in form or mode of expression from the prescribed form it is to be treated as sufficient in point of form and expression.

(5) A power of attorney cannot be an enduring power unless, when he executes the instrument creating it, the attorney is –

     (a)   an individual who has reached 18 and is not bankrupt, or

     (b)   a trust corporation.

(6) A power of attorney which gives the attorney a right to appoint a substitute or successor cannot be an enduring power.

(7) An enduring power is revoked by the bankruptcy of the donor or attorney.

(8) But where the donor or attorney is bankrupt merely because an interim bankruptcy restrictions order has effect in respect of him, the power is suspended for so long as the order has effect.

(9) An enduring power is revoked if the court –

     (a)   exercises a power under sections 16 to 20 in relation to the donor, and

     (b)   directs that the enduring power is to be revoked.

(10) No disclaimer of an enduring power, whether by deed or otherwise, is valid unless and until the attorney gives notice of it to the donor or, where paragraph 4(6) or 15(1) applies, to the Public Guardian.

Scope of authority etc. of attorney under enduring power

3   (1)   If the instrument which creates an enduring power of attorney is expressed to confer general authority on the attorney, the instrument operates to confer, subject to –

(a)   the restriction imposed by sub-paragraph (3), and

(b)   any conditions or restrictions contained in the instrument,

authority to do on behalf of the donor anything which the donor could lawfully do by an attorney at the time when the donor executed the instrument.

(2)   Subject to any conditions or restrictions contained in the instrument, an attorney under an enduring power, whether general or limited, may (without obtaining any consent) act under the power so as to benefit himself or other persons than the donor to the following extent but no further –

(a)   he may so act in relation to himself or in relation to any other person if the donor might be expected to provide for his or that person's needs respectively, and

(b)   he may do whatever the donor might be expected to do to meet those needs.

(3)   Without prejudice to sub-paragraph (2) but subject to any conditions or restrictions contained in the instrument, an attorney under an enduring power, whether general or limited, may (without obtaining any consent) dispose of the property of the donor by way of gift to the following extent but no further –

(a)   he may make gifts of a seasonal nature or at a time, or on an anniversary, of a birth, a marriage or the formation of a civil partnership, to persons (including himself) who are related to or connected with the donor, and

(b)   he may make gifts to any charity to whom the donor made or might be expected to make gifts,

provided that the value of each such gift is not unreasonable having regard to all the circumstances and in particular the size of the donor's estate.

PART 2   ACTION ON ACTUAL OR IMPENDING INCAPACITY OF DONOR

Duties of attorney in event of actual or impending incapacity of donor

4   (1)   Sub-paragraphs (2) to (6) apply if the attorney under an enduring power has reason to believe that the donor is or is becoming mentally incapable.

(2)   The attorney must, as soon as practicable, make an application to the Public Guardian for the registration of the instrument creating the power.

(3)   Before making an application for registration the attorney must comply with the provisions as to notice set out in Part 3 of this Schedule.

(4)   An application for registration –

(a)   must be made in the prescribed form, and

(b)   must contain such statements as may be prescribed.

(5)   The attorney –

(a)   may, before making an application for the registration of the instrument, refer to the court for its determination any question as to the validity of the power, and

(b)   must comply with any direction given to him by the court on that determination.

(6)   No disclaimer of the power is valid unless and until the attorney gives notice of

it to the Public Guardian; and the Public Guardian must notify the donor if he receives a notice under this sub-paragraph.

(7) A person who, in an application for registration, makes a statement which he knows to be false in a material particular is guilty of an offence and is liable –

(a) on summary conviction, to imprisonment for a term not exceeding 12 months or a fine not exceeding the statutory maximum or both;

(b) on conviction on indictment, to imprisonment for a term not exceeding 2 years or a fine or both.

(8) In this paragraph, 'prescribed' means prescribed by regulations made for the purposes of this Schedule by the Lord Chancellor.

PART 3   NOTIFICATION PRIOR TO REGISTRATION

Duty to give notice to relatives

5   Subject to paragraph 7, before making an application for registration the attorney must give notice of his intention to do so to all those persons (if any) who are entitled to receive notice by virtue of paragraph 6.

6   (1) Subject to sub-paragraphs (2) to (4), persons of the following classes ('relatives') are entitled to receive notice under paragraph 5 –

(a) the donor's spouse or civil partner,

(b) the donor's children,

(c) the donor's parents,

(d) the donor's brothers and sisters, whether of the whole or half blood,

(e) the widow, widower or surviving civil partner of a child of the donor,

(f) the donor's grandchildren,

(g) the children of the donor's brothers and sisters of the whole blood,

(h) the children of the donor's brothers and sisters of the half blood,

(i) the donor's uncles and aunts of the whole blood,

(j) the children of the donor's uncles and aunts of the whole blood.

(2) A person is not entitled to receive notice under paragraph 5 if –

(a) his name or address is not known to the attorney and cannot be reasonably ascertained by him, or

(b) the attorney has reason to believe that he has not reached 18 or is mentally incapable.

(3) Except where sub-paragraph (4) applies –

(a) no more than 3 persons are entitled to receive notice under paragraph 5, and

(b) in determining the persons who are so entitled, persons falling within the class in sub-paragraph (1)(a) are to be preferred to persons falling within the class in sub-paragraph (1)(b), those falling within the class in sub-paragraph (1)(b) are to be preferred to those falling within the class in sub-paragraph (1)(c), and so on.

(4) Despite the limit of 3 specified in sub-paragraph (3), where –

(a) there is more than one person falling within any of classes (a) to (j) of sub-paragraph (1), and

(b) at least one of those persons would be entitled to receive notice under paragraph 5,

then, subject to sub-paragraph (2), all the persons falling within that class are entitled to receive notice under paragraph 5.

7   (1) An attorney is not required to give notice under paragraph 5 –

(a)   to himself, or

(b)   to any other attorney under the power who is joining in making the application,

even though he or, as the case may be, the other attorney is entitled to receive notice by virtue of paragraph 6.

(2)   In the case of any person who is entitled to receive notice by virtue of paragraph 6, the attorney, before applying for registration, may make an application to the court to be dispensed from the requirement to give him notice; and the court must grant the application if it is satisfied –

(a)   that it would be undesirable or impracticable for the attorney to give him notice, or

(b)   that no useful purpose is likely to be served by giving him notice.

Duty to give notice to donor

8   (1)   Subject to sub-paragraph (2), before making an application for registration the attorney must give notice of his intention to do so to the donor.

(2)   Paragraph 7(2) applies in relation to the donor as it applies in relation to a person who is entitled to receive notice under paragraph 5.

Contents of notices

9   A notice to relatives under this Part of this Schedule must –

(a)   be in the prescribed form,

(b)   state that the attorney proposes to make an application to the Public Guardian for the registration of the instrument creating the enduring power in question,

(c)   inform the person to whom it is given of his right to object to the registration under paragraph 13(4), and

(d)   specify, as the grounds on which an objection to registration may be made, the grounds set out in paragraph 13(9).

10   A notice to the donor under this Part of this Schedule –

(a)   must be in the prescribed form,

(b)   must contain the statement mentioned in paragraph 9(b), and

(c)   must inform the donor that, while the instrument remains registered, any revocation of the power by him will be ineffective unless and until the revocation is confirmed by the court.

Duty to give notice to other attorneys

11   (1)   Subject to sub-paragraph (2), before making an application for registration an attorney under a joint and several power must give notice of his intention to do so to any other attorney under the power who is not joining in making the application; and paragraphs 7(2) and 9 apply in relation to attorneys entitled to receive notice by virtue of this paragraph as they apply in relation to persons entitled to receive notice by virtue of paragraph 6.

(2)   An attorney is not entitled to receive notice by virtue of this paragraph if –

(a)   his address is not known to the applying attorney and cannot reasonably be ascertained by him, or

(b)   the applying attorney has reason to believe that he has not reached 18 or is mentally incapable.

Supplementary

12   Despite section 7 of the Interpretation Act 1978 (c. 30) (construction of references to service by post), for the purposes of this Part of this Schedule a notice given by post is to be regarded as given on the date on which it was posted.

PART 4   REGISTRATION

Registration of instrument creating power

13   (1)   If an application is made in accordance with paragraph 4(3) and (4) the Public Guardian must, subject to the provisions of this paragraph, register the instrument to which the application relates.

(2)   If it appears to the Public Guardian that –

(a)   there is a deputy appointed for the donor of the power created by the instrument, and

(b)   the powers conferred on the deputy would, if the instrument were registered, to any extent conflict with the powers conferred on the attorney,

the Public Guardian must not register the instrument except in accordance with the court's directions.

(3)   The court may, on the application of the attorney, direct the Public Guardian to register an instrument even though notice has not been given as required by paragraph 4(3) and Part 3 of this Schedule to a person entitled to receive it, if the court is satisfied –

(a)   that it was undesirable or impracticable for the attorney to give notice to that person, or

(b)   that no useful purpose is likely to be served by giving him notice.

(4)   Sub-paragraph (5) applies if, before the end of the period of 5 weeks beginning with the date (or the latest date) on which the attorney gave notice under paragraph 5 of an application for registration, the Public Guardian receives a valid notice of objection to the registration from a person entitled to notice of the application.

(5)   The Public Guardian must not register the instrument except in accordance with the court's directions.

(6)   Sub-paragraph (7) applies if, in the case of an application for registration –

(a)   it appears from the application that there is no one to whom notice has been given under paragraph 5, or

(b)   the Public Guardian has reason to believe that appropriate inquiries might bring to light evidence on which he could be satisfied that one of the grounds of objection set out in sub-paragraph (9) was established.

(7)   The Public Guardian –

(a)   must not register the instrument, and

(b)   must undertake such inquiries as he thinks appropriate in all the circumstances.

(8)   If, having complied with sub-paragraph (7)(b), the Public Guardian is satisfied that one of the grounds of objection set out in sub-paragraph (9) is established –

(a)   the attorney may apply to the court for directions, and

(b)   the Public Guardian must not register the instrument except in accordance with the court's directions.

(9)   A notice of objection under this paragraph is valid if made on one or more of the following grounds –

(a)   that the power purported to have been created by the instrument was not valid as an enduring power of attorney,

(b)   that the power created by the instrument no longer subsists,

(c)   that the application is premature because the donor is not yet becoming mentally incapable,

(d)   that fraud or undue pressure was used to induce the donor to create the power,

(e)   that, having regard to all the circumstances and in particular the attorney's relationship to or connection with the donor, the attorney is unsuitable to be the donor's attorney.

(10) If any of those grounds is established to the satisfaction of the court it must direct the Public Guardian not to register the instrument, but if not so satisfied it must direct its registration.

(11) If the court directs the Public Guardian not to register an instrument because it is satisfied that the ground in sub-paragraph (9)(d) or (e) is established, it must by order revoke the power created by the instrument.

(12) If the court directs the Public Guardian not to register an instrument because it is satisfied that any ground in sub-paragraph (9) except that in paragraph (c) is established, the instrument must be delivered up to be cancelled unless the court otherwise directs.

Register of enduring powers

14   The Public Guardian has the function of establishing and maintaining a register of enduring powers for the purposes of this Schedule.

PART 5   LEGAL POSITION AFTER REGISTRATION

Effect and proof of registration

15   (1)   The effect of the registration of an instrument under paragraph 13 is that –

(a)   no revocation of the power by the donor is valid unless and until the court confirms the revocation under paragraph 16(3);

(b)   no disclaimer of the power is valid unless and until the attorney gives notice of it to the Public Guardian;

(c)   the donor may not extend or restrict the scope of the authority conferred by the instrument and no instruction or consent given by him after registration, in the case of a consent, confers any right and, in the case of an instruction, imposes or confers any obligation or right on or creates any liability of the attorney or other persons having notice of the instruction or consent.

(2)   Sub-paragraph (1) applies for so long as the instrument is registered under paragraph 13 whether or not the donor is for the time being mentally incapable.

(3)   A document purporting to be an office copy of an instrument registered under this Schedule is, in any part of the United Kingdom, evidence of –

(a)   the contents of the instrument, and

(b)   the fact that it has been so registered.

(4)   Sub-paragraph (3) is without prejudice to section 3 of the Powers of Attorney Act 1971 (c. 27) (proof by certified copies) and to any other method of proof authorised by law.

Functions of court with regard to registered power

16 (1) Where an instrument has been registered under paragraph 13, the court has the following functions with respect to the power and the donor of and the attorney appointed to act under the power.

(2) The court may –

(a) determine any question as to the meaning or effect of the instrument;

(b) give directions with respect to –

(i) the management or disposal by the attorney of the property and affairs of the donor;

(ii) the rendering of accounts by the attorney and the production of the records kept by him for the purpose;

(iii) the remuneration or expenses of the attorney whether or not in default of or in accordance with any provision made by the instrument, including directions for the repayment of excessive or the payment of additional remuneration;

(c) require the attorney to supply information or produce documents or things in his possession as attorney;

(d) give any consent or authorisation to act which the attorney would have to obtain from a mentally capable donor;

(e) authorise the attorney to act so as to benefit himself or other persons than the donor otherwise than in accordance with paragraph 3(2) and (3) (but subject to any conditions or restrictions contained in the instrument);

(f) relieve the attorney wholly or partly from any liability which he has or may have incurred on account of a breach of his duties as attorney.

(3) On application made for the purpose by or on behalf of the donor, the court must confirm the revocation of the power if satisfied that the donor –

(a) has done whatever is necessary in law to effect an express revocation of the power, and

(b) was mentally capable of revoking a power of attorney when he did so (whether or not he is so when the court considers the application).

(4) The court must direct the Public Guardian to cancel the registration of an instrument registered under paragraph 13 in any of the following circumstances –

(a) on confirming the revocation of the power under sub-paragraph (3),

(b) on directing under paragraph 2(9)(b) that the power is to be revoked,

(c) on being satisfied that the donor is and is likely to remain mentally capable,

(d) on being satisfied that the power has expired or has been revoked by the mental incapacity of the attorney,

(e) on being satisfied that the power was not a valid and subsisting enduring power when registration was effected,

(f) on being satisfied that fraud or undue pressure was used to induce the donor to create the power,

(g) on being satisfied that, having regard to all the circumstances and in particular the attorney's relationship to or connection with the donor, the attorney is unsuitable to be the donor's attorney.

(5) If the court directs the Public Guardian to cancel the registration of an instrument on being satisfied of the matters specified in sub-paragraph (4)(f) or (g) it must by order revoke the power created by the instrument.

(6) If the court directs the cancellation of the registration of an instrument under sub-paragraph (4) except paragraph (c) the instrument must be delivered up to the Public Guardian to be cancelled, unless the court otherwise directs.

Cancellation of registration by Public Guardian

17   The Public Guardian must cancel the registration of an instrument creating an enduring power of attorney –

    (a)   on receipt of a disclaimer signed by the attorney;

    (b)   if satisfied that the power has been revoked by the death or bankruptcy of the donor or attorney or, if the attorney is a body corporate, by its winding up or dissolution;

    (c)   on receipt of notification from the court that the court has revoked the power;

    (d)   on confirmation from the court that the donor has revoked the power.

PART 6   PROTECTION OF ATTORNEY AND THIRD PARTIES

Protection of attorney and third persons where power is invalid or revoked

18   (1)   Sub-paragraphs (2) and (3) apply where an instrument which did not create a valid power of attorney has been registered under paragraph 13 (whether or not the registration has been cancelled at the time of the act or transaction in question).

    (2)   An attorney who acts in pursuance of the power does not incur any liability (either to the donor or to any other person) because of the non-existence of the power unless at the time of acting he knows –

        (a)   that the instrument did not create a valid enduring power,

        (b)   that an event has occurred which, if the instrument had created a valid enduring power, would have had the effect of revoking the power, or

        (c)   that, if the instrument had created a valid enduring power, the power would have expired before that time.

    (3)   Any transaction between the attorney and another person is, in favour of that person, as valid as if the power had then been in existence, unless at the time of the transaction that person has knowledge of any of the matters mentioned in sub-paragraph (2).

    (4)   If the interest of a purchaser depends on whether a transaction between the attorney and another person was valid by virtue of sub-paragraph (3), it is conclusively presumed in favour of the purchaser that the transaction was valid if –

        (a)   the transaction between that person and the attorney was completed within 12 months of the date on which the instrument was registered, or

        (b)   that person makes a statutory declaration, before or within 3 months after the completion of the purchase, that he had no reason at the time of the transaction to doubt that the attorney had authority to dispose of the property which was the subject of the transaction.

    (5)   For the purposes of section 5 of the Powers of Attorney Act 1971 (c. 27) (protection where power is revoked) in its application to an enduring power the revocation of which by the donor is by virtue of paragraph 15 invalid unless and until confirmed by the court under paragraph 16 –

        (a)   knowledge of the confirmation of the revocation is knowledge of the revocation of the power, but

        (b)   knowledge of the unconfirmed revocation is not.

Further protection of attorney and third persons

19 (1) If –

   (a)   an instrument framed in a form prescribed as mentioned in paragraph 2(2) creates a power which is not a valid enduring power, and

   (b)   the power is revoked by the mental incapacity of the donor,

   sub-paragraphs (2) and (3) apply, whether or not the instrument has been registered.

   (2) An attorney who acts in pursuance of the power does not, by reason of the revocation, incur any liability (either to the donor or to any other person) unless at the time of acting he knows –

   (a)   that the instrument did not create a valid enduring power, and

   (b)   that the donor has become mentally incapable.

   (3) Any transaction between the attorney and another person is, in favour of that person, as valid as if the power had then been in existence, unless at the time of the transaction that person knows –

   (a)   that the instrument did not create a valid enduring power, and

   (b)   that the donor has become mentally incapable.

   (4) Paragraph 18(4) applies for the purpose of determining whether a transaction was valid by virtue of sub-paragraph (3) as it applies for the purpose or determining whether a transaction was valid by virtue of paragraph 18(3).

PART 7   JOINT AND JOINT AND SEVERAL ATTORNEYS

Application to joint and joint and several attorneys

20 (1) An instrument which appoints more than one person to be an attorney cannot create an enduring power unless the attorneys are appointed to act –

   (a)   jointly, or

   (b)   jointly and severally.

   (2) This Schedule, in its application to joint attorneys, applies to them collectively as it applies to a single attorney but subject to the modifications specified in paragraph 21.

   (3) This Schedule, in its application to joint and several attorneys, applies with the modifications specified in sub-paragraphs (4) to (7) and in paragraph 22.

   (4) A failure, as respects any one attorney, to comply with the requirements for the creation of enduring powers –

   (a)   prevents the instrument from creating such a power in his case, but

   (b)   does not affect its efficacy for that purpose as respects the other or others or its efficacy in his case for the purpose of creating a power of attorney which is not an enduring power.

   (5) If one or more but not both or all the attorneys makes or joins in making an application for registration of the instrument –

   (a)   an attorney who is not an applicant as well as one who is may act pending the registration of the instrument as provided in paragraph 1(2),

   (b)   notice of the application must also be given under Part 3 of this Schedule to the other attorney or attorneys, and

   (c)   objection may validly be taken to the registration on a ground relating to an attorney or to the power of an attorney who is not an applicant as well as to one or the power of one who is an applicant.

(6) The Public Guardian is not precluded by paragraph 13(5) or (8) from registering an instrument and the court must not direct him not to do so under paragraph 13(10) if an enduring power subsists as respects some attorney who is not affected by the ground or grounds of the objection in question; and where the Public Guardian registers an instrument in that case, he must make against the registration an entry in the prescribed form.

(7) Sub-paragraph (6) does not preclude the court from revoking a power in so far as it confers a power on any other attorney in respect of whom the ground in paragraph 13(9)(d) or (e) is established; and where any ground in paragraph 13(9) affecting any other attorney is established the court must direct the Public Guardian to make against the registration an entry in the prescribed form.

(8) In sub-paragraph (4), 'the requirements for the creation of enduring powers' means the provisions of –

(a) paragraph 2 other than sub-paragraphs (8) and (9), and
(b) the regulations mentioned in paragraph 2.

Joint attorneys

21 (1) In paragraph 2(5), the reference to the time when the attorney executes the instrument is to be read as a reference to the time when the second or last attorney executes the instrument.

(2) In paragraph 2(6) to (8), the reference to the attorney is to be read as a reference to any attorney under the power.

(3) Paragraph 13 has effect as if the ground of objection to the registration of the instrument specified in sub-paragraph (9)(e) applied to any attorney under the power.

(4) In paragraph 16(2), references to the attorney are to be read as including references to any attorney under the power.

(5) In paragraph 16(4), references to the attorney are to be read as including references to any attorney under the power.

(6) In paragraph 17, references to the attorney are to be read as including references to any attorney under the power.

Joint and several attorneys

22 (1) In paragraph 2(7), the reference to the bankruptcy of the attorney is to be read as a reference to the bankruptcy of the last remaining attorney under the power; and the bankruptcy of any other attorney under the power causes that person to cease to be an attorney under the power.

(2) In paragraph 2(8), the reference to the suspension of the power is to be read as a reference to its suspension in so far as it relates to the attorney in respect of whom the interim bankruptcy restrictions order has effect.

(3) The restriction upon disclaimer imposed by paragraph 4(6) applies only to those attorneys who have reason to believe that the donor is or is becoming mentally incapable.

PART 8   INTERPRETATION

23 (1) In this Schedule –

'enduring power' is to be construed in accordance with paragraph 2,
'mentally incapable' or 'mental incapacity', except where it refers to revocation at

common law, means in relation to any person, that he is incapable by reason of mental disorder (within the meaning of the Mental Health Act) of managing and administering his property and affairs and 'mentally capable' and 'mental capacity' are to be construed accordingly,

'notice' means notice in writing, and

'prescribed', except for the purposes of paragraph 2, means prescribed by regulations made for the purposes of this Schedule by the Lord Chancellor.

(2) Any question arising under or for the purposes of this Schedule as to what the donor of the power might at any time be expected to do is to be determined by assuming that he had full mental capacity at the time but otherwise by reference to the circumstances existing at that time.

SCHEDULE 5   TRANSITIONAL PROVISIONS AND SAVINGS

Section 66(4)

PART 1   REPEAL OF PART 7 OF THE MENTAL HEALTH ACT 1983

Existing receivers

1   (1) This paragraph applies where, immediately before the commencement day, there is a receiver ('R') for a person ('P') appointed under section 99 of the Mental Health Act.

(2) On and after that day –

(a) this Act applies as if R were a deputy appointed for P by the court, but with the functions that R had as receiver immediately before that day, and

(b) a reference in any other enactment to a deputy appointed by the court includes a person appointed as a deputy as a result of paragraph (a).

(3) On any application to it by R, the court may end R's appointment as P's deputy.

(4) Where, as a result of section 20(1), R may not make a decision on behalf of P in relation to a relevant matter, R must apply to the court.

(5) If, on the application, the court is satisfied that P is capable of managing his property and affairs in relation to the relevant matter –

(a) it must make an order ending R's appointment as P's deputy in relation to that matter, but

(b) it may, in relation to any other matter, exercise in relation to P any of the powers which it has under sections 15 to 19.

(6) If it is not satisfied, the court may exercise in relation to P any of the powers which it has under sections 15 to 19.

(7) R's appointment as P's deputy ceases to have effect if P dies.

(8) 'Relevant matter' means a matter in relation to which, immediately before the commencement day, R was authorised to act as P's receiver.

(9) In sub-paragraph (1), the reference to a receiver appointed under section 99 of the Mental Health Act includes a reference to a person who by virtue of Schedule 5 to that Act was deemed to be a receiver appointed under that section.

Orders, appointments etc.

2   (1) Any order or appointment made, direction or authority given or other thing done which has, or by virtue of Schedule 5 to the Mental Health Act was deemed to

have, effect under Part 7 of the Act immediately before the commencement day is to continue to have effect despite the repeal of Part 7.

(2) In so far as any such order, appointment, direction, authority or thing could have been made, given or done under sections 15 to 20 if those sections had then been in force –

(a) it is to be treated as made, given or done under those sections, and

(b) the powers of variation and discharge conferred by section 16(7) apply accordingly.

(3) Sub-paragraph (1) –

(a) does not apply to nominations under section 93(1) or (4) of the Mental Health Act, and

(b) as respects receivers, has effect subject to paragraph 1.

(4) This Act does not affect the operation of section 109 of the Mental Health Act (effect and proof of orders etc.) in relation to orders made and directions given under Part 7 of that Act.

(5) This paragraph is without prejudice to section 16 of the Interpretation Act 1978 (c. 30) (general savings on repeal).

Pending proceedings

3 (1) Any application for the exercise of a power under Part 7 of the Mental Health Act which is pending immediately before the commencement day is to be treated, in so far as a corresponding power is exercisable under sections 16 to 20, as an application for the exercise of that power.

(2) For the purposes of sub-paragraph (1) an application for the appointment of a receiver is to be treated as an application for the appointment of a deputy.

Appeals

4 (1) Part 7 of the Mental Health Act and the rules made under it are to continue to apply to any appeal brought by virtue of section 105 of that Act which has not been determined before the commencement day.

(2) If in the case of an appeal brought by virtue of section 105(1) (appeal to nominated judge) the judge nominated under section 93 of the Mental Health Act has begun to hear the appeal, he is to continue to do so but otherwise it is to be heard by a puisne judge of the High Court nominated under section 46.

Fees

5 All fees and other payments which, having become due, have not been paid to the former Court of Protection before the commencement day, are to be paid to the new Court of Protection.

Court records

6 (1) The records of the former Court of Protection are to be treated, on and after the commencement day, as records of the new Court of Protection and are to be dealt with accordingly under the Public Records Act 1958 (c. 51).

(2) On and after the commencement day, the Public Guardian is, for the purpose of exercising any of his functions, to be given such access as he may require to such

of the records mentioned in sub-paragraph (1) as relate to the appointment of receivers under section 99 of the Mental Health Act.

Existing charges

7   This Act does not affect the operation in relation to a charge created before the commencement day of –

(a)   so much of section 101(6) of the Mental Health Act as precludes a charge created under section 101(5) from conferring a right of sale or foreclosure during the lifetime of the patient, or

(b)   section 106(6) of the Mental Health Act (charge created by virtue of section 106(5) not to cause interest to fail etc.).

Preservation of interests on disposal of property

8   Paragraph 8(1) of Schedule 2 applies in relation to any disposal of property (within the meaning of that provision) by a person living on 1st November 1960, being a disposal effected under the Lunacy Act 1890 (c. 5) as it applies in relation to the disposal of property effected under sections 16 to 20.

Accounts

9   Court of Protection Rules may provide that, in a case where paragraph 1 applies, R is to have a duty to render accounts –

(a)   while he is receiver;

(b)   after he is discharged.

Interpretation

10   In this Part of this Schedule –

(a)   'the commencement day' means the day on which section 66(1)(a) (repeal of Part 7 of the Mental Health Act) comes into force,

(b)   'the former Court of Protection' means the office abolished by section 45, and

(c)   'the new Court of Protection' means the court established by that section.

PART 2   REPEAL OF THE ENDURING POWERS OF ATTORNEY ACT 1985

Orders, determinations, etc.

11   (1)   Any order or determination made, or other thing done, under the 1985 Act which has effect immediately before the commencement day continues to have effect despite the repeal of that Act.

(2)   In so far as any such order, determination or thing could have been made or done under Schedule 4 if it had then been in force –

(a)   it is to be treated as made or done under that Schedule, and

(b)   the powers of variation and discharge exercisable by the court apply accordingly.

(3) Any instrument registered under the 1985 Act is to be treated as having been registered by the Public Guardian under Schedule 4.

(4) This paragraph is without prejudice to section 16 of the Interpretation Act 1978 (c. 30) (general savings on repeal).

Pending proceedings

12 (1) An application for the exercise of a power under the 1985 Act which is pending immediately before the commencement day is to be treated, in so far as a corresponding power is exercisable under Schedule 4, as an application for the exercise of that power.

(2) For the purposes of sub-paragraph (1) –

(a) a pending application under section 4(2) of the 1985 Act for the registration of an instrument is to be treated as an application to the Public Guardian under paragraph 4 of Schedule 4 and any notice given in connection with that application under Schedule 1 to the 1985 Act is to be treated as given under Part 3 of Schedule 4,

(b) a notice of objection to the registration of an instrument is to be treated as a notice of objection under paragraph 13 of Schedule 4, and

(c) pending proceedings under section 5 of the 1985 Act are to be treated as proceedings on an application for the exercise by the court of a power which would become exercisable in relation to an instrument under paragraph 16(2) of Schedule 4 on its registration.

Appeals

13 (1) The 1985 Act and, so far as relevant, the provisions of Part 7 of the Mental Health Act and the rules made under it as applied by section 10 of the 1985 Act are to continue to have effect in relation to any appeal brought by virtue of section 10(1)(c) of the 1985 Act which has not been determined before the commencement day.

(2) If, in the case of an appeal brought by virtue of section 105(1) of the Mental Health Act as applied by section 10(1)(c) of the 1985 Act (appeal to nominated judge), the judge nominated under section 93 of the Mental Health Act has begun to hear the appeal, he is to continue to do so but otherwise the appeal is to be heard by a puisne judge of the High Court nominated under section 46.

Exercise of powers of donor as trustee

14 (1) Section 2(8) of the 1985 Act (which prevents a power of attorney under section 25 of the Trustee Act 1925 (c. 19) as enacted from being an enduring power) is to continue to apply to any enduring power –

(a) created before 1st March 2000, and

(b) having effect immediately before the commencement day.

(2) Section 3(3) of the 1985 Act (which entitles the donee of an enduring power to exercise the donor's powers as trustee) is to continue to apply to any enduring power to which, as a result of the provision mentioned in sub-paragraph (3), it applies immediately before the commencement day.

(3) The provision is section 4(3)(a) of the Trustee Delegation Act 1999 (c. 15) (which provides for section 3(3) of the 1985 Act to cease to apply to an enduring power when its registration is cancelled, if it was registered in response to an application made before 1st March 2001).

(4) Even though section 4 of the 1999 Act is repealed by this Act, that section is to continue to apply in relation to an enduring power –

    (a) to which section 3(3) of the 1985 Act applies as a result of sub-paragraph (2), or

    (b) to which, immediately before the repeal of section 4 of the 1999 Act, section 1 of that Act applies as a result of section 4 of it.

(5) The reference in section 1(9) of the 1999 Act to section 4(6) of that Act is to be read with sub-paragraphs (2) to (4).

Interpretation

15 In this Part of this Schedule, 'the commencement day' means the day on which section 66(1)(b) (repeal of the 1985 Act) comes into force.

SCHEDULE 6 MINOR AND CONSEQUENTIAL AMENDMENTS

Section 67(1)

Fines and Recoveries Act 1833 (c. 74)

1 (1) The Fines and Recoveries Act 1833 (c. 74) is amended as follows.

    (2) In section 33 (case where protector of settlement lacks capacity to act), for the words from 'shall be incapable' to 'is incapable as aforesaid' substitute 'lacks capacity (within the meaning of the Mental Capacity Act 2005) to manage his property and affairs, the Court of Protection is to take his place as protector of the settlement while he lacks capacity'.

    (3) In sections 48 and 49 (mental health jurisdiction), for each reference to the judge having jurisdiction under Part 7 of the Mental Health Act substitute a reference to the Court of Protection.

Improvement of Land Act 1864 (c. 114)

2 In section 68 of the Improvement of Land Act 1864 (c. 114) (apportionment of rentcharges) –

    (a) for ', curator, or receiver of' substitute 'or curator of, or a deputy with powers in relation to property and affairs appointed by the Court of Protection for,', and

    (b) for 'or patient within the meaning of Part VII of the Mental Health Act 1983' substitute 'person who lacks capacity (within the meaning of the Mental Capacity Act 2005) to receive the notice'.

Trustee Act 1925 (c. 19)

3 (1) The Trustee Act 1925 (c. 19) is amended as follows.

    (2) In section 36 (appointment of new trustee) –

        (a) in subsection (6C), for the words from 'a power of attorney' to the end, substitute 'an enduring power of attorney or lasting power of attorney registered under the Mental Capacity Act 2005', and

        (b) in subsection (9) –

            (i) for the words from 'is incapable' to 'exercising' substitute 'lacks capacity to exercise', and

(ii)   for the words from 'the authority' to the end substitute 'the Court of Protection'.

(3)   In section 41(1) (power of court to appoint new trustee) for the words from 'is incapable' to 'exercising' substitute 'lacks capacity to exercise'.

(4)   In section 54 (mental health jurisdiction) –

(a)   for subsection (1) substitute –

'(1)   Subject to subsection (2), the Court of Protection may not make an order, or give a direction or authority, in relation to a person who lacks capacity to exercise his functions as trustee, if the High Court may make an order to that effect under this Act.',

(b)   in subsection (2) –

(i)   for the words from the beginning to 'of a receiver' substitute 'Where a person lacks capacity to exercise his functions as a trustee and a deputy is appointed for him by the Court of Protection or an application for the appointment of a deputy',

(ii)   for 'the said authority', in each place, substitute 'the Court of Protection', and

(iii)   for 'the patient', in each place, substitute 'the person concerned', and

(c)   omit subsection (3).

(5)   In section 55 (order made on particular allegation to be conclusive evidence of it) –

(a)   for the words from 'Part VII' to 'Northern Ireland' substitute 'sections 15 to 20 of the Mental Capacity Act 2005 or any corresponding provisions having effect in Northern Ireland', and

(b)   for paragraph (a) substitute –

'(a)   that a trustee or mortgagee lacks capacity in relation to the matter in question;'.

(6)   In section 68 (definitions), at the end add –

'(3)   Any reference in this Act to a person who lacks capacity in relation to a matter is to a person –

(a)   who lacks capacity within the meaning of the Mental Capacity Act 2005 in relation to that matter, or

(b)   in respect of whom the powers conferred by section 48 of that Act are exercisable and have been exercised in relation to that matter.'.

Law of Property Act 1925 (c. 20)

4   (1)   The Law of Property Act 1925 (c. 20) is amended as follows.

(2)   In section 22 (conveyances on behalf of persons who lack capacity) –

(a)   in subsection (1) –

(i)   for the words from 'in a person suffering' to 'is acting' substitute ', either solely or jointly with any other person or persons, in a person lacking capacity (within the meaning of the Mental Capacity Act 2005) to convey or create a legal estate, a deputy appointed for him by the Court of Protection or (if no deputy is appointed', and

(ii)   for 'the authority having jurisdiction under Part VII of the Mental Health Act 1983' substitute 'the Court of Protection',

(b)   in subsection (2), for 'is incapable, by reason of mental disorder, of exercising' substitute 'lacks capacity (within the meaning of that Act) to exercise', and

(c)   in subsection (3), for the words from 'an enduring power' to the end substitute 'an enduring power of attorney or lasting power of attorney (within the meaning of the 2005 Act) is entitled to act for the trustee who lacks capacity in relation to the dealing.'.

(3) In section 205(1) (interpretation), omit paragraph (xiii).

Administration of Estates Act 1925 (c. 23)

5   (1) The Administration of Estates Act 1925 (c. 23) is amended as follows.

(2) In section 41(1) (powers of personal representatives to appropriate), in the proviso –

(a)   in paragraph (ii) –

(i)   for the words from 'is incapable' to 'the consent' substitute 'lacks capacity (within the meaning of the Mental Capacity Act 2005) to give the consent, it', and

(ii)   for 'or receiver' substitute 'or a person appointed as deputy for him by the Court of Protection', and

(b)   in paragraph (iv), for 'no receiver is acting for a person suffering from mental disorder' substitute 'no deputy is appointed for a person who lacks capacity to consent'.

(3) Omit section 55(1)(viii) (definitions of 'person of unsound mind' and 'defective').

National Assistance Act 1948 (c. 29)

6   In section 49 of the National Assistance Act 1948 (c. 29) (expenses of council officers acting for persons who lack capacity) –

(a)   for the words from 'applies' to 'affairs of a patient' substitute 'applies for appointment by the Court of Protection as a deputy', and

(b)   for 'such functions' substitute 'his functions as deputy'.

U.S.A. Veterans' Pensions (Administration) Act 1949 (c. 45)

7   In section 1 of the U.S.A. Veterans' Pensions (Administration) Act 1949 (c. 45) (administration of pensions) –

(a)   in subsection (4), omit the words from 'or for whom' to '1983', and

(b)   after subsection (4), insert –

'(4A) An agreement under subsection (1) is not to be made in relation to a person who lacks capacity (within the meaning of the Mental Capacity Act 2005) for the purposes of this Act if –

(a)   there is a donee of an enduring power of attorney or lasting power of attorney (within the meaning of the 2005 Act), or a deputy appointed for the person by the Court of Protection, and

(b)   the donee or deputy has power in relation to the person for the purposes of this Act.

(4B) The proviso at the end of subsection (4) also applies in relation to subsection (4A).'.

Intestates' Estates Act 1952 (c. 64)

8   In Schedule 2 to the Intestates' Estates Act 1952 (c. 64) (rights of surviving spouse or civil partner in relation to home), for paragraph 6(1) substitute –

'(1)   Where the surviving spouse or civil partner lacks capacity (within the meaning of the Mental Capacity Act 2005) to make a requirement or give a consent under this Schedule, the requirement or consent may be made or given by a deputy appointed by the Court of Protection with power in that respect or, if no deputy has that power, by that court.'.

Variation of Trusts Act 1958 (c. 53)

9   In section 1 of the Variation of Trusts Act 1958 (c. 53) (jurisdiction of courts to vary trusts) –

(a)   in subsection (3), for the words from 'shall be determined' to the end substitute 'who lacks capacity (within the meaning of the Mental Capacity Act 2005) to give his assent is to be determined by the Court of Protection', and

(b)   in subsection (6), for the words from 'the powers' to the end substitute 'the powers of the Court of Protection'.

Administration of Justice Act 1960 (c. 65)

10   In section 12(1)(b) of the Administration of Justice Act 1960 (c. 65) (contempt of court to publish information about proceedings in private relating to persons with incapacity) for the words from 'under Part VIII' to 'that Act' substitute 'under the Mental Capacity Act 2005, or under any provision of the Mental Health Act 1983'.

Industrial and Provident Societies Act 1965 (c. 12)

11   In section 26 of the Industrial and Provident Societies Act 1965 (c. 12) (payments for mentally incapable people), for subsection (2) substitute –

'(2)   Subsection (1) does not apply where the member or person concerned lacks capacity (within the meaning of the Mental Capacity Act 2005) for the purposes of this Act and –

(a)   there is a donee of an enduring power of attorney or lasting power of attorney (within the meaning of the 2005 Act), or a deputy appointed for the member or person by the Court of Protection, and

(b)   the donee or deputy has power in relation to the member or person for the purposes of this Act.'.

Compulsory Purchase Act 1965 (c. 56)

12   In Schedule 1 to the Compulsory Purchase Act 1965 (c. 56) (persons without power to sell their interests), for paragraph 1(2)(b) substitute –

'(b)   do not have effect in relation to a person who lacks capacity (within the meaning of the Mental Capacity Act 2005) for the purposes of this Act if –

(i)   there is a donee of an enduring power of attorney or lasting power of attorney (within the meaning of the 2005 Act), or a deputy appointed for the person by the Court of Protection, and

(ii)   the donee or deputy has power in relation to the person for the purposes of this Act.'.

Leasehold Reform Act 1967 (c. 88)

13 (1) For section 26(2) of the Leasehold Reform Act 1967 (c. 88) (landlord lacking capacity) substitute –

'(2) Where a landlord lacks capacity (within the meaning of the Mental Capacity Act 2005) to exercise his functions as a landlord, those functions are to be exercised –

(a) by a donee of an enduring power of attorney or lasting power of attorney (within the meaning of the 2005 Act), or a deputy appointed for him by the Court of Protection, with power to exercise those functions, or

(b) if no donee or deputy has that power, by a person authorised in that respect by that court.'.

(2) That amendment does not affect any proceedings pending at the commencement of this paragraph in which a receiver or a person authorised under Part 7 of the Mental Health Act is acting on behalf of the landlord.

Medicines Act 1968 (c. 67)

14 In section 72 of the Medicines Act 1968 (c. 67) (pharmacist lacking capacity) –

(a) in subsection (1)(c), for the words from 'a receiver' to '1959' substitute 'he becomes a person who lacks capacity (within the meaning of the Mental Capacity Act 2005) to carry on the business',

(b) after subsection (1) insert –

'(1A) In subsection (1)(c), the reference to a person who lacks capacity to carry on the business is to a person –

(a) in respect of whom there is a donee of an enduring power of attorney or lasting power of attorney (within the meaning of the Mental Capacity Act 2005), or

(b) for whom a deputy is appointed by the Court of Protection,

and in relation to whom the donee or deputy has power for the purposes of this Act.',

(c) in subsection (3)(d) –

(i) for 'receiver' substitute 'deputy', and

(ii) after 'guardian' insert 'or from the date of registration of the instrument appointing the donee', and

(d) in subsection (4)(c), for 'receiver' substitute 'donee, deputy'.

Family Law Reform Act 1969 (c. 46)

15 For section 21(4) of the Family Law Reform Act 1969 (c. 46) (consent required for taking of bodily sample from person lacking capacity), substitute –

'(4) A bodily sample may be taken from a person who lacks capacity (within the meaning of the Mental Capacity Act 2005) to give his consent, if consent is given by the court giving the direction under section 20 or by –

(a) a donee of an enduring power of attorney or lasting power of attorney (within the meaning of that Act), or

(b) a deputy appointed, or any other person authorised, by the Court of Protection,

with power in that respect.'.

Local Authority Social Services Act 1970 (c. 42)

16   (1)   Schedule 1 to the Local Authority Social Services Act 1970 (c. 42) (enactments conferring functions assigned to social services committee) is amended as follows.

(2)   In the entry for section 49 of the National Assistance Act 1948 (expenses of local authority officer appointed for person who lacks capacity) for 'receiver' substitute 'deputy'.

(3)   At the end, insert –

'Mental Capacity Act 2005	
Section 39	Instructing independent mental capacity advocate before providing accommodation for person lacking capacity.
Section 49	Reports in proceedings.'.

Courts Act 1971 (c. 23)

17   In Part 1A of Schedule 2 to the Courts Act 1971 (c. 23) (office-holders eligible for appointment as circuit judges), omit the reference to a Master of the Court of Protection.

Local Government Act 1972 (c. 70)

18   (1)   Omit section 118 of the Local Government Act 1972 (c. 70) (payment of pension etc. where recipient lacks capacity).

(2)   Sub-paragraph (3) applies where, before the commencement of this paragraph, a local authority has, in respect of a person referred to in that section as 'the patient', made payments under that section –

(a)   to an institution or person having the care of the patient, or
(b)   in accordance with subsection (1)(a) or (b) of that section.

(3)   The local authority may, in respect of the patient, continue to make payments under that section to that institution or person, or in accordance with subsection (1)(a) or (b) of that section, despite the repeal made by sub-paragraph (1).

Matrimonial Causes Act 1973 (c. 18)

19   In section 40 of the Matrimonial Causes Act 1973 (c. 18) (payments to person who lacks capacity) (which becomes subsection (1)) –

(a)   for the words from 'is incapable' to 'affairs' substitute '('P') lacks capacity (within the meaning of the Mental Capacity Act 2005) in relation to the provisions of the order',
(b)   for 'that person under Part VIII of that Act' substitute 'P under that Act',
(c)   for the words from 'such persons' to the end substitute 'such person ('D') as it may direct', and
(d)   at the end insert –

(2)   In carrying out any functions of his in relation to an order made under subsection (1), D must act in P's best interests (within the meaning of that Act).'.

Juries Act 1974 (c. 23)

20   In Schedule 1 to the Juries Act 1974 (c. 23) (disqualification for jury service), for paragraph 3 substitute –

'3   A person who lacks capacity, within the meaning of the Mental Capacity Act 2005, to serve as a juror.'.

Consumer Credit Act 1974 (c. 39)

21   For section 37(1)(c) of the Consumer Credit Act 1974 (c. 39) (termination of consumer credit licence if holder lacks capacity) substitute –

'(c)   becomes a person who lacks capacity (within the meaning of the Mental Capacity Act 2005) to carry on the activities covered by the licence.'.

Solicitors Act 1974 (c. 47)

22   (1)   The Solicitors Act 1974 (c. 47) is amended as follows.

(2)   For section 12(1)(j) (application for practising certificate by solicitor lacking capacity) substitute –

'(j)   while he lacks capacity (within the meaning of the Mental Capacity Act 2005) to act as a solicitor and powers under sections 15 to 20 or section 48 of that Act are exercisable in relation to him;'.

(3)   In section 62(4) (contentious business agreements made by clients) for paragraphs (c) and (d) substitute –

'(c)   as a deputy for him appointed by the Court of Protection with powers in relation to his property and affairs, or

(d)   as another person authorised under that Act to act on his behalf.'.

(4)   In paragraph 1(1) of Schedule 1 (circumstances in which Law Society may intervene in solicitor's practice), for paragraph (f) substitute –

'(f)   a solicitor lacks capacity (within the meaning of the Mental Capacity Act 2005) to act as a solicitor and powers under sections 15 to 20 or section 48 of that Act are exercisable in relation to him;'.

Local Government (Miscellaneous Provisions) Act 1976 (c. 57)

23   In section 31 of the Local Government (Miscellaneous Provisions) Act 1976 (c. 57) (the title to which becomes 'Indemnities for local authority officers appointed as deputies or administrators'), for the words from 'as a receiver' to '1959' substitute 'as a deputy for a person by the Court of Protection'.

Sale of Goods Act 1979 (c. 54)

24   In section 3(2) of the Sale of Goods Act 1979 (c. 54) (capacity to buy and sell) the words 'mental incapacity or' cease to have effect in England and Wales.

Limitation Act 1980 (c. 58)

25   In section 38 of the Limitation Act 1980 (c. 58) (interpretation) substitute –

(a)   in subsection (2) for 'of unsound mind' substitute 'lacks capacity (within

the meaning of the Mental Capacity Act 2005) to conduct legal proceedings',
and

(b)   omit subsections (3) and (4).

Public Passenger Vehicles Act 1981 (c. 14)

26   In section 57(2)(c) of the Public Passenger Vehicles Act 1981 (c. 14) (termination of
public service vehicle licence if holder lacks capacity) for the words from 'becomes a
patient' to 'or' substitute 'becomes a person who lacks capacity (within the meaning
of the Mental Capacity Act 2005) to use a vehicle under the licence, or'.

Judicial Pensions Act 1981 (c. 20)

27   In Schedule 1 to the Judicial Pensions Act 1981 (c. 20) (pensions of Supreme Court
officers, etc.), in paragraph 1, omit the reference to a Master of the Court of
Protection except in the case of a person holding that office immediately before the
commencement of this paragraph or who had previously retired from that office or
died.

Supreme Court Act 1981 (c. 54)

28   In Schedule 2 to the Supreme Court Act 1981 (c. 54) (qualifications for appointment
to office in Supreme Court), omit paragraph 11 (Master of the Court of Protection).

Mental Health Act 1983 (c. 20)

29   (1)   The Mental Health Act is amended as follows.

(2)   In section 134(3) (cases where correspondence of detained patients may not be
withheld) for paragraph (b) substitute –

'(b)   any judge or officer of the Court of Protection, any of the Court of
Protection Visitors or any person asked by that Court for a report under
section 49 of the Mental Capacity Act 2005 concerning the patient;'.

(3)   In section 139 (protection for acts done in pursuance of 1983 Act), in subsection
(1), omit from 'or in, or in pursuance' to 'Part VII of this Act,'.

(4)   Section 142 (payment of pension etc. where recipient lacks capacity) ceases to
have effect in England and Wales.

(5)   Sub-paragraph (6) applies where, before the commencement of sub-paragraph
(4), an authority has, in respect of a person referred to in that section as 'the
patient', made payments under that section –

(a)   to an institution or person having the care of the patient, or

(b)   in accordance with subsection (2)(a) or (b) of that section.

(6)   The authority may, in respect of the patient, continue to make payments under
that section to that institution or person, or in accordance with subsection (2)(a)
or (b) of that section, despite the amendment made by sub-paragraph (4).

(7)   In section 145(1) (interpretation), in the definition of 'patient', omit '(except in
Part VII of this Act)'.

(8)   In section 146 (provisions having effect in Scotland), omit from '104(4)' to
'section),'.

(9)   In section 147 (provisions having effect in Northern Ireland), omit from '104(4)'
to 'section),'.

Administration of Justice Act 1985 (c. 61)

30   In section 18(3) of the Administration of Justice Act 1985 (c. 61) (licensed conveyancer who lacks capacity), for the words from 'that person' to the end substitute
'he becomes a person who lacks capacity (within the meaning of the Mental Capacity
Act 2005) to practise as a licensed conveyancer.'.

Insolvency Act 1986 (c. 45)

31   (1) The Insolvency Act 1986 (c. 45) is amended as follows.
       (2) In section 389A (people not authorised to act as nominee or supervisor in
            voluntary arrangement), in subsection (3) –

       (a) omit the 'or' immediately after paragraph (b),
       (b) in paragraph (c), omit 'Part VII of the Mental Health Act 1983 or', and
       (c) after that paragraph, insert ', or

            (d) he lacks capacity (within the meaning of the Mental Capacity Act
                 2005) to act as nominee or supervisor'.

       (3) In section 390 (people not qualified to be insolvency practitioners), in subsection
            (4) –

       (a) omit the 'or' immediately after paragraph (b),
       (b) in paragraph (c), omit 'Part VII of the Mental Health Act 1983 or', and
       (c) after that paragraph, insert ', or

            (d) he lacks capacity (within the meaning of the Mental Capacity Act
                 2005) to act as an insolvency practitioner.'.

Building Societies Act 1986 (c. 53)

32   In section 102D(9) of the Building Societies Act 1986 (c. 53) (references to a person
holding an account on trust for another) –

       (a) in paragraph (a), for 'Part VII of the Mental Health Act 1983' substitute 'the
            Mental Capacity Act 2005', and
       (b) for paragraph (b) substitute –

            '(b) to an attorney holding an account for another person under –

                  (i)   an enduring power of attorney or lasting power of attorney
                        registered under the Mental Capacity Act 2005, or
                  (ii) an enduring power registered under the Enduring Powers of
                        Attorney (Northern Ireland) Order 1987;'.

Public Trustee and Administration of Funds Act 1986 (c. 57)

33   In section 3 of the Public Trustee and Administration of Funds Act 1986 (c. 57)
(functions of the Public Trustee) –

       (a) for subsections (1) to (5) substitute –

            '(1) The Public Trustee may exercise the functions of a deputy appointed
                  by the Court of Protection.',

       (b) in subsection (6), for 'the 1906 Act' substitute 'the Public Trustee Act 1906',
            and
       (c) omit subsection (7).

Patronage (Benefices) Measure 1986 (No.3)

34 (1) The Patronage (Benefices) Measure 1986 (No. 3) is amended as follows.

    (2) In section 5 (rights of patronage exercisable otherwise than by registered patron), after subsection (3) insert –

      (3A) The reference in subsection (3) to a power of attorney does not include an enduring power of attorney or lasting power of attorney (within the meaning of the Mental Capacity Act 2005).'

    (3) In section 9 (information to be sent to designated officer when benefice becomes vacant), after subsection (5) insert –

      '(5A) Subsections (5B) and (5C) apply where the functions of a registered patron are, as a result of paragraph 10 of Schedule 2 to the Mental Capacity Act 2005 (patron's loss of capacity to discharge functions), to be discharged by an individual appointed by the Court of Protection.

      (5B) If the individual is a clerk in Holy Orders, subsection (5) applies to him as it applies to the registered patron.

      (5C) If the individual is not a clerk in Holy Orders, subsection (1) (other than paragraph (b)) applies to him as it applies to the registered patron.'

Courts and Legal Services Act 1990 (c. 41)

35 (1) The Courts and Legal Services Act 1990 (c. 41) is amended as follows.

    (2) In Schedule 11 (judges etc. barred from legal practice), for the reference to a Master of the Court of Protection substitute a reference to each of the following –

      (a) Senior Judge of the Court of Protection,

      (b) President of the Court of Protection,

      (c) Vice-President of the Court of Protection.

    (3) In paragraph 5(3) of Schedule 14 (exercise of powers of intervention in registered foreign lawyer's practice), for paragraph (f) substitute –

      '(f) he lacks capacity (within the meaning of the Mental Capacity Act 2005) to act as a registered foreign lawyer and powers under sections 15 to 20 or section 48 are exercisable in relation to him;'.

Child Support Act 1991 (c. 48)

36 In section 50 of the Child Support Act 1991 (c. 48) (unauthorised disclosure of information) –

    (a) in subsection (8) –

      (i) immediately after paragraph (a), insert 'or',

      (ii) omit paragraphs (b) and (d) and the 'or' immediately after paragraph (c), and

      (iii) for ', receiver, custodian or appointee' substitute 'or custodian', and

    (b) after that subsection, insert –

      (9) Where the person to whom the information relates lacks capacity (within the meaning of the Mental Capacity Act 2005) to consent to its disclosure, the appropriate person is –

      (a) a donee of an enduring power of attorney or lasting power of attorney (within the meaning of that Act), or

      (b) a deputy appointed for him, or any other person authorised, by the Court of Protection,

      with power in that respect.'.

Social Security Administration Act 1992 (c. 5)

37   In section 123 of the Social Security Administration Act 1992 (c. 5) (unauthorised disclosure of information) –

(a)   in subsection (10), omit –

(i)   in paragraph (b), 'a receiver appointed under section 99 of the Mental Health Act 1983 or',

(ii)   in paragraph (d)(i), 'sub-paragraph (a) of rule 41(1) of the Court of Protection Rules 1984 or',

(iii)   in paragraph (d)(ii), 'a receiver ad interim appointed under sub-paragraph (b) of the said rule 41(1) or', and

(iv)   'receiver,', and

(b)   after that subsection, insert –

'(11) Where the person to whom the information relates lacks capacity (within the meaning of the Mental Capacity Act 2005) to consent to its disclosure, the appropriate person is –

(a)   a donee of an enduring power of attorney or lasting power of attorney (within the meaning of that Act), or

(b)   a deputy appointed for him, or any other person authorised, by the Court of Protection,

with power in that respect.'.

Judicial Pensions and Retirement Act 1993 (c. 8)

38   (1)   The Judicial Pensions and Retirement Act 1993 (c. 8) is amended as follows.

(2)   In Schedule 1 (qualifying judicial offices), in Part 2, under the cross-heading 'Court officers', omit the reference to a Master of the Court of Protection except in the case of a person holding that office immediately before the commencement of this sub-paragraph or who had previously retired from that office or died.

(3)   In Schedule 5 (retirement: the relevant offices), omit the entries relating to the Master and Deputy or temporary Master of the Court of Protection, except in the case of a person holding any of those offices immediately before the commencement of this sub-paragraph.

(4)   In Schedule 7 (retirement: transitional provisions), omit paragraph 5(5)(i)(g) except in the case of a person holding office as a deputy or temporary Master of the Court of Protection immediately before the commencement of this sub-paragraph.

Leasehold Reform, Housing and Urban Development Act 1993 (c. 28)

39   (1)   For paragraph 4 of Schedule 2 to the Leasehold Reform, Housing and Urban Development Act 1993 (c. 28) (landlord under a disability), substitute –

'4   (1)   This paragraph applies where a Chapter I or Chapter II landlord lacks capacity (within the meaning of the Mental Capacity Act 2005) to exercise his functions as a landlord.

(2)   For the purposes of the Chapter concerned, the landlord's place is to be taken –

(a)   by a donee of an enduring power of attorney or lasting power of attorney (within the meaning of the 2005 Act), or a deputy appointed for him by the Court of Protection, with power to exercise those functions, or

(b)   if no deputy or donee has that power, by a person authorised in that respect by that court.'.

(2)   That amendment does not affect any proceedings pending at the commencement of this paragraph in which a receiver or a person authorised under Part 7 of the Mental Health Act 1983 (c. 20) is acting on behalf of the landlord.

Goods Vehicles (Licensing of Operators) Act 1995 (c. 23)

40   (1)   The Goods Vehicles (Licensing of Operators) Act 1995 (c. 23) is amended as follows.

(2)   In section 16(5) (termination of licence), for 'he becomes a patient within the meaning of Part VII of the Mental Health Act 1983' substitute 'he becomes a person who lacks capacity (within the meaning of the Mental Capacity Act 2005) to use a vehicle under the licence'.

(3)   In section 48 (licence not to be transferable, etc.) –

(a)   in subsection (2) –

(i)   for 'or become a patient within the meaning of Part VII of the Mental Health Act 1983' substitute ', or become a person who lacks capacity (within the meaning of the Mental Capacity Act 2005) to use a vehicle under the licence,', and

(ii)   in paragraph (a), for 'became a patient' substitute 'became a person who lacked capacity in that respect', and

(b)   in subsection (5), for 'a patient within the meaning of Part VII of the Mental Health Act 1983' substitute 'a person lacking capacity'.

Disability Discrimination Act 1995 (c. 50)

41   In section 20(7) of the Disability Discrimination Act 1995 (c. 50) (regulations to disapply provisions about incapacity), in paragraph (b), for 'Part VII of the Mental Health Act 1983' substitute 'the Mental Capacity Act 2005'.

Trusts of Land and Appointment of Trustees Act 1996 (c. 47)

42   (1)   The Trusts of Land and Appointment of Trustees Act 1996 (c. 47) is amended as follows.

(2)   In section 9 (delegation by trustees), in subsection (6), for the words from 'an enduring power' to the end substitute 'an enduring power of attorney or lasting power of attorney within the meaning of the Mental Capacity Act 2005'.

(3)   In section 20 (the title to which becomes 'Appointment of substitute for trustee who lacks capacity') –

(a)   in subsection (1)(a), for 'is incapable by reason of mental disorder of exercising' substitute 'lacks capacity (within the meaning of the Mental Capacity Act 2005) to exercise', and

(b)   in subsection (2) –

(i)   for paragraph (a) substitute –

'(a)   a deputy appointed for the trustee by the Court of Protection,',

(ii)   in paragraph (b), for the words from 'a power of attorney' to the end substitute 'an enduring power of attorney or lasting power of attorney registered under the Mental Capacity Act 2005', and

(iii)   in paragraph (c), for the words from 'the authority' to the end substitute 'the Court of Protection'.

Human Rights Act 1998 (c. 42)

43 In section 4(5) of the Human Rights Act 1998 (c. 42) (courts which may make declarations of incompatibility), after paragraph (e) insert –

'(f) the Court of Protection, in any matter being dealt with by the President of the Family Division, the Vice-Chancellor or a puisne judge of the High Court.'

Access to Justice Act 1999 (c. 22)

44 In paragraph 1 of Schedule 2 to the Access to Justice Act 1999 (c. 22) (services excluded from the Community Legal Service), after paragraph (e) insert –

'(ea) the creation of lasting powers of attorney under the Mental Capacity Act 2005,

(eb) the making of advance decisions under that Act,'.

Adoption and Children Act 2002 (c. 38)

45 In section 52(1)(a) of the Adoption and Children Act 2002 (c. 38) (parental consent to adoption), for 'is incapable of giving consent' substitute 'lacks capacity (within the meaning of the Mental Capacity Act 2005) to give consent'.

Licensing Act 2003 (c. 17)

46 (1) The Licensing Act 2003 (c.17) is amended as follows.

(2) In section 27(1) (lapse of premises licence), for paragraph (b) substitute –

'(b) becomes a person who lacks capacity (within the meaning of the Mental Capacity Act 2005) to hold the licence,'.

(3) In section 47 (interim authority notice in relation to premises licence) –

(a) in subsection (5), for paragraph (b) substitute –

'(b) the former holder lacks capacity (within the meaning of the Mental Capacity Act 2005) to hold the licence and that person acts for him under an enduring power of attorney or lasting power of attorney registered under that Act,', and

(b) in subsection (10), omit the definition of 'mentally incapable'.

Courts Act 2003 (c. 39)

47 (1) The Courts Act 2003 (c. 39) is amended as follows.

(2) In section 1(1) (the courts in relation to which the Lord Chancellor must discharge his general duty), after paragraph (a) insert –

'(aa) the Court of Protection,'.

(3) In section 64(2) (judicial titles which the Lord Chancellor may by order alter) –

(a) omit the reference to a Master of the Court of Protection, and

(b) at the appropriate place insert a reference to each of the following –

(i) Senior Judge of the Court of Protection,

(ii) President of the Court of Protection,

(iii) Vice-president of the Court of Protection.

SCHEDULE 7   REPEALS

Section 67(2)

Short title and chapter	Extent of repeal
Trustee Act 1925 (c. 19)	Section 54(3).
Law of Property Act 1925 (c. 20)	Section 205(1)(xiii).
Administration of Estates Act 1925 (c. 23)	Section 55(1)(viii)
U.S.A. Veterans' Pensions (Administration) Act 1949 (c. 45)	In section 1(4), the words from 'or for whom' to '1983'.
Mental Health Act 1959 (c. 72)	In Schedule 7, in Part 1, the entries relating to– section 33 of the Fines and Recoveries Act 1833, section 68 of the Improvement of Land Act 1864, section 55 of the Trustee Act 1925, section 205(1) of the Law of Property Act 1925, section 49 of the National Assistance Act 1948, and section 1 of the Variation of Trusts Act 1958.
Courts Act 1971 (c. 23)	In Schedule 2, in Part 1A, the words 'Master of the Court of Protection'.
Local Government Act 1972 (c. 70)	Section 118.
Limitation Act 1980 (c. 58)	Section 38(3) and (4).
Supreme Court Act 1981 (c. 54)	In Schedule 2, in Part 2, paragraph 11.
Mental Health Act 1983 (c. 20)	Part 7. In section 139(1) the words from 'or in, or in pursuance' to 'Part VII of this Act,'. In section 145(1), in the definition of 'patient' the words '(except in Part VII of this Act)'. In sections 146 and 147 the words from '104(4)' to 'section),'. Schedule 3. In Schedule 4, paragraphs 1, 2, 4, 5, 7, 9, 14, 20, 22, 25, 32, 38, 55 and 56. In Schedule 5, paragraphs 26, 43, 44 and 45.
Enduring Powers of Attorney Act 1985 (c. 29)	The whole Act.
Insolvency Act 1986 (c. 45)	In section 389A(3)– the 'or' immediately after paragraph (b), and in paragraph (c), the words 'Part VII of the Mental Health Act 1983 or'. In section 390(4)– the 'or' immediately after paragraph (b), and in paragraph (c), the words 'Part VII of the Mental Health Act 1983 or'.
Public Trustee and Administration of Funds Act 1986 (c. 57)	Section 2. Section 3(7).
Child Support Act 1991 (c. 48)	In section 50(8)– paragraphs (b) and (d), and the 'or' immediately after paragraph (c).

Short title and chapter	Extent of repeal
Social Security Administration Act 1992 (c. 5)	In section 123(10)– in paragraph (b), 'a receiver appointed under section 99 of the Mental Health Act 1983 or', in paragraph (d)(i), 'sub-paragraph (a) of rule 41(1) of the Court of Protection Rules Act 1984 or', in paragraph (d)(ii), 'a receiver ad interim appointed under sub-paragraph (b) of the said rule 41(1) or', and 'receiver,'.
Trustee Delegation Act 1999 (c. 15)	Section 4. Section 6. In section 7(3), the words 'in accordance with section 4 above'.
Care Standards Act 2000 (c. 14)	In Schedule 4, paragraph 8.
Licensing Act 2003 (c. 17)	In section 47(10), the definition of 'mentally incapable'.
Courts Act 2003 (c. 64)	In section 64(2), the words 'Master of the Court of Protection'.

Appendix 2
EXPLANATORY NOTES TO THE MENTAL CAPACITY ACT 2005

These notes refer to the Mental Capacity Act 2005 (c.9)
which received Royal Assent on 7 April 2005

EXPLANATORY NOTES

INTRODUCTION

1. These explanatory notes relate to the Mental Capacity Act 2005 which received Royal Assent on 7 April 2005. They have been prepared by the Department for Constitutional Affairs and the Department of Health in order to assist the reader in understanding the Act. They do not form part of the Act and have not been endorsed by Parliament.

2. The notes need to be read in conjunction with the Act. They are not, and are not meant to be, a comprehensive description of the Act. So where a provision or part of a provision does not seem to require any explanation or comment, none is given.

SUMMARY AND BACKGROUND

3. The Act has its basis in the Law Commission Report No.231 on Mental Incapacity, which was published in February 1995 after extensive consultation. The Government consulted further and published a Policy Statement, *Making Decisions,* in October 1999, setting out proposals to reform the law in order to improve and clarify the decision-making process for people unable to make decisions for themselves. On 27 June 2003 the Government published a draft Mental Incapacity Bill and accompanying notes (Cm 5859–I & II) which was subject to pre-legislative scrutiny by a Joint Committee of both Houses. The Joint Committee published their report on 28 November 2003 (HL Paper 189-I & HC 1083-I). The Government's response to the Joint Committee report was presented to Parliament in February 2004 (Cm 6121). The renamed Mental Capacity Bill was introduced in Parliament on 17 June 2004 and received Royal Assent on 7 April 2005, having been carried over from the previous session.

4. The Act aims to clarify a number of legal uncertainties and to reform and update the current law where decisions need to be made on behalf of others. The Act will govern decision-making on behalf of adults, both where they lose mental capacity at some point in their lives, for example as a result of dementia or brain injury, and where the incapacitating condition has been present since birth. It covers a wide range of decisions, on personal welfare as well as financial matters and substitute decision-making by attorneys or court-appointed 'deputies', and clarifies the position where no such formal process has been adopted. The Act includes new rules to

govern research involving people who lack capacity and provides for new independent mental capacity advocates to represent and provide support to such people in relation to certain decisions. The Act provides recourse, where necessary, and at the appropriate level, to a court with power to deal with all personal welfare (including health care) and financial decisions on behalf of adults lacking capacity.

5.   The Act replaces Part 7 of the Mental Health Act 1983 and the whole of the Enduring Powers of Attorney Act 1985. A new Court of Protection with more comprehensive powers will replace the current Court of Protection, which is an office of the Supreme Court.

The Act

6.   The Act is divided into 3 parts.

Part 1: Persons who lack capacity

7.   Part 1 contains provisions defining 'persons who lack capacity'. It contains a set of key principles and sets out a checklist to be used in ascertaining a person's best interests. It deals with liability for actions in connection with the care or treatment of a person who lacks capacity to consent to what is done. Part 1 also establishes a new statutory scheme for 'lasting' powers of attorney which may extend to personal welfare (including health care) matters. It sets out the jurisdiction of the new Court of Protection to make declarations and orders and to appoint substitute decision-makers ('deputies'), where a person lacks capacity. This Part also sets out rules about advance decisions to refuse medical treatment and creates new safeguards controlling many types of research involving people who lack capacity. It establishes a system for providing independent mental capacity advocates for particularly vulnerable people. It also provides for codes of practice to give guidance about the legislation and creates a new offence of neglect or ill-treatment.

Part 2: The Court of Protection and the Public Guardian

8.   Part 2 establishes a new superior court of record, to be known as the Court of Protection, and provides for its judges and procedures. It also establishes a new statutory official, the Public Guardian, to support the work of the court. Provision is also made for Court of Protection Visitors.

Part 3: Miscellaneous and General

9.   Part 3 deals with private international law and transitional and other technical provisions and includes a declaratory provision that nothing in the Act is to be taken to affect the law relating to unlawful killing or assisting suicide. ECHR issues arise in relation to a number of provisions.

COMPATIBILITY WITH ECHR

10.   The Act meets the state's positive obligation under Article 8 of the European Convention on Human Rights ('ECHR') to ensure respect for private life. ECHR issues arise in relation to a number of provisions.

11.   Article 8 issues in relation to private life are engaged in connection with *sections 5, 6, 9* and *11* and could also be engaged as a result of *section 20* and a court order made under *section 16(2)*. Any interference pursues the legitimate aim of protecting the health and wellbeing of the person lacking capacity and ensures that those who care for and treat persons who lack capacity are protected from certain liabilities where appropriate. The principles in *section 1*, the criteria for lack of capacity (*section 2*), the checklist as to best interests (*section 4*) and the safeguards within the sections themselves create a framework within which any interference will be

proportionate to this legitimate aim. Article 8 rights may also be engaged by *section 49(7)* to *(9)*, which allows the court to direct a medical examination or interview of the person concerned and the examination of his health and social services records: the court is bound by the principles in *section 1* and the best interests checklist. *Sections 35(6)*, *58(5)* and *(6)* and *61(5)* and *(6)* also make provision whereby particular persons may interview the person concerned and examine relevant records. Again, any interference is justified as being for the protection of that person's own health and welfare and proportionate to that aim. The powers are given to the relevant officials for the purpose of enabling them to carry out their functions, which are directed to the protection of the interests of the person who lacks capacity.

12.   Rights under Article 1 of the First Protocol may be engaged in connection with *sections 7 to 9* and *12* which provide for the control of a person's property and affairs and payment on his behalf for necessary goods and services. The statutory rules are intended to be clear and precise and are designed to strike a fair balance between the property interests of the person lacking capacity, his own wider welfare interests and the interests of others (persons supplying necessary goods and services to the person lacking capacity, anyone bearing the cost and, in the case of *section 12*, persons related to or connected with him).

13.   *Sections 10(2)* and *13(8)* and *(9)* prevent a bankrupt from acting as a donee of a lasting power of attorney (an 'LPA') where the power covers property and affairs and suspend that power where there is an interim bankruptcy restrictions order. Interim bankruptcy restrictions orders will not bring an LPA to an end; but the appointment and power would be suspended (as far as it concerns the donor's property and affairs) so long as the order has effect. Bankruptcy restrictions orders are provided for in Schedule 4A to the Insolvency Act 1986. Article 8 and Article 14 rights may be engaged but any difference of treatment has the legitimate aim of protecting an incapacitated donor from the possibility of financial abuse and is proportionate to that end.

14.   A donee of an LPA can be given power to refuse to give consent to life-sustaining treatment on behalf of the donor (see *section 11(7)* and *(8)*). The donor's Article 2 and Article 3 rights could be engaged. A person can also make an advance decision to refuse treatment, including life-sustaining treatment. *Section 25(5)* provides that an advance decision will not apply to any treatment necessary to sustain life unless the advance decision is in writing and is signed and the signature is witnessed. Further, there must be a statement that the decision stands even if life is at risk (and this statement must also be in writing and be signed and the signature must be witnessed). *Sections 6(7)* and *26(5)* provide that action can be taken to preserve life or prevent serious deterioration while the court resolves any dispute or difficulty. These provisions are designed to protect a person's Article 2 and 3 rights, while also discharging the obligation to respect the Article 8 rights of those who choose to give powers to a donee under an LPA or to make an advance decision.

15.   *Sections 35 to 39* may engage Article 14 rights in connection with Article 8 by providing for an independent mental capacity advocate to represent and support people who lack capacity where they are being treated and cared for by the NHS or a local authority and there is no one who could be consulted about that treatment or care. Any relevant difference in treatment which there might be would have the legitimate aim of protecting the Article 8 rights of incapacitated persons.

16.   The comprehensive jurisdiction of the new Court of Protection (*sections 15 to 21* and *45 to 56*) ensures protection for any rights engaged in connection with the provisions of the Act. The Government is satisfied that *sections 50* (certain applicants to obtain permission to apply), *51(2)(d)* (exercise of jurisdiction by officers or staff) and *54* (court fees) do not breach Article 6 rights.

TERRITORIAL EXTENT

17.   The Act extends only to England and Wales. Two exceptions are set out in *section 68(5)* and concern evidence of instruments and registration of LPAs. The amendments and repeals made by *Schedules 6* and *7* will have the same extent as the enactments concerned.

18.   Similar legislation has already been passed in Scotland in the form of the Adults with Incapacity (Scotland) Act 2000.

TERRITORIAL APPLICATION: WALES

19.   The National Assembly for Wales may make regulations under *section 30* (research) and *section 34* (loss of capacity during research project) and issue guidance under *section 32(3)*. It may also make regulations under *section 35* (appointment of independent mental capacity advocates), *section 36* (functions of independent mental capacity advocates), *section 37* (provision of serious medical treatment by NHS body) and *41* (power to adjust role of independent mental capacity advocate). *Section 68(2)* provides that sections *30* to *41* will come into force by order made by the National Assembly. *Section 43(1)* provides that the National Assembly must be consulted by the Lord Chancellor before a code of practice is prepared or revised.

COMMENTARY ON SECTIONS

PART 1: PERSONS WHO LACK CAPACITY

The principles

Section 1: The principles

20.   This sets out key principles applying to decisions and actions taken under the Act. The starting point is a presumption of capacity. A person must be assumed to have capacity until it is proved otherwise. A person must also be supported to make his own decision, as far it is practicable to do so. The Act requires 'all practicable steps' to be taken to help the person. This could include, for example, making sure that the person is in an environment in which he is comfortable or involving an expert in helping him express his views. It is expressly provided that a person is not to be treated as lacking capacity to make a decision simply because he makes an unwise decision. This means that a person who has the necessary ability to make the decision has the right to make irrational or eccentric decisions that others may not judge to be in his best interests (see *section 3*). Everything done, or decision made, under the Act for a person who lacks capacity must be done in that person's best interests. This principle is expanded upon in *section 4*. In addition, the 'least restrictive option' principle must always be considered. The person making the decision or acting must think whether it is possible to decide or act in a way that would interfere less with the rights and freedom of action of the person who lacks capacity.

Preliminary

Section 2: People who lack capacity

21.   This sets out the Act's definition of a person who lacks capacity. It focuses on the particular time when a decision has to be made and on the particular matter to

which the decision relates, not on any theoretical ability to make decisions generally. It follows that a person can lack capacity for the purposes of the Act even if the loss of capacity is partial or temporary or if his capacity fluctuates. It also follows that a person may lack capacity in relation to one matter but not in relation to another matter.

22. The inability to make a decision must be caused by an impairment of or disturbance in the functioning of the mind or brain. This is the so-called 'diagnostic test'. This could cover a range of problems, such as psychiatric illness, learning disability, dementia, brain damage or even a toxic confusional state, as long as it has the necessary effect on the functioning of the mind or brain, causing the person to be unable to make the decision.

23. *Subsection (3)* introduces a principle of equal consideration in relation to determinations of a person's capacity. It makes it clear that such determinations should not merely be made on the basis of a person's age, appearance or unjustified assumptions about capacity based on the person's condition or behaviour. Any preconceptions and prejudicial assumptions held by a person making the assessment of capacity must therefore have no input into the assessment of capacity. The reference to 'condition' captures a range of factors, including any physical disability a person may have. So, in making an assessment of capacity, the fact that the person in question has a learning difficulty should not in itself lead the person making the assessment to assume that the person with the learning difficulty would lack capacity to decide, for example, where to live. The reference to 'appearance' would also include skin colour.

24. *Subsection (5)* makes it clear that powers under the Act generally only arise where the person lacking capacity is 16 or over (although powers in relation to property might be exercised in relation to a younger person who has disabilities which will cause the incapacity to last into adulthood: see *section 18(3)*). Any overlap with the jurisdiction under the Children Act 1989 can be dealt with by orders about the transfer of proceedings to the more appropriate court (see *section 21*).

25. *Subsection (5)* has the first use of the capital letter 'D' to refer to a person exercising powers in relation to a person who lacks capacity. The use of capital letters sometimes makes complex provisions easier to follow (particularly where a number of different people are being referred to), and is a technique often adopted in recent legislation. In this Act, the fact that lack of capacity is specific to particular decisions and that there are many reasons why a person may lack capacity makes it necessary to use a neutral, rather than descriptive, label for the person concerned.

Section 3: Inability to make decisions

26. This sets out the test for assessing whether a person is unable to make a decision about a matter and therefore lacks capacity in relation to that matter. It is a 'functional' test, looking at the decision-making process itself. Four reasons are given why a person may be unable to make a decision. The first three (*subsection (1)(a)* to *(c)*) will cover the vast majority of cases. To make a decision, a person must first be able to comprehend the information relevant to the decision (further defined in *subsection (4)*). *Subsection (2)* makes clear that a determination of incapacity may not be reached without the relevant information having been presented to the person in a way that is appropriate to his circumstances. Secondly, the person must be able to retain this information (for long enough to make the decision, as explained in *subsection (3)*). And thirdly, he must be able to use and weigh it to arrive at a choice. If the person cannot undertake one of these three aspects of the decision-making process then he is unable to make the decision.

27. *Subsection (1)(d)* provides for the fourth situation where someone is unable to make a decision namely where he cannot communicate it in any way. This is intended to be a residual category and will only affect a small number of persons, in particular some of those with the very rare condition of 'locked-in syndrome'. It seems likely

that people suffering from this condition can in fact still understand, retain and use information and so would not be regarded as lacking capacity under subsection (1)(a) to (c). Some people who suffer from this condition can communicate by blinking an eye, but it seems that others cannot communicate at all. *Subsection (1)(d)* treats those who are completely unable to communicate their decisions as unable to make a decision. Any residual ability to communicate (such as blinking an eye to indicate 'yes' or 'no' in answer to a question) would exclude a person from this category.

Section 4: Best interests

28.   It is a key principle of the Act that all steps and decisions taken for someone who lacks capacity must be taken in the person's best interests. The best interests principle is an essential aspect of the Act and builds on the common law while offering further guidance. Given the wide range of acts, decisions and circumstances that the Act will cover, the notion of 'best interests' is not defined in the Act. Rather, *subsection (2)* makes clear that determining what is in a person's best interests requires a consideration of all relevant circumstances (defined in *subsection (11)*). *Subsection (1)* makes clear that best interests determinations must not be based merely on a person's age, appearance, or unjustified assumptions about what might be in a person's best interests based on the person's condition or behaviour. Best interests determinations must not therefore be made on the basis of any unjustified and prejudicial assumptions. For example, in making a best interests determination for a person who has a physical disability it would not be acceptable to assume that, because of this disability, they will not have a good quality of life and should therefore not receive treatment. As with *section 2(3)* the references to 'condition' and 'appearance' capture a range of factors. The section goes on to list particular steps that must be taken. Best interests is not a test of 'substituted judgement' (what the person would have wanted), but rather it requires a determination to be made by applying an objective test as to what would be in the person's best interests. All the relevant circumstances, including the factors mentioned in the section must be considered, but none carries any more weight or priority than another. They must all be balanced in order to determine what would be in the best interests of the person concerned. The factors in this section do not provide a definition of best interests and are not exhaustive.

29.   The decision-maker must consider whether the individual concerned is likely to have capacity at some future date (*subsection (3)*). This is in case the decision can be put off, until the person can make it himself. Even if the decision cannot be put off, the decision is likely to be influenced by whether the person will always lack capacity or is likely to regain capacity.

30.   *Subsection (4)* provides that the person concerned must so far as possible be involved in the process. Even where a person lacks capacity he should not be excluded from the decision-making process.

31.   *Subsection (5)* applies to determinations as to whether treatment that is necessary to sustain life is in the best interests of the person concerned. It provides that the decision-maker must not be motivated by a desire to bring about the person's death. This means that whatever a decision-maker personally feels about, or wants for, the person concerned this must not affect his assessment of whether a particular treatment is in the person's best interests. This subsection does not change the previously understood common law on best interests. It does not mean that doctors are under an obligation to provide, or to continue to provide, life-sustaining treatment where that treatment is not in the best interests of the person.

32.   The decision-maker must also consider, as far as is reasonably ascertainable, the 'past and present wishes and feelings' of the person concerned (*subsection (6)*). Such wishes and feelings would include any relevant written statement. Even where people cannot make their own decisions, they can express preferences and feelings

which should be taken seriously. For those who have lost capacity (for example because of progressive dementia) it may be particularly important to consider past wishes and feelings as well as current ones. In particular, there must be consideration of written statements made by the person whilst he had capacity. Such statements may be about what sort of care or treatment the person would wish to have in the case of future illness. Where written statements are well-thought out and considered, they are likely to carry particular weight for the purposes of best interests determinations. There must also be consideration of the person's beliefs and values – religious beliefs, cultural values and lifestyle choices are obvious aspects of this. There may also be other factors that the person would have been likely to consider if able to do so. For example, a person with capacity will often consider emotional bonds or family obligations when deciding how to spend his money or where to live.

33.   *Subsection (7)* specifies who should be consulted when making a best interests determination, recognising that they will often have important information and views as to what would be in the person's best interests. They will also often have information about the past and present wishes and feelings of the person concerned, his beliefs and values and other factors he would be likely to consider were he able to do so. The decision-maker should consult anyone the person concerned has named as someone to consult and anyone who has a caring role or is interested in his welfare. This will include informal carers, family and friends and others who care for the person in a professional or voluntary capacity, including any kind of existing advocate. Anyone appointed under an LPA and any deputy appointed by the court (dealt with later in Part 1) should also be consulted. Consultation is required where it is 'practicable and appropriate'. For example, no consultation may be possible in an emergency situation and it might not be appropriate for every day-to-day decision (such as whether to watch television). For significant, non-urgent, decisions, including where there is a series of minor decisions that cumulatively become significant, consultation will be required, as being both practicable and appropriate.

34.   *Subsection (8)* applies the best interests principle to situations where the person concerned may not lack capacity. A donee may be acting under a lasting power of attorney while the donor still has capacity. The subsection makes clear that the obligation also applies where the person concerned does not in fact lack capacity but where the other person reasonably believes that he does lack capacity. There would otherwise be a lacuna in the applicability of the best interests test.

35.   *Subsection (9)* offers appropriate protection to those who act in the reasonable belief that they are doing so in the other person's best interests. It should be remembered that 'reasonable belief' is an objective test. Where the court makes a decision it must of course be satisfied that its decision is indeed in the person's best interests.

36.   *Subsection (11)* explains what relevant circumstances means in the context of considering a person's best interests. The person making the determination must consider those circumstances of which he is aware and which it would be reasonable to regard as relevant. This strikes a balance by acknowledging that the decision-maker cannot be expected to be aware of everything whilst stipulating that he must take into account factors that it is reasonable to regard as relevant.

Section 5: Acts in connection with care or treatment

37.   This provides statutory protection against liability for certain acts done in connection with the care or treatment of another person. If an act qualifies as a 'section 5 act' then a carer can be confident that he will not face civil liability or criminal prosecution. Civil liability could involve being sued for committing a tort such as battery, false imprisonment or breach of confidence. Criminal prosecution might be for an offence against the person (assault or causing actual bodily harm) or for an offence against property (theft).

38.   A qualifying 'section 5 act' may be performed by a range of people on any one day. The key requirements are that the person ('D') acts in connection with the care or treatment of another person ('P') and that D has formed a reasonable belief as to P's lack of capacity and best interests.

39.   D will not incur any liability which would not have arisen if P, with capacity to do so, had in fact consented to D's act. Consent is a complete defence to a wide range of torts (battery, false imprisonment, trespass to land or goods, breach of confidence) and to many offences against the person or against property. Many people who are fully capable will regularly consent (expressly or impliedly) to others touching them, locking the doors of a car or dealing with their property. If a person takes someone else's unwanted clothes to a charity shop he could, in the absence of the owner's consent, in principle face civil liability for trespass to goods or criminal prosecution for theft. This section offers protection against liability where the owner is unable to give a valid consent, as long as the step is taken in connection with caring for him and is in his best interests.

40.   Consent is not a defence to a claim in the tort of negligence. There are some offences which depend on a finding of negligence as defined in civil law (most notably, manslaughter where the element of unlawful killing may be made out by grossly negligent behaviour, whether an act or an omission to act in breach of duty). Consent might be relevant to issues of contributory negligence. *Subsection (3)* therefore makes it clear that liability for negligence is unaffected by the section.

41.   This section does not affect the operation of advance decisions to refuse treatment, as covered by *sections 24 to 26*. If a person has made a valid and applicable advance decision then that takes priority over the rules in this section.

Section 6: Section 5 acts: limitations

42.   This sets two limitations to 'section 5 acts'. *Subsections (1)* to *(4)* deal with restraint, which is defined as the use or threat of force where P is resisting and any restriction of liberty of movement, whether or not P resists. This will include actions such as pulling someone away from the road, putting a seat belt on someone in a car or administering sedatives in order to undertake treatment. Restraint is permitted only when the person using it reasonably believes it is necessary to prevent harm to P. The restraint used must be proportionate both to the likelihood of the harm and the seriousness of the harm. It follows that the minimum level of restraint must be used; if the risk of harm diminishes, the restraint used must be reduced. It should be remembered that the principles in *section 1* also apply when restraint is proposed. The principle of the 'least restrictive option' in *section 1(6)* is likely to be particularly significant here.

43.   Decisions of the European Court of Human Rights draw a clear distinction between acts which restrict a person's liberty of movement and those which deprive a person of his liberty within the meaning of Article 5 of the ECHR. *Subsection (4)(b)* refers only to restriction of the person's liberty of movement. *Subsection (5)* makes clear that for *section 6* a deprivation of liberty, within the ECHR meaning, amounts to more than mere restraint. *Section 6* will therefore not provide protection for an action that amounts to a deprivation of liberty for the purposes of Article 5.

44.   The second limitation is in *subsection (6)* which makes it clear that a valid decision by an attorney or a deputy takes priority over any action which might be taken under section 5. However, there is a limitation on the authority of an attorney or deputy. There could be a dispute or difficulty over a decision made by an attorney or deputy. For example, a doctor might be concerned that the attorney is not acting in P's best interests. *Subsection (7)* makes it clear that action can be taken to sustain life or prevent serious deterioration while any such dispute is referred to the court.

Section 7: Payment for necessary goods and services

45.   This revises and extends the statutory rule in section 3(2) of the Sale of Goods Act 1979 insofar as it applies to people who lack capacity to contract. In general, a contract entered into by a person who lacks capacity to contract is voidable if the other person knew or must be taken to have known of the lack of capacity. This does not apply if 'necessaries' are supplied. In those circumstances, the person lacking capacity must still pay a reasonable price. The rule in section 3(2) of the 1979 Act only applies to 'necessary' goods, but there is a matching common law rule about 'necessary' services. This section combines these rules to set out a single statutory rule to cover 'necessary' goods and services. *Subsection (2)* repeats the established legal definition of what is 'necessary'. Thus, for example, if the milkman carries on delivering milk to the house of someone who has a progressive dementia, he can expect to be paid. If, however, a roofer puts a completely unnecessary new roof on to that person's house, when all that was required was a minor repair, then the rule will operate to prevent the roofer from being able to recover his charges.

Section 8: Expenditure

46.   This is to be read with *sections 5* and *7*. It allows a person who is acting under *section 5* and who arranges something for P's care or treatment that costs money to do certain things. He can promise that P will pay, use money which P has in his possession and pay himself back from P's money in his possession or consider himself owed by P. This restates existing common law rules which provide that a person acting as an 'agent of necessity' for another person should not be out of pocket as a result. A carer might, acting in P's best interests, arrange the delivery of disability aids or household items. Nothing in this section allows a carer to gain access to P's funds where they are held by a third party such as a bank or building society. The bank or building society would remain bound by contractual obligations to P until formal steps were taken (for example, registering a relevant power of attorney, or obtaining a court order).

47.   *Subsection (3)* recognises that some people may have control over P's money or property by other routes, for example under the Social Security (Claims and Payments) Regulations 1987 (SI 1987/1968) or by way of banking arrangements.

Lasting powers of attorney

Section 9: Lasting powers of attorney

48.   *Sections 9* to *14* create a new statutory form of power of attorney, the 'lasting power of attorney' (or LPA). This replaces the 'enduring power of attorney' (or EPA) provided for by the Enduring Powers of Attorney Act 1985. The 1985 Act is repealed by section 66(1)(b), but the legal effect of an EPA already made under the current law is preserved and integrated into the scheme of the Act by *section 66(3)* and *Schedule 4*.

49.   *Section 9* sets out the key aspects of an LPA. Unlike an EPA, it can extend to personal welfare matters (*(subsection (1)(a)*) as well as to property and affairs. By making an LPA, an individual (the donor) confers on another individual or individuals (donee/s) authority to make decisions about the donor's personal welfare and/or property and affairs or specified matters concerning those areas. Power to make decisions includes, by virtue of *section 64(2)*, acting on decisions made where appropriate.

50.   *Subsection (1)* also makes clear that to be valid an LPA must include authority to make decisions when the donor no longer has capacity to make those decisions himself. An LPA can, in certain circumstances, operate as an 'ordinary' power of attorney when the donor has full mental capacity but it will also continue to operate after the donor has lost capacity.

51.   *Subsection (2)* deals with the creation of an LPA. The donor must be aged 18 or over and have capacity to execute an LPA. The rules in section 10 about who can be a donee must be complied with. Detailed provisions about the making and registration of the instrument, as set out in *Schedule 1*, must be complied with. If the rules are not complied with the document created will not be a valid LPA and cannot be lawfully used to make decisions on behalf of the donor (*subsection (3)*).

52.   *Subsection (4)* reiterates that any donee must apply the principles set out in *section 1* and act in the donor's best interests. A donee's authority is also subject to any conditions or restrictions that the donor may choose to put in the LPA document itself.

Section 10: Appointment of donees

53.   This sets out certain requirements relating to donees and how they should act. A donee must be aged 18 or over. Someone who is bankrupt cannot be appointed as the donee of an LPA relating to property and affairs. If the LPA relates only to property and affairs, the donee can be either an individual or a trust corporation (defined in section 68(1) of the Trustee Act 1925 as the Public Trustee or a corporation appointed by the court in any particular case to be a trustee, or entitled by rules made under section 4(3) of the Public Trustee Act 1906, to act as custodian trustee).

54.   *Subsection (4)* provides that where two or more people are appointed as donees, they may be appointed either to act jointly (so that they must all join together in any decision) or to act jointly and severally (which means they can act all together or each of them can act independently). The donor may also appoint two or more persons to act jointly in respect of some matters and jointly and severally in respect of others. To the extent that the donor does not specify in the instrument whether donees are to act jointly or jointly and severally, it will be assumed from the instrument that they are appointed to act jointly (*subsection (5)*).

55.   For joint attorneys, any breach of the relevant rules about how lasting powers of attorney are made will prevent a valid LPA being created (*subsection (6)*). For 'joint and several' attorneys, a breach only affects the attorney who is in breach; a valid LPA is still created in respect of the other donee(s) (*subsection (7)*).

56.   *Subsection (8)* allows a donor to provide for the replacement of the donee(s) on the occurrence of a specified event which would normally terminate a donee's powers. The specified events are: the donee renouncing his appointment, the donee's death or insolvency, the dissolution or annulment of a marriage or civil partnership between the donor and the donee or the lack of capacity of the donee. For example, an older donor might wish to appoint his spouse, but nominate a son or daughter as a replacement donee. A donee cannot be given power to choose a successor (*subsection (8)(a)*) as this would be inconsistent with the core principle that the donor is giving authority to a chosen attorney. A civil partnership is a registered relationship between two people of the same sex which ends only on death, dissolution or annulment, as provided for in the Civil Partnership Act 2004.

Section 11: Lasting powers of attorney: restrictions

57.   *Subsections (1)* to *(4)* place restrictions on the use of restraint by attorneys, matching those applying in relation to 'section 5 acts' (*see section 6*) and deputies (*see section 20*). Restraint can only be used to prevent harm, and must be proportionate. *Subsection (6)* makes clear that for *section 11* a deprivation of liberty within the ECHR meaning amounts to more than mere restraint.

58.   Further restrictions are set out in *subsection (7)*. An attorney cannot act where the donor has capacity, or where the donor has made a qualifying advance decision (*see sections 24 to 26*). *Subsection 7(c)* has to be read with *subsection (8)*. Thus, although an attorney may give or refuse consent to the carrying out or continuation of health care, this would not extend to refusing life-sustaining treatment unless the LPA expressly said so, and is subject to any conditions or restrictions in the LPA.

Section 12: Scope of lasting powers of attorney: gifts

59.   This is similar to section 3(5) of the Enduring Powers of Attorney Act 1985 and deals with an attorney's power to make gifts of the donor's property. The attorney can only do something that is in the donor's best interests but this section operates as a specific restriction in relation to gifts. It allows modest gifts proportionate to the donor's assets to people related or connected to the donor (including himself) on 'customary occasions', as defined; and to charities (subject to any conditions or restrictions in the LPA itself). The court has power to authorise more substantial gifts (see *section 23(4)*) if satisfied this would be in the donor's best interests. For example, if an older person has substantial assets then tax planning might be a reason for the making of gifts.

Section 13: Revocation of lasting powers of attorney

60.   This deals with the ways in which LPAs may cease to be effective, whether before or after registration. A donor may revoke an LPA at any time while he has capacity to do so (*subsection (2)*). Other events will automatically terminate an LPA.

61.   The bankruptcy of either the donor or the attorney will terminate any financial powers granted. *Section 64(3)* provides that all references to the bankruptcy of an individual include a case where a bankruptcy restrictions order is in force in respect of him. Bankruptcy restrictions orders are provided for in Schedule 4A to the Insolvency Act 1986. Interim bankruptcy restrictions orders do not bring a power of attorney to an end; they just have a suspensive effect (*subsections (4)* and *(9)*).

62.   An LPA also comes to an end if the donee disclaims, dies or loses capacity. The dissolution or annulment of a marriage or civil partnership between the donee and the donor will terminate the donee's powers unless the donor has specified that it should not (*subsection (11)*).

63.   *Subsections (7)* and *(10)* provide for situations where there is a replacement or a 'joint and several' attorney (in respect of any matter) who can continue to act.

Section 14: Protection of donee and others if no power created or power revoked

64.   This sets out the legal consequences when a registered LPA turns out to be invalid. There is similar provision in relation to EPAs in section 9 of the 1985 Act. Broadly, both attorneys and third parties are given protection from liability if they were unaware that the LPA was invalid or had come to an end.

General powers of the court and appointment of deputies

Section 15: Power to make declarations

65.   This gives the court power to make declarations, if necessary, about whether an individual has capacity, either in relation to a specific decision that needs to be made, or in relation to decisions on such matters as are described in the declaration. It also gives the court power to make declarations about whether an act or proposed act was or would be lawful. The Court of Protection would have this latter power as a superior court of record which, under *section 47*, has the same powers, rights, privileges and authority as the High Court, but it is considered helpful to spell this out. *Subsection (2)* confirms that the court can be asked to adjudicate on omissions to act (for example, the withholding or withdrawing of medical treatment) and a course of conduct.

Section 16: Powers to make decisions and appoint deputies: general

66.   This sets out the core jurisdiction of the court, which is to make decisions about personal welfare or property and affairs for persons lacking capacity or to appoint a deputy to do so.

67. *Subsection (3)* confirms that the principles in *section 1* and the best interests checklist will govern the court's exercise of its powers.

68. *Subsection (4)* requires the court to consider two additional principles, further emphasising the 'least restrictive intervention' principle mentioned in *section 1(6)*. The first additional principle is that a decision of the court is preferable to the appointment of a deputy and the second is that, if a deputy is appointed, the appointment should be as limited in scope and duration as is reasonably practicable in the circumstances. In welfare (including health care) matters a deputy is never required in order for care or treatment to be given to a person because *section 5* provides sufficient scope for carers and professionals to act. Nevertheless, a deputy may be particularly helpful in cases of dispute. For matters concerning property and affairs, a deputy may be needed in order to provide the authority to deal with contractual matters and where there is an on-going need for such decisions to be taken. *Subsection (5)* enables the court to grant the deputy powers or impose duties on him as it thinks necessary to avoid repeated applications to the court. However, it also enables the court to require the deputy to seek consent before taking certain actions. *Subsection (6)* gives the court an 'own motion' power to make whatever order is in the person's best interests.

69. The court can always vary or discharge its orders and *subsection (8)* provides that it has power to take away or alter a deputy's powers if the deputy is overstepping his powers or not adhering to his best interests obligations.

Section 17: Section 16 powers: personal welfare

70. The powers created by *section 16* in relation to making orders and appointing deputies will extend to a wide range of personal welfare issues. Particular mention is made in this section of issues which have arisen in the past and been dealt with by the High Court in the exercise of its inherent jurisdiction and may be most likely to arise in future. This is not an exhaustive, merely an indicative, list. It is not a list of decisions that must always go to court, rather it provides examples of where the court can act if it would be appropriate, and beneficial to the person, for the court to do so. There are restrictions on what may be delegated to a deputy, set out in *section 20(2)*.

Section 18: Section 16 powers: property and affairs

71. *Subsection (1)* indicates the extent of the court's powers with regard to property and affairs. Again it provides a non-exhaustive, indicative list of the matters within the powers relating to property and affairs. This largely reproduces the list which applies to the original Court of Protection in section 96 of the Mental Health Act 1983. Again, this is not a list of matters which must always go to the new Court of Protection but rather an indication of the types of order the court might make if an application were made. Where property and financial matters are concerned the effect of the general law relating to contract and property will often be to create a need for formal powers. So if the person concerned has lost capacity to enter into a contract for the sale of his house no purchaser is going to accept a contract or Land Registry transfer document signed by someone who is not the registered owner, unless the proposed purchaser sees a document proving that someone else has formal authority to contract to sell and transfer the property on his behalf. Equally, the person's bank will be bound by the terms of its contract with him not to hand his money over to someone else. If he can no longer give a valid instruction or valid receipt to the bank then his money will have to be held by the bank until formal authority is provided. If a valid power of attorney exists then this would probably remove any need for the Court of Protection to make orders. Again, not all of the powers can be given to deputies (see *section 20(3)*). These correspond to matters which, under the current law, always have to be dealt with by the court itself.

Section 19: Appointment of deputies

72.   This deals with deputies appointed by the court. The general rule is that a deputy must be at least 18 years of age. If a trust corporation is appointed deputy it can only act in respect of property and affairs. The court may appoint the holder of a specified office as deputy (this is different to LPAs where the attorney must be an individual). Before being appointed deputy, a person must consent to being appointed. The court will be able to appoint more than one deputy to act on behalf of an individual who lacks capacity and these deputies can act jointly, jointly and severally, or jointly for some matters and jointly and severally for other matters. That is, the court can specify that they must all act together, that each can act independently of the other or that they can act either way, depending on the matter in question. When appointing a deputy, the court will also have the power to appoint a successor or successors to the original appointees. The court will specify the circumstances under which this could occur.

73.   *Subsection (6)* provides that a deputy will be treated as an 'agent' of the adult who lacks capacity. The law of agency imposes a range of duties on those who act as agents for someone else. For example, an agent must act with 'due care and skill' and is bound by fiduciary duties amongst other duties. Case law has established that receivers appointed by the original Court of Protection under Part 7 of the Mental Health Act 1983 are agents but it is considered helpful to make statutory provision to that effect in relation to deputies.

74.   All deputies will be able to claim reasonable expenses from the estate of the adult lacking capacity and if the court directs, the deputy can be paid for his services from the estate. The court will be able to give a deputy the power to deal with all matters concerning the control and management of any property belonging to the adult lacking capacity, including being able to invest. The court will also be able to require a deputy to give the Public Guardian security against misbehaviour (that is, either a deposit of money or a guarantee bond) and to direct the deputy to file with the Public Guardian reports and accounts as it sees fit. These provisions are broadly in line with arrangements in the original Court of Protection (Mental Health Act 1983, Part 7).

Section 20: Restrictions on deputies

75.   This sets a number of limitations on the powers of deputies. *Subsection (1)* specifies that a deputy cannot act where the person concerned is able to act for himself. In some cases the person may have fluctuating capacity, for example as a result of mental health problems, and it is not acceptable for a deputy to carry on making substitute decisions when the person concerned has in fact recovered. *Subsection (6)* reiterates that a deputy must act in accordance with *section 1* (principles) and *section 4* (best interests).

76.   *Subsections (2) and (3)* relate back to *sections 16* to *17* and list certain matters which must always be dealt with by the court, not a deputy. The powers to prohibit a person from having contact with an adult lacking capacity or to direct a person responsible for his health care to allow a different person to take over are, of course, powers which have to be exercised by the court itself. As under the current law, deputies will also be restricted from making certain financial decisions in connection with wills and trusts.

77.   *Subsection (4)* makes it clear that a deputy cannot be given power to 'trump' an attorney (who will have been chosen by the donor himself, at a time when he had capacity). If there is a concern or a dispute about the way an attorney is behaving the court must use its powers in *sections 22* and *23*, rather than seeking to appoint a deputy. *Subsection (5)* restricts deputies from refusing consent to the carrying out or continuation of treatment that is necessary to sustain life. *Subsection (6)* clarifies that the principles in *section 1* and the considerations as to best interests as set out in *section 4* apply to deputies.

78.   *Subsections (7)* to *(11)* impose limitations on deputies in relation to restraint, matching those imposed in relation to 'section 5 acts' by *section 6* and on attorneys by *section 11*. A deputy will have to be acting within the scope of an authority expressly conferred on him by the court. Restraint can only be used to prevent harm and must be proportionate. *Subsection (13)* makes clear that for *section 20* a deprivation of liberty within the ECHR meaning amounts to more than mere restraint.

Section 21: Transfer of proceedings relating to people under 18

79.   The Act deals with people aged 16 and over (and with the property of younger children – see *section 18(3)*), while the Children Act 1989 deals with people under the age of 18. There will be some overlap between the jurisdictions and the Lord Chancellor is therefore given power by this section to make transfer of proceedings orders. It is intended that the order will indicate that a case should be transferred to the court most suitable to deal with the issues. One factor is likely to be the prospect of a person under 18 who is the subject of a dispute still lacking capacity when an adult. For example, if the parents of a 17–year old with profound learning difficulties are in dispute about residence or contact then it may be more appropriate for the Court of Protection to deal with the case, since an order made under the Children Act 1989 would expire on the child's 18th birthday at the latest.

Powers of the court in relation to lasting powers of attorney

Section 22: Powers of court in relation to validity of lasting powers of attorney

80.   This section and *section 23* set out what the Court of Protection can do in relation to LPAs. The powers are similar to those in section 8 of the Enduring Powers of Attorney Act 1985, except that administrative functions connected with registration will be performed by the Public Guardian.

81.   The court can determine questions about validity and revocation (*subsection (2)*). It can direct that an instrument should not be registered or (if it is unregistered) revoke it on the grounds set out in *subsection (3)* (fraud or undue pressure, or misbehaviour by the attorney).

82.   *Subsection (5)* provides that where there is more than one donee the court may revoke the instrument or the LPA so far as it relates to any of them.

Section 23: Powers of court in relation to operation of lasting powers of attorney

83.   This allows the court to decide questions about the meaning or effect of an LPA (or an instrument purporting to create an LPA) and to give directions to attorneys where the donor lacks capacity. The court may also give the attorney directions about producing reports, accounts, records and information and about his remuneration and expenses. The court has power to relieve a donee from some or all of the liabilities arising from a breach of duty (cf Enduring Powers of Attorney Act 1985, section 8(2)(f)). It may also authorise gifts beyond the scope of what is permitted by *section 12(2)* (for example, for tax planning purposes).

Advance decisions to refuse treatment

Section 24: Advance decisions to refuse treatment: general

84.   *Sections 24* to *26* deal with advance decisions to refuse treatment. Some people already choose to make such decisions and their legal effect has been analysed in a number of judicial decisions. It has been confirmed by the High Court that a competent adult patient's anticipatory refusal of consent remains binding and effective notwithstanding that he has subsequently become incompetent (*HE v. NHS*

Trust A and AE [2003] EWHC 1017 (Fam), a case concerning a refusal of blood transfusion). Broadly, the sections seek to codify and clarify the current common law rules, integrating them into the broader scheme of the Act. There would otherwise be a lacuna in the scheme of the Act and the powers of the new court. Many general forms of advance statement or 'living will' will be important and relevant as 'past wishes' of the person for the purposes of the best interests checklist in *section 4*. An 'advance decision' as defined in these sections is a special type of advance statement that represents an actual decision to refuse treatment, albeit at an earlier date. As now, it will therefore be decisive in certain circumstances.

85.   The key characteristics of an 'advance decision' for the purposes of the Act are set out in *subsection (1)* of this section. It must be made by a person who is 18 or over and at a time when the person has capacity to make it. A qualifying advance decision must specify the treatment that is being refused, although this can be in lay terms (for example using 'tummy' instead of stomach). It may specify particular circumstances, again in lay terms, in which the refusal will apply. A person can change or completely withdraw the advance decision if he has capacity to do so (*subsection (3)*). *Subsection (4)* confirms that the withdrawal, including a partial withdrawal, of an advance decision does not need to be in writing and can be by any means. *Subsection (5)* confirms that an alteration of an advance decision does not need to be in writing, unless it applies to an advance decision refusing life-sustaining treatment, in which case formalities will need to be satisfied in order for it to apply.

Section 25: Validity and applicability of advance decisions

86.   This introduces the two important safeguards of validity and applicability in relation to advance decisions to refuse treatment.

87.   To be valid the advance decision must not have been withdrawn or overridden by a subsequent LPA giving a donee the authority to consent or refuse consent to the treatment (other LPAs will not override – see *subsection ((7)*). Also, if the person has acted in a way that is clearly inconsistent with the advance decision remaining his fixed decision, then the advance decision is invalid. An example of an inconsistent action might be a former Jehovah's Witness converting to Islam and marrying a Muslim man. Even if she had forgotten to destroy a written advance decision refusing blood transfusion, her actions could be taken into account in determining whether that earlier refusal remained her fixed decision.

88.   An advance decision will not be applicable if the person actually has capacity to make the decision when the treatment concerned is proposed. It will also not be applicable to treatments, or in circumstances, not specified in the decision. Furthermore the decision will not be applicable if there are reasonable grounds for believing that the current circumstances were not anticipated by the person and, if they had been anticipated by him, would have affected his decision. For example, there may be new medications available that radically change the outlook for a particular condition and make treatment much less burdensome than was previously the case.

89.   *Subsection (5)* introduces further rules about the applicability of advance decisions to refuse treatment that is necessary to sustain life. An advance decision will not apply to life-sustaining treatment unless it is verified by a statement confirming that the decision is to apply to that treatment even if life is at risk. The reference to 'life' includes the life of an unborn child. Both the decision and the statement verifying it must be in writing and be signed and the signature must be witnessed. It is important to note that a person does not physically need to write his advance decision himself. This means that advance decisions recorded in medical notes are considered to be in writing. Writing can also include electronic records.

90.   If the maker of the advance decision cannot sign then another person can sign for him at his direction and in his presence (*section 25(6)(b)*). As with a signature by the person himself, the witness must be present when the third party signs.

Section 26: Effect of advance decisions

91.   This deals with the legal effect of a qualifying advance decision. If it is both valid and applicable it has the same effect as a contemporaneous refusal of treatment by a person with capacity. That is, the treatment cannot lawfully be given. If given, the person refusing would be able to claim damages for the tort of battery and the treatment-provider might face criminal liability for assault. *Subsections* (2) and (3) clarify the rules about liability. A treatment-provider may safely treat unless satisfied that there is a valid and applicable qualifying advance refusal; and a treatment-provider may safely withhold or withdraw treatment as long as he has reasonable grounds for believing that there is a valid and applicable qualifying advance decision.

92.   If there is doubt or a dispute about the existence, validity or applicability of an advance decision then the Court of Protection can determine the issue. There is an important proviso to the general rule that an advance refusal is legally effective. There may be a doubt or dispute about whether a particular refusal is in fact one which meets all the tests (existence, validity and applicability). As with decisions by donees or deputies in *section 6(7)*, action may be taken to prevent the death of the person concerned, or a serious deterioration in his condition, whilst any such doubt or dispute is referred to the court.

Excluded decisions

Section 27: Family relationships etc.

93.   This lists certain decisions that can never be made under the Act on behalf of a person who lacks capacity. For example, in relation to adoption, if a birth parent lacks capacity to consent to an adoption order the rules as to dispensing with consent in the adoption legislation will apply. There will be no question of an attorney consenting or of the Court of Protection making an order or appointing a deputy to provide the requisite consent.

Section 28: Mental Health Act matters

94.   This deals with the question of people who are detained for psychiatric treatment pursuant to the Mental Health Act 1983. The section ensures that the Mental Capacity Act does not apply to any treatment for mental disorder which is being given in accordance with the rules about compulsory treatment set out in Part 4 of the 1983 Act. The specific statutory safeguards which the 1983 Act gives in relation to compulsory psychiatric treatment must always be afforded to those patients to whom that Act applies.

Section 29: Voting rights

95.   This provides that the Act does not apply to decisions on voting.

Research

Section 30: Research

96.   This section and *sections 31 to 33* allow intrusive research to be lawfully carried out on, or in relation to, a person who lacks capacity, where the research is part of a research project approved by an appropriate body and it is carried out in accordance with the conditions set out in *sections 32 and 33*. The provisions are based on long-standing international standards, for example, those laid down by the World Medical Association and the Council of Europe Convention on Human Rights and Biomedicine.

97.   This section relates to intrusive research, which means research that would normally need consent if it involved an adult with capacity. Clinical trials that are currently regulated under the Medicines for Human Use (Clinical Trials) Regulations 2004 (SI 2004/1031) (or regulations succeeding or amending them) are excluded from the Act because those Regulations already make provision for trials involving participants who lack capacity. Research on anonymised medical data or tissue is also not included, but may be subject to controls under the Data Protection Act 1998 or the Human Tissue Act 2004.

98.   The appropriate authority (the Secretary of State in relation to research in England and the National Assembly for Wales in relation to research in Wales) must specify an appropriate body for approving research projects, such as a Research Ethics Committee (REC).

Section 31: Requirements for approval

99.   This section sets out the matters of which the appropriate body – such as an REC- must satisfy itself before approving a research project involving a person who lacks capacity.

100.   Subsection (2) requires that the research must be connected with an impairing condition that affects the person participating in the research or with the treatment of the condition. Impairing condition means one that is, or may be, attributable to or causes or contributes to the impairment of or disturbance in the functioning of the person's mind or brain. This limits the sort of research projects that the person may be involved in but will include research into the effects of the impairment on his health and day-to-day life as well as into the causes or possible causes of the impairment and its treatment. *Subsection (4)* requires that there are reasonable grounds for believing that there is no alternative to the involvement of the person in the research, that is, it cannot be carried out as effectively if it only involves people who have capacity.

101.   *Subsections (5)* and *(6)* deal with the anticipated benefits and risks of the research. There are two alternatives: either the research has the potential to benefit the person without imposing a burden disproportionate to that benefit (this type of research is sometimes called 'therapeutic research'); or the research is to provide knowledge of the causes of the person's condition, its treatment or the care of people who have the same or similar condition now or who may develop it in the future. In relation to this latter category, there must be reasonable grounds for believing that the risk to the person is negligible and the research must not interfere with the person's freedom of action or privacy in a significant way or be unduly invasive or restrictive. This latter category of research might include indirect research on medical notes or on tissue already taken for other purposes. It may also include interviews or questionnaires with carers about health or social-care services received by the person or limited observation of the person. And it could include taking samples from the person, e.g. blood samples, specifically for the research project.

Section 32: Consulting carers etc

102.   Before any decision is taken to involve a particular person in approved research, the researcher must take reasonable steps to identify a person close to the person (this could include an attorney or deputy but not someone acting in a professional capacity or for payment, such as a paid carer) who is prepared to be consulted about the person's involvement in the research (*subsection (2)*). If there is no such person, then the researcher must nominate a person independent of the research in accordance with guidance issued by the appropriate authority (see paragraph 99).

103. *Subsection (4)* requires the researcher to give the consultee information about the research and to ask him or her for advice as to whether the person should take part in the research and what, in his opinion, the consultee's wishes and feelings would be about taking part in the research. If at any time the person consulted advises the researcher that in his opinion the person's wishes and feelings would be likely to lead him to decline to take part in the project then the researcher must ensure that the person does not take part in the project, or if it is already underway must ensure that the person is withdrawn from it. But the person may still receive treatment he was receiving during the research if withdrawal would create a significant risk to his health *(subsection (6))*.

104. *Subsections (8)* and *(9)* allow for action to be taken in relation to the research where treatment is to be provided to the person urgently and there is insufficient opportunity to consult. The researcher may proceed if he has the agreement of a doctor who is not connected to the project or in accordance with a procedure agreed by the appropriate body at the time of approval. However *subsection (10)* makes it clear that the researcher may only rely on *subsection (9)* while there is an urgent need to treat. Examples of this type of research may involve action by a paramedic or doctor to make measurements in the first few minutes following a serious head injury or stroke. These arrangements are similar to those provided for in the Clinical Trials Regulations.

Section 33: Additional safeguards

105. The purpose of *section 33* is to provide additional safeguards for the person participating in the research once the research has begun. It requires the researcher to respect any signs of resistance from the person (except where this would conflict with procedures designed to protect him from harm or injury), and not to involve the person in research that would be contrary to an advance decision or any other form of statement. The person's interests must be assumed to outweigh those of science and society *(subsection (3))*.

106. The person must be withdrawn from the project without delay if he indicates that he wishes to be withdrawn from it or if the researcher has reasonable grounds for believing that any of the requirements for approval of the project as set out at in *section 31(2)* to *(7)* are no longer met. As in *section 32*, the person may still receive treatment he was receiving during the research if withdrawal would create a significant risk to his health *(subsection (6))*.

Section 34: Loss of capacity during research project

107. This section provides for a transitional regulation-making power to cover research started before *section 30* comes into force and which involves people who had capacity when enrolled but who lose capacity before the end of the project. The regulations will lay down the conditions on which such research may continue; the research must meet prescribed requirements, the information or material used in the research must have been obtained before the loss of capacity and certain steps must be taken to protect the person participating *(subsection (2))*.

108. The regulations will set out these requirements and steps and may include safeguards similar to those provided for in *sections 31 to 33* but with any necessary alterations to the requirements for approval by an appropriate body, consultation with carers or the additional safeguards *(subsection (3))*. Regulations made by the Secretary of State will be subject to the affirmative procedure in Parliament (see *section 65*).

Independent mental capacity advocate service

Section 35: Appointment of independent mental capacity advocates

109.   *Sections 35* to *41* create a new scheme designed to provide the input of an independent mental capacity advocate ('IMCA') where certain decisions need to be taken for particularly vulnerable people who lack capacity. This may include older people with dementia who have lost contact with all friends and family, or people with severe learning disabilities or long term mental health problems who have been in residential institutions for long periods and lack outside contacts. Such people will be represented and provided with support when decisions are to be made about serious medical treatment or significant changes of residence provided by public bodies.

110.   *Subsection (1)* places a duty on the appropriate authority to make arrangements for the provision of a new independent mental capacity advocacy service. The appropriate authority is, in relation to England, the Secretary of State and, in relation to Wales, the National Assembly for Wales.

111.   *Subsection (2)* allows the appropriate authority to make regulations setting out how the IMCA will be appointed. This will ensure that an individual will need to meet common standards in order to be approved as an IMCA. *Subsection (4)* provides that, as far as practicable, the IMCA should be independent of the person who is making the decision concerned. *Subsection (5)* provides that the arrangements may include provision for payments to be made to, or in relation to, the IMCA. *Subsection (6)* stipulates that an IMCA must be able to meet the person concerned in private and see relevant health, social services and care home records. This is to enable the IMCA to be able to perform properly his function of representing and supporting the person who lacks capacity.

Section 36: Functions of independent mental capacity advocates

112.   This section allows the appropriate authority to make regulations setting out the functions of IMCAs. *Subsection (2)* provides that those regulations may set out the steps which an IMCA needs to take in fulfilling those functions. These steps should ensure that the IMCA supports the person to participate as fully as possible in the decision; obtains and evaluates relevant information; ascertains and represents the person's wishes, feelings, beliefs and values; finds out about all the available options; and seeks a second medical opinion if necessary. *Subsection (3)* provides that the regulations may also set out the circumstances in which the IMCA may challenge the decision-maker on behalf of the person, if appropriate.

Section 37: Provision of serious medical treatment by NHS body

113.   This section applies where 'serious medical treatment' is to be provided or arranged by the NHS for a person who lacks capacity, and there is no one for the treatment-provider to discuss it with. If there is neither a person from the list in *section 40* (such as an attorney under an LPA or deputy) nor a non-professional carer or friend whom it is appropriate to consult, then an IMCA is to be instructed.

114.   The role of the IMCA will be both to represent and to support the person in accordance with the regulations made under *section 36*. The information and submissions provided by the IMCA must be taken into account by the decision-maker.

115.   *Subsection (2)* provides that where the person's treatment is regulated under Part 4 of the Mental Health Act 1983, the IMCA does not need to be instructed under *section 37(3)*. That Act already contains its own safeguards.

116.   *Subsection (4)* makes provision in relation to urgent treatment. *Subsection (6)* provides that the types of 'serious medical treatment' to be covered will be set out in regulations. *Subsection (7)* provides that regulations will also define the particular NHS bodies who will become subject to the duties. The intention is that this will cover the bodies responsible for direct provision or funding of treatment as appropriate.

Section 38: Provision of accommodation by NHS body

117. This section applies to long-stay accommodation in a hospital or a care home, or a move between such accommodation, where this accommodation is provided or arranged by the NHS. *Subsection (9)* clarifies that this section only applies when the accommodation is to be provided for more than 28 days in relation to accommodation in hospital or more than 8 weeks in relation to accommodation in a care home. The IMCA is to be instructed where such accommodation is being proposed and a person lacks capacity to agree to the arrangements and there is no other person to discuss it with. Again the role of the IMCA is both to support and to represent the person concerned. Any information or submissions from the IMCA must be taken into account by the NHS body.

118. *Subsection (2)* provides that where the person concerned is to be detained in hospital or otherwise required to live in the accommodation in question under the Mental Health Act 1983, the IMCA does not need to be consulted, as that Act already contains its own safeguards. *Subsection (3)* makes provision in relation to urgent placements.

119. *Subsection (4)* is intended to ensure that an IMCA is involved in relation to people whose residence is initially intended to be less than 28 days/8 weeks (see paragraph 118) if the period is later extended beyond the applicable period.

120. *Subsections (6)* and *(7)* define the types of care homes and hospitals which are covered under by this section. *Subsection (8)* provides that regulations will also define the particular NHS bodies who will become subject to the duties.

Section 39: Provision of accommodation by local authority

121. This section applies to long-stay accommodation (8 weeks or more) arranged by a local authority or a change in such accommodation. It applies to residential accommodation provided in accordance with *section 21* or *29* of the National Assistance Act 1948. This may be accommodation in a care home, nursing home, ordinary and sheltered housing, housing association or other registered social housing, or in private sector housing provided by a local authority or in hostel accommodation. The IMCA safeguard will also apply to people accommodated following discharge under section 117 of the Mental Health Act 1983.

122. The IMCA is to be instructed where a person lacks capacity to agree to the arrangements and there is no other person to discuss it with. Again the role of the IMCA is both to support and to represent the person concerned. Any information or submissions from the IMCA must be taken into account by the local authority.

123. *Subsection (3)* provides that the IMCA does not need to be instructed where the person is to be required under the Mental Health Act 1983 to live in the accommodation in question (for example, as a requirement of conditional discharge). *Subsection (4)* makes provision in relation to urgent placements.

124. *Subsection (5)* is intended to ensure that an IMCA is involved in relation to people whose residence is initially intended to be less than 8 weeks if the period is later extended.

Section 40: Exceptions

125. This section provides that the independent mental capacity advocacy service does not have a role when the person concerned already has somebody who can speak with the provider of treatment or accommodation (e.g. a person chosen in advance, an attorney under an EPA or LPA, or a deputy). This overrides *sections 37(3)*, *38(3)* and *(4)* and *39(4)* and *(5)*, which generally trigger the involvement of an IMCA when there is no one appropriate to consult about the person's interests, other than a paid or professional carer.

Section 41: Power to adjust role of independent mental capacity advocate

126.   This section provides that the scope of the independent mental capacity advocacy service can be extended, by regulations made for England by the Secretary of State or for Wales by the National Assembly for Wales, to other sets of circumstances. Such regulations would follow consultation about where the involvement of an IMCA might prove useful. Regulations made by the Secretary of State will be subject to the affirmative procedure in Parliament (see *section 65*).

Miscellaneous and supplementary

Section 42: Codes of practice

127.   This section provides for the Lord Chancellor to make and revise a code or codes of practice to supplement the Act. Attorneys, deputies, professionals, paid workers, researchers and IMCAs acting on behalf of adults who lack capacity will be under an obligation to have regard to any relevant code. Any codes of practice issued will be allowed to be used as evidence in court or tribunal proceedings.

Section 43: Codes of practice: procedure

128.   This section sets out the procedure for issuing and revising any codes of practice. The Lord Chancellor will have to consult the National Assembly for Wales and other appropriate persons before preparing or revising a code. Draft codes will have to be laid before both Houses of Parliament for 40 days. They may then be issued, provided that neither House has resolved to reject the draft. The Lord Chancellor must arrange for the code to be brought to the attention of people who may need to know about it.

Section 44: Ill-treatment or neglect

129.   This section creates an offence of ill-treatment or wilful neglect of a person lacking capacity by anyone responsible for that person's care, donees of LPAs or EPAs, or deputies appointed by the court.

PART 2: THE COURT OF PROTECTION AND THE PUBLIC GUARDIAN

The Court of Protection

Section 45: The Court of Protection

130.   This section establishes a superior court of record, called the Court of Protection, which will be able to sit anywhere in England and Wales. Welfare matters previously referred to the High Court may be referred to this court. It is intended that the Court of Protection will have a regional presence but will have a central office and registry as designated by the Lord Chancellor. Additional registries (being High Court district registries or county courts) may also be designated. *Subsection (6)* provides that the former office of the Supreme Court known as the Court of Protection will cease to exist.

Section 46: The judges of the Court of Protection

131.   The Lord Chancellor or an appropriate person acting on his behalf will nominate judges to exercise the jurisdiction of the Court of Protection. *Subsection (2)* sets out which judges may be nominated. *Subsection (3)* gives the Lord Chancellor the power to appoint one of the senior nominated judges to be designated President of

the Court of Protection and another to be Vice-President of the Court of Protection. *Subsection (4)* gives the Lord Chancellor the power to appoint a judge to be Senior Judge of the Court of Protection, with various administrative functions.

Supplementary powers

Section 47: General powers and effect of orders etc.

132. *Subsection (1)* gives the Court of Protection the same powers as the High Court, for example in relation to witnesses, contempt and enforcement.

Section 48: Interim orders and directions

133. This section allows the court to make interim orders even if evidence as to lack of capacity is not yet available, where there is reason for the court to believe that the person lacks capacity in respect of a particular matter and it is in his best interests for the court to act without delay.

Section 49: Power to call for reports

134. This section makes provision for reports to assist the court in determining a case. Such reports can be commissioned from the Public Guardian, local authorities, NHS bodies or Court of Protection Visitors. The Public Guardian is a new statutory official (see *section 57*) and the Court of Protection Visitors replace current 'Lord Chancellor's Visitors' (see section 102 of the Mental Health Act 1983 and *section 61*). Local authority staff or NHS staff may already be providing services to the person concerned and be able to report to the court on the basis of their existing involvement.

135. *Subsections (7)* to *(9)* allow the Public Guardian or Court of Protection Visitor who is reporting to the court to have access to health, social services or care records relating to the person and interview him in private. Where a Court of Protection Visitor is a Special Visitor (e.g. a registered medical practitioner or someone with other suitable qualifications or training) he may, on the directions of the court, carry out medical, psychiatric or psychological examinations.

Practice and procedure

Section 50: Applications to the Court of Protection

136. This section provides that persons listed in *subsection (1)* can apply to the Court of Protection as of right while others generally will be required to obtain permission from the court. Court of Protection Rules can, however, provide that certain types of application will not require permission. The factors that the court must have regard to when considering whether to grant permission are listed in *subsection (3)* and are designed to ensure that any proposed application will promote the interests of the person concerned, rather than causing unnecessary distress or difficulty for him.

Section 51: Court of Protection Rules

137. The specialist jurisdiction of the new court calls for specialist rules of court, which will be made by the Lord Chancellor. *Subsection (2)* lists different matters in relation to which rules may be made and *subsection (4)* permits different provisions to be made for different geographical areas.

Section 52: Practice directions

138.   This section gives power to make practice directions. These are directions about a court's practices and procedures, issued for the assistance and guidance of litigants. They often support and add detail to rules of court. Practice directions for the Court of Protection will have to be made by the President with the approval of the Lord Chancellor or by another person (for example, the Vice-President) with the approval of the President and the Lord Chancellor. *Subsection* (3) provides that the Lord Chancellor need not approve any directions giving guidance about the law or the making of judicial decisions. *Section 51(3)* enables Court of Protection Rules, instead of providing for any matter, to refer to provision made or to be made by these directions. The intention is to make rules accompanied by practice directions, on the model of the Civil Procedure Rules 1998.

Section 53: Rights of appeal

139.   This section concerns appeals from the Court of Protection and will be supplemented by Court of Protection Rules. Subject to such rules, an appeal will lie from any decision of the court to the Court of Appeal. However, the Court of Protection will comprise a range of judges at different levels. It is therefore intended to make provision by rules of court, by virtue of *subsection* (2), so that decisions made at a lower level of the Court of Protection are appealed to a higher judge within the Court of Protection. Rules may make further detailed provision as to permission to appeal and may provide that where an appeal has already been made to a higher judge of the Court of Protection no appeal may be made to the Court of Appeal from that decision unless the Court of Appeal considers that the appeal would raise an important point of principle or practice or there is some other compelling reason to hear the appeal. This matches the '2nd appeal' test in the Civil Procedures Rules 1998, Rule 52.13.

Fees and costs

Section 54: Fees

140.   This section concerns the setting of fees chargeable by the Court of Protection (which will be by order of the Lord Chancellor with the consent of the Treasury). The order will be subject to the negative resolution procedure (see *section 65(2)*). The order may set the level of fees, any exemptions from and reductions in the fees and any partial or whole remission of fees. Prior to making the order the Lord Chancellor must consult with the President, Vice-President and Senior Judge of the Court of Protection. The Lord Chancellor must take reasonably practicable steps to give out information about fees. Similar provision is made about other court fees in section 92 of the Courts Act 2003.

Section 55: Costs

141.   This section concerns the costs of Court of Protection proceedings and will be supplemented by Court of Protection Rules. Subject to such rules, the court will have discretion to make costs orders, including wasted costs orders, against legal or other representatives. It seeks to put the new court in the same position as the other civil courts.

Section 56: Fees and costs: supplementary

142. This section provides that the Court of Protection rules can deal with the way in which, and funds from which, fees and costs are to be paid and make provision for them to be charged against the estate of the person concerned. It is modelled on the Mental Health Act 1983, section 106.

The Public Guardian

Section 57: The Public Guardian

143. This section provides for a new public official, the Public Guardian, to be appointed by the Lord Chancellor. The Public Guardian will have staff and officers so that he can discharge his duties. The Lord Chancellor may also enter into contracts with other persons for the provision of officers, staff or services for the discharge of the Public Guardian's functions.

Section 58: Functions of the Public Guardian

144. This section sets out the role of the Public Guardian and may be supplemented by regulations made by the Lord Chancellor. It is intended that regulations will set out in more detail how the Public Guardian will exercise his administrative duties in connection with court-ordered security and reports. The regulations will also deal with fees and the sources from which they may be met.

145. The functions of the Public Guardian are set out in *subsection (1)*. They include establishing and maintaining registers of lasting powers of attorney and of orders appointing deputies and supervising deputies. He may also direct Court of Protection Visitors to visit donors or donees of LPAs, deputies or those appointing them. He may deal with complaints and concerns expressed to him about how an attorney or deputy is exercising his powers. He may also publish any information he thinks appropriate about his work.

146. *Subsection (2)* provides that certain functions may be discharged in co-operation with any other person who has functions in relation to the care or treatment of the person to whom the power of attorney or appointment of a deputy relates. It is intended that the Public Guardian will work closely with organisations such as local authorities and NHS bodies.

147. *Subsection (4)* provides for regulations made by the Lord Chancellor to make provision for the setting of fees which may be charged by the Public Guardian, and for any exemptions from and reductions in the fees and any partial or whole remission of fees.

148. *Subsections (5)* and *(6)* allow the Public Guardian to examine and take copies of relevant health, social services or care records, and to interview the person concerned in private. This is to ensure that the Public Guardian will be able to carry out his functions. The Public Guardian has similar rights when reporting to the Court of Protection (see *section 49(7)* and *(8)*). Court of Protection Visitors are given similar rights (see *section 61(5)* and *(6)*).

Section 59: Public Guardian Board

149. This section provides for a body, to be known as the Public Guardian Board, members of which are to be appointed by the Lord Chancellor. The Board will scrutinise and review the Public Guardian's work and make recommendations to the Lord Chancellor.

150. The Board must have at least one member who is a judge of the Court of Protection and at least four members with appropriate knowledge or experience of the Public Guardian's work. *Subsection (6)* provides a regulation-making power that will allow

the Lord Chancellor to set out in more detail how members will be appointed and how the Board will operate.

151.   *Subsection (8)* provides for the Lord Chancellor to make payments to members of the Board for reimbursement of expenses, allowances and remuneration. *Subsection (9)* requires the Board to make an annual report to the Lord Chancellor.

Section 60: Annual report

152.   This requires the Public Guardian to make an annual report about his work to the Lord Chancellor, who must within one month of receipt lay a copy of the report before both Houses of Parliament.

Court of Protection Visitors

Section 61: Court of Protection Visitors

153.   Court of Protection Visitors are appointed to carry out visits and produce reports, as directed by the court (*section 49(2)*) or the Public Guardian (*section 58(1)(d)*) in relation to those who lack capacity. Their functions and powers are similar to those of Lord Chancellor's Visitors appointed under Part 7 of the Mental Health Act 1983.

PART 3: MISCELLANEOUS AND GENERAL

Declaratory provision

Section 62: Scope of the Act

154.   This confirms that the Act has no effect on the law relating to unlawful killing or assisting suicide.

Private international law

Section 63: International Protection of Adults

155.   This introduces *Schedule 3* which makes provision as to the private international law of England and Wales in relation to persons who cannot protect their interests. For example it determines which jurisdiction should apply when a national of one country is in another.

General

Section 66: Existing receivers and enduring powers of attorney etc.

156.   This repeals Part 7 of the Mental Health Act 1983 (management of property and affairs of patients) and the whole of the Enduring Powers of Attorney Act 1985, but introduces transitional provisions.

Section 67: Minor consequential amendments and repeals

157.   This section enables the Lord Chancellor to make secondary legislation (orders) to give effect to the Act. Any such order which amends or repeals primary legislation (an Act of Parliament or General Synod Measure) will be subject to the affirmative resolution procedure in Parliament.

SCHEDULES

SCHEDULE 1: LASTING POWERS OF ATTORNEY: FORMALITIES

Part 1: Making instruments

158. This Part sets out the requirements with regard to the form and execution of an LPA. A document which fails to comply with the provisions of this Schedule or regulations made under it will not generally create an LPA and consequently will not give any powers to the donee. An LPA must be in the form prescribed by regulations. The form must also contain statements by both the donor and the donee of the power to the effect that they have read, or have had read to them, such information as may be prescribed. The LPA must include names of any persons whom the donor wishes to be notified of any application to register the LPA ('named persons') or a statement that there are no such persons.

159. The form must also include a certificate by a person of a prescribed description that, in his opinion, at the time when the donor executes the instrument he understands the purpose of the instrument and the scope of the authority conferred, that no fraud or undue pressure is being used to induce him to create an LPA, and that there is nothing else that would prevent an LPA from being created by the instrument. The Public Guardian may treat an LPA differing in an immaterial respect from the prescribed form as sufficient to create an LPA. The Court of Protection has the power to make a declaration that an instrument not in the prescribed form is to be treated as if it were, if satisfied that the persons executing the instrument intended to create an LPA.

Part 2: Registration

160. The powers given in an LPA to the donee cannot be exercised until the document has been registered. In order to register an LPA an application must be made by the donor or donee(s) to the Public Guardian. When about to apply to register the LPA, the donor or donee(s) must notify the named persons to inform them of the pending registration. The Public Guardian is required to notify the donor or donee(s) (depending on who makes the application). The court will have the power to dispense with the notification requirement on the application of either the donor or donee.

161. If the instrument received by the Public Guardian is flawed in some way (that is, it is ineffective, or contains a provision that would make it inoperable as an LPA), the Public Guardian must refer it to the Court of Protection and must not register the instrument in the interim. The court can either remove (or 'sever') the offending provision from the instrument or direct the Public Guardian not to register the LPA instrument. If the court severs a provision, the Public Guardian can then register the instrument, but must attach a note to that effect to it.

162. Objections can be made to the registration of the LPA within a prescribed period. An objection by a donor to registration by the donee(s) must be made to the Public Guardian and the court will only direct him to register the LPA if satisfied that the donor lacks capacity to object. An objection by a donee or named person on the basis that the LPA has been revoked (for example, because of bankruptcy of the donee) must also be made to the Public Guardian who, if satisfied, will not register the LPA. If the person wishing to register the LPA disagrees with the Public Guardian's decision not to register the instrument, he can apply to the court. If the court finds that the grounds for the Public Guardian objecting to registration are not established, the court can direct the Public Guardian to register the LPA. An objection by a donee or named person on such other grounds as may be prescribed must

be made to the court. The Public Guardian must not register the instrument, unless told to do so by the court, where it appears to him that there is a deputy appointed for the donor and that the powers of the deputy would conflict with the powers to be conferred on the donee.

Part 3: Cancellation of registration and notification of severance

163   The Public Guardian will cancel an LPA if he is satisfied that the power has been revoked on the basis of:

- the donor's bankruptcy;
- the donee giving up his/her appointment by exercising a disclaimer;
- the death of the donee;
- the insolvency of the donee;
- the dissolution or annulment of a marriage or civil partnership between donor and donee; and
- the lack of capacity of the donee.

164.   The court must direct the Public Guardian to cancel the registration of an LPA if the court:

- decides that a requirement for creating the LPA was not met;
- decides that the power has been revoked or otherwise come to an end; or
- revokes the power on fraud or undue pressure grounds.

165.   On cancellation of the registration of an LPA the Public Guardian will notify both the donor and donee to this effect. Where the court has removed a provision from an instrument, *paragraph 19(2)(a)* requires the court to notify the Public Guardian of the severance of that provision. And where the court determines that a provision in an instrument means that instrument cannot operate as a valid LPA, *paragraph 19(2)(b)* requires the court to direct the Public Guardian to cancel the registration of that instrument as an LPA.

Part 4: Records of alterations in registered powers

166.   A note of any revocation of an LPA, because of the donor or donee's bankruptcy, which only takes effect in so far as the power relates to the property and affairs of the donor will be attached to the LPA by the Public Guardian. The Public Guardian must also attach a note to an instrument if an event has terminated the appointment of the donee but not revoked the instrument (for example, if there is more than one donee), where a donee's ability to act has been suspended by the making of an interim bankruptcy restrictions order or the appointment of the donee has been replaced under the terms of the LPA. The Public Guardian must give the donor and donee notice of any notes attached to the LPA. Where the court has notified the Public Guardian that it has removed a provision from an instrument, *paragraph 24* requires that the Public Guardian must attach a note to that effect to the instrument.

SCHEDULE 2: PROPERTY AND AFFAIRS: SUPPLEMENTARY PROVISIONS

167.   This contains detailed provisions relating to the court's powers in relation to property and affairs, in particular the making of wills and settlements. *Paragraphs 1 to 4* deal with wills that can be made on behalf of an adult lacking capacity. These are generally known as 'statutory wills' when made under the Mental Health Act 1983, Part 7. *Paragraphs 5 and 6* concern settlements, that is putting a person's property into a trust. *Paragraph 7* enables the court to direct the transfer of stocks to a person appointed outside England and Wales.

168. *Paragraph 10* specifies that only a representative appointed by the Court of
      Protection may exercise the powers which the person concerned has as patron of a
      benefice. A benefice is a freehold office in the Church of England, such as the vicar
      or rector of a parish, and the patron of a benefice has the right to present a priest
      for admission to that benefice. The representative must be an individual capable of
      appointment by a patron as his representative under section 8(1)(b) of the
      Patronage (Benefices) Measure 1986. This means he must be a communicant mem-
      ber of the Church of England (or of a Church in communion with it) or a clerk in
      Holy Orders. The representative will discharge the person's functions as patron of
      the benefice not only presenting a priest to a vacant benefice, but also performing
      other functions of the patron such as acting as a consultee when there is a proposal
      to suspend presentation under section 67 of the Pastoral Measure 1983. In dis-
      charging his functions, the representative is subject to the provisions of the 1986
      Measure in the same way that a representative appointed by a patron with capacity
      would be.

SCHEDULE 3: INTERNATIONAL PROTECTION OF ADULTS

169. This makes provision as to the private international law of England and Wales in
      relation to persons who cannot protect their interests. In particular, it gives effect in
      England and Wales to the Convention on the International Protection of Adults
      signed at the Hague on 13th January 2000 (Cm. 5881) (the 'Hague Convention') (the
      text of which is available at: http://www.hcch.net/e/conventions/menu35e.html.).
170. It should be noted that for the purposes of the Hague Convention, England and
      Wales, Scotland and Northern Ireland are treated separately because they constitute
      separate jurisdictions. The provisions of *Schedule 3* are intended to be compatible
      with the provisions of Schedule 3 to the Adults with Incapacity (Scotland) Act 2000
      which provided for the private international law of Scotland in this field and imple-
      mented the Hague Convention for Scotland. Scotland is as yet the only country to
      have ratified the Convention, which will enter into force only once it has been rat-
      ified by three states. However, *Schedule 3* provides private international law rules to
      govern jurisdictional issues between Scotland and England/Wales, irrespective of
      whether the Convention is in force.

Part 1: Preliminary

171. This Part contains relevant definitions and introductory provisions. The definition of
      'adult' in *paragraph 4* is consistent with the Act but is not the same as the definition
      provided in the Hague Convention.

Part 2: Jurisdiction of competent authority

172. Part 2 of the Schedule provides the grounds, based on Articles 5 to 11 of the Hague
      Convention, on which the Court of Protection will exercise its jurisdiction under
      the Act when dealing with cases with an international element. *Paragraph 7(1)* pro-
      vides that the court may exercise its jurisdiction in relation to: an adult habitually
      resident in England and Wales; an adult's property in England and Wales; an adult
      present in England or Wales or who has property there, if the matter is urgent; or
      an adult present in England and Wales, if a protective measure which is temporary
      and limited in its effect to England and Wales is proposed in relation to him.
173. *Paragraph 7(2)* provides that an adult present in England and Wales is to be treated
      as habitually resident if his habitual residence cannot be ascertained, he is a refugee
      or he has been displaced as a result of disturbance in the country of his habitual
      residence.

174.   Once the provisions of the Convention are in force the court will also be able to exercise jurisdiction, in so far as it cannot otherwise do so under the provisions of *paragraph 7*, in relation to a British citizen with a closer connection with England and Wales than with Scotland or Northern Ireland. The jurisdiction may be exercised provided that the court considers that it is in a better position to assess the interests of the adult, that certain requirements as to notification of other Convention countries are complied with and that other Convention countries which may have jurisdiction on certain grounds have not dealt, or are not dealing with the matter (*paragraph 8(2)(c)* and Article 7 of the Hague Convention).

Part 3: Applicable law

175.   *Part 3* of the Schedule makes provision as to which law is to apply in various situations. Although the Court of Protection will normally apply the law of England and Wales, and the conditions of implementation of any protective measure taken abroad will be governed by the law of England and Wales if implemented here, the court may apply the law of another country if it thinks that a matter has a substantial connection with that country (*paragraphs 11* and *12*).

176.   In addition the donor of a foreign power akin to an LPA may specify that the law applicable to the existence, extent, modification or extinction of the power is to be the law of a country of which he is a national, in which he is habitually resident, or in which he has property. If the power is exercised in England and Wales the law of England and Wales shall, however, apply to the manner of the exercise of the power. Regulations may apply the provisions of *Schedule 1* (lasting powers of attorney: formalities) to such foreign powers (*paragraphs 15*).

177.   The court may disapply or modify a lasting power (including a foreign power) where the power is not exercised in a manner sufficient to guarantee the protection of the donor or his property. In these circumstances the court must, so far as possible, have regard to any foreign law applicable by virtue of this (*paragraph 14*).

178.   This Part provides protection for a third party who enters into a transaction with a representative on behalf of a person, where that representative was actually not entitled so to act under the law of a country other than England and Wales applicable by virtue of this Part. Protection is provided if the third party neither knew nor ought to have known that such a law was applicable (*paragraph 16*); ensures that mandatory provisions of the law of England and Wales apply regardless of any other system of law that would apply (*paragraph 17*); and provides that nothing in this Part of the Schedule requires or enables the application in England and Wales of a provision of the law of another country that is manifestly contrary to public policy (*paragraph 18*).

Part 4: Recognition and enforcement

179.   *Part 4* of the Schedule provides for the recognition and enforcement of protective measures taken in other countries. It provides that a protective measure is to be recognised in England and Wales if it was taken on the ground that the adult is habitually resident in the other country. It also provides that a protective measure taken in another Convention country is to be recognised provided that it was taken on a ground provided for in the Convention (the same grounds on which the Court of Protection will exercise jurisdiction under Part 2) (*paragraph 19(1)* and (2)).

180.   However the court may refuse to recognise a protective measure where it thinks that the case in which the measure was taken was not urgent, the adult was not given an opportunity to be heard, and that omission amounted to a breach of natural justice. The court may also refuse to recognise a protective measure if recognition of the measure would be manifestly contrary to public policy, the measure would be inconsistent with a mandatory provision of the law of England and Wales, or the

measure is inconsistent with one subsequently taken or recognised in relation to the adult (*paragraph 19(3) and (4)*).

181.   *Paragraph 20* provides for any interested person to apply to the court for a declaration as to whether a protective measure taken under the law of a country other than England and Wales is to be recognised in England and Wales.

182.   *Paragraph 22* provides for an interested person to apply to the court for a declaration as to whether a protective measure taken under the law of, and enforceable in, a country other than England and Wales is enforceable, or to be registered, in England and Wales in accordance with Court of Protection Rules.

Part 5: Co-operation

183.   *Part 5* of the Schedule provides for co-operation between authorities in England and Wales and authorities in other Convention countries.

Part 6: General

184.   *Part 6* includes powers to make further provision as to private international law by Order in Council and regulations (*paragraphs 31 and 32*). An Order in Council under paragraph 31 will be subject to the negative resolution procedure in Parliament. Regulations under *paragraph 32(1)(b)* will be subject to the affirmative resolution procedure (see *section 65*).

SCHEDULE 4: PROVISIONS APPLYING TO EXISTING ENDURING POWERS OF ATTORNEY

185.   This Schedule has effect in relation to any EPAs remaining at the time of the repeal of the Enduring Powers of Attorney Act 1985. It ensures that such instruments will continue to have the same legal effect as they had at the time they were made. They will also continue to be governed by the legal rules and procedures which were in place at the time they were made. The Schedule therefore restates with amendments the relevant provisions of the Enduring Powers of Attorney Act 1985. The amendments relate to the distribution of the functions of the original Court of Protection between the new Court of Protection and the new office of the Public Guardian.

Part 1: Enduring powers of attorney

186.   Part 1 sets out the main elements of EPAs. They are not revoked by any subsequent mental incapacity of the donor of the power, unlike ordinary powers of attorney. Such a power is only created if it is in the prescribed form and complies with the provisions in *paragraph 2* of this Part. This Part also deals with the scope of EPAs. Both general and specific powers may be subject to conditions and restrictions as set out by the donor. A donee may from time to time make gifts from the donor's property to people connected to the donor (including himself) and to any charity the donor may have been expected to make gifts to. This is subject to any conditions or restrictions as mentioned above and also to the reasonableness of such gifts with regard to the size of the donor's estate.

Part 2: Action on actual or impending incapacity of donor

187.   This Part outlines the steps which should be taken on the actual or impending incapacity of the donor. Once the attorney believes that the donor is or is becoming mentally incapacitated he or she must immediately make an application to the Public Guardian to register the power. Part 3 deals with the steps which must be taken before the application to the Public Guardian is made. The application for

registration must be made in the prescribed form and must contain the appropriate statements (as prescribed by regulations).

Part 3: Notification prior to registration

188.   Part 3 sets out the steps which should be taken by the attorney before making an application to the Public Guardian to register the power. The attorney must give notice of his intention to register the power to all those entitled to receive notice. These people can include the donor's spouse or current partner, the donor's children and the donor's parents. The attorney is also under a duty to give notice of his intention to register to the donor. The attorney may apply to the court to dispense with this requirement to give notice to entitled persons. Notices should be in the prescribed form and must contain specific information, especially with regard to the right of that person to object to registration.

Part 4: Registration

189.   Where an application for registration is made in accordance with the provisions of Part 2, the Public Guardian must register the instrument unless a valid notice of objection has been made in accordance with the provisions of this part. A notice of objection is valid if made on one or more of the following grounds:

- that the power was not valid as an EPA;
- that the power created no longer exists;
- that the application is premature because the donor is not yet becoming mentally incapable;
- that fraud or undue pressure was used to induce the donor to create the power;
- that, having regard to all the circumstances, the donee is unsuitable to be the donor's attorney.

190.   It is for the court to decide whether any of those grounds is actually made out and if so it must direct the Public Guardian not to register the instrument. If the court is satisfied that fraud or undue pressure was used or that the donee is unsuitable, then it must also order the revocation of the power created by the instrument.

191.   Where it appears that there is no one to whom notice has been given or the Public Guardian has reason to believe that appropriate inquiries might bring to light evidence on which he could be satisfied that one of the valid grounds of objection was established, he must not register the instrument and must undertake such inquiries as he thinks appropriate. If, after those inquiries, he considers one of the grounds of objection to be made out, he must apply to the court for directions and must not register the instrument except in accordance with such directions. The Public Guardian must not register an EPA if a deputy has been appointed and the powers of the attorney would conflict. Again, the court may give directions.

Part 5: Legal position after registration

192.   Once an EPA has been registered any revocation of the power must be confirmed by the court. A disclaimer by the attorney is not valid until the attorney has given notice of such to the Public Guardian. Furthermore, the donor cannot alter in any way the scope of the power given in the registered power. This Part also sets out the role of the court with regard to registered powers. The court has a number of functions, not least the power to decide any question about the meaning or effect of an EPA. The court is also under an obligation to direct the Public Guardian to cancel the registration of a power in a number of circumstances (for example, if it is satisfied that the donor is and is likely to remain capable or that undue force or pressure was put on the donor to create the power). The full list of circumstances is given in *paragraph 16(4)*. This Part also lists the circumstances under which the Public

Guardian is obliged to cancel the registration of a power, such as on receipt of a disclaimer from the attorney.

Part 6: Protection of attorney and third parties

193. This Part provides protection for those who act under a power which is invalid as long as at the time of acting they did not know that the power was invalid or that, had the EPA been valid, either an event had occurred which would have revoked the power or that the power would have expired. Any transaction between an attorney and another person is valid unless that person is aware of any of those matters.

Part 7: Joint and joint and several attorneys

194. A document which appoints more than one attorney cannot create an EPA unless the attorneys are appointed to act jointly or jointly and severally. Where attorneys are appointed to act jointly and severally, if one of them fails to comply with the necessary requirements for the creation of an EPA, then the document will not create a power in his case. But this will not affect the creation of a power in relation to the other attorneys. If one or more (but not both or all) of the attorneys applies to register the document, they must notify the other attorney(s) of this.

SCHEDULE 5: TRANSITIONAL PROVISIONS AND SAVINGS

195. *Schedule 5* sets out transitional arrangements arising from the repeal of Part 7 of the Mental Health Act 1983 and repeal of the Enduring Powers of Attorney Act 1985.

196. In particular, Part 1 sets out provisions for enabling receivers appointed under the Mental Health Act 1983 to continue. *Paragraph 1(2)* provides that after implementation the Act shall apply as if any receiver for the person were, in fact, a deputy appointed in relation to that person, but only with the functions he had as a receiver. Part 2 allows for the continuation of procedural matters (e.g. appeals and other legal proceedings) relating to EPAs which remain in place by the time the Enduring Powers of Attorney Act 1985 is repealed.

COMMENCEMENT

197. The Act (with the exception of *sections 30* to *41*) will come into force on dates appointed by the Lord Chancellor. *Sections 30* to *41* will come into force on dates appointed by the Secretary of State (in relation to England) and the National Assembly for Wales (in relation to Wales).

PARLIAMENTARY STAGES

198.   The following table sets out the dates for each stage of this Act's passage through Parliament.

Stage	Date	Hansard Reference
House of Commons		
Introduction	17 June 2004	Vol.422(no.603)Col 928
Second Reading	11 October 2004	Vol.425 (no.134) Col 22
Standing Committee A	Day 1 – 19 October 2004	First Sitting (Morning) Second Sitting (Afternoon)
	Day 2 – 21 October 2004	Third Sitting (Morning) Fourth Sitting (Afternoon)
	Day 3 – 26 October 2004	Fifth Sitting (Morning) Sixth Sitting (Afternoon)
	Day 4 – 28 October 2004	Seventh Sitting (Morning) Eighth Sitting (Afternoon)
	Day 5 – 2 November 2004	Ninth Sitting (Morning) Tenth Sitting (Afternoon)
	Day 6 – 5 November 2004	Eleventh Sitting (Morning) Twelfth Sitting (Afternoon)
Re-introduction (following carry-over)	24 November 2004	Vol. 428 (No. 2) Col. 101
Report and Third Reading	14 December 2004	Vol. 428 (No.13) Col.1531
House of Lords		
Introduction	15 December 2005	Vol. 667 (No.14) Col. 1333
Second Reading	10 January 2005	Vol.668 (No.18) Col. 11
Committee	25 January 2005 27 January 2005 1 February 2005 8 February 2005	Vol. 668 (No.28) Col.1143 Vol. 668 (No.30) Col.1395 Vol. 669 (No.32) Col.102 Vol. 669 (No.37) Col.734
Report	Day 1 – 15 March 2005	Vol. 670 (No.53) Col. 1275
	Day 2 – 17 March 2005	Vol. 670 (No.55) Col. 1441
Third Reading	24 March 2005	Vol. 671 (No.59) Col. 412
Commons Consideration of Lords Amendments	5 April 2005	Vol. 432 (No.63) Col. 1362

Royal Assent – 7 April 2005   House of Commons Hansard Vol. 432 Col. 1641

House of Lords Hansard Vol. 671 Col. 950

Appendix 3
MENTAL CAPACITY BILL: DRAFT CODE OF PRACTICE

PREFACE

This document represents a preliminary draft of a Code of Practice to accompany the Mental Capacity Bill, when enacted.

Last year a Parliamentary pre-legislative scrutiny committee considered the Bill, and in their report they specifically recommended that the Bill should not be introduced to Parliament until it could be considered alongside draft Codes of Practice. It is unusual to provide a draft Code at such an early stage in the legislative process. However, the Government accepted this recommendation and undertook to provide a first draft in time for Committee stage in Parliament.

We are now fulfilling this commitment, though I must emphasise that this draft represents the first stage in what will be a lengthy and thorough process to produce a final Code of Practice. It may be that the final Code of Practice will look quite different, both to reflect changes in the Bill that Parliament decides to make, and also as a result of the formal consultation that must follow the passing of any Act. Such consultation will be vital in ensuring that the ultimate code is helpful to stakeholders and others who will be responsible for implementing future legislation. And unlike this first draft, the final Code will contain extensive cross-referencing and signposts to other relevant guidance and sources of information.

That said, I very much hope that this first draft will help the Committee and Parliament as a whole by giving a clearer idea of our current thinking on the role and content of the Code. I also hope that it will assist the Committee and Parliament when scrutinising and debating the Bill since it gives a greater level of detail on many of the Bill's provisions and demonstrates how we think those acting under the Bill will need to be guided when putting these provisions into practice. The Government will take full account of all comments and suggestions that are made about the Code during the course of debate on the Bill.

Finally, I want to record how very grateful I am to a wide range of interested stakeholders, including voluntary sector organisations, professional bodies, academics and lobby groups, who have helped to prepare this first draft. They have provided an significant number of useful and insightful comments and the draft owes a great deal to their goodwill and commitment.

Lord Filkin

MENTAL CAPACITY BILL – CODE OF PRACTICE

Contents of the Code of Practice

[. . .]

CHAPTER 1: THE SCOPE AND PURPOSE OF THE CODE OF PRACTICE TO THE MENTAL CAPACITY ACT

INTRODUCTION

1.1　The Mental Capacity Act (the Act) provides a framework for acting and making decisions on behalf of individuals who lack the mental capacity to do these acts and make these decisions for themselves.

1.2　The Act represents the legal framework and is accompanied by a Code of Practice which provides guidance and information to those acting under the terms of the legislation.

1.3　There will also be guidance and explanatory information targeted at specific groups of people who need to know about the new law. This will include specialist information for professionals (for example on how the Act will affect day-to-day clinical decisions), literature for informal carers and basic information of interest to the general public (for example on the role of the Public Guardian and how to make a Lasting Power of Attorney).

THE ROLE OF THE CODE

1.4　The Code provides guidance to all those working with and/or caring for adults who lack capacity, including family members, professionals and carers and describes their responsibilities when acting or making decisions with, or on behalf of, individuals who lack the capacity to do these things themselves. As noted above, however, relevant messages for those affected by the Act will also be provided in other formats suitable for their audience. In effect, the Code explains how the legal rules set out in legislation will work in practice.

1.5　Where necessary and relevant, the Code provides information on how to obtain further, more detailed, guidance.

STATUS OF THE CODE

1.6　Section 40 of the Act sets out the purpose of the Code of Practice which is to provide guidance for specific people in specific circumstances.

1.7　Section 41 sets out procedures for the preparation of and consultation about drafts of the Code of Practice, and for parliamentary consideration.

1.8　Sections 40, subsections (4) and (5), set out categories of people who are placed under a duty to have regard to the Code and give further information about the status of the Code. The following categories of people are under a duty to have regard to the Code when acting in relation to a person who lacks capacity:

■　People working in a professional capacity (for example, a doctor who is assessing a person's capacity to make a particular decision or a social worker who is arranging for a person lacking capacity to move into a supported living arrangement)

- People who are receiving payment for work in acting in relation to the person without capacity (for example, a care assistant working in a residential care home for people with learning disabilities)
- Anyone who is a donee of a Lasting Power of Attorney (LPA) (LPAs are discussed in more detail at Chapter 6) and
- Anyone who is a deputy appointed by the Court of Protection (the Court of Protection and deputies are discussed in more detail at Chapter 7)

1.9 These categories of people must be able to demonstrate that they are familiar (in broad terms) with relevant parts of the Code or with the guidance produced on particular parts of the Code and aimed at, for example, non-professional carers. If they have not followed the guidance contained in the Code, or supporting guidance, then they will be expected to give reasons why they have departed from it.

1.10 Failure to comply with the Code can be used in evidence in civil or criminal proceedings, if relevant. It is therefore important that anyone working with or caring for a person who lacks capacity should become familiar with it.

1.11 Other people, who are not placed under this legal duty, will still be expected to follow the guidance in the Code. The Act applies to *everyone* who looks after, or cares for, someone who lacks capacity, including informal carers and family members, and the Code will help them to understand the Act and apply it.

REFERENCES IN THE CODE

1.12 Throughout the Code, the Mental Capacity Act is referred to as 'the Act'. Where reference is made to provisions from other legislation, the title and date of the relevant Act will be set out. Where reference is made to regulations or other secondary legislation made under the Act the name, number and date of the Statutory Instrument is indicated.

FURTHER INFORMATION

1.13 The Code has been published in alternative formats and these are available from the DCA. In accordance with the Welsh Language Act, the Code is available in the Welsh language

CHAPTER 2: GUIDING PRINCIPLES OF THE MENTAL CAPACITY ACT AND RELATIONSHIP OF THE ACT TO OTHER RELEVANT LEGISLATION

INTRODUCTION

2.1 This chapter provides a general introduction to the Mental Capacity Act (the Act). **Part 1** of this Chapter provides a brief overview of the Act and a commentary on its guiding principles. **Part 2** provides brief pointers to how the Act relates to other relevant legislation, namely the Mental Health Act 1983.

PART 1: OUTLINE OF THE ACT

2.2 This Act sets out a framework for acting and making decisions on behalf of adults aged 16 years and over who lack the mental capacity to act or make such decisions for themselves. It provides mechanisms for decision-making in relation to individuals' welfare (including health care) and financial affairs.

WHAT ACTS AND DECISIONS DOES THE ACT COVER?

2.3   The Act covers decisions made, or actions taken, on behalf of people lacking capacity, whether they relate to day-to-day matters or represent major life-changing events. Actions or decisions may range from choosing what to wear or doing the weekly shopping to carrying out a routine dental check-up, to deciding whether the person should move into residential care or deciding to undertake a major surgical operation.

Who is affected by the Act?

2.4   The Act sets out fundamental legal rules which apply to everyone working with and/or caring for adults who lack capacity, including relatives, professionals and other carers. It also provides mechanisms for resolving disputes or difficulties which are important for all professionals and carers, as well as for people who are being treated as lacking capacity themselves.

What changes will the Act introduce?

2.5   Many of the provisions in the Act are based upon existing common law principles (i.e. principles that have been established through decisions made by courts in individual cases). The Act seeks to clarify and improve upon these existing principles and build upon current good practice which has derived from them. The underlying philosophy of the Act is to ensure that individuals who lack capacity are the focus of any decisions made, or actions taken, on their behalf. The interests of the person who lacks capacity should prevail; not the views or convenience of those caring for that person.

Consultation process

2.6   The Act is the result of several years of preparation, consultation and review. In 1995, following five years research and consultation, the Law Commission published Mental Incapacity, which set out detailed recommendations for the introduction of comprehensive legislation for making decisions on behalf of people who lack capacity. The Government's Green paper, Who Decides? Making Decisions on Behalf of Mentally Incapacitated People (1997) sought views on these proposals for reform. In the light of the responses to this consultation document, the Lord Chancellor's Department published Making Decisions in 1999 which set out the areas intended to be covered in future legislation. This was followed by the publication of the draft Mental Incapacity Bill in June 2003.

2.7   The House of Lords and House of Commons Joint Committee on the Draft Mental Incapacity Bill made substantial recommendations for improving the draft Bill, having received over 1,200 written submissions and heard evidence from over 60 witnesses. In response to such recommendations, the Government revised the Bill and prepared a first draft Code of Practice.

Guiding Principles

2.8   In order to underline the Act's fundamental concepts, section 1 of the Act sets out a number of key principles. These principles apply to all actions and decisions taken under the Act and are described below.

- **The presumption of capacity:** '*A person must be assumed to have capacity unless it is established that he lacks capacity.*'

2.9 A fundamental principle of common law is that every adult has the right to make his or her own decisions and is assumed to have capacity to do so unless it is proved otherwise. This principle underpins a key message of the Act – that everyone has the right to make choices and decisions for themselves (the right to autonomy) unless it has been shown that the person lacks capacity to make these particular choices and decisions themselves. More information about the presumption of capacity is given in Chapter 3 of the Code.

- **Maximising decision-making capacity:** '*A person is not to be treated as unable to make a decision unless all practicable steps to help him to do so have been taken without success.*'

2.10 This is linked to the presumption of capacity. Individuals who have an illness or disability that might affect their ability to make decisions for themselves should be enabled and encouraged to take as many decisions for themselves as they can. The aim is to ensure that people who can make decisions for themselves, but may need help and support to do so, are not automatically labelled as incapable of making these decisions and therefore subject to unnecessary interventions. Such help and support might include using specific communication strategies, providing information in an accessible form, or treating an underlying mental disorder to enable a person to regain capacity. More information on the ways in which people can be helped to make decisions for themselves is given in Chapter 3.

- **Unwise decisions:** '*A person is not to be treated as unable to make a decision merely because he makes an unwise decision.*'

2.11 This principle again underpins the right to autonomy and reflects the fact that each one of us is an individual with our own values, beliefs, preferences and attitude to risk, which may not be the same as those of other people. Thus, even if a person makes a decision which others, including their family and friends, regard as unwise, unusual or irrational, this does not necessarily mean that the person lacks capacity to make that decision. This is considered in more detail in Chapter 3.

- **Best interests:** '*An act done, or decision made, under this Act for or on behalf of a person who lacks capacity must be done, or made, in his best interests.*'

2.12 The requirement that all actions and decisions taken for someone who lacks capacity should be in that person's 'best interests' is a well established principle of common-law. The concept of 'best interests' must guide all actions taken or decisions made on behalf of a person who lacks capacity under the Act. It is not possible for statute to give a single all-encompassing definition of 'best interests' because what will be in a person's best interests will depend on that particular individual and his or her personal circumstances. However, the Act sets out certain steps that must be taken in order to decide what is in a person's best interests each time an act or decision is being taken on behalf of an individual who lacks capacity. Chapter 4 provides more detailed guidance on best interests and factors to be taken into account when deciding what will be in the person's best interests.

- **Least restrictive alternative:** '*Before the act is done, or the decision is made, regard must be had to whether the purpose for which it is needed can be as effectively achieved in a way that is less restrictive of the person's rights and freedom of action.*'

2.13 One of the key principles of the Act is that before any action is taken, or decision made, on behalf of a person lacking capacity, people must consider whether it is possible to decide or act in a way that would interfere less with the person's rights and freedoms. This means that people should consider whether there is a need to act at all or make a decision. This key principle again seeks to protect the rights and freedoms of those lacking capacity.

PART 2: HOW THE MENTAL CAPACITY ACT RELATES TO OTHER RELEVANT LEGISLATION

[N.B. This section will be substantially updated if the Mental Health Bill 2005 is passed.]

2.14   The Mental Health and Mental Capacity Acts have different purposes. The Mental Capacity Act has a broad scope and provides a legal framework for acting and decision-making which applies in many situations where adults are unable to take decisions and act for themselves due to a lack of capacity. The Mental Health Act provides a much narrower legal authority for the admission to hospital and treatment (where appropriate without consent) of people with a mental disorder when this is necessary in certain circumstances, because of the risk posed to themselves or others.

2.15   Since lack of capacity is not the basis for treatment under mental health legislation, treatment delivered in accordance with the Mental Health Act 1983 is specifically excluded from the scope of the Mental Capacity Act (in section 28). This clause ensures that the Act does not apply to any treatment for a mental disorder which is safeguarded by the provisions in Part 4 of the Mental Health Act. The procedural safeguards in that Act take precedence and must be followed when treating patients to whom that part applies.

2.16   The Mental Health Act 1983 only deals with treatment 'for mental disorder'. A person detained under the Mental Health Act may also lack capacity in relation to some other form of medical treatment or some other issues. For example, someone may be detained for treatment for a mental disorder but also require dental treatment. In these cases, the Mental Capacity Act will apply to decisions about dental treatment.

CHAPTER 3: CAPACITY TO MAKE A DECISION

INTRODUCTION

3.1   This chapter deals with the provisions of the Act about capacity, lack of capacity and assessment of capacity.

PART 1: WHAT IS MENTAL CAPACITY?

3.2   In a day-to-day context, mental capacity means the ability to make decisions or take actions affecting daily life – when to get up, what to wear, what to eat, whether to go to the doctor when feeling ill etc. In a legal context, it refers to a person's ability to do something, including making a decision, which may have legal consequences for the person themselves or for other people.

Presumption of capacity

S1 (2)   'A person must be assumed to have capacity unless it is established that he lacks capacity'

3.3   The Act provides that the starting-point should be a *presumption of capacity*. Some people may need help or support to be able to make a decision or communicate a decision (see Part 3 below), but the need for help and support does not automatically mean that they cannot make that decision.

3.4   The starting point for assessing someone's capacity to make a particular decision is always the assumption that the individual does have capacity. In legal proceedings, the burden of proof will fall on any person who asserts that capacity is lacking. A court must be satisfied that, on the balance of probabilities, capacity has been shown to be lacking.

Mrs A has been diagnosed as being in the early stages of dementia and her son is worried that she is becoming confused about money. She knows her pension is paid into the bank every month but cannot always remember which bills she has to pay or how to pay them. Her son must first assume she has capacity to manage her affairs and look at each financial decision as it has to be made, giving his mother the help and support she may need to make these decisions for herself. As a start, he offers to help make arrangements to pay the bills by direct debit and explains to her what this means. Mrs A agrees this would be helpful and signs the relevant forms because she is able to understand what she is doing. He goes shopping with her and sees she is quite capable of finding the goods she needs and making sure she gets the correct change when paying for them. But when it comes to deciding how to get the best returns from her investments, Mrs A gets confused about the different options, no matter how they are explained to her, even though she had been able to make such decisions in the past. Her son concludes that she has capacity to deal with everyday financial matters but not more complex affairs. He therefore considers making an application to the Court of Protection.

PART 2: LACK OF CAPACITY

Defining lack of capacity – the 'functional' approach – decision specific

S2 (1) 'For the purposes of this Act, a person lacks capacity in relation to a Matter if at the material time he is unable to make a decision for himself in relation to the matter because of an impairment of, or a disturbance in the functioning of, the mind or brain.

(2) It does not matter whether the impairment or disturbance is permanent or temporary.

S3 (1) For the purposes of section 2, a person is unable to make a decision for himself if he is unable –

(a)   to understand the information relevant to the decision,

(b)   to retain that information

(c)   to use or weigh that information as part of the process of making the decision or

(d)   to communicate his decision (whether by talking, using sign language or any other means).'

The two-stage test of capacity

3.5   In order to decide whether an individual has capacity to make a particular decision, a two-stage test must be applied:

(i)   is there an impairment of or disturbance in the functioning of the person's mind or brain? If so,

(ii)   has it made the person unable to make a particular decision?

The diagnostic threshold

3.6   The requirement to show that the inability to decide is caused by a form of mental disability sets a diagnostic threshold for a finding of incapacity. If there is no such impairment or disturbance, the individual cannot lack capacity within the meaning of the Act.

> Mr B is 48 and has lived in a London suburb with his wife and two children for the past 20 years, while working in a City bank. He decides to leave his job and wants to spend a year travelling. He feels his children are now old enough to fend for themselves and wants more adventure in his life. His wife is shocked that her reliable and cautious husband could make such a decision and is worried about their future financial security. She persuades him to talk things over with their family doctor. The doctor can find no indication that Mr B is suffering from the effects of stress, any mental illness, such as depression, or any other impairment of, or disturbance in, the functioning of his mind or brain. Therefore there appears to be no reason to doubt Mr B's capacity to make each of these decisions.

3.7   The diagnostic threshold is intended to cover a wide range of situations. Examples include people who are affected by the symptoms of alcohol or drug mis-use, delirium, or following head injury, as well as the more obvious categories of mental illness, dementia, learning disabilities, or the long-term effects of brain damage.

Inability to make decisions

3.8   Section 3 of the Act sets out the test for assessing whether a person is unable to make a decision for him/herself and therefore lacks capacity. This is a 'functional' test, focussing on how the decision is made rather than the outcome. The Act says that a person is unable to make a decision if s/he is unable to:

(a)   understand the information relevant to the decision or
(b)   retain that information or
(c)   use or weigh that information as part of the process of making the decision or
(d)   communicate the decision (whether by talking, using sign language or any other means)

S2 (1)(A) UNDERSTAND THE INFORMATION RELEVANT TO THE DECISION

3.9   In deciding whether the person is able to *understand the information relevant to a decision*, every effort must first be made to provide that information and explain it to the person in a way that is most appropriate for that individual and will assist his/her understanding. Such information will include the particular nature of the decision in question, the purpose for which the decision is needed and the likely effects of making or not making the decision. The steps set out below in relation to taking all practicable steps to enable someone to make a decision themselves should also be considered when assessing someone's capacity to understand all information relevant to a decision.

3.10   Section 2(5) stipulates that the information relevant to a decision includes information about the likely consequences of deciding one way or another or of making no decision at all. The explanation of what is proposed, and any possible consequences, should be given in given in broad terms and simple language (or whatever method of communication the person requires). It will not always be necessary to explain all the minutiae.

S3 (1)(B) RETAIN THE INFORMATION RELEVANT TO THE DECISION

3.11   Section 3(4) stipulates that the ability to retain information for a short period only should not automatically disqualify the person from making the decision – it will depend on what is necessary for the decision in question. Aids, such as videos and voice recorders, may also be used to assist retention and recording of information.

S2 (1)(C) USE OR WEIGH THE INFORMATION AS PART OF THE PROCESS OF MAKING THE DECISION;

3.12   This has been described in the courts as the ability to weigh all relevant information in the balance as part of the process of making a decision and then use that information to arrive at a decision. There are cases where the person concerned can understand the information but where the effects of a mental impairment or disturbance prevents him or her using the information or taking it into account in making a decision. For example, certain disorders cause people, who are able to understand and absorb information, to make decisions which are inevitable, regardless of the information and their understanding of it. For example, a person suffering from anorexia may be able to understand rationally the consequences of not eating, but lack the capacity to weigh them against the desire not to eat and will decide not to eat regardless of whether he or she feels hungry, the time of day etc. Certain types of pathology seen after catastrophic brain damage, such as a massive stroke, can cause people, who are able to understand and absorb information, to take decisions or to act impulsively, regardless of the information available or their understanding of it.

S2 (1)(D) UNABLE TO COMMUNICATE THE DECISION (WHETHER BY TALKING, USING SIGN LANGUAGE OR ANY OTHER MEANS)

3.13   The final criterion that would indicate an inability to make a decision is the fact that the person is *unable to communicate the decision* by any possible means. Very few people will fall within this criterion. In particular it will affect those with the condition known as 'locked-in syndrome'.

3.14   Before concluding that someone is totally unable to communicate and therefore lacks capacity, strenuous efforts must first be made to assist and facilitate communication. In addition to the pointers set out in paragraph 3.10, it is very likely in cases of this sort that professionals with specialised skills in verbal and non-verbal communication will be required. Communication by simple muscle movements, such as blinking an eye, or squeezing a hand, to indicate 'yes' or 'no,' should be sufficient to indicate that the person has capacity.

PART 3: HELPING SOMEONE TO MAKE THEIR OWN DECISIONS

Steps to help someone make a decision

S1 (3)   'A person is not to be treated as unable to make a decision unless all practicable steps to help him to do so have been taken without success'

3.15   There are a number of ways in which people can be helped and supported to enable them to make their own decisions. These will vary depending on the decision to be

made, the timescale for making the decision and the individual circumstances of
the person wishing to make it.

3.16   The Act applies to a wide variety of people with a range of conditions which may
affect their decision-making capacity. Different methods may apply when seeking
to give appropriate explanations, help and support to a person with learning disabilities, for example, compared to those that will help to stimulate memory recall
and recognition in a person with dementia. In the following paragraphs, some
pointers are given in order to prompt consideration of all relevant factors, but only
some of these will be relevant to any particular situation and the examples are not
exhaustive.

Providing all relevant information

3.17   The provision of relevant information is essential for any type of decision-making,
no matter how simple the decision or capable the decision-maker. If someone is
asked what they want to have for breakfast on a particular day, they need to know
what food is available before making that decision. If the decision concerns consent
to medical treatment, the doctor will need to explain what is involved in the proposed course of treatment, why it is considered necessary, any alternatives to it and
the consequences of consenting, or refusing consent, to treatment.

3.18   All practicable steps must be taken to help the person to make a decision themselves. This includes providing all information relevant to the decision in question
in a way the particular individual can understand. It is important to choose the
means of communication that is easiest and most appropriate for the person
concerned. Consideration may be given to the following:

Relevant information

■   Take time to explain anything you think might be relevant or might help the person
make the decision in question, but:

   ■   try not to burden the person with more information than is required. This may
   be confusing – an explanation in broad terms may be sufficient for the decision
   to be made

   ■   describe any foreseeable consequences of making the decision, or of not making
   any decision at all; what are the risks and benefits?

   ■   explain the effects the decision might have on the person him/herself and on
   others, particularly those who have a close relationship with the person

   ■   if there is a choice, give the same information in a balanced way on any
   alternative options.

Communication: general points to consider

■   Consult family members, carers or whoever knows the person well on the best
methods of communication (for example, using pictures or signing) with the person concerned, the best times to communicate and the best people to be involved
in doing this

■   Use simple language and, where appropriate, use pictures and objects rather than
words

■   Speak at the right volume and speed with appropriate vocabulary and sentence
structure

■   Enlist the help of others who know and are trusted by the person, such as relatives,
friends, GP, social worker, religious or community leaders

- Be aware of any cultural or religious factors which may have a bearing on the person's way of thinking, behaviour or communication
- Consider whether the services of an independent advocate might be helpful in assisting communication

Communication: aids for people with specific communication or cognitive problems

- Use any aids which might be helpful, such as pictures, photographs, pointing boards or other signalling tools, symbols and objects, videos or tapes
- Find out what the person is used to – for example Makaton or some way of communicating that is only known to those who are close to them
- If the person has hearing difficulties, consider using appropriate visual aids or sign language
- Consider using any appropriate mechanical devices such as voice synthesisers or other computer equipment
- In cases of extreme communication or cognitive difficulties, consider other forms of professional help, such as an expert in clinical neuropsychology

Choosing the best time and location

3.19   Most people find it easier to make decisions if they are in an environment where they feel at ease or if the location is relevant to the decision in question. It is also important to recognise that some people are more alert or able to pay attention at different times of day. A judgement must be made as to which of the following pointers may be helpful and are possible and practicable in each situation:

Location

- Where possible, choose the best location where the person feels most at ease – usually, people will feel more comfortable in their own home than in, say, a doctor's surgery or a lawyer's office, but
- Consider whether it may be easier to make the decision in a different location more relevant to that decision – for example a decision about consenting to treatment in hospital may be made easier by a visit to hospital to see what is involved
- Choose a quiet location where interruptions are unlikely. Try to eliminate any background noise or distractions, such as the television or radio, or people talking

Timing

- If possible, try to choose the best time of day when the person is most alert – some people are better in the mornings, others are more lively in the afternoon or early evening. Other considerations may include:
- If the person's capacity is likely to improve, for whatever reason (for example, after treatment for depression or a psychotic episode) wherever possible wait until it has done so. Clearly this may not be possible if the decision is urgent
- Some medication could affect capacity (e.g. medication which causes drowsiness or affects memory). Consider delaying the decision until any negative effects of medication have subsided.
- Take one decision at a time – be careful to avoid tiring or confusing the person
- Don't rush – allow time for reflection or clarification where appropriate
- Be prepared to abandon the first attempt and try at other times

Enabling decision-making

3.20   Having done everything practicable to provide all relevant information and to create the best possible environment for decision-making, there are other techniques
and support mechanisms which may be useful in helping people to make decisions.
Illustrative examples are given below.

- Many people find it helpful to be able to talk things over with people they trust
or who have been in a similar situation or faced similar dilemmas. For example, people with learning difficulties may benefit from the help of a designated
support worker or being part of a support network with their peers
- When someone is in an acute state of distress, e.g. following bereavement, or
where there are long-standing issues influencing someone's understanding,
decision-making may be delayed to give the individual the opportunity to
undertake a recognised psychological therapy
- It may be helpful for the person to have assistance from an advocate who is
independent of the family or other agencies involved in the person's care. An
advocate could help the person express wishes and aspirations and make real
choices. Information about advocacy services is given on page xx
- Some voluntary organisations and charities have produced publications, tapes
and other materials to help people who need support to make decisions, or
those who provide support. Some of this material is designed to help people
with specific conditions, such as Alzheimer's disease or profound learning
disability. Details are given on page xx.

Unwise or unusual decisions

**S1 (4) A PERSON IS NOT TO BE TREATED AS UNABLE TO MAKE A DECISION
MERELY BECAUSE HE MAKES AN UNWISE DECISION**

3.21   Different people, who have capacity, will make different decisions because they give
greater weight to some factors than to others, taking account of their own values
and preferences. Some people are keener to express their own individuality or more
willing to take risks than others.

> A person with mental health problems smokes cigarettes and continues to do so
> even though he has a severe chest condition. Doctors have explained to him the
> risks of continuing to smoke and have advised him to give up. He should not be
> assumed to lack capacity to decide whether to smoke or not simply because
> smoking is generally regarded as an unwise thing to do.

3.22   There may however be a cause for concern if an individual repeatedly makes
unwise decisions which will place him/her at a significant risk of harm or serious
exploitation. Concern may also be triggered if a person makes a particular decision
which defies all notions of rationality and/or is markedly out of character. In these
situations, it would be relevant to look at the person's past decisions and choices.
While such situations should not automatically lead to the conclusion that capacity is lacking, they might raise doubts about capacity and indicate the need for
further investigation.

> An elderly woman with vascular dementia spends nearly £500 on fresh fish from
> a door-to-door salesman. She is very fond of fish but there is far too much to fit
> into her freezer. Before the onset of dementia, she was always very thrifty and
> careful with her money and would never dream of buying such expensive fish

or spending this amount in one go. This decision does not automatically mean she lacks capacity to manage all aspects of her finances but suggests the need for further and more detailed assessment.

PART 4: ADDITIONAL ISSUES SURROUNDING CAPACITY

Fluctuating capacity

3.23   Some people may at times be quite capable of making their own decisions and running their own lives, but have a mental health problem or other condition which affects their decision-making abilities and therefore their capacity during acute phases. For example, someone with a bi-polar illness may spend money unwisely and get into debt during a hypomanic phase, which they may regret later when they become more lucid. A person with a psychotic illness may have delusions affecting their judgement, which may disappear after treatment. Temporary factors may also affect someone's ability to make decisions, such as acute illness, the effect of medication, or distress caused by bereavement or a sudden shock.

3.24   In cases of fluctuating or temporary incapacity, as in any other case, an assessment must be made of the person's capacity to make a particular decision at the time the decision has to be made. It may be possible to put off the decision until such time as the person has recovered and regained capacity to make their own decision (see also chapter 4 on 'Best interests'). It should also be remembered that many people with learning disabilities are often able to learn new skills and abilities throughout their lives so assessments of their capacity to make certain decisions may need to be made and reviewed periodically.

'On-going' incapacity

3.25   Although as a general rule capacity should be assessed in relation to a particular decision or a specific issue, there may be circumstances where a person has an on-going condition which affects his/her capacity to make a type of decision or a range of inter-related or sequential decisions. One decision on its own may make sense but the combination of decisions can indicate that a person may lack capacity. It is important to recognise that capacity should be reviewed over a period of time since, with experience and time, a person can improve his or her decision-making capabilities.

A young man sustained a head injury during an accident at work. In the personal injury litigation which followed he was awarded a significant amount of damages intended to cover the costs of his future care for the rest of his life. An application was made to the Court of Protection to appoint a deputy to manage his financial affairs. The young man objected to the proposed appointment saying that he was capable of managing his own money and affairs and that as he was now a multi-millionaire, he should be able to spend his money as he wished. He presented the Court with a list of what he intended to do with his damages award; this included fully-staffed luxury properties and holiday villas in several countries, cars with chauffeurs, jewellery and various other items for himself and his family. Although he could afford a number of these luxuries, he could not afford all of them and also be able to cover his care needs for the coming decades. The Court judged that the young man did not have capacity to understand the purpose for which damages were awarded or to manage the amount of money involved and therefore made an order appointing a deputy.

Existing common law tests of capacity

3.26   The definition and two-stage test of capacity set out in the Act are expressed to apply 'for the purposes of this Act'. Schedule 6 also makes consequential amendments to existing statutes in order to ensure that the definition and two-stage test of capacity is used, as appropriate, in relation to other proceedings. For example, this will ensure that inability to act as a juror is assessed according to a person's capacity to do the very specific tasks involved in acting as a juror. There are also several *common law* tests of capacity set out in case law. Examples include:

- capacity to make a will
- capacity to marry
- capacity to make a gift
- contractual capacity
- capacity to litigate

3.27   The new definition of capacity is intended to build on the terms of existing common law tests. As cases come before the court, it may be likely that judges will consider the new statutory definition and they may use it to develop common law rules in particular cases.

PART 5: ASSESSMENT OF CAPACITY

3.28   After a person makes an assessment that an individual lacks decision-making capacity with respect to a particular matter, that person may then perform acts that are in respect of the care or treatment, and in the best interests of, the person lacking capacity (or take decisions where they have formal authority to do so in matters where the person lacks capacity to make the decision for himself).

Reasonable belief of lack of capacity

3.29   It is sufficient for a person to hold a 'reasonable belief' that another person lacks capacity with regard to a particular matter. This means that they will be expected to have reasonable grounds for believing that someone lacks capacity to do the action or make the decision in question. It also means that they must be able to point to objective reasons as to why they believe the person is lacking capacity.

Who assesses capacity?

3.30   In keeping with the functional approach to capacity (see paragraph 3.14) the question of who assesses an individual's capacity will depend on the particular decision to be made. Set procedures and processes are rarely required unless the assessment is challenged, or there is reason for doubt, for example by the person whose capacity is being assessed or by another family member. In most circumstances, it is sufficient for the person assessing capacity to hold a reasonable belief, as described above, that the person lacks capacity.

> Ms C suffered brain damage in a road accident and is unable to speak. She is cared for at home by her family who at first thought she was unable to make any decisions, but soon discovered that she was able to express her choices by pointing at the clothes she wants to wear or selecting the types of food she prefers. She is also able to indicate by her behaviour that she enjoys attending the day centre but she refuses to go swimming and her carers have assessed her as capable of making these decisions. Ms C needs further hospital treatment but she gets very distressed when away from home. Her mother feels that this should be

> taken as an indication that Ms C is refusing consent to the treatment in question, but her father thinks she lacks capacity to refuse consent to potentially beneficial treatment. The clinician who is proposing the treatment will have to assess Mrs C's capacity. When doing so, he will need to take account of the views of both parents.

3.31   Where consent to medical treatment or examination is required, the doctor or clinician proposing the treatment must decide whether the patient has capacity to consent and should record his findings in the person's medical notes. Where a legal transaction is involved, such as making a will or a power of attorney, the solicitor handling the transaction will need to assess whether the client has the required capacity to satisfy the relevant legal test, perhaps assisted by an opinion from a doctor. In making such an assessment, the doctor may need to seek others' views as to the person's capacity. Where the person's capacity is borderline or may be challenged, a doctor, or other appropriate professional, who has carried out an assessment of capacity may, for example, be asked to witness the will or other legal document or otherwise attest to the person's capacity (see paragraphs 3.35–3.37). A person who has fluctuating capacity may him or herself ask for professional confirmation of their capacity (for example, to make a will), if they feel that someone may, at a future date, challenge their capacity to have done this at that particular time. If a person's capacity to do something is disputed, ultimately the question of their capacity may be put before the court to decide.

3.32   Whoever is carrying out an assessment of capacity, the processes involved are similar and require a number of factors to be taken into account. The following questions must first be considered:

- Does the person have all the information relevant to the decision? If there is a choice, has information been given on any alternatives?
- Could the information be explained or presented in a way that is easier for the person to understand?
- Are there particular times of day when the person's understanding is better, or particular locations where they may feel more at ease? Can the decision be delayed until the circumstances are right for the person concerned?
- Can anyone else help or support the person to make choices (or express a view), such as an advocate or someone to assist communication?

3.33   Where there are doubts about capacity, it is important that people are assessed when they are at their highest level of functioning for the decision in question because this is the only realistic way of determining what they may or may not be capable of doing.

3.34   In many cases, it may seem, or will be obvious, whether there is any impairment or disturbance which could affect the person's decision-making capacity. For example, there may have been a previous diagnosis of a mental illness or disability, or recognisable symptoms to indicate the recurrence of illness or the disabling effects of a head injury. Any assumptions should however be revisited and reviewed. In other cases, such as dementia, the onset of debilitating illness is gradual and the point at which capacity is affected (or is potentially affected) is hard to define. During the period when capacity is borderline, a medical opinion may be required (see paragraph 3.35 to 3.37 below).

> Mr D is 87 years old and has lived alone since his wife died 3 years ago. He is supported by his daughter who visits every evening and a home carer who comes for an hour each morning to help him get up. Mr D has little short-term memory and is often confused about the time of day, so he forgets to eat. He also neglects his personal hygiene but usually agrees to have a bath when his daughter persuades him. She would like him to move to residential care, but having

discussed it with him, she feels satisfied that he understands the risks involved in staying at home and is capable of deciding to take those risks.

Two months later, Mr D has a fall and breaks his leg. While being treated in hospital, he becomes more confused and depressed. Although he says he wants to go home, this time his daughter feels he cannot understand the consequences or weigh up the risks. She takes steps to have his capacity to make this decision assessed by relevant professionals.

The need for involving professionals when assessing capacity

3.35   The majority of decisions made on behalf of people lacking capacity will be day-to-day decisions and as such, those caring for them on a day-to-day basis will be able to assess their capacity to make these decisions. However, certain more complex or serious decisions may require the involvement of different people in order to assess capacity. Where the person has been diagnosed with a particular condition or disorder, it may be appropriate to seek an opinion as to the person's capacity from a specialist, such as a consultant psychiatrist or psychologist, who has extensive clinical experience of the disorder and is familiar with caring for patients with that condition.

3.36   Where professionals are involved in assessing a person's capacity, it is a matter of good practice that a full assessment is made and the findings recorded in the relevant professional records.

3.37   In other cases, a judgement will need to be made as to whether it is appropriate or necessary to involve a doctor or other expert in assessing the person. Any of the following factors might indicate the need for professional involvement:

- The gravity of the decision or its consequences
- Where the person concerned disputes a finding of incapacity
- Where there is disagreement between family members, carers and/or professionals as to the person's capacity
- Where the person concerned is expressing different views to different people, perhaps through trying to please each or tell them what s/he thinks they want to hear
- Where the person's capacity to make a particular decision may be subject to challenge, either at the time the decision is made or in the future – for example a person's testamentary capacity may be challenged after his or her death by someone seeking to contest the will
- Where there may be legal consequences of a finding of capacity – for example in a settlement of damages following a claim for personal injury
- The person concerned is repeatedly making decisions that put him/her at risk or resulted in preventable suffering or damage.

Refusal to be assessed

3.38   There may be circumstances in which a person whose capacity is in doubt refuses to undergo an assessment of capacity or refuses to be examined by a doctor. It will usually be possible to persuade someone to agree to an assessment if the consequences of refusal are carefully explained. For example, it could be explained to a person wishing to make a will that the will could be challenged and held to be invalid after their death, while evidence of their capacity to make a will could prevent this from happening.

3.39   If the person lacks capacity to consent to or refuse that actual assessment itself, it will normally be possible for an assessment to proceed so long as the person is compliant and this is considered to be in the person's best interests (see chapter 4).

However, in the face of an outright refusal, in the majority of circumstances no one can be forced to undergo an assessment of capacity unless required to do so by a court in legal proceedings. Even then, entry to a person's home cannot be forced and a refusal to open the door to the doctor may be the end of the matter. Where there are serious concerns about the person's mental health, forcing an entry and making an assessment under mental health legislation may be warranted, so long as the statutory grounds are fulfilled (a refusal to be assessed is in no way sufficient grounds for an assessment under the Mental Health Act).

CHAPTER 4: THE LEAST RESTRICTIVE OPTION AND BEST INTERESTS

INTRODUCTION

4.1 Where a person lacks capacity to make a particular decision, it may be necessary for a decision to be made by someone else on the person's behalf. One of the key principles of the Act are that any such decision must take account of the least restrictive option principle and be made in the person's best interests. **Part 1** of this chapter explains the principle of the least restrictive option and what this means in practice. **Part 2** explains the concept of best interests and when the best interests principle must be applied. **Part 3** describes the factors which must be considered when trying to determine what is in a person's best interests and how determinations on best interests may be reached. **Part 4** considers some problems which may arise when determining best interests, such as dealing with competing or conflicting concerns and balancing a person's right to confidentiality with the need for appropriate consultation.

PART 1: THE LEAST RESTRICTIVE OPTION PRINCIPLE

4.2 S1 (6) 'Before the act is done, or the decision is made, regard must be had to whether the purpose for which it is needed can be as effectively achieved in a way that is less restrictive of the person's rights and freedom of action'.

4.3 It is a key principle of the Act that before any action is taken or decision made on behalf of a person lacking capacity, the person taking the action or making the decision must consider whether it is possible to decide or act in a way that would interfere less with the other person's rights and freedoms. This means that people must consider whether there is a need to act at all or make a decision.

4.4 If it is established that there is a need to act or make a particular decision, the person responsible for taking the decision or doing the action must then consider which action or decision would be in the person's best interests. In practice, the process of deciding whether or not to act, and how to act, will be intermingled; there will not be a clear-cut two-stage process involving the application of the 'least restrictive option' principle, followed by the 'best interests' principle. However, it is important to remember that both these key principles of the Bill must be applied each time a decision or action may need to be taken on behalf of a person lacking capacity.

John has a learning disability. He has recently moved into supported accommodation with three other young men and they are all doing well. John's Dad has power of attorney over his finances.

Recently John's grandfather died and left him £1000. John's Dad thinks the money should be invested for his future care. John wants to use it to take his friends for holiday to the seaside in a posh hotel. One of their support workers says he will come too to help make sure they are OK. Other people in their block have done this before and had a good time. But John's Dad thinks this is a waste of money, and he does not trust the care worker as he lets John drink beer, and once John was very ill afterwards. John says he wants to have some fun now whilst he's still young. The drinking episode didn't do him any lasting harm, he won't do it again, and why shouldn't he be allowed to spend the money on what he wants instead of saving it all as his Dad suggests? John's dad thinks this over. He agrees a compromise: he will give John half the money to spend on a weekend away with two or three of his close friends, and invest the rest.

Mr S has learning disabilities and although he can do some everyday things for himself, e.g. dressing, he needs quite a lot of support in doing so. He has just moved to a new residential care home. In his last home, there were simple push-button showers which gave out water at a set temperature for a couple of minutes at a time. Mr S was happy to use these by himself. However, the new home has modern showers that give residents control over the temperature. Mr S's carers are worried that he will not be able to operate the new showers safely; he is not very confident about running a bath for himself and once scalded his foot. The carers start by trying to teach Mr S how to adjust the shower himself. But although Mr S can say whether something is too hot or too cold, and can copy the carers when they adjust the shower, it becomes clear that he is not able to understand that moving the dial is what changes the temperature of the water.

PART 2: THE BEST INTERESTS PRINCIPLE

S1 (5) 'An act done, or decision made, under this Act for or on behalf of a person who lacks capacity must be done, or made, in his best interests.'

4.5 The principle of acting in the best interests of a person who lacks capacity has become well established in the common law and the concept has been developed by the courts in cases relating to incapacitated adults. Section 1(5) of the Act enshrines this principle in statute as the overriding principle that must guide all actions done for or decisions made on behalf of someone lacking capacity.

4.6 It is also important to recognise that consideration of a person's best interests is only relevant once it has been shown that the person lacks capacity to make the decision in question. People with capacity are able to decide for themselves what is best, and may even choose an option which others consider to be unwise or not in their best interests. That is their prerogative as competent and autonomous adults. However, once capacity is lost, it is the best interest's of the person who may lack capacity which govern how decisions or actions may be taken on his/her behalf.

4.7 In considering what might be in a person's best interests, regard must be had to what is best for that person in those particular circumstances. This will involve consideration of a number of factors. It is that person's best interests that are relevant, not those of the decision-maker or anyone else. While the views of other people will need to be taken into account in determining best interests (see paragraphs 4.17–4.18 below), it is important to place the focus firmly on the person lacking capacity and to give priority to what is objectively the best course of action for him or her in that particular situation.

Ben is cared for by his mother after having suffered severe head injuries in a car accident a number of years ago. Ben lacks capacity to do many everyday things for himself, including buying clothes and dressing himself. In deciding what clothes to buy Ben and what he should wear each day, his mother thinks about what sort of clothes would be best for Ben. For example, she knows that Ben cannot fasten buttons but can do up zips. She chooses clothes with zips that Ben can put on himself and that are also similar to clothes that he used to wear before his accident. By acting in this way, she is allowing Ben to be as self-sufficient as possible and is acting in his best interests.

PART 3: DETERMINING BEST INTERESTS

4.8   Section 4 of the Act sets out some statutory guidance on how a person's best interests should be determined. It must be recognised that statute cannot give an exhaustive account of what is in a person's best interests, since this will vary with each individual person and the particular circumstances of the particular decision. Acting in someone's best interests simply means doing what is best for him or her.

4.9   However, the Act also sets out a checklist of common factors which must *always* be taken into account. These are explained in paragraphs 4.10 to 4.30 below). Decision-makers must work their way through the checklist, which provides a common standard to ensure consistency in how substitute decisions are approached. It is important to remember that the checklist is not a definition of best interests nor an exhaustive list of factors to be taken into account when determining best interests. Rather they are factors that must always be considered in determining what is in a person's best interests.

THE CHECKLIST OF RELEVANT CIRCUMSTANCES

S4 (1)   'In determining for the purposes of this Act what is in a person's best interests, the person making the determination must consider all the circumstances appearing to him to be relevant.'

4.10   The Act specifies that the person making the determination must consider all the relevant circumstances. As the Act potentially applies to every situation in a person's life it is not possible to list every relevant circumstance. These will necessary vary from case to case. For example, when making a decision about medical treatment, a doctor would need to consider the clinical needs of the patient, together with the potential benefits and burdens of the treatment on the person's health and life expectancy. In a recent case concerning a possible kidney transplantation, the President of the Family Division said that, when considering the best interests of a patient, it is the duty of the court 'to assess the advantages and disadvantages of the various treatments and management options, the viability of each such option and the likely effect each would have on the patient's best interests and, I would add, his enjoyment of life.'[1]

4.11   Similar concerns apply where a financial decision needs to be made on behalf of a person lacking capacity. For example, if a person had received a substantial sum of money as compensation for an accident resulting in brain injury, the decision-maker would have to consider all relevant circumstances. For example, they would need to think about whether it would be best to invest in a new property that could be easily adapted to the person's needs, or to keep the person where (s)he is and invest the money for future care if perhaps their condition may improve and needs change over the next couple of years.

Richard has learning disabilities and has been diagnosed as having cancer. His healthcare team has to decide what treatment to provide in the light of his diagnosis. Richard lacks the capacity to make decisions about what treatment he should receive for the cancer so the doctor talks through several options with

[1] (An Hospital NHS Trust v. S [2003] EWHC 365 (Fam), paragraph 47)

Richard's parents, his best friend, and his main carer. He lacks capacity to make decisions about what treatment he should receive for the cancer, has never had capacity to make an LPA or advance decision, and has no court appointed deputy, so his healthcare team have to decide themselves what treatment to provide in the light of his diagnosis and according to best interests. It is decided that Richard should be given a course of chemotherapy. Although this will involve unpleasant side-effects, the team decides that these are justified in view of the benefits that the treatment will bring in terms of giving Richard a good quality of life for an extended period of time. By weighing up these, and other relevant considerations, including any wishes or feelings that Richard has indicated, the team reaches a decision on what course of action is in Richard's best interests.

4.12   It is important to remember that the Act does not give priority to any particular considerations or factors which appear in the best interests checklist. The checklist acts as a mandatory starting point in determining best interests and does not in any way preclude the consideration of other factors which may apply in a particular case. For example, as the preceding case study sets out, a doctor would consider his patient's prognosis and the possible side-effects of treatment when determining that patient's best interests.

4.13   The following paragraphs describe the factors in the checklist as set out in section 4(2) of the Act.

Regaining capacity

S4 (3) 'He must consider:

    (a)   whether it is likely that the person in question will at some time have capacity in relation to the matter in question, and

    (b)   If it appears likely that he will, when that is likely to be.'

4.14   The checklist requires a decision-maker determining what is in someone's best interests to consider whether the individual concerned is likely to have capacity to make that particular decision in the future and if so, when that is likely to be. It is important to consider whether the decision can be put off until the person can make it him/herself. This delay may allow further time for additional steps to be taken to restore the person's capacity or to provide support and assistance which would enable the person to make the decision themselves.

4.15   Even if the decision cannot be put off, how the decision is made is likely to be influenced by whether the person will always lack capacity for this and/or other decisions or is likely to regain capacity at some point.

A young woman is seriously injured in a car accident and sustains severe injuries to her left leg. She is unconscious following the accident although doctors expect her to regain consciousness in a few days time. Her doctors want to perform surgery on her injured leg although this does carry with it certain risks and there is a possibility that the leg may need to be amputated if the surgery is unsuccessful. Doctors decide that, as she is expected to regain consciousness within the next few days, the decision on whether to operate on her leg can wait until she is able to make the decision herself.

4.16   The factors which may indicate that a person may regain capacity include the following:

    ■   The cause of the incapacity can be treated, either by medication or some other form of treatment or therapy

- The incapacity may decrease in time (for example where caused by the effects of medication or alcohol, or following a sudden shock)
- People may learn new skills or be subject to new experiences which increase their capacity to make certain decisions, for example, a young adult with learning disabilities who leaves his parental home to live in supported accommodation and gains new skills as a result
- The person may have a condition which causes capacity to fluctuate (such as some forms of mental illness) so it may be possible to arrange for the decision to be made during a lucid interval
- A person previously unable to communicate may learn a new form of communication

Permitting and encouraging participation

S4 (4) 'He must, so far as reasonably practicable, permit and encourage the person to participate, or to improve his ability to participate, as fully as possible in any act done for him and any decision affecting him.'

4.17   In considering what might be in a person's best interests, the person must be involved in the decision-making process to the fullest possible extent. The fact that the person lacks capacity does not mean that s/he can be cut out or ignored. It is important always to consult the person on the particular decision to be made and to try to seek their views. This will involve taking time to explain what is happening and the decision which needs to be made, and using all possible means to encourage the maximum involvement and participation. The practicable steps discussed in chapter 3 (see paragraphs 3.15–3.20) will also be helpful here.

4.18   Even if the person lacks capacity to make the decision in question, s/he may have views on issues which affect the decision, and on what outcome would be preferred. A trusted relative or friend, or an independent advocate may be able to help the person to express wishes or aspirations or to indicate a choice between different options.

> The parents of a young woman with learning difficulties are going through a bitter divorce and are arguing about who should continue to care for their daughter. She cannot understand what is happening but attempts are made to see if she can give some indication of where she would prefer to live. An independent advocate is appointed to work with her to help her understand and to find out her likes and dislikes and matters which are important to her. With the advocate's help, she is able to participate in decisions about her future care.

The person's wishes and feelings

S4 (5) 'He must consider, so far as is reasonably ascertainable –

(i) The person's past and present wishes and feelings,
(ii) The beliefs and values that would be likely to influence his decision if he had capacity, and
(iii) The other factors that he would be likely to consider if he were able to do so'

4.19   This element of the checklist establishes the importance of individual views. Every attempt must be made to find out the person's current wishes and feelings. People who cannot express their wishes and feelings in words or other conventional ways can still express their wishes and feelings through their behaviour. Expressions of pleasure or distress and their emotional responses will also be relevant in deciding what is in their best interests. It is important to ensure that these are the person's true wishes and have not been influenced by others. An independent advocate could provide support to enable the person to express their views without the risk of being influenced by others involved in the decision.

4.20   Of equal importance are the person's values and beliefs. We are all influenced by values and beliefs in making decisions. This factor may be of particular significance for people who have lost capacity, for example because of a progressive illness such as dementia. Values and beliefs may be indicated by the person's cultural background, or known past behaviour or expressions, such as religious or political conviction Specific views may have been set out in a document, such as an advance decision about medical treatment, or 'living will', or expressed informally to relatives or carers.

4.21   However, it is important to recognise that the person's wishes and feelings will not automatically control the outcome. The 'best interests' principle is a fundamental principle, requiring what is best for the person. In some cases, **past** wishes and feelings may conflict with **current** wishes and feelings. While neither past nor present wishes can determine the decision which is now to be made, both are important and must be weighed against each other and considered alongside other factors in the checklist.

4.22   When making a decision, people with capacity will take account of a range of factors including the consequences of the decision for themselves and the effects of the decision on other people, particularly family members or close friends. The second element of section 4(5)(c) allows for similar factors to be taken into account in relation to decisions made on behalf of an person who may lack capacity. Reference must be made to any of the factors the person who may lack capacity would consider if able to do so. This might include, for example, altruistic motives and concern for others as well as duties and obligations towards dependants or future beneficiaries.

Mrs F, a widow in her late 80s with no children, lives in a private nursing home. The home provides a choice of main course and many residents can decide for themselves what to order each morning. Mrs F has dementia and often gets flustered at having to choose. Her care assistants ask her friends what she liked eating before she moved and they tell them she ate meat because her husband liked it, but always chose vegetarian options when she came out with them. The carers therefore order the vegetarian options for her on the days she can't decide for herself.

The views of other people

S4 (6) 'He must take into account, if it is practicable and appropriate to consult them, the views of –

(i) anyone named by the person as someone to be consulted on the matter in question or on matters of that kind,

(ii) anyone engaged in caring for the person or interested in his welfare,

(iii) any donee of a lasting power of attorney granted by the person, and

(iv) any deputy appointed for the person by the court as to what would be in the person's best interests and, in particular, as to the matters mentioned in subsection (5).'

4.23   In considering a person's best interests, it will be important to consult with all relevant people, in particular those who are close to the person concerned, including close relatives, partners, or other carers. The Act requires such consultation to take place, but only if it is 'practicable and appropriate' in the particular circumstances where a decision needs to be made. This is not intended to give absolute discretion to the decision-maker about whom to consult, rather decision-makers will need to show they have thought carefully about whom to consult and be prepared to explain why a consultation which they declined to carry out was either impracticable or inappropriate.

4.24   Similarly, prior to losing capacity, the person may have expressed a wish that certain people should always be consulted in the event of loss of capacity or in relation to specific matters. The first subsection of this part of the checklist requires that such a wish should be respected.

4.25   The person's GP, close relatives and friends, particularly those involved in caring for the person, or who have an interest in his or her welfare, may know the person's wishes and feelings (past or present) and any values, beliefs or important factors which the person would have considered if able to do so. They may also have different but equally valid views of what may be in the person's best interests (conflicting views are dealt with further in paragraph 4.31 below). Such views should also be taken into account and weighed against the person's own views and other factors relevant to the decision in question.

A young woman with a history of political activity sustains serious brain damage during a car accident. The court appoints her father as deputy to invest the compensation she received. As the decision-maker he is obliged to take into account the views of others before deciding how to invest the money. He talks to her friends from college who tell him more about her political beliefs. This persuades him that choosing the option favoured by the bank's financial adviser would not be in her overall best interests, as although it gives the highest return, the fund includes bonds and shares from specific multi-national companies that he knows she disapproved of. Instead he employs an ethical investment advisor to choose appropriate companies in line with her beliefs.

4.26   Any donee appointed by the person under a Lasting Power of Attorney, and any court-appointed deputy, should be consulted whenever the person's best interests are being considered, if practicable and appropriate. Even if the donee has only been appointed to manage the person's financial affairs, the donee may have some knowledge about the person's wishes and feelings which are relevant to his/her best interests and could affect personal or healthcare decisions.

Reasonable belief as to best interests

S4 (8) 'In the case of an act done, or a decision made, by a person other than the court, there is sufficient compliance with this section if (having complied with the requirements of subsections (1) to (6) he reasonably believes that what he does or decides is in the best interests of the person concerned.'

4.27   The need to determine the best interests of a person lacking capacity, and to act in accordance with them, applies in relation to all decisions made or actions taken under the Act, extending from informal decisions to court based powers. Where there is a need for a court decision, the Court may clearly require formal documentary evidence, including from those with relevant professional expertise (in psychiatry and/or social work) as to what course of action might be in the person's best interests. However, in many day-to-day situations, such formality is neither required nor appropriate and in emergency cases may not be possible.

4.28   Where the court is not involved, carers, relatives and others can only be expected to have *reasonable grounds for believing* that what they are doing or deciding is in the best interests of the person concerned. This does not mean that informal decision-makers can merely impose their own views. Rather, they must be able to point to objective reasons to demonstrate why they believe they are acting in the person's best interests. They must consider all relevant circumstances and the four elements of the checklist.

4.29   It may be shown subsequently that someone was mistaken in his/her opinion of best interests and that the actual decision or action taken was not the best thing for the person lacking capacity. Coming to an incorrect conclusion does not necessarily mean that the decision-maker was acting unlawfully. He or she does, however, have to be able to show that it was reasonable, in the particular circumstances which applied at the time, for him/her to believe that the action taken or the decision made was in the person's best interests.

> A woman is knocked unconscious after being mugged and is rushed to hospital by ambulance. She has sustained head injuries and a stab wound and has lost a lot of blood so the casualty doctor arranges an urgent blood transfusion, believing this to be necessary to save her life and therefore in her best interests. When her relatives are finally contacted, they say the woman is a Jehovah's Witness and would have refused all blood products. There was no prior indication of who she was, or her beliefs, as her handbag had been stolen. The doctor therefore had reasonable grounds for believing that his action was in his patient's best interests and so was justified in taking that action. If, however, a document had been available that confirmed her religion and her refusal of blood products, the doctor would not have been acting in her best interests in failing to take that into account when deciding what treatment to give.

PART 4: PROBLEMS IN DETERMINING BEST INTERESTS

4.30   The purpose of the best interests principle and the statutory checklist is to ensure that when decisions are taken or acts done for those lacking capacity, the outcome is the best one available for the person concerned. Complex decisions, for example decisions surrounding serious medical treatment, will require a balancing exercise of the pros and cons, and of all other relevant factors.

Dealing with competing or conflicting concerns

4.31   When trying to determine the best interests of a person lacking capacity, a decision-maker may be faced with competing or conflicting concerns. For example, family members or other consultees may disagree between themselves about their relative's best interests or may have different memories as to the previously expressed views of the person concerned. The decision-maker will need to find a way of balancing these concerns or deciding between them. The first approach should be to try to seek a consensus between everyone involved – including the person who may lack capacity so far as s/he is able to participate and anyone who has been involved in the consultations. It is important that everyone focuses on what would be best for the person who lacks capacity, and strives to reach agreement about the best solution.

> Some time ago, Mr H made a Lasting Power of Attorney appointing his son and daughter as joint attorneys to manage his finances. He now has Alzheimer's Disease and has moved into private residential care. The LPA has been registered and a decision needs to be made about Mr H's house, a country cottage which has important associations for all the family. His son wants to sell it and invest the money for Mr H's future care. His daughter wants to keep the property, at least for the present, as she and other relatives spend holidays there and often arrange for Mr H to visit and spend time in his old home. She also thinks he would have wanted to keep the cottage for as long as possible so it can continue to be used and enjoyed by family members. After efforts are made to seek Mr H's

views, the family meets to discuss all the issues involved. After hearing other family views, the attorneys agree that it would be in their father's best interests to keep the property for so long as he is able to enjoy visiting it.

4.32   If consensus is not possible, it is up to the person charged with making the decision or carrying out the act in question to reach a conclusion about the incapacitated adult's best interests, having considered all relevant circumstances and worked though the statutory checklist.

4.33   Ultimately, the question of what is in the best interests of a person lacking capacity may be one for the court to decide. If consensus cannot be reached or if someone wishes to challenge a determination about best interests made by a decision-maker, an application may be made to the Court of Protection if all other attempts to resolve the situation fail. The application procedures and the powers of the Court of Protection are explained in chapter 7.

Confidentiality

4.34   The best interests checklist requires consultation with a range of relevant people (see paragraphs 4.17 – 4.18) but only where it is 'practicable and appropriate' to consult them. The right to confidentiality of the person lacking capacity should be protected, unless it is in his or her best interests for specific acts of information-sharing to take place, or there is some strong reason to override it, such as when it is in the public interest. If professionals are involved in the decision in question, they will also need to comply with their own duties of confidentiality in accordance with their professional codes of conduct. Further guidance is given in chapter 13.

Independent Advocacy

4.35   Reference has been made in this chapter to the potentially useful role of independent advocacy services in providing a focus on the views and wishes of a person who may lack capacity in the determination of their best interests. The following situations might indicate the need for the involvement of an independent advocate when determining best interests:

- Where the person lacking capacity has no close family or friends to take an interest in his/her welfare
- Where family members are in dispute or disagree about the person's best interests
- Where the person lacking capacity is already in contact with an advocate

CHAPTER 5: ACTS IN CONNECTION WITH CARE OR TREATMENT

INTRODUCTION

5.1   **Part 1** of this chapter describes provisions in the Act (at section 5) that may apply in circumstances when carers (both family members and paid carers) and health and social care professionals carry out certain acts in connection with the personal care, healthcare or medical treatment of a person lacking capacity to consent to these acts. These provisions are intended to give legal backing, in the form of protection from liability, for actions considered to be in the best interests of someone who lacks capacity. **Part 2** explains the restrictions and limitations on this protection from liability. **Part 3** explains the circumstances in which a carer, acting without formal authority, can buy goods or organise necessary services for a person lacking capacity, and arrange for these to be paid for out of the person's money.

PART 1: PROTECTION FOR ACTS DONE FOR PERSONS WHO LACK CAPACITY

5.2   Every day, millions of acts are done to and for people with impaired capacity and who can neither care for themselves nor give consent to someone else caring for them. Examples might be actions such as helping individuals to wash, dress, eat or attend to their personal hygiene, taking them to see the doctor or dentist, or helping them buy food or have gas and electricity supplied to their home. Sometimes, carers and professionals have to take serious steps to preserve or enhance a person's health, such as surgery or the administration of powerful medication, even where the patient lacks capacity to consent to it.

5.3   According to basic legal principles, many of these actions, particularly those which involve touching a person or interfering with their property, could be unlawful. People have the right to freedom from interference with their body or their possessions unless they give permission for that interference. A problem arises when a person lacks capacity to give that permission or consent to having things done to or for them. For example, if a person lacks the necessary capacity to dress themselves and a carer dresses them, the carer is potentially committing assault in touching the person without their consent (even if the action did not involve any violence or harm the person in any way). Or if a neighbour enters the house of a person lacking capacity in order to do housework etc, they could be trespassing on the person's property.

5.4   The purpose of the provisions discussed in this chapter is to ensure that when people need to perform such acts and they follow the principles of the Act, they will be protected from liability for committing acts which could otherwise amount to civil wrongs or crimes, such as assault or trespass for example. By offering protection from liability, we enable caring actions to take place in the absence of consent.

What type of acts would potentially attract protection from liability?

5.5   The types of action which may be permitted under section 5 are those carried out *in connection with the care or treatment* of a person who is believed to lack capacity in relation to the matter in question. The category is intentionally wide, the key issue simply being whether the act has a connection with the 'care' or 'treatment' of the other person. The Act does not define these ordinary words, but does specify that 'treatment' covers a diagnostic or other procedures (section 60(1)). Examples of acts in connection with care or treatment (but which do not form an exhaustive list) might be:

a)   *Acts in connection with personal care* –

   (i)   acts of physical assistance such as washing, dressing, attending to personal hygiene, feeding, physically putting someone in a car (e.g. in order to take them to see their doctor).

   (ii)   other assistance, such as doing the shopping, buying essential goods, arranging services required for the person's care

   (iii)   clearing someone's house when they have moved into residential care, washing someone's clothes, taking their car to a garage to be repaired.

b)   *Acts in connection with health care and treatment*

   (i)   diagnostic examinations and tests

   (ii)   medical and dental treatment

(iii) other healthcare procedures (such as the taking of a blood or other bodily samples, chiropody, physiotherapy)

(iv) nursing care

5.6   Moving a person's residence may or may not involve one or more acts in connection with care or treatment. It is not always clear whether:

i)   the move involves any acts which call for the person's formal consent, or

ii)   the move is a single action or a series of individual actions, performed by different people.

It may be important to consider and compare what forms of consent would be sought from a person in similar circumstances who had no impairment to his or her capacity.

5.7   If consent would be sought from a person of full capacity, carers and professionals should comply with the section 5 requirements as this will help to ensure they are acting within the law when moving a person to different accommodation.

Who can take action?

5.8   Section 5 of the Act refers to a person who 'does an act in connection with the care or treatment of another person'. The section can apply to any person and the likelihood is that a number of people may be acting in accordance with it at any particular time. There is no question of one person having a statutory power which excludes all others. The provisions in section 5 do not confer any special powers on anyone to make substitute decisions or to give substitute consent. Nor do they specify *who* has the authority to act in a particular instance. They simply allow carers and healthcare professionals who have a responsibility to care for a person who lacks capacity to be able to carry out that caring obligation without incurring liability.

5.9   For example, someone may provide personal care for an individual lacking capacity (whether as part of a paid job, or an unpaid or voluntary responsibility), including any necessary assistance with washing, dressing, toileting or eating. This could include family members who look after their relative who lacks capacity at home or paid care assistants working in a care home or nursing home where the person lives. Section 5 may also cover the acts of care assistants in a day centre if a person lacking capacity needs assistance with personal care while attending the centre. It may also cover nurses providing personal care in hospitals.

On any one day, an older person with early onset dementia who lives at home may have help with breakfast from a family member in the morning, a regular injection from a nurse in the afternoon and be taken to the park by a friend later in the day. Each of these individuals, provided they have taken reasonable steps to see if the person lacked capacity and are acting in the person's best interests, would be protected from any liability in relation to the act performed under section 5 of the Act.

5.10   Also in connection with a person's care, a carer may have to deal with some financial matters, for example using the money of the person lacking capacity to pay for necessary goods or services, such as buying food, paying the electricity bill or paying for home care services. However, access to a person's bank account or savings will not be given without formal authority, for example under a Lasting Power of Attorney (see chapter 6) or an order of the Court of Protection (see chapter 7). Access to benefits will require an appointee under the Social Security Regulations. These issues are discussed further in Part 3 of this chapter.

The steps required for people to be protected from liability for their actions

5.11   A step-by-step approach must be taken by anyone wishing to take action in connection with the care or treatment of another person in order to benefit from protection from liability.

First, reasonable steps must be taken to ascertain whether the person concerned has capacity in relation to the matter in question (see chapter 3, in particular paragraphs 3.31–3.39) – if the person has capacity, his/her consent to the action will be required to provide protection from liability. In accordance with section 1, the starting-point is a presumption of capacity and unwise decisions must not be treated as made without capacity. All practicable steps must be taken to help the person make his or her own decision.

Second, where there are reasonable grounds for believing that the person lacks capacity, the carer must then consider whether there are reasonable grounds for believing that it will be in the person's best interests for the act to be done (see chapter 4). All relevant circumstances must be considered, and the best interests checklist followed. In accordance with section 1, the principle of taking the least restrictive option must be considered.

5.12   As explained in chapter 3, the Act requires a functional approach when deciding whether a person lacks decision-making capacity – this means that capacity is decision-specific and must therefore be assessed in relation to the particular decision an individual purports to make, at the time the decision needs to be made. In day-to-day situations, the carer attending to personal care needs must consider whether the person has capacity in relation to the matter in question. For example, a carer intending to help a compliant person to dress must consider whether that person has capacity to make a decision to remain in his or her night clothes all day. If they cannot, it may be appropriate to intervene. It may be in the best interests of a person to be dressed in day clothes so as to be able to join other residents or go on an outing. A carer wanting to help someone to wash must consider whether that person has capacity to make a decision about whether or not to wash. Carers acting informally are not expected to be experts in assessing capacity, but they must be able to show that they have *reasonable grounds for believing* the person lacks capacity in relation to that particular matter, at that particular time. Formal assessment processes are rarely required but there must be some evidence leading to a belief of lack of capacity. If the carer's assessment is challenged, s/he will be protected from liability so long as s/he can point to the grounds which justified a reasonable belief of lack of capacity.

5.13   Similarly, carers, relatives and others who are acting informally can only be expected to have *reasonable grounds for believing* that what they are doing is in the best interests of the person concerned. This means that informal carers should not merely impose their own views; rather they must be able to demonstrate that they have considered all relevant circumstances, and explain why they believe they are acting in the person's best interests. If their determination of best interests is challenged, they will be protected if they can show that it was reasonable in all the circumstances of that particular case for them to have done this.

5.14   Where professionals are involved, their professional skills will be taken into account in determining whether they took 'reasonable steps' to establish lack of capacity and had a reasonable belief as to lack of capacity and best interests. For example, a psychiatrist who provides medical treatment without consent would be expected to demonstrate more specialist knowledge of the assessment of capacity than a lay person, by recording in the person's medical notes the steps taken in the original assessment and the reasons he or she assessed the treatment as being in the patient's best interest. In determining what treatments should be offered, professionals must apply normal clinical and professional standards. In giving treatment to a patient who lacks capacity, they must act in the patient's best interests, taking all relevant circumstances into account, including the best interests principle and the elements of the Best Interests checklist set out in the Act.

5.15   There may be circumstances where it is necessary to give emergency medical treatment in order to save the life or prevent serious harm to a person who lacks capacity to consent to such treatment. In such emergencies what are reasonable steps and reasonable grounds for belief will be adjusted.

No protection in cases of negligence

5.16   Section 5 operates in conjunction with other provisions of the law. Professionals and others have duties of care which, if breached, give rise to liability in the tort of negligence. The Act states explicitly that section 5 does not provide a defence to negligent acts. So, section 5 may provide a doctor with protection against liability in the tort of battery if the doctor carries out an operation which is in a person's best interests, even though the person lacks capacity to consent. If, however, the doctor then performs the operation in a negligent fashion then there will still be liability in the tort of negligence. So, the person who lacks capacity is in the same position as a person who (with capacity) had consented to the operation to begin with.

> A surgeon carried out a lumpectomy operation on a young woman who lacked capacity to consent to the operation, having established that this would be in her best interests. Following the operation, she suffered serious life-threatening complications and it was discovered that the surgeon had not followed proper procedures during the operation causing her some permanent damage. While the surgeon was protected from liability for performing the act of the lumpectomy operation, as this was in the young woman's best interests, he would still be liable in any claim for damages resulting from his clinical negligence in the way he had performed the operation.

Effect of an advance decision to refuse treatment

5.17   When providing healthcare or treatment for a person lacking capacity to consent to those medical procedures, health professionals must act in accordance with any advance decision to refuse treatment made by that person with capacity, so long as the advance decision is both valid and applicable to the proposed treatment (see chapter 8).

5.18   Where a health professional is satisfied that an advance decision as defined in the Act exists and is valid and applicable in the circumstances which have arisen, then section 5 does not give protection from liability (See further detail in chapter 8).

Effect of formal decision-making powers

5.19   Section 5 provides protection from liability to carers and professionals in circumstances where no formal powers are required. However, where formal powers already exist, for example under a Lasting Power of Attorney (see chapter 6), or through an order made by the Court of Protection (see chapter 7), these decision-making powers will take precedence. This is because an LPA, the court or a deputy can provide consent on behalf of the person who lacks capacity, so it is no longer necessary to act in the absence of consent. Anyone acting contrary to a decision of a donee or deputy will not have protection from liability.

5.20   There may be occasions when carers or health professionals feel that a donee or deputy is acting outside the scope of their authority, or contrary to the best interests of the person lacking capacity. An application to the Court of Protection may be necessary if the problem cannot be resolved. Section 6(6) clarifies that life-sustaining treatment, or treatment necessary to prevent a serious deterioration in the person's condition, can be given pending a ruling from the court.

Serious healthcare and treatment decisions

5.21   Before the Act came into force, the courts decided that some decisions relating to the provision of medical treatment were so serious that each case should be brought before the court so that a declaration could be made that the proposed action was lawful. The categories were:

- The proposed withholding or withdrawal of artificial nutrition and hydration (ANH) from patients in a permanent vegetative state (PVS)
- The proposed non-therapeutic sterilisation of a person lacking capacity to consent to this (e.g. for contraceptive purposes)

5.22   In any case where there is a doubt or dispute about whether a particular treatment will be in a patient's best interests, the Court of Protection will have jurisdiction to resolve that doubt or dispute.

5.23   The case-law requirement to seek a declaration in PVS cases is unaffected by the Act and we anticipate that a practice direction by the new President of the Court of Protection will confirm this. Non-therapeutic sterilisation may, by definition, involve a doubt as to best interests and such cases should also continue to be referred to the court.

5.24   Other cases likely to be referred to the Court include those involving ethical dilemmas in untested areas, or where there are otherwise irresolvable conflicts between professionals, or between professionals and family members. (See chapter 7.)

PART 2: LIMITATIONS ON SECTION 5 ACTS

5.25   Section 6 imposes certain limitations on the protection from liability described in the first part of this chapter. In particular, no protection is offered to people who use or threaten violence in order to carry out any action in connection with the care or treatment of a person lacking capacity or to force that person to comply with the carers' actions. However, there may be limited circumstances when the use of some form of restraint or physical intervention may be permitted in order to protect the person from harm. This is described in paragraphs 5.26–5.30 below.

The use of restraint

5.26   As a general rule, any act that is intended to restrain a person lacking capacity will not attract protection from liability. However, section 6 specifies certain conditions, which if satisfied, will serve to provide protection from liability for someone who uses restraint

What is restraint?

5.27   Section 6(4) provides that someone restrains a person lacking capacity if he uses, or threatens to use, force to do an act which the person resists, or restricts the liberty of movement of someone who lacks capacity, whether or not he or she resists.

5.28   Restraint may take many forms. It may be both verbal and physical and may vary from shouting threats at someone, to holding them down, to locking them in a room. It may also include chemical restraint, for example giving someone a large amount of sleeping pills in order to sedate them and thereby restrict their liberty of movement.

The conditions which may justify the use of restraint

5.29   Since the Act has the best interests of people who lack capacity as its key principle, the use of any sort of threat or force or restriction of liberty is generally not permitted. However, the practicalities of caring for and providing protection for people who lack capacity are also recognised. A line needs to be drawn between justifiable protection of people who have impaired decision-making capacity on the one hand and unjustifiable force or coercion on the other. The Act draws this line by setting out two conditions which, if satisfied, may provide protection from liability to carers and others who need to use restraint:

- The first condition is that the person taking action must reasonably believe that it is necessary to do an act which involves restraint in order to *prevent harm* to the person lacking capacity.
- The second condition is that the act is a *proportionate response* (in terms of both the degree and the duration of the restraint) to the likelihood of the person who may lack capacity suffering harm and the seriousness of that harm.

5.30   The onus is on the person doing the act to identify reasons which objectively justify his or her belief that the person being cared for is likely to suffer harm unless some sort of physical intervention or other restraining action is taken. Where restraint is necessary to prevent the person from coming to any harm, only the minimum of force may be used and for the shortest possible duration.

An elderly man with dementia has been prescribed medication for a heart condition which requires his blood pressure to be monitored regularly and occasional blood tests to be carried out. He does not like being 'messed about with' and also is unable to keep still for long enough for the tests to be done. Both his GP and the district nurse are concerned that his medication may do more harm than good if it is not prescribed at the correct level and balanced against other drugs he has been prescribed. After trying, without success, all possible means to explain to the man what is happening and why, the nurse asks her colleagues to hold him still just for long enough for the tests to be carried out. In doing so, they are acting proportionately and would be protected from liability in restraining him in this way.

What is harm?

5.31   The Act does not define 'harm' since it is likely to vary according to the individual circumstances of the person lacking capacity. For example, a person with learning disabilities may run into a busy road without warning, unaware of the danger; a person with dementia may wander away from home and be unable to find the way back; a person with bi-polar affective disorder may run up huge debts through spending money excessively when going through a hypomaniac phase or may be at risk of self-harm when depressed. In many cases, the risk of harm can be prevented by common sense measures (such as locking away poisonous chemicals or removing obstacles) as well as care planning for people being cared for by health or social services authorities, taking account of any risk assessments. However, it is impossible to eliminate all risk, and if a risk arises then a proportionate response is required.

What is a 'proportionate response'?

5.32   The scale and nature of any form of restraint must be a *proportionate response* to the likelihood of the person who may lack capacity suffering harm and to the seriousness of that harm. The means of restraint should be commensurate with the desired outcome, using the minimum necessary force or intervention and for the shortest possible time. For example, a carer may need to keep hold of the arm of a person with learning disabilities while crossing a road, but it would not be a proportionate response to stop the person going outdoors at all. It may be appropriate to have a secure lock on a door leading to a road, but it would not be a proportionate response to lock someone in a bedroom all the time because they have a tendency to wander out onto the busy main road.

5.33   Special care is needed when dealing with people who have particularly challenging behaviour. Guidance has already been issued by the Department of Health and Department for Education and Skills on the use of restrictive physical interventions for people with learning disability and autistic spectrum disorder in health, education and social care settings (see page xx).

> A young man with a learning difficulty sometimes gets distressed in his college class and hits the wall in frustration. Sometimes he hurts himself. Staff are concerned about how to tackle this. They don't want to take him out of the class because although it sometimes upsets him, he says he enjoys it, is keen to get on the bus in the morning, and is learning new skills. They have tried having a support worker sit with him in class, but he still gets upset. The support worker could try to hold him back but thinks this would be inappropriately invasive, even though it would prevent him from hurting himself in the short term. Instead staff decide to give the man a restrictive arm cuff for a few weeks whilst they work with him to find ways of managing his emotions without harming himself. This means he can carry on coming to the class.

PART 3: PAYING FOR GOODS, SERVICES AND OTHER EXPENDITURE

5.34   It is recognised that people who care for others with impaired decision-making capacity often have to spend money on their behalf in order to provide that care. For example, carers may arrange for milk to be delivered or for a chiropodist to call to provide a service to the person at home. More costly arrangements might be for house repairs or organising a holiday. Where it is appropriate for carers to arrange such matters, and so long as the arrangements made are in the best interests of the person lacking capacity, the carers' actions are likely to be protected from liability if their actions were to be challenged. The following paragraphs explain the legal obligations for payment and the circumstances in which any expenditure incurred by carers can be reclaimed from a person lacking capacity.

Who pays for necessary goods and services?

5.35   In general, a contract entered into by a person who lacks capacity to contract is voidable if the other person knows or must be taken to have known of the lack of capacity. However, the Sale of Goods Act 1979 modified this rule where goods which are 'necessaries' are supplied to a person who lacks the capacity to enter into a contract for them. There is a similar modification, at common law, in relation to services. Section 7 of the Act brings both modifications together and provides that in these circumstances, a person is legally obliged to pay a reasonable price for such goods and services.

What is necessary?

5.36   Section 7(2) sets out the definition of 'necessary', which means suitable to the person who may lack capacity's condition in life (i.e. his or her place in society, rather than any mental or physical condition) and his/her actual requirements at the time when the goods are supplied or the services are provided. Thus, while food, drink and clothing are necessary for everyone, the actual requirements for the type of food or the style or amount of clothing will vary according to their individual circumstances or 'condition in life'. Goods will not be necessary if the person's existing supply is sufficient. For instance, buying smart new evening clothes for someone moving into residential care might be necessary if she always dressed for dinner at home and would be distressed at not being well-presented in front of other people, but not if the person had lived in the same much-loved jeans and t-shirts for years and always had to be coaxed to smarten up for special occasions.

Arranging for payment to be made

5.37   As explained above, the legal responsibility for paying for necessary goods and services lies with the person for whom they are supplied, even though that person lacks the capacity to contract for them. Where that person also lacks the capacity to arrange for such payment to be made, section 5 and section 8 of the Act operate together to allow a carer who arranges for goods and services also to arrange settlement of the bill. Section 5 requires the carer to have assessed capacity and best interests. Section 8 then confirms that the carer can lawfully deal with payment in one of three ways:

- If neither the person lacking capacity nor the carer who has arranged for the goods or services can produce the necessary funds, then the carer may promise that the person who may lack capacity will pay (i.e. the carer may pledge the credit of the person who lacks capacity). Of course, it may be that a supplier will not be happy with such a promise, in which case formal steps will be required.
- If the person lacking capacity has cash in his/her possession, then the carer may use that money to pay for goods or services (e.g. to pay the milkman or the hairdresser).
- The carer may choose to pay for the goods or services with his/her own money and is then entitled to be reimbursed or otherwise indemnified from the money of the person lacking capacity. Again, this may involve using cash in the person's possession, or running up an IOU. Formal steps would be required before a carer could gain access to any money held by a third party such as a bank or building society.

An elderly woman was recently admitted to hospital as a result of medical problems although she also has severe dementia. She now requires turning every two hours and nursing care to ensure that her skin does not break down and pressure sores develop. Her family are keen for her to return home and an enhanced package of care is proposed. Her daughter makes the necessary arrangements and pays for the equipment that is needed immediately to enable her mother to be discharged from hospital. The daughter is then entitled to be reimbursed from her mother's money (but not, without formal steps, to take any money out of the bank to settle that debt).

5.38   The intention of these provisions is to make it possible for ordinary but necessary goods and services to be provided for people who lack the capacity to organise and pay for them. However, section 8 does not give any authorisation to a carer to gain access to the income or assets of, or to sell the property of, the person who lacks capacity. A distinction is drawn between the use of available cash already in the possession of the person lacking capacity on the one hand and the removal of money from a bank account or selling valuable items of property on the other.

5.39   Where the assets of a person lacking capacity to manage them are held in a bank or building society account or are invested, specific authority (in the form of a Lasting Power of Attorney, a Deputyship or a single order of the Court of Protection) will generally be required before the bank or building society can give access to them to anyone other than the legal owner.

During some very severe storms, several tiles were blown off the roof of the house owned by a man with Alzheimer's disease and it is clear to his family that urgent repairs are needed to make the roof watertight. He is incapable of making the arrangements for the work to be done and also lacks capacity to make a claim on his insurance. The repairs are likely to be costly because scaffolding has to be erected. His son decides to go ahead with organising the repairs and agrees to pay the cost himself. The son must then apply to the Court of Protection for authority to make the insurance claim on his father's behalf and for him to be reimbursed from his father's bank account to cover the cost of the repairs.

5.40   Some carers may already have lawful control over money belonging to a person lacking capacity. For example, a carer may have been appointed as a financial donee under a Lasting Power of Attorney (see chapter 6) or as a deputy appointed by the Court of Protection to make financial decisions on behalf of a person lacking capacity (see chapter 7). Alternatively, a carer may be appointed under Social Security regulations to act as 'appointee' to claim benefits for a person lacking capacity to make his/her own claim and to use the money on the person's behalf. Section 6(5) makes clear that an informal carer cannot make arrangements for goods or services to be supplied to a person lacking capacity if this conflicts with a decision made by someone who has formal powers over the person's money and property.

CHAPTER 6: LASTING POWERS OF ATTORNEY

This chapter describes the main provisions relating to LPAs and provides basic guidance on their practical implications. The Office of the Public Guardian will produce detailed guidance, in due course, on explaining the procedures involved in making an LPA and important issues to consider when making an LPA. Guidance will also explain the registration process for LPAs and the circumstances in which it may be necessary to revoke a power.

INTRODUCTION

6.1   Part 1 of this chapter explains what is meant by a Lasting Power of Attorney (LPA), describes the types of decisions that donors (those making the power) can delegate to their attorneys (known in the Bill as donees) and sets out the circumstances in which an LPA can and cannot be used. Part 2 sets out the duties and responsibilities of donees, describes the standards of conduct expected of donees and explains the actions which can be taken against a donee who fails to meet appropriate standards. **Part 3** briefly considers the transitional arrangements which will apply to Enduring Powers of Attorney (EPAs) created before the implementation of this Act.

PART 1: WHAT IS A LASTING POWER OF ATTORNEY?

6.2 A power of attorney is a legal document by which one person (the donor) gives another person (the attorney or donee) or persons the authority to act in the donor's name and on his or her behalf. Prior to the introduction of the Enduring Powers of Attorney Act 1985, every power was automatically revoked once the donor lacked capacity. That Act, however, introduced the Enduring Power of Attorney (EPA) which was a particular type of power of attorney that allowed the attorney(s) to continue to act on behalf of the donor in relation to property and financial affairs even after the donor ceased to have capacity.

6.3 The Mental Capacity Act introduces a new form of power of attorney, a *Lasting Power of Attorney (LPA)*, to replace EPAs and to extend the areas in which donors can authorise others to make decisions on their behalf in the event of them losing capacity. In addition to property and financial affairs, donors can now choose to delegate decisions affecting their personal welfare, including healthcare and consent to medical treatment. Different donees may be appointed to take different types of decisions.

6.4 LPAs dealing with property and financial affairs (referred to here as financial LPAs) can be used both before and after the donor loses capacity, according to the donor's wishes. However, welfare LPAs (including those relating to healthcare decisions) can only be used once the donor has lost capacity. To be valid, both types of LPA must be set out in the prescribed form and must be registered with the Public Guardian. The different types of LPAs are described in more detail in the next section.

Lasting Powers of Attorney

6.5 Section 9 of the Act defines an LPA and specifies the requirements and procedures that must be followed in order to create a valid LPA. These requirements are set out in section 9 and Schedule 1 of the Act and include the requirement that only adults aged 18 or over and who have capacity can appoint an LPA. In all cases, the LPA must be registered with the Public Guardian before it can be used.

6.6 Of particular importance is section 9(4) which specifies that, when acting under an LPA, donees must comply with all the provisions in Part 1 of the Act and in particular, must always act in the *best interests* of the donor. This involves, amongst other considerations, permitting and encouraging the donor to participate as fully as possible in any decisions affecting him/her and consulting, where appropriate, with relatives, carers and others who have an interest in the donor's welfare (see chapter 4).

Lasting Powers of Attorney: Personal welfare

6.7 Donors can authorise the donee(s) to act in relation to all matters concerning their personal welfare or they can list specific matters where they wish the donee(s) to have power to act. The types of decisions that welfare donees could be authorised to take, and the powers an LPA would confer on them, might include any or all of the following:

- Decisions on where the donor should live;
- Giving or refusing consent to medical examination and/or treatment;
- Arranging for the donor to access medical, dental or optical treatment;

- Applying for and having access to confidential documents and personal information relating to the donor held by any organisation, such as medical records or personal files held by social services authorities.

6.8   The list above gives examples of the types of powers that might be included in a welfare LPA and is not intended to be exhaustive. A general LPA in respect of personal welfare will authorise the donee to make all of the decisions set out above. In any particular case, specific powers may need to be included. The donor may wish to specify the types of powers s/he wishes the donee to have, or to exclude particular types of decisions or acts. Before using any power under an LPA, a donee must first be satisfied that the decision being made is in the donor's best interests. This will include consideration of whether the donor has the capacity to make the decision in question themselves.

Mrs P has recently been diagnosed as being in the very early stages of Alzheimer's disease. She is anxious to get all her affairs in order while she is still able to do so. She decides to make a welfare LPA, appointing her daughter as donee so that when she no longer has capacity, her daughter can make decisions on her behalf concerning the care she receives, including deciding if residential or nursing home care is necessary (in other words, where Mrs P will live). However, Mrs P has always believed quite strongly that doctors should be the ones who should decide whether a person receives particular medical treatments if that person cannot make those decisions themselves. She does not think it is right for her daughter to be able to make such decisions and so she states in the LPA that her daughter cannot make decisions on her behalf relating to medical treatment.

Restrictions on personal welfare LPAs

6.9   Section 11 of the Act imposes certain restrictions on the powers of welfare donees. Subsection (1) provides that an LPA does not authorise the donee to use, or threaten to use force in order to do something which the donor resists or does not authorise him to restrict the donor's liberty, whether or not he resists, unless three conditions are satisfied. These are that a) the donee reasonably believes that the donor lacks capacity b) the donee reasonably believes that it is necessary to do the act in order to prevent harm to the donor and c) the act is proportionate response to the likelihood and the seriousness of that harm.

Mrs S has severe dementia and is looked after by her son who is her attorney under a welfare LPA. She has complained of very bad toothache for several days and it appears to be getting worse. Her son takes her to the dentist who finds that Mrs S's toothache is being caused by a rotten tooth which needs to be extracted. Her son and her dentist both try to explain that this needs to be done in order to make Mrs S's pain go away but Mrs S lacks capacity to consent to the treatment and becomes very distressed and resists physically when the dentist attempts to give her an anaesthetic. Her son and the dentist discuss the need to remove the tooth and her son agrees that Mrs S should be gently but firmly held down in the dentist's chair so that the dentist can give her an anaesthetic and remove the rotten tooth.

LPAs authorising healthcare decisions

6.10   As indicated above, an LPA which authorises the donee to make personal welfare decisions including the authority to give or refuse consent to medical treatment or make other healthcare decisions (section 11(6)(c)), can only be used when the donor has lost capacity. The donee will be able to make all welfare decisions unless any decisions are specifically excluded by the donor when creating the power. However, the donee may only make decisions about the carrying out or continuation of life-sustaining treatment in circumstances if the donor has included a clear statement to this effect in the LPA document.

6.11 It is also important to remember that, in the same way that a person with capacity cannot demand a particular treatment, LPAs cannot give donees the power to demand specific forms of medical treatments that doctors or other health professionals may not agree with

> Mrs R has never trusted doctors and prefers to rely on alternative therapies and remedies. Having seen her father suffer for many years after invasive treatment for cancer, she is clear that she would not accept such treatment for herself, even with the knowledge that she may die without it. When she is diagnosed with bowel cancer, Mrs R again discusses this issue with her husband. Mrs R trusts her husband more than anyone else and knows he will respect her wishes about the forms of treatment she would or would not accept. She therefore asks him to act as her donee to make welfare and healthcare decisions on her behalf, should she lose the capacity to make her own decisions. Mrs R makes a general LPA appointing her husband to make all her welfare decisions, and includes a specific statement authorising him to refuse life-sustaining treatment on her behalf, if that is in her best interests. He will then be able to make decisions about treatment in her best interests, including using what he knows about his wife's feelings.

Lasting Powers of Attorney: Property and financial affairs

6.12 While still retaining capacity, an adult aged 18 or over can make an LPA appointing one or more donees to make decisions relating to the management of the donor's property and financial affairs on his/her behalf. The LPA may be used while the donor still retains capacity if s/he so wishes, and will continue to have effect when the donor is unable to make some types of decisions. Alternatively, the donor can specify that the LPA can only be used after s/he no longer has capacity. In either case, the LPA must be registered with the Public Guardian before it can be used.

6.13 Donors can authorise the donee(s) to act in relation to all matters concerning their property and financial affairs or they can list specific matters where they wish the donee(s) to have power to act. The types of decisions or actions financial donees could be authorised to take, and the powers an LPA would confer on them, might include any or all of the following:

- Buying or selling property (land, buildings or other assets);
- Opening, closing or operating any bank, building society or other account containing the donor's funds;
- Giving access to financial information to others concerning the donor;
- Claiming, receiving and using on the donor's behalf all benefits, pensions, allowances, rebates etc to which the donor may be entitled (unless someone else had already been appointed to do this and everyone wanted that arrangement to continue)
- Receiving any income, inheritance or other entitlement of the donor;
- Dealing with the donor's tax affairs;
- Paying the donor's mortgage, rent and/or household expenses;
- Making appropriate arrangements to insure, maintain and repair the donor's property;

- Investing the donor's savings in interest bearing accounts, bonds, stocks and shares or any other form of investment;
- Making gifts on the donor's behalf (but see paragraph 6.15 below);
- Pay for private medical care and/or residential care or nursing home fees;
- Using the donor's income or capital to purchase a vehicle or any aids, adaptations or equipment required by the donor where these are not provided free or charge;
- Borrowing money on behalf of the donor and repaying interest and capital on any loan taken out by the donor or donee on his/her behalf;
- Making provision for any person for whom the donor might be expected to provide if he did not lack capacity, such as a spouse and dependant children;

6.14   The above list gives examples of the types of powers that might be included in a financial LPA and again, is not intended to be exhaustive. A general LPA in respect of property and financial affairs will authorise the donee to undertake any of the acts set out above. The donor may wish to specify the types of powers s/he wishes the donee to have, or to exclude particular types of decisions or acts. In using any power under an LPA, a donee must first be satisfied that the decision being made or the action taken will be in the donor's best interests. Again, this will include consideration of whether the donor has the capacity to make the decision in question themselves.

A long-time member of the Green Party appoints his solicitor as his donee under a financial LPA. While he has confidence in his solicitor to manage his affairs efficiently, he stipulates in the LPA that any investments made on his behalf must be ethical investments in companies which operate in a socially and environmentally responsible manner.

Scope of financial LPAs: gifts

6.15   Section 12 of the Act imposes limitations on the donee's powers to make gifts from the property and estate of the donor. A donee is only permitted to make gifts to people who are related to or connected with the donor (including the donee him/herself) on 'customary occasions' (section 12(1)(a)). These are defined as being the occasion of or the anniversary of a birth, marriage, civil partnership or any other occasion when presents are usually given among families, friends or associates (section 12(3)(b)), which would include for example Christmas, Diwali or other religious festivals that the person lacking capacity would be likely to celebrate, or the giving of house-warming presents. If the donor had previously made regular or periodic donations to any charity, the donee would also be permitted to continue to make such donations from the donor's funds. However, the value of any gift or charitable donation must be reasonable in the particular circumstances and taking account of the size of the donor's estate. For example, it may not be reasonable to buy distant relations expensive gifts at Christmas if the donor was living on modest means and had to do without essential items in order to pay for them.

6.16   In addition to the above limitations, the donor may impose any other conditions or restrictions on the donee's powers to make gifts, which must be specified in the LPA document at the time the LPA is created. However, it is also important to note that the donee's power to act in the donor's best interests is flexible. As it requires the donee to consider the donor's wishes and feelings and the factors that he or she would have taken into account, the donee would be able to meet another person's needs in an appropriate case or make appropriate gifts.

Mr S made an LPA appointing his son as his financial donee. When he lost capacity to manage his own affairs, the LPA was registered and his son took over as his donee. Before he lost capacity, Mr S had always been very close to his only grandson and had often expressed his wish that his grandson attend the same fee-paying school that both he and his son had attended. When his grandson reached the right age, Mr S's son decided to use his father's money to pay the school fees so his son could attend the school in question. By doing so, Mr S's son felt that he was acting in his father's best interests as this was something that he thought he would have done himself if he had still been able.

PART 2: DUTIES AND RESPONSIBILITIES OF DONEES

6.17 When a donor chooses a particular person to act as his/her donee under a Lasting Power of Attorney, s/he does not have the right to insist that the donee accepts the appointment. The provisions of the Act do not impose a duty on donees to act, but merely authorise donees to act if they wish to do so. However, once a donee starts to act under an LPA, s/he will assume a number of duties and responsibilities, both as a result of the Act and as a result of common law principles that apply under the law of agency and will be required to act in accordance with certain standards. Failure to comply with the duties set out below could result in an application being made to the Court of Protection for the donee to be removed, and in some circumstances the donee could be personally liable to criminal charges of fraud or negligence.

Duty to act in the donor's best interests

6.18 Section 9(4)(a) stipulates that the authority conferred by an LPA is subject to the provisions of Part 1 of the Act, and in particular section 4, requiring the donee always to act in the best interests of the donor. Donees must therefore take account of the guidance set out in chapter 4 in determining the donor's best interests in relation to any particular decision taken under the LPA. This will include considering whether the donor will have capacity at some point in the future to make the decision themselves and if so, whether the decision can be delayed until that time.

Duty of care and fiduciary duties

6.19 A donee of an LPA is acting as the agent of the donor and therefore, under the law of agency, the donee has certain obligations and duties towards the donor. The donee owes a duty of care to the donor and, in particular regarding duties of a fiduciary nature to respect the degree of trust the donor has placed in the donee.

6.20 When agreeing to act as donee under a Lasting Power of Attorney, whether a personal welfare or a financial LPA, the donee is taking on a role which carries a great deal of power which s/he must use carefully and responsibly. The standard of conduct expected of donees involves compliance with the following fiduciary and other duties. There is a duty:

- to act within the scope of the LPA
- of care
- not to delegate unless authorised to do so
- not to take advantage of the position of donee
- of good faith
- of confidentiality
- to comply with the directions of the Court of Protection

■   not to disclaim without complying with the relevant regulations (*add ref when known*)

And specifically in relation to financial LPAs:

■   to keep accounts
■   to keep the donor's money and property separate

These duties are described in more detail in the following paragraphs.

Duty to act within the scope of the LPA

6.21   A donee has a duty to act only within the scope of the actual powers set out in the LPA. Thus a welfare donee has no authority to act in relation to the donor's property and affairs, or vice versa, unless the LPA authorises this. The scope of the donee's powers will be quite broad where the LPA is expressed in general terms. But where a donor has specified any conditions or restrictions in the LPA, the donee must respect the donor's wishes and act only within the authority conferred by the LPA (section 9(4)(b). If the donee considers that additional powers are needed and the donor no longer has capacity to amend the LPA, an application may be made to the Court of Protection (see chapter 7).

Duty of care

6.22   A donee of an LPA owes a duty of care to the donor in carrying out his/her functions under the LPA. This means meeting a certain standard of care depending on whether the donee is being paid for his/her services or holds relevant professional qualifications.

■   Donees who are not being paid must act with due care, skill and diligence as they would do in making their own decisions and conducting their own affairs. A donee who claims to have particular skills must show greater skill in those particular areas than someone who does not make such claims.

■   If donees are being paid for their services, this is taken into account in determining the degree of care or skill expected for the proper performance of their duties and will mean that a higher degree of care and skill is expected from them.

■   Donees who undertake their duties in the course of their professional work (such as solicitors or accountants) must display professional competence and abide by their own profession's rules and standards.

Duty not to delegate

6.23   It is a basic principle of the law of agency that an agent cannot delegate his/her authority. Since a donee is the chosen agent of the donor, s/he must carry out the functions under the LPA personally and cannot, as a general rule, delegate those functions to anyone else. The donor must make specific provision in the LPA to authorise the donee to have any wider powers of delegation.

Duty not to take advantage of the position of donee

6.24   A donee has a duty not to take advantage of his/her position. Donees must avoid any conflicts of interest between their responsibilities towards the donor and their own personal interests. They must constantly be guided by the principles of the Bill, notably the requirement to act in the donor's best interests and not allow any other influences to affect the way in which they exercise the powers delegated under the LPA.

Duty of good faith

6.25 Donees must act in good faith in exercising their authority under an LPA. An act carried out in good faith means an act that is carried out honestly. For example, a donee must try to ensure his/her actions do not negate previous decisions made by the person while still competent.

Duty of confidentiality

6.26 Donees have a duty to keep the donor's affairs confidential, unless the donor has consented to disclosure of personal or financial information, or unless there is some other good reason to release it, such as the public interest, that overrides the duty of confidentiality. The ethical considerations raised by this duty are discussed in more detail in chapter 13.

Duty to comply with the directions of the Court of Protection

6.27 Under sections 22 and 23 of the Act, the Court of Protection has wide powers to determine any question as to the meaning or effect of an LPA. The Court may also give specific directions to extend the powers available to donees under an LPA, or to require donees to keep records (such as financial accounts) or provide specific information or documentation to the Court. Donees have a duty to comply with any direction given by the Court.

Duty not to disclaim without notifying the donor and the Court

6.28 If a donee wishes to disclaim his or her appointment, the disclaimer must be in accordance with certain requirements which are prescribed in regulations .

Duty to keep accounts

6.29 A financial donee is expected to keep, and be constantly ready to produce, correct accounts of all his/her dealings and transactions on the donor's behalf. Where a lay person, such as a family member, is acting as donee, and the donor's affairs are relatively straightforward, all that may be required is a record of the donor's income, any major or regular expenditure and details of the donor's bank accounts. The more complicated the donor's affairs, the more detailed the accounts may need to be. As indicated above, the Court of Protection can give directions requiring the submitting of accounts and the production of records kept by the donee.

Duty to keep the donor's money and property separate

6.30 Donees should, in general, keep the donor's money and property separate from their own or anyone else's. There may be occasions, for example where a husband is acting as his wife's donee or vice versa, where a prior arrangement was made to keep their money in a joint bank account and it may be appropriate for this to continue under the LPA. But in most circumstances, donees must keep everything separate to avoid any possibility of mistakes or confusion in handling the donor's affairs.

Protection against abuse

6.31   Because donees are in a position of trust there is always the potential for abuse to take place. The main protection from abuse is for the donor to choose carefully in selecting a suitable donee. But others have a role to play in looking out for possible signs of abuse or exploitation and reporting any concerns to the Office of the Public Guardian, who will then follow this up in co-operation with relevant agencies.

6.32   There are some signs that are sufficient to raise concerns that a donee may be exploiting the donor or failing to act in the donor's best interests, for example:

■   The denial of relatives or friends of access to the donor – either active denial by the donee or where the donor suddenly refuses visits or telephone calls from family members or longstanding friends for no apparent reason;

■   Sudden unexplained changes in living arrangements, such as where someone moves in to care for an elderly person with whom they have had little previous contact;

■   The denial of access to a medical practitioner or care worker to see the donor;

■   Unpaid bills, such as arrears of residential care or nursing home fees;

■   The opening of credit card accounts for the donor by the donee;

■   Expenditure that is not obviously related to the donor's needs;

■   Unusual or extravagant expenditure by the donee;

■   The transfer of assets to another country.

6.33   Any concerns or suspicions of abuse should be raised immediately with the OPG, which has specific responsibilities in respect of donees of LPAs (section 56). The OPG may direct a Court of Protection Visitor to visit a donee to investigate any matter of concern. The OPG will be able to investigate any concerns or complaints against donees but in serious cases, where physical abuse or serious fraud is suspected, the matter should be referred directly to the police.

6.34   The protection of vulnerable people from the risk of abuse, ill-treatment or neglect and the duties and responsibilities of the various agencies involved, including the OPG and local authorities, are discussed in more detail in chapter 9.

PART 3: ARRANGEMENTS FOR EXISTING ENDURING POWERS OF ATTORNEY

6.35   The scheme for LPAs described in this chapter is designed to replace Enduring Powers of Attorney (EPAs) since the Act repeals the Enduring Powers of Attorney Act 1985. It will no longer be possible to execute an EPA once the Act is in force. However, many EPAs will have been created before the Act came into force, with the expectation that attorneys appointed by them will have authority to manage the donor's property and financial affairs after the donor has lost capacity.

6.36   Many donors of EPAs who still have capacity when the Act comes into effect may prefer to destroy the EPA and make an LPA under the new statutory provisions, as described above. Some donors will not have capacity to make an LPA and others will omit, or choose not, to do so. The Act therefore makes transitional provisions for existing EPAs, whether registered or not, to continue to be valid so that the donors' expectations in making them can continue to be met.

Enduring Powers of Attorney

6.37   Schedule 5 reproduces the Enduring Powers of Attorney Act 1985 in its entirety with some minor amendments to take account of changes to the Court of Protection and the new role of the Public Guardian. The provisions are not described in detail here, since they are covered in guidance issued by the former Public Guardianship Office and other more detailed publications on EPAs. References to these publications and details of how to get copies are given on page xx.

CHAPTER 7: THE COURT OF PROTECTION AND COURT-APPOINTED DEPUTIES

INTRODUCTION

7.1   This chapter gives guidance to professionals and others using the Code of Practice about the role of the court, with particular detail about deputies appointed by the Court. Official guidance and information will also be contained in Rules of Court, Regulations and Practice Directions issued by the Court and the Office of the Public Guardian.

- Part 1 explains the powers of the Court and describes the circumstances where it may be necessary, or there is a requirement, to apply to the court. Part 1 also broadly explains how to go about obtaining such an order.
- Part 2 looks in more detail at the appointment of deputies to act and make decisions on behalf of people lacking capacity and sets out the duties and responsibilities of deputies appointed by the Court. It describes the standards of conduct expected of deputies and explains the actions that can be taken against a deputy who fails to meet appropriate standards.

PART 1: THE COURT OF PROTECTION

7.2   Section 43 of the Act establishes a specialised court, known as the Court of Protection, with a new jurisdiction to deal with decision-making for adults who lack capacity. The new Court takes over the role and functions of the former Court of Protection in relation to the management of property and financial affairs of people lacking capacity. It also deals with serious decisions affecting healthcare and personal welfare matters that were previously dealt with by the High Court under its inherent jurisdiction. The Court is supported in its role by the Office of the Public Guardian.

7.3   While it is expected that, in the vast majority of cases, the structures for decision-making set out in Part 1 of the Act will enable appropriate decisions to be made or any concerns or disputes to be easily resolved, the Court of Protection provides a judicial forum of last resort to deal with particularly complex decisions or difficult disputes which cannot be resolved in any other way. (See also chapter 10).

When should an application be made to the Court of Protection?

7.4   The Court of Protection will have comprehensive jurisdiction in relation to welfare and financial matters. The President of the Court of Protection has issued a Practice Direction (ref. to be added here) specifying in some detail the circumstances in which cases should be referred to the Court and setting out the types of cases which are likely to require a hearing before the Court and those which may be resolved without recourse to the Court.

Who should make the application?

7.5   The Act makes flexible provision as to who can make an application to the Court, since this will depend on the type and circumstances of the case under consideration. For example, in relation to disputes between family members, it will be a decision for the aggrieved family member as to whether court action is warranted, bearing in mind the need in most cases to obtain permission beforehand (see paragraph 7.6 below). Where the dispute relates to the provision of medical treatment, the NHS Trust or other body responsible for the patient's care should in most cases make the application to the Court. A local authority wishing to intervene in decisions affecting the personal welfare of a person lacking capacity should make the application. Regardless of who makes the application, the person lacking capacity in relation to the matter in question should in most cases be a party to the proceedings. The Court may appoint the Official Solicitor to act for the person lacking capacity. The friend will then make the application on his behalf.

Permission to apply to the Court of Protection

7.6   Section 48 of the Act sets out specific requirements relating to applications to the Court of Protection. As a general rule, the Court's permission must first be sought before an application can be made. Some categories of people can apply as of right without the need to obtain permission from the Court. These include:

- a person who lacks, or who is alleged to lack, capacity (or anyone with parental responsibility if the person is under 18 years)
- the donor or donee of a Lasting Power of Attorney to which the application relates
- a court-appointed deputy acting for the person concerned
- a person named in an existing court order to which the application relates.

7.7   In all other cases, subject to the Court of Protection rules and paragraph 21 (2) of Schedule 3 (declarations relating to private international law), permission will be required before an application can be made to the court. In deciding whether to grant permission, the Court must take account of a number of factors designed to ensure that any application will promote the interests of the person lacking capacity (or alleged to lack capacity) who is the subject of the proceedings. In particular, the Court must consider:

- The applicant's connection with the person lacking capacity to whom the application relates
- The reasons for the application
- The benefit to the person lacking capacity to whom the application relates of any proposed order or direction of the Court
- Whether that benefit can be achieved in any other way.

A charity providing outdoor adventure holidays for adults with learning disabilities wishes to take a young man on a mountaineering holiday but his mother objects, as she thinks it would be too dangerous. Local authority care workers wish to support this opportunity for the young man's personal development and seek permission to apply to the Court of Protection on his behalf. The Court decides that the benefit could be achieved in another way through negotiation and mediation, taking account of the young man's own views and wishes, and therefore refuses permission for the application to be made.

Powers of the Court of Protection

7.8   The Court of Protection has wide ranging powers to make declarations, decisions and orders affecting people who lack, or are alleged to lack, capacity. It may also appoint deputies to act and make decisions on behalf of people lacking capacity, and has the power to remove deputies or donees acting under a Lasting Power of Attorney (LPA) who act improperly. The various powers are briefly described in the following paragraphs, covering:

- Power to make declarations
- Power to make orders (section 16)

- Power to appoint deputies (section 16)
- Powers in relation to Lasting Powers of Attorney (clause 23)

POWER TO MAKE DECLARATIONS

7.9   In some cases, it may be helpful to ask the Court to make a ruling on whether or not a person has capacity in relation to make a particular decision. In order to make such a ruling, the Court will require specific evidence of lack of capacity over the matter in question. Where the Court decides that the person has capacity to make the relevant decision(s), the Court has no further role in the matter since the person has the right to decide for him/herself.

7.10   There will be relatively few circumstances where there will be a need to apply to the court asking for a declaration as to capacity or a lack of capacity. Often these questions can be resolved informally (see chapter 10). However, recourse to the Court may be appropriate in the following circumstances:

- Where there is a dispute between professionals over a person's capacity to make a particular (invariably serious) decision. For example, where professionals disagree as to whether a person with learning disabilities has the capacity to refuse consent to major heart surgery.
- Where there is a more wide-ranging dispute; for example, between family members over whether an elderly member of the family has the capacity to make an LPA and there is also disagreement as to the person appointed as the donee under the power. Or where a particularly novel treatment has been proposed and there is a dispute about whether this is in a person's best interests. In these circumstances, a declaration as to capacity may be needed in order to settle the dispute.

7.11   In addition to establishing whether or not someone has capacity, the Court may also make declarations as to:

- Whether an act done, in relation to a person lacking capacity was lawful (for example by a carer acting without formal powers) or whether a proposed act would be lawful.

7.12   This ability to make declarations as to the lawfulness of an act particularly concerns serious medical treatment cases, where there is doubt or disagreement. The Act provides for life-sustaining treatment or other actions to be taken to stop the deterioration of a person's condition pending a court decision.

Serious healthcare and treatment decisions

7.13   Before the Act came into force, the courts decided that some decisions relating to the provision of medical treatment were so serious that each case should have a declaration that the proposed action was lawful before that action was taken.

7.14   The case law requirement to seek a declaration in cases involving people in a persistent vegetative state (PVS) is unaffected by the Act and we anticipate that a practice direction by the new President of the Court of Protection will confirm this. Non-therapeutic sterilisation may, by definition, involve a doubt as to best interests and such cases should also continue to be referred to the court.

7.15   Other cases likely to be referred to the Court include those involving ethical dilemmas in untested areas, or where there are otherwise irresolvable conflicts between professionals, or between professionals and family members.

Single orders of the Court

7.16   In cases of serious dispute, where there is no other way of finding a solution or when the authority of the court is needed in order to make a particular decision or take a particular action, it may be appropriate to ask the Court to state its decision in the form of a single order (see below).

7.17   Examples of the types of cases when an application for a single order may be appropriate are as follows:

■   When there is genuine doubt or disagreement about the existence, validity or applicability of an advance decision to refuse treatment (see chapter 8).

■   Where there is a major dispute regarding a serious decision for example about where a person lacking capacity should live

■   Where it is suspected that a person lacking capacity is at risk of harm or abuse from a named individual, the Court could be asked to make an order prohibiting that individual from having contact with the person who lacks capacity.

■   Where formal authority is needed to deal with significant one-off financial decisions for a person lacking capacity to manage financial affairs (such as paying a costly bill for house repairs or selling a valuable item of property), but there is no need for on-going financial powers, the Court could be asked to make an order providing the necessary authority.

■   Where it is necessary to make a will, or amend an existing will, on behalf of a person lacking testamentary capacity, this can only be done by order of the Court.

The son and daughter of a woman with Alzheimer's disease, who live some distance apart, argue over which care home their mother should move to. Although she is incapable of making this decision herself, she has enough money to pay the fees. Her solicitor acts as attorney in relation to her financial affairs under a registered Enduring Power of Attorney, but has no power, and is unwilling, to get involved in this family dispute, which is becoming increasingly bitter. The Court of Protection makes a single order in the mother's best interests, having taken account of her relationship with her children and decides which care home can best meet her needs. Once this matter is resolved, there is no need to appoint a deputy.

Powers in relation to Lasting Powers of Attorney

7.18   As described in chapter 6, the Court of Protection has a range of powers to determine the validity of an LPA and to give directions as to how the LPA should be operated. In particular, where the donor no longer has capacity, the Court has power to revoke an LPA with the effect of terminating the donee's appointment.

7.19   For example, where there are concerns about the validity of the LPA, the Court may be asked to:

■   decide whether the requirements for making an LPA have been met
■   decide whether the LPA has been revoked or otherwise come to an end.

The Court also has power to direct that an LPA should not be registered, or if it has already been registered, that an LPA should be revoked in circumstances where:

■   the LPA was made as a result of undue pressure or fraud
■   the donee has behaved, is behaving or proposes to behave, in a way that contravenes his/her authority or is not in the donor's best interests

7.20   If someone feels that the drafting of an LPA is not entirely clear, the Court can be asked to clarify the meaning or effect of the LPA. It may give specific directions to donees as to how an LPA should be operated. If a donee considers that the powers available under the LPA are insufficient, s/he may apply to the Court for an extension of powers where the donor no longer has capacity to grant authority for such an extension. In particular, the Court may authorise the making of gifts of the donor's property which donees are not otherwise permitted to make under section 12(2) (see paragraph 6.15).

7.21   The Court also has powers to require donees to keep and produce records (such as financial accounts) and to provide specific reports, information or documentation as directed by the Court. If concerns are raised about any remuneration or expenses claimed by donees in carrying out their duties, the Court can give directions to resolve the matter. Part 2. Deputies appointed by the Court of Protection

PART 2: DEPUTIES APPOINTED BY THE COURT OF PROTECTION

7.22   Where the Court believes that there is a need for on-going decision-making powers for a person lacking capacity, it may under section 16(2) appoint a deputy to act for and make such decisions on behalf of the person. When the Court decides that the appointment of a deputy is in the best interests of a person lacking capacity, a decision by the Court must be preferred to the appointment of a deputy to make a decision. Section 16(4)(b) also requires the Court to have regard to the principle that the powers conferred on a deputy should be as limited in scope and duration as is reasonably practicable in the circumstances. (see paragraph 7.24 below).

Appointment of deputies

7.23   It is for the Court to decide who to appoint as a deputy. The Court will consider whether the proposed deputy is reliable and trustworthy and has an appropriate level of skill and competence to carry out the necessary tasks. Different skills may be required according to whether the deputy is appointed to make welfare (including healthcare) decisions or financial decisions or both.

When might a deputy need to be appointed?

7.24   The Court must consider the principle that a decision by the Court is to be preferred to the appointment of a deputy to make a decision when deciding if it is in the best interests of the person lacking capacity to appoint a deputy. The need for a deputy to be appointed will vary according to the individual circumstances of the person lacking capacity and whether the appointment relates to property and affairs or personal welfare matters.

Property and affairs

7.25   The appointment of a deputy to manage the person's property and financial affairs is likely to be needed in similar circumstances to those that previously governed the appointment of a receiver under Part VII of the Mental Health Act 1983 (which this Act repeals). There may be a need to apply to the Court for an order appointing a deputy when:

- more than a specified amount of cash assets remain to be dealt with after any debts have been paid; or
- there is property to be sold; or
- the person has a level of income or capital that the Court considers requires to be managed by a deputy.

7.26   A deputy may be appointed in a situation where there is already a benefits appointee in existence (i.e. an individual who has been appointed under social security legislation to receive and deal with benefits on behalf of a person who lacks capacity to do this himself or herself). The deputy may be the same person as the benefits appointee or someone else. Although the appointeeship scheme remains completely outside the legal framework created by the Mental Capacity Act, the deputy would be expected to act in close conjunction with the appointee regarding actions taken on behalf of the person lacking capacity.

7.27   The proposed deputy will need to sign a declaration giving details of his/her own personal circumstances and ability to manage financial affairs. The declaration will include details of the tasks and duties the deputy will be required to carry out, and the deputy is required to give a personal undertaking that s/he has the skills, knowledge and time to perform and complete each task and to carry out his/her duties as deputy.

Personal welfare

7.28   It is expected that the appointment of a deputy to make personal welfare or health-care decisions is likely to be needed only in the most extreme cases, when necessary action cannot be taken without the need for formal powers and/or there is no other way of making a decision that is in the best interests of the person lacking capacity. As noted above, where possible, the Court will seek to make a single order. Examples of circumstances which may require the appointment of a personal welfare deputy for a person lacking capacity are as follows:

■   Where there is a history of acrimonious and serious family disputes which could have a detrimental effect on decisions about the person's future care

■   Where the person's best interests are best met by a deputy consulting with everyone concerned and having the final authority to make the necessary decisions

■   In exceptional cases where the person is felt to be at risk of serious harm if left in the care of family members, a local authority officer or other independent person could be appointed as deputy to make personal care decisions – this could, for example, be combined with a Court order prohibiting those family members from having contact with the person

■   When a series of linked welfare decisions need to be made over time, for which single orders of the Court are not appropriate.

Having spent most of her childhood in care, a young woman with learning disabilities goes to live with her father when she becomes 18. Staff at the day centre she attends notice that she is becoming increasingly disturbed and often has bruises on her arms and legs. They arrange for her to be seen by a doctor who finds signs of physical and sexual abuse. The father denies this and criminal proceedings against him fail for lack of evidence. The local authority social services try to persuade him that a move to independent supported housing would be in his daughter's best interests, but he objects. The authority therefore applies to the Court for a deputy to be appointed to make decisions about the woman's future care and welfare.

Who can be a deputy?

7.29   Section 19(1) clarifies that deputies appointed by the Court must be individuals who are at least 18 years of age. Where appointed to make decisions in relation to property and affairs, the deputy can be either an individual or a trust corporation (often parts of banks or other financial institutions). It is also possible for the Court to appoint as deputy someone who holds a specified office or position, such as a Director of Social Services. No-one can be appointed as a deputy without their consent.

7.30 Section 19(4) also makes provision for two or more deputies to be appointed and for the Court to specify whether they should act 'jointly' or 'jointly and severally'.

- **Joint deputies** must always act together and the agreement (and in some circumstances, the signature) of all deputies must be obtained before a decision can be made or an act carried out
- **Joint and several deputies** can act together but may also act independently if they wish, so that any action taken by any deputy alone would be as valid as if s/he were the sole deputy

---

A young woman receives a significant award of damages following an accident at work which resulted in serious brain damage and other disabilities. Her parents have recently divorced and are arguing about how the money should be used and where their daughter should live. She has always been close to her sister, who is keen to be involved but is anxious about dealing with such a large amount of money. The Court decides to appoint the sister and a solicitor as joint and several deputies to decide where the young woman will live and how to manage her property and affairs.

Successor deputies

7.31 When appointing a deputy or deputies, the Court will also have the power to appoint a successor or successors to the original deputy(s). The Court will specify the circumstances under which this could occur and in some cases, the period, when the substitute deputy may be appointed to act. This arrangement may be particularly helpful when the best candidate for appointment is already elderly and wishes to be sure that someone else will take over in the future.

A man with Down's Syndrome inherits a substantial amount of money and property from his grandfather. His parents were already retired when they were appointed as deputies to manage his property and affairs. They have always been worried about what will happen to their son when they are no longer able to cope. The Court agrees that other specified relatives should be appointed to act as successors to the deputyship and take over following the parents' death or when they are no longer able to carry out their responsibilities as deputies.

Powers of court-appointed deputies

7.32 The Court will decide the extent of powers it wishes to confer on a deputy and the order of appointment will specify the particular decisions or actions the deputy is authorised to take, the powers available to him/her as deputy and the duration of the appointment.

Restrictions on deputies

7.33 Section 20 sets out some specific restrictions and limitations on deputies' powers. In particular, a deputy has no authority to make decisions in the following circumstances:

- Where the deputy does an act that is intended to restrain the person concerned except if certain conditions are satisfied
- If the deputy knows or has reason to believe that the person concerned has capacity to make the decision(s) or do the act in question
- Where the deputy's decisions are inconsistent with a decision made by the donee of a Lasting Power of Attorney granted by the person before s/he lost capacity.
- A deputy cannot refuse consent to the carrying out or continuation of life-sustaining treatment for a person lacking capacity unless the court has expressly given the deputy this power.

7.34   If a deputy considers that the powers conferred on him/her are insufficient for carrying out necessary duties towards the person lacking capacity, the deputy must apply to the Court either for the Court to make the decision in question or for a variation of powers in his/her order of appointment.

Requirement to give security

7.35   Under section 19(9)(a), the Court may require a deputy to give to the Public Guardian whatever type of security the Court considers appropriate. For example, deputies appointed to deal with property and affairs may be required to deposit an amount of money, or to purchase insurance such as a guarantee bond, to cover any loss to the person lacking capacity as a result of the deputy's misbehaviour in his role. Under section 19(9)(b) the Court may also require a deputy to submit to the Public Guardian reports and accounts as it sees fit.

Duties and responsibilities of deputies

7.36   Once an order has been made by the Court setting out the deputy's powers, the deputy will assume a number of duties and responsibilities and will be required to act in accordance with certain standards. Failure to comply with the duties set out below could result in the Court of Protection revoking the order appointing the deputy and, in some circumstances, the deputy could be personally liable to claims for negligence or criminal charges of fraud.

7.37   In order to make their position clear at the outset, deputies should always notify any third party with whom they are dealing that they have been appointed by the Court of Protection to act as deputy on behalf of the person lacking capacity.

Duty to act

7.38   An order appointing a deputy imposes on the deputy a duty to act where necessary, and to take decisions on behalf of the person lacking capacity, as required under the order. A deputy who fails to act at all when a decision which falls within the scope of his/her authority is called for could be in breach of duty.

Duty to act in the donor's best interests

7.39   The principle set out in section 1(5) means that anyone using the provisions of the Act to do any act or make any decision for a person who lacks capacity, is required to act in the person's best interests. This requirement applies equally to court-appointed deputies and any other decision-maker. Deputies must therefore have regard to the guidance set out in chapter 4 on determining the person's best interests in relation to any particular decision or action taken on the person's behalf.

Duty of care and duties of trust (fiduciary duties)

7.40 Section 19(6) clarifies that a deputy is to be treated as the agent of the person lacking capacity in relation to anything done or decided by him/her within the scope of his/her appointment. Under the law of agency, the deputy has certain obligations and duties towards the person, including duties of a fiduciary nature to respect the degree of trust the Court has placed in the deputy to act as statutory agent on the person's behalf.

7.41 When agreeing to act as deputy whether in relation to welfare or financial affairs, the deputy is taking on a role which carries power that s/he must use carefully and responsibly. The standard of conduct expected of deputies involves compliance with the following fiduciary duties and statutory requirements:

■ Duty to act within the scope of his/her authority
■ Duty of care
■ Duty not to delegate unless authorised to do so
■ Duty not to take advantage of the position of deputy
■ Duty of good faith
■ Duty of confidentiality
■ Duty to comply with the directions of the Court of Protection

And specifically in relation to property and affairs:

■ Duty to keep accounts
■ Duty to keep the person's money and property separate from own finances

These duties are described in more detail in the following paragraphs.

Duty to act within the scope of the authority granted by the Court

7.42 A deputy has a duty to act only within the scope of the actual powers conferred by the Court and set out in the order of appointment. If the deputy considers that additional powers are needed, an application must be made to the Court of Protection for the scope of the order to be varied.

Duty of care

7.43 A deputy owes a duty of care to the person lacking capacity in carrying out his/her functions as deputy. However deputies may have different obligations depending on whether they are undertaking the role in a paid capacity or as a professional.

■ Deputies who are not being paid must act with due care, skill and diligence, as they would do in making their own decisions and conducting their own affairs. A deputy who holds him/herself out as having particular skills must show they have such particular skills.
■ If deputies are being paid for their services, this is taken into account in determining the degree of care or skill expected for the proper performance of their duties
■ Deputies who undertake their duties in the course of their professional work (such as solicitors or accountants) must display normal professional competence and abide by their own professional rules and standards.

Duty not to delegate

7.44   It is a basic principle of the law of agency that in general an agent cannot delegate his/her authority unless the delegation is permitted by the express authority of the principal or statutory authority. Since a deputy is the agent appointed by the Court to undertake specific functions on behalf of the person lacking capacity, s/he must carry out those functions personally and cannot, as a general rule, delegate those functions to anyone else. In certain circumstances, the Court will authorise the delegation of specific matters, for example where professional assistance is needed for conduct of investment business.

Duty not to take advantage of the position of deputy

7.45   A deputy has a duty not to take advantage of his/her position. Deputies must avoid any conflicts of interest between their responsibilities towards the person lacking capacity and their own personal interests. They must not allow any other influences to affect the way in which they exercise the powers conferred by the Court. In particular, deputies cannot use their position to acquire any personal benefit, whether or not at the person's expense.

7.46   It is also important to be aware that certain local authorities may impose restrictions on paid carers acting as court-appointed deputies to avoid any conflict of interest. For example, there may be restrictions imposed on managers of residential care homes acting as financial deputies, and therefore making decisions about disposing of the property of a person who lacks capacity when this may then affect that person's liability to pay for the care they are receiving. (Although it should be noted that a care home manager would not usually be appointed as a deputy.)

Duty of good faith

7.47   In exercising his or her authority, a deputy must look after the interests of the person lacking capacity, and act dutifully and in good faith. An act carried out in good faith means an act that is carried out honestly. For example, a deputy must try to ensure his/her actions do not negate previous decisions made by the person while still competent.

Duty of confidentiality

7.48   Deputies have a duty to keep the person's affairs confidential, unless the person, before losing capacity, consented to the disclosure of personal or financial information, or unless there is some other good reason to release it, such as the public interest, that overrides the duty of confidentiality. The ethical problems raised by this duty are discussed in more detail in chapter 13.

Duty to comply with the directions of the Court of Protection

7.49   The Court of Protection may give specific directions to deputies as to how they should exercise their powers. The Court may also require deputies to submit to the Public Guardian specific reports (such as financial accounts or reports on the welfare of the person lacking capacity) at any time or at such intervals as the Court directs. Deputies have a duty to comply with any direction given by the Court.

Duty to keep accounts

7.50   A deputy appointed to manage property and affairs is expected to keep, and periodically submit to the Public Guardian, correct accounts of all his/her dealings and transactions on the person's behalf. Where a lay person, such as a family member, is acting as deputy, and the person's affairs are relatively straightforward, all that may be required is a record of the person's income, any major or regular expenditure and details of any bank accounts. The more complicated the donor's affairs, the more detailed the accounts may need to be.

Duty to keep the person's money and property separate from their own

7.51   Deputies should, in general, keep the person's money and property separate from their own or anyone else's except where there is good reason not to do so, for example where a husband is acting as his wife's deputy and they have, for many years, had a shared bank account in both their names. But in most circumstances, deputies must keep everything separate to avoid any possibility of mistakes or confusion in handling the person's affairs.

Supervision of deputies

7.52   Since deputies are appointed by the Court of Protection, they remain accountable to the Court for their actions in carrying out their duties during the duration of their appointment. The Court has power to discharge the order appointing a deputy at any time if it decides the appointment is no longer in the best interests of the person lacking capacity.

7.53   The Public Guardian is responsible for the supervision of deputies appointed by the Court and for supporting deputies in their role. However, the Public Guardian also has a role in protecting people subject to the Court's powers from possible abuse or exploitation. Any concerns or suspicions of abuse by deputies should be raised immediately with the Office of the Public Guardian (OPG). The OPG may also direct a Court of Protection Visitor to visit a deputy to investigate any matter of concern. The supervisory duties of the OPG are described in more detail in chapter 9.

7.54   The Public Guardian will also be able to investigate any concerns or complaints against deputies. However, in serious cases, where physical abuse or serious fraud is suspected, the matter should be referred directly to the police and/or social services, and the Public Guardian informed.

7.55   The protection of vulnerable people from the risk of abuse, ill treatment or neglect and the duties and responsibilities of the various agencies involved are discussed in detail in chapter 9.

CHAPTER 8: ADVANCE DECISIONS TO REFUSE TREATMENT

8.1   This chapter describes the main provisions in the Act relating to advance decisions to refuse treatment and provides basic guidance on their practical implications.

INTRODUCTION

8.2   **Part 1** of this chapter concerns what constitutes an advance decision to refuse medical treatment. It sets out guidance on formatting, updating and withdrawing advance decisions. It also provides guidance on advance decisions concerning life-sustaining treatment. **Part 2** sets out the safeguards in the Act aimed at ensuring an advance decision exists, is valid and applicable and the relationship with other decision-making mechanisms. **Part 3** looks at the effects of advance decision and the duties and responsibilities of healthcare professionals. **Part 4** describes the actions that can be taken in the event of a dispute or disagreement about an advance decision.

PART 1: WHAT CONSTITUTES AN ADVANCE DECISION TO REFUSE TREATMENT

8.3   Some essential principles of the ethical practice of medicine are that doctors and other health professionals have a duty to provide a good standard of care and treatment, to show respect for human life and to exercise their duties in a fair, unprejudiced and non-discriminatory way. All patients, whether or not they lack capacity, have the right to expect the same standards of care and the duties and responsibilities placed on health professionals apply equally in their care of both capable people and people who may lack capacity. No assumption should be made that life and health have any less value for those who lack capacity.

8.4   One particular duty of health professionals is to respect competent patients' autonomy to make decisions in relation to their treatment. Competent and informed adults who are capable of understanding the implications of their decisions have an established legal right in common law to refuse medical procedures or treatment. Before the Act came into force, some people made advance decisions and a number of judicial decisions have analysed the legal effect of these decisions. A recent case confirmed that a competent adult patient's anticipatory refusal remains binding and effective if the patient subsequently loses capacity to make medical decisions.

8.5   Sections 24 – 26 set out the arrangements which enable adults aged 18 or over, having the capacity, to make an advance decision to refuse medical treatment. The Act also prescribes important safeguards and procedures in relation to advance decisions to protect the rights and interests of people lacking capacity while enabling any advance decisions they have made about the medical treatment to be respected.

8.6   No patient, whether he has or lacks capacity, has the right, in law, to demand specific forms of medical treatment and therefore no-one can insist, either at the time or in advance, on being given treatments that doctors consider to be clinically unnecessary, futile or inappropriate.

8.7   It must also be stressed that no one can ask for and be given unlawful procedures, such as assistance in suicide. As section 58 sets out, the law relating to murder, manslaughter or assisting suicide is unchanged by any provision in the Act.

8.8   It is entirely a matter for individual choice as to whether or not a person wishes to make plans for possible future lack of capacity by making an advance refusal of treatment. There is absolutely no obligation to make an advance decision. Many people prefer to leave treatment decisions to their doctors at the time any treatment might need to be considered. Others may prefer to appoint a trusted family member to make decisions on their behalf (see Chapter 6 on LPAs). Individuals who choose to make advance refusals of treatment must do so voluntarily while they have capacity to make such a decision. This means, among other things, that they must be able to understand and retain the information relevant to the decision, be able to use and weigh details of benefits and burdens of the different options, and not be subject to any form of undue pressure from others. (See chapter on capacity.)

Definition of an advance decision to refuse treatment

8.9   Section 24(1) of the Act sets out the definition of an advance decision to refuse treatment. An *advance decision* for the purposes of the Act is a decision made by a person after s/he has reached the age of 18 and when s/he has capacity to make such a decision (see chapter 3). The effect of an advance decision will be to enable that person to refuse specified medical treatment at a point in the future when that person has lost the capacity to give or refuse consent to that treatment.

8.10   An advance decision to refuse treatment:

- must specify the treatment that is to be refused – this can be expressed in medical language or lay terms, as long as it is clear what is meant
- may set out the circumstances in which the refusal will apply. It is helpful to include as much detail as possible on the circumstances in which the refusal will apply; for example, to say it should apply if there is no chance of a cure.
- will only apply when the person lacks capacity to consent to the specified treatment

Life-sustaining treatment

8.11   If the person intends the advance decision to apply to the refusal of life sustaining treatment, section 25(5) of the Act requires that this **must** be explicitly stated in the advance decision. This is a vital safeguard concerning the applicability of advance decisions that concern life-sustaining treatment. Many advance decisions may be concerned with situations where the end of life is foreseeable (for example an inoperable brain tumour) and with refusal of treatment that might prolong a person's life. Factors involved in making an advance decision are considered in more detail below.

General advance statements about medical treatment

8.12   There is a clear distinction between the legal status of a general advance statement reflecting an individual's wishes and feelings about how s/he wishes to be treated and a valid and applicable **advance decision** to refuse a specified medical procedure or treatment. Both general advance statements and advance decisions are a means whereby patients, through advance planning, can continue to influence the treatment they receive in the event that they lack capacity to express their views in the future. A general advance statement about wishes and feelings operates in a different way by influencing the way doctors determine best interests (see chapters 3 and 4). A general advance statement is an expression of past wishes and feelings and so forms part of the best interests checklist.

> Mr Y is suffering from MS with some early cognitive problems. Having discussed his prognosis and all treatment options with his healthcare team, he sets out a preferred treatment plan in a general advance statement. Whilst he knows that, during times when he does not have the capacity to consent to treatment himself, doctors will decide on the course of treatment that is in his best interests, he feels reassured that his wishes as set out in the general advance statement are documented and will need to be taken into account.

Format of advance decisions to refuse treatment

8.13   The Act sets out that valid and applicable advance decisions (as defined in the Act) are as effective as contemporaneous decisions. No specific legal requirements have been imposed concerning their format. Both written and oral advance decisions are capable of being legally effective at common law and both written and oral advance decisions will continue to be capable of being legally effective under the provisions of the Act.

8.14   Similarly, the Act does not impose any particular formalities on the format of procedures involved in making advance decisions to refuse treatment. However, it requires not only that an advance decision (as defined) exists but that it is valid and applicable.

8.15   There is no prescribed statutory form on which a written advance decision must be made, since the contents of advance decisions will vary considerably according to the wishes and circumstances of individual makers. It is strongly advised that discussions are held with the relevant health professional when making either an oral or a written advance decision. It is helpful for the following information to be included in a written advance decision:

- Full details of maker, including date of birth, home address, and any distinguishing features (so that an unconscious person, for example, might be identified).
- Name and address of General Practitioner and whether they have a copy.
- [Where relevant] information on where the advance decision is stored and list of people who are aware of its existence and should be contacted.
- A statement that the decision is intended to have effect if the maker lacks capacity to make treatment decisions.
- A clear statement of the decision, specifying the treatment to be refused and the circumstances in which the decision will apply or which will trigger a particular course of actions.
- [Where relevant] a clear statement that the decision is intended to apply even if the treatment in question is necessary to sustain life.
- Date the document was written (or reviewed) and, if appropriate, the time interval between creation and review.
- The signature of the witness who witnessed the maker's signature.
- Information on the independence of witness, including details of their relationship with the maker.

8.16   The witness should only witness the signature of the person making the advance decision and attest that it appears that they intend their signature to give effect to the advance decision. The role of the witness does not involve certifying the capacity of the person making the advance decision even though in some situations, a professional such as a doctor may be asked to act as a witness.

8.17   There is also no prescribed statutory style for how oral advance decisions to refuse treatment should be made. Again this is because the contents of the advance decision will vary considerably according to the situations of the individual makers. For example, the nature of an oral advance decision of a person made shortly before going into the operating theatre, who verbally informs his healthcare team that he wants to impose limitations on the surgery he is facing, may differ from that of a person who makes an oral advance decision during ongoing medical treatment. Such oral advance decisions must be documented in the patient's medical notes, which will then form a written record of the oral advance decision. The following information should be included in such a written record:

- A note that the decision is intended to have effect if the maker lacks capacity to make treatment decisions in the future;
- A clear note of the decision, specifying the treatment to be refused and the circumstances in which the decision will apply;
- Details of a witness to the decision;
- [Where relevant] a clear note that the decision is intended to apply even if the treatment in question is necessary to sustain life.

Reviewing and updating advance decisions

8.18   Patients should be advised that it is a good idea that an advance decision to refuse treatment should be kept under review and regularly updated. Decisions made a long time in advance are not automatically invalid or inapplicable, but there may be doubts over the validity and applicability of such advance decisions. A regularly reviewed, witnessed and written advance decision is more likely to be both valid and applicable as it will have been possible to reflect circumstances that may have changed since it was first made.

8.19   Views and circumstances may change over time. It is important that people take the time to discuss the situation with their health care professional and to amend an advance decision accordingly. In particular, a new stage in a patient's illness or a major change in personal circumstances may be appropriate times to review treatment decisions made in advance. An advance decision is more likely to be both valid and applicable if it is shown that the maker had on-going discussions with their health care professional about the practical aspects and consequences of their treatment and clearly takes account of circumstances that have changed since it was first made.

Withdrawing or amending an advance decision

8.20   The person's views may well change to such an extent that s/he wishes to withdraw the advance decision altogether. There is nothing to stop the person withdrawing or destroying a written advance decision at any time while s/he has capacity to do so. No formal procedures are required. Whether or not advance decisions are set out in writing, they can be altered or withdrawn either orally or in writing, as the person's particular situation requires. For example, someone who becomes severely disabled after they have made an advance decision may change their views on what treatments they would be prepared to have, and what they see as a good quality of life. They might therefore decide to change or withdraw an advance decision they have already made.

PART 2: ADVANCE DECISIONS TO REFUSE TREATMENT: EXISTENCE, VALIDITY AND APPLICABILITY

Capacity to make an advance decision

8.21   Only people aged 18 and over and who have capacity can make an advance decision. Capacity to make a decision and how capacity is assessed are discussed in chapter 3. For most people planning in advance for possible future lack of capacity, their capacity to make an advance decision will be obvious. But in some cases it may be helpful to obtain evidence to confirm the person's capacity to make the advance decision, for example if there is a possibility that the advance decision may be challenged in the future.

> Mrs P, a 38-year-old woman, has been suffering from serious lower abdominal pain. During discussions her doctor informs her that it is possible that there may be a problem with her ovaries and that he wants to her to undergo an exploratory operation, his advice is that if the ovaries are cancerous it is important to remove them. Mrs P states categorically that under no circumstances should both ovaries be removed, even if it means there is a risk of the cancer spreading. Her doctor is not sure that Mrs P has the capacity to make such a decision because she appears to be having a depressive response and is refusing to discuss the possible consequences of her refusal and the possible alternatives. With her agreement, he therefore speaks to her husband and sister in an attempt to ascertain whether she fully understands the consequences of her decision and asks a colleague to talk her, explain the situation and give a second opinion on her capacity to make that decision. After discussions it is accepted that Mrs P

can understand and weigh the information needed to make this treatment decision, even though her conclusion may not necessarily seem rational to others.
Mrs P's oral advance decision is then recorded in her medical notes.

SAFEGUARDS: VALIDITY AND APPLICABILITY OF ADVANCE DECISIONS

8.22   An advance decision to refuse treatment is a major step and could have serious and
significant consequences for the maker. It could also have a significant impact on
their family and friends and for professionals involved in their care and treatment.
Section 25 therefore makes provision for two important safeguards in relation to
advance decisions to refuse treatment. In order for the refusal to be legally effective
at the time when it is proposed to carry out or continue medical treatment, an
advance decision must be both *valid* and *applicable* to the proposed treatment.
These tests are crucial.

Validity

8.23   The first consideration is to decide whether an advance decision is valid, in order
to establish that it is in fact an advance decision to refuse treatment, as defined in
section 24.

8.24   Events that would make an advance decision invalid are set out in section 25(2).
These are:

■   That the person has withdrawn the decision while s/he still had capacity to do
so;

■   That after making the advance decision, the person has created a Lasting
Power of Attorney (LPA) giving power to a donee to give or refuse consent to
the treatment specified in the advance decision (an LPA conferring different
powers would not affect the advance decision); or

■   That the person has done something which is clearly inconsistent with the
advance decision which implies that s/he has had a change of mind.

A young man, whose friend had been in PVS for a number of years, made a written advance decision refusing any treatment to keep him alive by artificial
means. A few years later, he is seriously injured in a road traffic accident and is
paralysed from the neck down and is only able to breathe with artificial ventila-
tion. Initially he remains conscious and is able to consent to treatment on being
taken to hospital. He participates actively in a rehabilitation programme. Some
months later he loses consciousness. It is at this point that his written advance
decision is located, though he has not mentioned it during his treatment. His
previous consent to treatment and rehabilitation place considerable doubt on
the validity of the advance decision because it is clearly inconsistent with his
actions prior to his lack of capacity.

Applicability

8.25   The next consideration, once the advance decision is established as valid, is
whether it is applicable to the situation in question. The first consideration must be
to determine whether or not the person still has capacity to give or refuse consent
to the treatment in question at the time the treatment is proposed (section 25(3)).
If the person has capacity, s/he can refuse the treatment there and then – or s/he can
change the decision and consent to the treatment if s/he so wishes. The advance
decision is not relevant and not applicable in those circumstances.

8.26   The advance decision must also be applicable to the treatment proposed to be given. Under section 25(4), an advance decision is not applicable to the treatment in question if:

- The proposed treatment is not the treatment specified in the advance decision;
- The circumstances are different from those set out in the advance decision; or
- There are reasonable grounds for believing that circumstances have now arisen which were not anticipated by the person when making the advance decision and which would have affected their advance decision had s/he anticipated them at the time.

8.27   In relation to the first two bullet points above, it will be important to consider how long ago the advance decision was made and whether, for instance, there have been changes in the patient's personal life or developments in medical treatment. It will also be important to consider specifically whether the decision reflects adequately the treatment now proposed and the specific circumstances which have now arisen.

8.28   The third bullet point is mainly intended to cover advances in medical science and the development of new medications or other forms of treatment or therapies not available at the time when the advance decision was made. Such developments might extend the treatment options available and could have affected the person's decision to refuse treatment. But it may also include changes in personal circumstances which might affect the person's decision.

Mr A is HIV positive and some years ago began to experience AIDS-related symptoms. Though willing to consent to standard treatment, for instance during a bout of pneumonia, he was initially unwilling to try the new retro-viral treatments, saying he didn't want to be a guinea pig for the medical profession. He made an advance decision refusing specific retro-virals were he to be incapable of giving or refusing consent in the future. Five years later he was suddenly admitted to hospital seriously ill and was drifting in and out of consciousness. Doctors examining his advance decision considered that the advances in knowledge surrounding the retro-viral options had been significant since Mr A made his advance decision. They talked to his partner about the advance decision. Both parties agreed that Mr A was not fully up-to-date on the research in this area and would have changed his mind if he had capacity to discuss it with the doctors on this occasion. They decided the advance decision to refuse was therefore invalid and gave him retrovirals as part of his treatment.

Relationship of Advance Decisions to other Decision-Making Mechanisms

8.29   A valid and applicable advance decision to refuse treatment will be as effective as a contemporaneous refusal of consent and will therefore take precedence over:

- Any attempt to give consent by a donee acting under a welfare LPA made before the advance decision was made;
- Any attempt to give consent by a court-appointed deputy;
- The provisions of section 5, as far as they would otherwise allow a doctor to provide treatment which is considered to be in the patient's best interests.

8.30   While the Court of Protection may make declarations as to the existence, validity and applicability of an advance decision, it will have no power to override an effective advance decision.

Advance decisions regarding treatment for mental disorder

8.31   Where a patient is liable to be detained under the Mental Health Act 1983, the contents of any advance decision to refuse treatment for mental disorder may be overridden by the compulsory treatment provisions of section 63 of that Act which provides that 'the consent of a patient shall not be required for any medical treatment given to him for the mental disorder from which he is suffering' [and is not treatment that falls under section 57 or 58 of the 1983 Act]. Treatment for mental disorder may therefore be given under the 1983 Act without the patient's consent and even where the patient is making or has made a decision to refuse a particular treatment for that particular condition. However, an advance decision to refuse treatment for a physical condition, as opposed to a mental disorder that falls within the application of section 63 of the 1983 Act, could still be valid and effective regardless of whether the patient was liable to be detained or compulsorily treated under mental health legislation.

PART 3: EFFECT OF ADVANCE DECISIONS TO REFUSE TREATMENT FOR HEALTHCARE PROFESSIONALS

8.32   This section summarises the effects of advance decisions on the duties and responsibilities of healthcare professionals.

Responsibilities of health care professionals

8.33   Health care professionals should be aware of the possibility that a patient may have made an advance decision. If, during the course of diagnosing and treating their patient, a health care professional has reasonable grounds to believe or is alerted to the existence of a relevant written or oral advance decision they should, if time permits, make reasonable efforts to find out what that decision was. Reasonable efforts might include having discussions with relatives of the patient, looking in the patient's clinical notes held in the hospital or contacting the patient's GP.

8.34   Once health care professionals who are considering treatment have been informed of the existence of an oral advance decision or presented with a written advance decision, they need to consider (1) whether it is an advance decision within the meaning of the Act (2) whether it is valid and (3) whether it is applicable to the treatment.

8.35   Health care professionals must also consider whether the advance decision is applicable in the circumstances which have now arisen (see paragraph 8.24 above). Particular care will need to be taken for advance decisions that do not appear to have been reviewed or updated, for instance, in the light of changes in personal circumstances or developments in medical treatment. If the current situation does not involve circumstances identical to those specified in the advance decision, the decision may not be applicable. If any individuals have been named in the advance decision as people to contact or be consulted, they may be able to clarify the patient's wishes or help in determining his/her best interests.

Emergency situations

8.36   A doctor may safely treat unless satisfied that there is (1) a qualifying advance decision which is (2) valid and (3) applicable in the circumstances. Emergency treatment should not be delayed in order to look for an advance decision to refuse treatment if there is no clear indication that one exists.

8.37   Where there is doubt about the existence or validity and applicability of an advance decision within the meaning of the Act, a declaration can be sought from the court as to whether a valid and applicable advance decision exists. Section 26 of the Act provides that a doctor may provide necessary treatment to prevent serious deterioration in the person's condition or life-sustaining treatment while a decision is being sought from the court.

Liability of health care professionals

8.38   A health care professional may safely treat someone unless they are satisfied that there is (1) a qualifying advance decision which is (2) valid and (3) applicable in the circumstances. They may also safely withhold or withdraw treatment as long as they have reasonable grounds for believing that a valid and applicable advance decision exists.

8.39   Health care professionals need to be aware of the potential liability for treating without consent. Where a health professional treats someone, even though he is satisfied that an advance decision to refuse that particular treatment exists, and is valid and applicable in the circumstances, that have arisen, he may be subject to a claim for damages for battery or to criminal liability for assault.

8.40   Health care professionals also need to be aware of their potential liability in negligence if they follow an apparent advance decision. In order to avoid liability for not providing treatment, a health professional must be able to demonstrate that he had a reasonable belief that there was a valid and applicable advance decision within the meaning of the Act.

8.41   Having a 'reasonable belief' means that health care professionals must be able to point to reasonable grounds as to why they believe that a valid and applicable advance decision exists rather than being satisfied that a valid and applicable advance decision exists. Reasonable grounds might arise if a decision is recent, in writing, countersigned by a health professional who certifies that he gave advice about available treatments, and the maker's signature has been witnessed by a family member with no interest in the patient's estate.

8.42   There are some situations which may be sufficient to raise concerns about the existence, validity or applicability of an advance decision to refuse treatment, which might alert health professionals to the need to make more careful enquiries. In cases where serious doubt remains, it will be possible to seek a declaration from the court. Grounds for concern might include:

- A disagreement between relatives and health professionals about whether the person's oral comments really amounted to a qualifying advance decision.
- Evidence about the person's state of mind at the time of making the advance decision that raised questions about his/her capacity to have made the advance decision.
- Evidence of significant changes in the person's behaviour prior to lacking capacity that might indicate a change of mind since the advance decision was made.

Conscientious objection

8.43   Some health professionals may disagree in principle with patients' rights to refuse life-sustaining treatment or may have moral objections to withdrawing or withholding life-prolonging treatment in some circumstances. The current position on issues of conscience remains unchanged under the Act.

8.44   This means that doctors or health care professionals with a conscientious objection to limiting treatment in line with their patients' advance decision should make their views clear when the matter is initially raised. Patients should then be given the option of their care and treatment being transferred to another doctor or health professional, where this is feasible without jeopardising the patient's care. In cases where the patient lacks capacity but has made a clear advance decision to refuse treatment which a doctor or health professional cannot, for reasons of conscience, accede to, management of the patient's care should be transferred to another health professional. Doctors are entitled to have their personal beliefs respected and will not be pressurised to act contrary to those beliefs.

PART 4: DISPUTES AND DISAGREEMENTS ABOUT ADVANCE DECISIONS

8.45   It is ultimately the responsibility of the relevant health care professional who is in charge of the patient's care, when the treatment is required, to decide whether there is a qualifying advance decision which is valid and applicable in the circumstances. In the event of disagreement between health professionals, or between health professionals and family members or others close to the patient about an advance decision, the senior clinician must consider all the available evidence.

8.46   The senior clinician may need to consult with relevant colleagues and others who are close to or familiar with the patient. All staff involved in the patient's care should be given the opportunity to express their views. The patient's GP may also have relevant information.

8.47   The point of such discussions should not be to try to overrule the patient's advance decision but rather to seek evidence concerning its validity and to confirm its scope and its applicability to the current circumstances. Details of these discussions should be recorded in the patient's medical notes. Where the senior clinician has a reasonable belief that a qualifying advance decision to refuse medical treatment is both valid and applicable, the patient's advance decision should be complied with.

Applications to the Court of Protection

8.48   Where there continues to be genuine doubt or disagreement about the existence, validity or applicability of an advance decision to refuse treatment and the matter cannot be resolved in any other way, a declaration should be sought from the Court of Protection.

CHAPTER 9: PROTECTION AND SUPERVISION

INTRODUCTION

9.1   This chapter is addressed to those people who make decisions for and act for people lacking capacity, whether this is done on a formal or informal basis and whether or not they are formally bound by the Code.

PURPOSE OF THIS CHAPTER

9.2   This chapter explains how professionals and people acting under the formal powers of the Act (i.e. attorneys and deputies) are expected to interact with the relevant agencies responsible for the protection of adults lacking capacity. This information will also be useful to everyone who cares for people who lack capacity, whether this is on a formal or informal basis. The chapter therefore explains the relevant services that those organisations provide in relation to protecting adults who lack capacity and those who care for them.

9.3   The Mental Capacity Act provides for the supervision, by the Office of the Public Guardian (the OPG), of attorneys acting under LPAs and court-appointed deputies in co-operation with other relevant bodies. The Act works together with existing initiatives put in place by the Department of Health to protect vulnerable adults.

9.4   This chapter has four parts:

- Part 1 – a brief explanation of what is meant by abuse
- Part 2 – an overview of the supervisory functions of the Office of the Public Guardian and an explanation of how we expect those acting under the legislation to interact with the OPG
- Part 3 – a brief overview of the criminal offence of ill treatment or wilful neglect
- Part 4 – a brief overview of other measures put in place to protect adults lacking capacity

PART 1: WHAT DO WE MEAN BY ABUSE?

9.5   Abuse can cover a wide spectrum of actions. In some cases, abuse is clearly a deliberate act or omission, done with a malicious intent. But, sometimes, abuse is not intentional and may occur because the carer or decision-maker does not know how to act correctly or has not accessed appropriate help and support. In all cases, it is important that abuse is prevented if at all possible, and investigated and dealt with effectively.

9.6   The English 'No Secrets' and the Welsh 'In Safe Hands' guidance define abuse as any violation of an individual's human and civil rights by any other person or persons. Both documents describe a variety of forms of abuse, such as sexual, physical, verbal, financial or emotional abuse. It can be a single act, a series of repeated acts or failure to act, or neglect. Abuse can take place in any setting, for example in a person's own home, a care home or a hospital.

'No Secrets' and 'In Safe Hands' set out multi-agency procedures that must be followed when allegation of abuse is made or suspected. These documents are available on (DH website, WAG website)

Examples of abuse

9.7   The main forms of abuse are as follows:

- **Financial abuse:** such as theft, fraud, undue pressure or the misuse or misappropriation of property, possessions or benefits.
- **Physical abuse:** such as slapping, pushing and kicking. It also includes the misuse of medication (for example, giving someone a high dose of medication in order to make them drowsy and 'less difficult') and placing inappropriate sanctions on an individual, for example refusing to give food at meal times because the person being cared for has been 'bad'.
- **Sexual abuse:** such as rape and sexual assault. It also includes sexual acts to which the person has not consented, or could not consent or was pressurised into consenting.
- **Psychological abuse:** such as emotional abuse, threats of harm or abandonment, deprivation of contact and intimidation,
- **Neglect and acts of omission:** such as ignoring the person's medical or physical care needs, failure to provide access to appropriate health or social care and the withholding of medication, adequate nutrition and heating

PART 2: MENTAL CAPACITY ACT – PROVISIONS FOR SUPERVISION

THE ROLE OF THE PUBLIC GUARDIAN

9.8   Functions of the Public Guardian

The Act creates a new public office – the Public Guardian. The Public Guardian has a range of functions that contribute to the protection of people who lack capacity including:

- establishing and maintaining a register of Lasting Powers of Attorney (LPAs);
- establishing and maintaining a register of orders appointing deputies;
- supervising, in co-operation with other relevant authorities (such as social services if the person who lacks capacity is receiving social care) deputies appointed by the court;
- directing Court of Protection Visitors to visit people lacking capacity and those who have formal powers to act on their behalf;
- receiving reports from donees of LPAs and deputies;
- providing reports to the Court as requested, for example on the suitability of a proposed deputy prior to their appointment; and
- dealing with representations (including complaints) about the way in which donees of LPAs or deputies exercise their powers.

Court of Protection Visitors

9.9   The Court of Protection Visitors are individuals who have been appointed by the Lord Chancellor to a panel either of Special Visitors (approved healthcare practitioners with relevant expertise) or General Visitors. Their role is to provide independent advice to the Court and the Public Guardian on matters relating to the exercise of powers under the Act.

Mrs G made an LPA some time ago, appointing her nephew, Ian, as her attorney with a general power to make personal welfare and financial decisions on her behalf. The power has now been registered on the basis that Mrs G no longer has the capacity to make many of these decisions herself. However, Mrs G's niece is concerned that Ian is not acting in Mrs G's best interests. In particular, she suspects that Ian is using much of Mrs G's income to pay off debts that he has incurred. She addresses these concerns to the Public Guardian which first directs Ian to give a report, and then directs a General Visitor to visit Mrs G and Ian. The Visitor duly produces a report recommending that the LPA be revoked, as Ian is not acting in Mrs G's best interests. On receipt of the report, the Court makes an order revoking the LPA.

Functions in respect of Lasting Powers of Attorneys (LPAs)

9.10   An LPA is a private arrangement between the person who makes the LPA ('the donor') and the person who is appointed to act on behalf of the donor under this arrangement ('the donee'). It will be important for individuals to choose someone in whom they have trust and confidence. The Public Guardian will provide information that will help potential donors understand the impact of making an LPA, what powers they could consider granting and what to consider when choosing who may act as a donee.

9.11   The Act seeks to protect potential donors from abuse by requiring the Public Guardian to ensure that the appointment of the LPA complies with the statutory requirements, for example by checking, in certain cases, that potential financial donees do not have criminal convictions for fraud or deception. The Public Guardian will not generally be involved once the LPA has been registered unless concerns are raised about the way in which the donee or donees are exercising their powers under the LPA. Chapter 6 gives detailed information about the duties and responsibilities of attorneys.

Functions in respect of Court-Appointed Deputies

9.12   Whereas the execution of an LPA involves appointing a donee of the person's choice, individuals are not able to choose the deputy appointed to make financial and/or welfare decisions on their behalf, as the appointment is made by the Court at a time when they do not have capacity. There are therefore more stringent safeguards to protect individuals who lack capacity from possible abuse by deputies.

9.13   As explained in Chapter 6, deputies will most frequently be appointed for financial matters where there is likely to be a need for ongoing significant decisions. There will be far fewer appointments to make health and/or welfare decisions as in these cases, the Court is more likely to be able to make a single order where there is difficulty over a significant decision.

Peter has sustained serious head injuries in a motorbike accident which has left him permanently and severely brain-damaged. His condition has been stabilised but he has minimal awareness of his surroundings and has been assessed as being incapable of making any decisions for himself. A number of important decisions need to be made about where Peter is treated and what sort of treatment he receives. Peter's parents are concerned that their views are not always fully taken into account when discussing what treatment is in Peter's best interests with his healthcare team. They want to ensure that their views are formally recognised. They therefore make an application to the Court to be appointed as joint-personal welfare deputies. The court considers that as there are likely to be many healthcare decisions that need to be made for Peter over a number of years, it would be impracticable to make a single order in each case. Also, as the members of the healthcare team may change, it would also be advantageous to retain some continuity in decision-making and lastly, an appointment would ensure that Peter's parents are formally involved in healthcare decisions made for their son. The court therefore grants the application and appoints Peter's parents as joint welfare deputies.

9.14   Where the appointment of a deputy is suggested, a major focus of protection from abuse will be at the application stage. In particular, the OPG will carry out a risk assessment of the case to ensure that the level of future supervision of the deputy and the amount and type of checks on the deputy are proportionate to the level of risk involved (for example, it would probably not be appropriate to carry out a criminal records check on a local authority official who was applying to be appointed as a deputy).

Chapter 7 gives detailed information about the duties and responsibilities of deputies.

Where concerns are raised

9.15   Many people who lack capacity are likely to have some support from a range of agencies. These agencies and their staff retain those responsibilities on the registration of a LPA or the appointment of a deputy. Thus, although concerns about the way in which LPAs or deputies exercise their powers may be directed to the Public Guardian, the Public Guardian will not be the most appropriate body to investigate all of them. The Act states that the Public Guardian may co-operate with relevant agencies to ensure that concerns and complaints are referred to the right agency. In practice, this will most commonly include social services, NHS bodies and the police.

9.16   The OPG may itself carry out investigations where there are allegations of financial abuse on the part of the LPA, the deputy or some other third party. Where the concerns relate to personal welfare LPAs or personal welfare deputies, the Public Guardian will refer them to the relevant health or social care agency. Where the concern suggests that a criminal offence has been committed, this will be referred to the police. However, where the Public Guardian has made such a referral, it will ensure that it is kept informed of the action taken by the relevant agency and will ultimately ensure that the Court has all the information it needs in order to take possible sanctions against the attorney or deputy. It should also be remembered that other agencies may also need to be involved, for example the relevant social services department, in situations where alternative care arrangements may need to be made for the person lacking capacity.

Referrals will take place in a wide range of situations. Some possible examples are:

9.17   Where a complaint has been raised that a welfare attorney is physically abusing a donor (his spouse). This would be referred to the relevant local authority adult protection committee and/or the police.

9.18   Where a solicitor appointed as a financial deputy for an elderly person with dementia has been found to be defrauding that person's estate resulting in the loss of several thousand pounds. This would be referred to the police although the OPG, which would also conduct its own investigation, would prepare a report for the Court recommending that the deputy's appointment be revoked.

PART 3: CRIMINAL OFFENCE: ILL-TREATMENT OR NEGLECT

9.19   The Act introduces a new criminal offence of ill treatment or wilful neglect which applies to the following individuals:

- a person who has the care of a person who lacks capacity or is reasonably believed to lack capacity; or
- a person who is the donee of a LPA; or
- a person who is a deputy appointed for the person by the court.

9.20   Such individuals will be guilty of an offence if they ill-treat or wilfully neglect the person they have care of, or to whom the LPA or deputy appointment relates. The penalty for such an offence is a fine and/or a sentence of imprisonment of up to 5 years. The following example illustrates the type of actions that may lead to a prosecution under this offence.

Norma is 95 and suffering from Alzheimer's disease. She lives with her son, Brendan, who is her principal carer and who has also been appointed as her welfare attorney under an LPA. A district nurse regularly visits Norma at home to give her medication for arthritis. She is concerned that recently, Norma is displaying bruises and other injuries. She also suspects that Brendan may be assaulting his mother when drunk. She alerts the police and the local Adult Protection Committee. Following this, a number of things happen: following a criminal investigation, Brendan is charged with the ill treatment of his mother.

In addition, the Court, in conjunction with the Public Guardian, also takes steps to revoke the LPA. Lastly, local Social Services are alerted and procedures are set in motion to place Norma in appropriate residential care.

PART 4: OTHER PROTECTIVE MEASURES

9.21   The provisions of the Act are intended to complement and enhance existing measures to protect vulnerable adults. Vulnerable adults are defined as people who are or may be in need of community care services due to having some form of mental or other disability, age or illness and who may be unable to take care of themselves or protect themselves against significant harm or exploitation. This group obviously encompasses many of the people who lack capacity and will have people acting for them under the terms of the Mental Capacity Act.

Multi-agency policies and procedures

9.22   Following the publication of 'No Secrets' – guidance on Developing Multi-Agency Policies and Procedures to Protect Vulnerable Adults from Abuse, (March 2000) (titled 'In Safe Hands' in Wales) local agencies, under the leadership of local councils have developed and implemented multi-agency policies and procedures to protect vulnerable adults from abuse, both in care settings and elsewhere. Many localities have established Adult Protection Committees. These are cross-agency management committees that determine policy, co-ordinate activity between agencies, facilitate joint training and monitor and review progress.

9.23   This multi-agency approach will aid the Public Guardian in providing a single point of contact for the referral of allegations of abuse and ill treatment. It will also aid those acting under the provisions of the legislation in crystallising the various procedures and bodies which they will be expected to be aware of.

Employment checks for care staff

9.24   The following systems have been introduced:

9.25   The **Protection of Vulnerable Adults (POVA)** list provides details of those individuals who have been judged unsuitable to work with vulnerable adults. All providers of care who employ staff are required to check whether potential employees are on this list and to refuse employment to anyone whose name is on the list.

9.26   The Public Guardian will be able to check whether a potential deputy is on the POVA list and take appropriate action as a result.

9.27   **Criminal record checks** must now be made on all staff working in care homes. Potential employers must conduct a pre-employment criminal record with the Criminal Records Bureau (CRB) for all potential new health and social care staff, including nurses' agency and domiciliary care agency staff (who provide personal care). Again, the Public Guardian will be able to conduct criminal record checks when investigating potential deputies

9.28   **Commission for Social Care Inspection and the Social Care Inspectorate for Wales and the Social Services Inspectorate for Wales** All care providers are required to register with the Commission for Social Care Inspection in England (CSCI) and the Social Care and Social Services Inspectorate for Wales, which will work with care providers to ensure that the standards are met. Regulations require procedures to protect service users from harm or abuse to be put in place. In particular, their task is to take swift action if they identify any dangerous or unsafe practices that could place service users and residents at risk. The standards also guarantee that service users have access to effective complaints procedures and, if complaints cannot be resolved locally, they can be referred to CSCI. CSCI also has a role in supporting and encouraging improvement across the country. They work with others, including the Social Care Institute for Excellence, in spreading best practice.

OTHER INITIATIVES

9.29   There are a number of additional initiatives and requirements which people acting under the legislation will need to be aware of (although many will already be aware). These include:

- National Minimum Standards (for care homes, domiciliary care agencies etc) which apply to both England and Wales
- National Service Frameworks (NSFs) which set out national standards for specific services or care groups for example older people
- Complaints mechanisms relating to all NHS bodies and local councils.

9.30   Further information about these initiatives is available from xxx.

CHAPTER 10: RESOLVING DISAGREEMENTS

INTRODUCTION

10.1   Despite efforts to determine what a person who lacks capacity would want in relation to a particular decision and what would be in their best interests, sometimes disagreements may arise in the course of taking a decision for or acting for a person lacking capacity. It is generally in the interests of all involved to resolve the problem in a way that is quick, effective, involves minimal stress and is cost effective.

10.2   While the Mental Capacity Act (the Act) establishes a new, dedicated Court of Protection to settle serious and complex disputes, it may often be more appropriate to explore alternative solutions to solving problems. In some cases it would also be inappropriate to take the matter to court, for example, a complaint about the health care that the person who lacks capacity has received, as there are more appropriate complaints mechanisms specifically for these type of situations.

10.3   This Code of Practice provides information about avenues to resolve disagreements, complaints procedures, and guidance on what is likely to be the appropriate or most desirable route to take. People assessing whether a person has capacity, people acting in connection with the care or treatment of another person, donees acting under a Lasting Power of Attorney and those acting as deputies must all have regard to the Code of Practice.

10.4   Part 1 of this chapter describes existing complaint and dispute resolution mechanisms including advocacy services. Accessing legal funding is considered in Part 2.

PART 1: METHODS OF RESOLVING DISAGREEMENTS

10.5   The best way of resolving a disagreement or concern will depend on the people involved, the type of disagreement, its severity and the urgency. Disagreements may be:

- between family members or other individuals – these can often be dealt with via informal routes or through mediation;
- about health, social or other welfare services – these can usually be dealt with through informal or formal complaints processes;
- about very serious issues requiring resolution by the Court of Protection.

Mediation

10.6   This section discusses mediation where informal attempts to resolve matters – perhaps by third parties or other family members – have not succeeded.

10.7   Many disputes arising under the Act will be between individuals – often family members – who disagree on what is in the best interests of the person who lacks capacity. Depending on the type of issue involved, these disagreements are more likely to find a lasting resolution if agreement is reached without resort to the courts. Mediation can help to forge better relationships between the parties and so avoid future disputes. While there is no guarantee that the parties will be able to reach an agreement via mediation, if they can do so they are more likely to keep to it since they have agreed something rather than having it imposed on them.

10.8   Potentially, any case that is capable of settlement through negotiation may be suitable for mediation. Mediation will be most suitable when the dispute is between individuals who are failing to communicate with each other or to understand each other's point of view. It is a good option when it is in the person's interests for those involved to maintain a relationship in the future. In order for mediation to take place, everyone involved in the decision must be willing to try. The mediator should be able to decide whether the case is suitable for mediation, taking account of the likely chances of success and the need to safeguard the person lacking capacity. If all parties agree to mediation, it suggests that they are prepared to talk and possibly to make compromises. Even if mediation does not produce a solution, it can help to define and narrow the issues so that when the case comes to court it can be dealt with more easily.

Mrs A, who has dementia and lives with her son and daughter-in-law, spends a holiday with her daughter who lives 200 miles away. After the holiday her daughter refuses to bring her mother back, having found a care home nearby where she thinks her mother will be better looked after. Her brother disagrees. Mrs A is upset by this family dispute, and so her son and daughter decide to try mediation. The mediator believes that Mrs A is able to make her wishes known and agrees to take on the case. A decision is reached for Mrs A to continue to live with her son but to review the situation again in six months to see if her needs might be better met elsewhere.

10.9   A number of providers of community and family mediation have relevant experience of cases involving disputes where one person lacks mental capacity.

Mr B has learning disabilities. His parents are divorced and he lives in a residential care home although this is soon to close. Mr B does not have capacity to decide where he would like to live and his parents cannot agree as to where she should move to. Ms B's social worker resolves the dispute by arranging counselling, advice and mediation and a consensus decision is reached: namely, that Mr B will move into supported housing.

10.10   The mediation process requires all parties to take part as equally as possible so that a mediator is able to ascertain the person's best interests. It might be appropriate to involve an independent advocate to try to ascertain their wishes.

10.11   In some cases mediation may be funded through public legal funding. Anyone can apply for legal funding, but certain conditions will need to be satisfied in order for an application to be successful (see Part 2). Details of where to find a local, suitably qualified mediator, are available at advice centres and on the internet (at xxx)

10.12   While health and social services might be involved in a case, and might be included in the mediation process, most disputes will be between individuals, rather than between an individual and an agency. In the case of the latter, the route of health and social care complaints procedures may be more appropriate (see paragraph 18 onwards).

Advocacy

10.13   Family members, friends, care managers, social workers, health care professionals and others may support and speak for a person, but where there are differences of opinion, or conflicting interests, the person might benefit from independent advocacy.

Independent advocacy

10.14   An independent advocate acts on behalf of and in the interests of a person who has difficulty speaking up for him/herself and is independent of any statutory agency or other party involved with the person. Most advocacy services are provided by the voluntary sector and are arranged at a local level. Most receive some statutory (local and/or health authority) and voluntary (charitable trust or national lottery grants) funding.

10.15   When disagreements arise, an independent advocate may be able to help resolve the dispute without the use of a mediator or complaints process, simply by presenting the person's feelings to his family, carers or professionals. Advocates may also be involved during mediation or complaints proceedings. In certain specific, defined circumstances, people who lack capacity have a statutory right to advocacy, for example, to support a person in making a formal complaint against the NHS.

10.16   The Government commissions advocacy services through two routes:

- advocacy which is provided for in statute, and
- advocacy which is not provided for in statute.

Complaints about health care

10.17   Formal and informal mechanisms exist to resolve complaints about the health care received by patients, including those who lack capacity. Health care professionals and others need to be aware of these methods and in which situations their use is appropriate. The Patient Advice and Liaison Service (PALS) provides an informal way of dealing with problems before they reach the complaints stage. There is a PALS in each NHS and primary care trust in England which can provide advice and information to patients or their relatives/carers in order to try to resolve problems quickly. Where appropriate, they are able to sign-post people to local specialist support services, for example, health advocates, mental health support teams, social services and interpreting services. PALS can provide explanations of complaints procedures and, if appropriate, can direct patients, their relatives or carers to the formal complaints process. A similar service is being piloted in parts of Wales.

10.18   A complaint about something that happened in the past, requiring for example an apology or explanation, should be dealt with by NHS complaints procedures since a court cannot provide these solutions.

Disagreements about proposed treatments

10.19   If a case is not urgent, it may be possible for it to be dealt with in the supportive atmosphere that the Patient Advice and Liaison Service can provide. Urgent cases about serious proposed treatment may need to go directly to the Court of Protection.

Mrs C, who has Alzheimer's, does not want a flu jab. Her daughter thinks she should have the injection. The doctor does not want to go against the wishes of his patient, as he believes she has capacity to give an informed refusal of treatment and does not consider that there is a risk of serious consequences if the jab is not given. Mrs C's daughter goes to the Patient Advice and Liaison Service (PALS) since she does not agree with the doctor's assessment or that he is acting in her mother's best interests. PALS provide information and advice about consent, and how to find more information about the flu jab. PALS speak to the doctor, and explain his point of view to the family. The daughter remains unhappy. PALS advises her that the Independent Complaints Advocacy Service (see paragraph 10.20) can help if she wishes to make a formal complaint.

NHS complaints procedure

10.20 The NHS has a formal procedure for resolving complaints about care and services. The procedure covers complaints made by an individual about any matter connected with the provision of NHS services by NHS organisations or primary care practitioners. The Independent Complaints Advocacy Service (ICAS) provides advice and support to people who want to take forward formal NHS complaints, making the system more accessible to those who lack mental capacity. Complaints are first investigated and responded to at a local level. The complainant can request an independent review by the Commission for Healthcare Audit and Inspection (also known as the Healthcare Commission) if he or she remains unhappy after local resolution. If a complainant remains unhappy after the NHS complaints procedure has been exhausted, he or she (or the person acting on their behalf) can take the case to the Health Service Ombudsman. In Wales, complaints advocates based at Community Health Councils provide advice and support to people wanting to complain about the NHS, and independent review is undertaken by lay reviewers appointed by the Welsh Assembly Government.

10.21 NHS Foundation Trusts are not covered by the regulations setting out the framework for the local resolution stage of the NHS complaints procedure. However, they are covered by the independent review stage operated by the Healthcare Commission and by the Health Service Ombudsman. Where someone has a complaint about an NHS Foundation Trust they should contact the Trust for advice on how to make this.

Clinical negligence cases

10.22 The NHS Litigation Authority has an overview of all clinical negligence cases brought against the NHS in England and actively encourages the use of alternative dispute resolution by both the NHS and claimants to enable cases to be settled effectively and without the need for resort to the courts.

10.23 On 30 June 2003, the Chief Medical Officer published *Making Amends*. This sets out proposals for reforming the approach to clinical negligence in the NHS including a new NHS redress scheme and greater use of Alternative Dispute Resolution. Work is ongoing to develop these proposals further in England and its implementation in Wales is being considered by the Welsh Assembly Government.

Complaints about social care

10.24   A complaint about the way in which care services are delivered, the type of services provided, or failure to provide services, should be dealt with through the local authority's procedures for handling concerns and complaints.

10.25   An attempt should initially be made to resolve a complaint through an informal discussion between professionals, the person (with support if necessary) and their carers and/or relatives. If the complainant is not satisfied, the local authority will conduct a formal investigation according to its complaints procedures. If the complaint is still not resolved, it can be referred, in England, to the Commission for Social Care Inspection (CSCI) for an independent review. Complaints may be referred to the Local Government Ombudsman for Wales or England where appropriate.

10.26   If someone is unhappy with care provided by a private or local authority care home, they should use the care home's own complaints procedure (required under the Care Homes Regulations 2001). If they are dissatisfied with either the complaints procedure, or the response to their complaint, they may approach the CSCI in England, or the Care Standards Inspectorate for Wales – depending on where it is – as regulator of the home. If the person was placed in the home by the local authority, it might be more appropriate to use the social services complaint procedure if the concern is with that placement and the authority's assessment of the person's needs, rather than the services provided by the home.

Following a social services assessment Mr E was placed in a care home. However, Mr E's family believe that the standard of care provided by the home is insufficient to meet his assessed needs. The family file a formal complaint with the care home and, following investigation by the home manager, additional support for Mr E is offered.

Other welfare issues

10.27   The Independent Housing Ombudsman deals with complaints about registered social landlords in England. This applies mostly to housing associations, but also many landlords who manage homes that were formerly run by local authorities and some private landlords. Complaints about local authorities are referred to the Local Government Ombudsman in England or the Local Government Ombudsman for Wales. They look at complaints about decisions on council housing, social services, Housing Benefit and planning applications.

Disagreements regarding financial matters

10.28   Disagreements about the financial affairs of a person who lacks capacity in relation to those affairs might include the following:

■   Disputes between family members or other individuals, for example over the size of an allowance to be paid by the person lacking capacity to a family member who acts as carer

■   Disputes over whether a house should be sold

■   Disputes involving a third party questioning the actions of an LPA donee or a deputy

10.29   In all of the above circumstances, the most appropriate action would be to contact the OPG for guidance and advice. Staff at the OPG will be able to provide advice and guidance on the appropriate steps to take, according to the circumstances of each case.

Access to the Court of Protection

10.30   The new Court of Protection has powers to make decisions in relation to all areas of decision-making for adults who lack capacity. Chapter 7 of the Code describes the role, functions, operation and powers of the Court, and sets out the duties and responsibilities of deputies appointed by the Court to make decisions on behalf of a person lacking capacity.

10.31   The creation of a new Court of Protection, however, does not imply that all problems involving people who lack capacity will or should be determined by the court. Although the Court will be relatively accessible and informal, other methods of solving problems will generally be more appropriate, faster and less distressing for all parties.

10.32   There are a few types of cases that should be dealt with by the court, and when another form of dispute resolution would generally not be suitable. These include:

- Where it is unclear whether proposed serious and/or invasive medical treatment is likely to be in the best interests of the person lacking capacity to consent.
- Where formal authority is needed to deal with one-off significant financial decisions for a person lacking capacity to manage financial affairs (such as paying a costly bill for house repairs or selling a valuable item of property), but there is no need for on-going financial powers, the Court could be asked to make an order providing the necessary authority.
- Where it is necessary to make a will, or amend an existing will, on behalf of a person lacking testamentary capacity, this can only be done by order of the Court.

Ms F is a young woman who has been diagnosed as suffering from variant CJD. Her prognosis is poor but healthcare professionals and family members have become aware of a new treatment for her condition that is relatively untested but has been reported to produce improvements in some patients. However, there are side-effects related to the treatment and both her healthcare team and members of her family are divided as to whether it would be in her best interests to receive the treatment. Given the division of opinion, an application is made to the Court of Protection for a declaration that it would be lawful, and in Ms F's best interests, to receive the treatment. The Court, after considering evidence from all relevant parties, makes such a declaration and the treatment is given to Ms F.

Leave to apply

10.33   Clause 48 of the Act specifies persons who are not required to seek permission before making an application to the Court of Protection. If a case is not brought by the person lacking capacity, a deputy or attorney or someone named in an existing court order to which this application relates, permission will be required. This will only be granted if the case is suitable for resolution at court and the court will decide whether the benefit can be achieved in any other way.

PART 2: PUBLIC LEGAL FUNDING

10.34   Every effort should be made to resolve disputes at an early stage through taking advice (including advice on complaint and dispute resolution mechanisms from the Office of the Public Guardian), discussion and agreement if possible (including mediation and PALS – see part 1 above). Legal Funding is available through the Legal Services Commission (LSC) to ensure that people who lack capacity are able to get Legal Help and where necessary Legal Representation at the Court of Protection. Those who lack capacity may need a litigation friend, such as the Official Solicitor, to enable them to take a case and funding will then be paid to the friend, rather than direct to the applicant.

The means and merits tests

10.35 Applicants for Legal Help will need to satisfy the standard 'means test' (confirming receipt of specified benefits or income and capital below a specified amount) and 'merits test' (confirming that there is sufficient benefit to the applicant to justify providing the advice and that no other source of funding is available). People in receipt of 'passported' benefits (including income support) automatically qualify financially for legal aid.

Legal Help

10.36 Legal Help can cover advice and assistance on matters relating to mental incapacity including preparation work for Court hearings. It will generally be available if an applicant satisfies the means and merit tests. Under the Legal Help scheme, applicants can receive up to £500 for initial assistance, to cover help from a solicitor in writing letters, getting a barrister's opinion, help with mediation and preparation for Court of Protection hearings. If necessary, additional funding can be applied for. People will not be able to get Legal Help to make a Lasting Power of Attorney or an advance decision to refuse treatment. Staff at the Office of the Public Guardian will be able to give general and procedural assistance on these matters, if required, but they will not be able to give legal or other specialised advice. For example, they will not be able to advise someone on what powers they should delegate to the person they want to appoint as their LPA.

Legal Representation

10.37 Legal Representation will only be available for representation at Court of Protection hearings for the most serious cases. That is, cases that were previously heard by the High Court would continue to attract Legal Representation when such cases are transferred to the Court of Protection. Primarily, these proceedings relate to the personal liberty or medical treatment of a person who lacks capacity. It is proposed that a Direction will be issued to the Legal Services Commission to ensure that Legal Representation is available for serious cases that meet the specified criteria. The Direction cannot be framed until the legislation is settled by Parliament.

CHAPTER 11: SAFEGUARDS FOR VULNERABLE PEOPLE

This chapter deals with the provisions in the Mental Capacity Bill that establish the independent consultee service. These provisions represent the most recently developed area of policy in the Bill and as such, have not been subject to formal consultation as the other areas of the Bill have been. In addition, much of the detail as to how the independent consultee system will operate will not be contained in the Bill itself but will instead by brought about by regulations made under the Bill. For both these reasons, this chapter is likely to be subject to further development as more work is done on the independent consultee service. However, we felt that it was still important at this early stage to give at least a preliminary idea of how we expect guidance on these provisions to look.

INTRODUCTION

11.1   Part 1 of this chapter describes the additional safeguards provided under the Act
for particularly vulnerable people who lack capacity to take decisions in certain
serious, potentially life-changing situations. These will be provided through the
appointment of an 'independent consultee' whose role will be to provide advice on
the person's best interests. Part 2 explains the particular situations which will
require the appointment of an independent consultee and the categories of vulnerable people to whom the safeguard will apply. Part 3 describes the obligations
placed on public authorities (relevant NHS bodies or local authorities) relating to
the requirement to consult with independent consultees and take account of their
advice.

PART 1: THE INDEPENDENT CONSULTEE SERVICE

11.2   Sections 34–39 of the Mental Capacity Act establish a new statutory scheme,
known as the 'independent consultee service', to provide additional safeguards for
people who lack capacity to take decisions in certain specific, serious situations and
who are particularly vulnerable because they have no close relatives, friends or any
other person to help protect their interests. The categories of people who qualify
for additional safeguards and the particular situations which will trigger them are
described in Part 2 below. The Act also makes provision for extension of the scheme
by regulations where future needs are identified.

The need for additional safeguards

11.3   In the vast majority of cases, individuals with capacity problems will have a network of support, whether from family members or friends who take an interest in
their welfare, from a donee appointed under a Lasting Power of Attorney (see chapter 6) or from a deputy appointed by the Court of Protection (see chapter 7). When
determining what would be in the best interests of a person lacking capacity in relation to a particular decision or course of action, all those people in the person's network of support must be consulted where it is appropriate or practicable to do so
(see chapter 4).

11.4   Where there is a dispute about an individual's best interests, the independent consultee will be able to pursue a complaint or challenge a particular decision or action
affecting that individual in the same way that a concerned family member may take
action on behalf of an incapacitated relative via existing complaint mechanisms.
The role of the Independent Consultee will be to give advice. There may be situations where the NHS body or local authority will take action even where the
Independent Consultee advises that this is not in the best interests of the person
lacking capacity. In these circumstances, the Independent Consultee could make a
complaint as the person's representative or someone acting on his behalf under
existing procedures.

Appointment of independent consultees

11.5   Section 34 of the Act sets out the arrangements for the appointment of independent consultees to be available to assist where necessary to protect the interests of
vulnerable people who qualify for the service. This places an obligation on the
'appropriate authority' (in England, the Secretary of State for Health; in Wales, the
National Assembly for Wales) to ensure that arrangements are in place to ensure
that independent consultees are available.

Who can be an independent consultee?

11.6   The particular qualifications, experience and training requirements necessary for approval of independent consultees are set out in Regulations [Add ref and details when known)

11.7   In order to ensure their independence, people approved to act as independent consultees:

■   must not have any professional or paid involvement with the provision of care or treatment for any vulnerable person for whom they may be appointed to act; and

■   must be completely independent of the person responsible for making the decision or doing the act in question.

The role and functions of the independent consultee

11.8   The actual role and functions of independent consultees are set out in Regulations [Add ref and details when known].

Providing advice about best interests

11.9   The primary role of the independent consultee is to advise on what is in a vulnerable person's best interests. There is already an obligation on the decision-maker or actor to try to determine the best interests of the person lacking capacity in relation to the matter in question (see chapter 4). Part of the best interests checklist requires consultation with specified people, including any person previously named by the person lacking capacity, any person engaged in caring for the person or interested in his/her welfare and any donee or deputy appointed to act on the person's behalf. Where there is no-one other than a paid carer who fits into any of these categories, that role is fulfilled by the independent consultee.

11.10   In order to carry out this task, the consultee will need to investigate the particular circumstances of the vulnerable person in relation to other aspects of the best interests checklist. These include:

■   whether the person is likely to regain capacity in relation to the matter in question, and if so, when that is likely to be;

■   the need to permit and encourage the person to participate, or to improve his/her ability to participate, as fully as possible in any act done for and any decision affecting him/her;

■   so far as these can be ascertained, the past and present wishes and feelings of the person concerned, any beliefs and values that may have influenced the decision in question, and the factors which the person would consider if able to do so;

■   any other relevant factors, including for example, the need to promote the human rights of the person concerned.

11.11   In addition, the consultee will need to consider whether the principles set out in section 1 of the Act have been complied with. In particular, where there is more than one course of action or a choice of decisions to be made, the consultee will need to check whether all possible options or alternatives have been explored and whether the proposed option would be least restrictive of the person's future choices or would allow him/her the most freedom. They should also check that the person has been given adequate support to try to make his or her own decision and that he or she does in fact lack capacity in relation to the decision in question.

11.12   Section 34(6) therefore provides independent consultees with certain powers to enable them to carry out their functions under the Act. These include:

- the right to visit and have a private discussion with the vulnerable person concerned; and
- the right to examine any records (such as clinical records, care plans or social care assessment documents) which are considered relevant to the decision or action in question.

11.13 If the independent consultee considers that further information is required in order to form a view as to the person's best interests, the following courses of action may be appropriate, according to the particular circumstances of the case:

- Where the vulnerable person has communication difficulties, the consultee may consider seeking specialist help, for example from a speech therapist or translator;
- The consultee may wish to discuss possible options with other professionals or paid carers directly involved in providing care or treatment for the vulnerable person, bearing in mind the duty of confidentiality towards the person concerned;
- where the decision or action concerns medical treatment, the consultee may consider seeking a second opinion from a doctor with an appropriate specialism as to whether the proposed treatment is necessary and in the person's best interests.

An independent consultee is appointed in relation to a young man who has been in hospital for voluntary treatment for a mental disorder. It is now proposed to discharge him into a specialist care home, as he is liable to self-harm and will need to be kept under observation. He lacks capacity to agree to the move and has no outside contacts other than with his carers. An independent consultee is appointed to advise on his best interests. The consultee will wish to visit the young man, look at his clinical records and care plans and discuss the proposals for his future care with a multi-disciplinary team and with staff at the care home. The consultee may also wish to obtain specialist advice.

11.14 In some situations, particularly where the matter is urgent, it may not be possible or practicable for the independent consultee to carry out extensive investigations. The consultee will therefore need to make a judgement about what investigations are necessary and appropriate in the particular circumstances in order to reach a view as to the person's best interests. There may be rare occasions when, despite their best efforts, independent consultees are unable to form an opinion about an individual's best interests. Nevertheless, they will usually be able to raise relevant issues and questions, and provide additional information to ensure that all relevant factors are taken into account in determining the person's best interests.

11.15 It is ultimately the responsibility of the person proposing an action or decision to decide what is in the best interests of the person lacking capacity to make the decision or agree to the action, but the decision-maker has a duty to take account of the advice given by the independent consultee. In most cases, a determination of best interests will be achieved through discussion and consensus of all involved, including, so far as possible, the person lacking capacity.

Resolving disagreements

11.16 Having offered advice or information about the best interests of a vulnerable person lacking capacity in relation to a specific matter, there may be occasions when the independent consultee feels that insufficient regard has been given to that advice. In some cases, there may be significant disagreement between the consultee and the decision-maker about whether the proposed course of action is actually in the person's best interests. In such cases, the independent consultee may need to take steps to try to resolve the disagreement.

11.17 Different methods of resolving disagreements are set out in chapter 10, which will vary depending on the type and urgency of the particular dispute. Every effort should be made to resolve disputes at the earliest possible stage. Possibilities include:

- In relation to disagreements about health care or treatment:

  - involving the Patient Advice and Liaison Service (PALS) (in England)
  - using the NHS Complaints Procedure
  - continuing care review panels

- In relation to disagreements about social care:

  - if the person is in a care home, using the care home's own complaints procedure
  - using the local authority complaints procedure

- In particularly serious cases where there is no other way of resolving the matter, an independent consultee may, as a last resort:

  - seek permission to refer the matter to the Court of Protection (see chapter 7).

Additional functions of independent consultees

11.18 We intend to give Independent consultees an additional role under statutory guidance issued to local authorities (under section 7, Local Authority Social Services Act 1970) and to NHS bodies (under section 17, National Health Service Act 1977), but this is subject to clearance. The guidance will require the relevant local authority, and the Directions will require the NHS body, to involve an independent consultee in the annual reviews of people in long-term care (whether in hospital or care home in relation to accommodation provided by an NHS body, or any residential accommodation provided by a local authority, irrespective of whether it is owned independently or not) in circumstances where the person concerned lacks capacity to participate in the review and has no relative, friend or other person to take an interest in his/her welfare and be consulted on his/her best interests. This would apply only where an IC was involved in the original decision.

11.19 In order to ensure sufficient flexibility to meet any additional needs for safeguards which may be identified in future, the Act allows for the scheme to be extended, or additional functions to be ascribed to independent consultees by amendment to the Regulations.

PART 2: SITUATIONS REQUIRING AN INDEPENDENT CONSULTEE

11.20 The independent consultee will provide protection for people who have nobody to speak for them when serious decisions need to be made. The following paragraphs provide further details of a) the specific situations in which an independent consultee will be required and b) the categories of people who qualify for the additional safeguards provided by the independent consultee service.

What acts or decisions require additional safeguards?

11.21 The need for additional safeguards for particularly vulnerable people has been identified in the following situations:

- decisions relating to providing, withholding or withdrawing serious medical treatment;
- where it is proposed to move a person lacking capacity to agree to the move into long-term care in a hospital or care home; or
- where a move to a different care establishment is proposed.

Serious healthcare and treatment decisions

11.22   Where a serious healthcare or treatment decision is contemplated for a person lacking capacity to consent, who qualifies for additional safeguards, section 35 imposes a duty on the NHS body responsible for the patient's treatment to make sure that advice about the person's best interests is sought from an independent consultee (Part 3 below explains which NHS body may be responsible). The particular types of healthcare or treatment decision which will trigger the need for an independent consultee are prescribed in Regulations [Add ref when known].

> A man with Down's Syndrome has been in care for most of his life and has lost touch with his family. He now has Alzheimer's disease which has also led to a weakening of his swallowing reflex. In other ways he is healthy and he has been referred to a specialist with a view to him going onto artificial feeding (directly into his stomach). He lacks capacity to consent. An independent consultee is appointed to advise clinicians and other staff as to his best interests.

11.23   The only situation in which the duty to seek advice from an independent consultee could be dispensed with is where the proposed treatment needs to be provided as a matter of urgency, for example to save the person's life or prevent a serious deterioration in his/her condition (Section 35(3)).

11.24   Regulations will set out types of serious health care or treatment decisions which will require an independent consultee. Regulations can be amended more easily to take account of new treatment techniques and procedures which may be developed in the future

Decisions about accommodation/changes of residence

11.25   Sections 36–37 impose similar duties on NHS bodies or local authorities which are responsible for the placement in accommodation of a person lacking capacity to agree to the placement, and who also qualifies for the additional safeguards of an independent consultee. These duties will be triggered where:

- an NHS body proposes to place a person, who lacks the capacity to agree, in a hospital or care home for a period likely to exceed 28 days;
- an NHS body proposes to move the person to another hospital or care home for a period likely to exceed 28 days;
- during an assessment under the NHS and Community Care Act 1990 of a person who lacks the capacity to agree to accommodation arrangements, a local authority proposes to provide community care services in the form of residential accommodation and to place the person in accommodation for a period likely to exceed 8 weeks;
- a local authority proposes to move the person to another care home for a period likely to exceed 8 weeks.

An NHS Trust has a long stay ward which houses 28 older people with mental health problems in less than adequate accommodation. Plans have been made to close the ward and make new placements for the residents. One of the residents has been on this same ward for the last ten years and no longer has any contact with the outside world. An independent consultee is appointed to advise on her best interests.

11.26   The only situation in which the duty to seek advice from an independent consultee can be dispensed with is where the proposed placement or move needs to be made as a matter of urgency, for example an emergency admission to hospital, or where the person lacking capacity would be made homeless unless admitted immediately to a care home.

11.27   In addition to these particular situations set out in the Act which relate to placements in hospital or care homes, changes in the Regulations may provide for the extension of the independent consultee scheme to other types of situations, should a need be identified in the future.

Who qualifies for additional safeguards?

11.28   The additional safeguards are intended to apply to people who have no network of support and no-one close to them who takes an interest in their welfare. This lack of support makes the determination of best interests particularly difficult since there is no-one who can be consulted, other than people who provide care or treatment in a professional capacity or for remuneration, who have a different role to play in deciding the best interests of a person lacking capacity. A further disadvantage is that there is no-one to support the incapacitated person in communicating his/her own wishes and feelings or participating so far as possible in the decision in question.

11.29   Therefore, the people who qualify for the additional safeguards provided by an independent consultee are those who:

- lack capacity in relation to one of the decisions or acts described in paragraphs 11.21–11.27 above; and
- have no-one close to them who can be consulted about their best interests, other than people engaged in their care or treatment in a professional or paid capacity.

11.30   Section 38 clarifies the particular categories of people who will not require the services of an independent consultee, since there will always be someone else who can be consulted about the person's best interests. These include the following:

- where a person who now lacks capacity in relation to a particular matter has previously expressed a wish that a named person should be consulted in matters affecting his/her interests, and that person is available and willing to be consulted;
- where there is a donee appointed under a Lasting Power of Attorney;
- where there is an attorney appointed under an Enduring Power of Attorney, and the attorney continues to manage person's affairs;
- where a deputy (or before the Act came into effect, a receiver) has been appointed by the Court of Protection.

11.31   Even if the donee or deputy has been appointed to manage the person's financial affairs, they are likely to have some knowledge about the person's wishes and feelings and about their particular circumstances which are relevant to his/her best interests.

11.32 The Act provides for extension of the categories of people who qualify for these additional safeguards through changes in the Regulations, should further needs be identified in the future.

DUTIES OF PUBLIC AUTHORITIES

11.33 The duty to make sure that arrangements for the independent consultee service are put in place lies with the 'appropriate authority' Secretary of State for Health in England, and in Wales, with the National Assembly for Wales. The appointment of independent consultees and management of the service must be carried out in accordance with the Regulations. *[Add ref when known]*

11.34 The duty to consult an independent consultee in the situations described n Part 2 above lies with the relevant public authority, the 'responsible body' which is responsible for the proposed decision or course of action.

Which is the 'responsible body'?

11.35 This will depend on the type of decision or proposed course of action.

- In relation to healthcare or treatment decisions, the responsible body that will have a duty to consult with an independent consultee will normally be the NHS body involved in providing healthcare or treatment for the person concerned. In most cases, this will be the relevant local NHS Trust, but could also be a Primary Care Trust (PCT) (for example where the PCT runs a small community hospital). However, where the healthcare or treatment is being carried out in an independent (private) hospital, the responsible authority in those cases will be the NHS body which agreed to fund the person's care in that hospital. This could be either an NHS Trust, a PCT, or in Wales, a Local Health Board.
- In relation to decisions about admission to hospital, the responsible body, again with the duty to consult, will be the NHS body which either manages the hospital to which it is proposed to admit the person or agrees to fund the person's care in an independent hospital
- In relation to decisions about moves into long-term care, the responsible body will be the local authority which carried out the assessment of the person under the NHS and Community Care Act 1990 and has decided to provide community care services in the form of residential accommodation.

Duties of the responsible body

11.36 The responsible body is under a statutory duty to

- Consult the independent consultee and make sure that the particular decision-maker or person proposing to take the action in question takes account of the advice given by the independent consultee in determining the best interests of the person concerned.

11.37 In order to comply with these duties, the responsible body must have in place procedures to ensure that:

- All relevant staff are aware of the particular situations requiring an independent consultee (see Part 2 above);
- All relevant staff are aware of how to access the independent consultee service;
- All reasonable requests for information or access to records made by independent consultees in carrying out their functions under the Act are complied with;

- Proper records are made of the involvement of a consultee and the advice given by the consultee as to the person's best interests;
- Proper records are made by the person proposing the decision or action as to how the consultee's advice has been taken into account and, where relevant, his/her reasons for disagreeing with or ignoring that advice.

11.38   Where a disagreement arises between the independent consultee and anyone employed by or acting on behalf of the responsible body, every effort must be made to resolve the disagreement at the earliest possible stage, where necessary using the authority's dispute resolution or complaints procedures (see paragraphs 11.16–11.17 above).

CHAPTER 12: RESEARCH

INTRODUCTION

12.1   **Part 1** of this chapter sets out the reasons for including provisions for research in the Act, clarifies what is meant by research, and provides some background information on research governance arrangements. **Part 2** lists the different parties that must be involved under such circumstances, specifically those individuals who are proposing to undertake the research, bodies such as research ethics committees, and any third party consulted about the participation of a person lacking capacity in the research. The responsibilities of each of these parties are outlined. **Part 3** sets out the requirements for approval and **Part 4** identifies the processes that need to be followed in order to ensure that such research is lawful.

PART 1: WHY IS RESEARCH INCLUDED IN THE ACT?

12.2   The Mental Capacity Act ('the Act') enables substitute decision-making under those circumstances where a person is found to lack decision-making capacity. The guiding principle is that any decision taken on behalf of the person lacking capacity must be in that person's best interests.

12.3   The Act and the Code of Practice aim to establish the right balance between the need for research to bring benefit or information and the need for protection against exploitation and abuse. It also seeks to ensure that any increased risk of the research, over and above that risk associated with the condition or treatment itself, is either proportionate to the potential benefit to that individuals, or, in the case of research to provide knowledge, the risk is minimal.

Definition and examples of research covered by Sections 31 to 33 of the Act

12.4   The term 'intrusive research' used in Section 31 of the Mental Capacity Act refers to research that can normally only lawfully take place if the participant concerned, having the capacity to consent, has consented to it. In these circumstances to proceed with the research, in the absence of consent, would be unlawful. Section 31 also states that the Act and its guidance does not apply to clinical trials of medication. These trials are subject to the Medicines for Human Use (Clinical Trials) Regulations 2004 ('Clinical Trials Regulations').

12.5   Research has been defined as an activity that attempts to derive new knowledge by addressing clearly defined questions (hypotheses) using systematic and rigorous methods. The knowledge gained may provide information that can be generalised to the particular illness, disorder, or circumstances under investigation. Such knowledge may inform further research, may lead directly to the use of new medical treatments or other interventions (e.g. surgical procedure, psychological treatments), or may have wider implications, such as informing health or social care policy and practice (e.g. investigating factors that influence or maximise a potentially incapacitated person's decision-making capacity).

12.6   Health research in particular is usually a process that progresses from investigations that are not of immediate therapeutic value (non-therapeutic research), that aims, for example, to identify the potential cause of an illness; to the testing of new treatments or intervention strategies usually in comparison to an existing treatment or a placebo (referred to as therapeutic research). Whilst a distinction is drawn between therapeutic and non-therapeutic research, in practice many research programmes are likely to include both forms of research and the former (therapeutic) would not have been possible without the latter.

Research Governance

12.7   All research should be conducted to an acceptable ethical standard and those engaged in research must be able to demonstrate that the necessary procedures have been complied with. These procedures have been set down by international, national, and professional bodies and by institutions such as Hospital Trusts and Universities where research takes place. All researchers must be familiar with such guidance. The main principles are given in this Code of Practice but in addition all researchers are expected to be familiar with relevant guidance in line with local and professional research governance arrangements.

12.8   Research in the NHS and other organisations is governed by specific procedures and the requirement that an appropriately established and independent ethics committee considers and approves the protocol before the project commences (now co-ordinated through the Central Office for Research Ethics Committees). The involvement of humans in research is governed by these procedural safeguards and by the requirement that the potential participants in a research project are properly informed about the research and the potential risks and benefits, and have given informed and voluntary consent. The main safeguards to protect against unethical and inappropriate research practices are therefore the following:

- research governance arrangements;
- the regulatory framework of the Research Ethics Committees (RECs);
- the informed and voluntary consent of potential participants.

12.9   The absence of one such safeguard (consent), because of the participant's incapacity to consent, requires additional provisions to ensure that the research is appropriate and not exploitative.

PART 2: WHO DO THESE PROVISIONS APPLY TO?

12.10   In the context of research the following determines whether this Act applies:

- the proposed research is defined as 'intrusive' i.e. it is of a kind that would require the consent of the potential participant in order to be lawful;
- the research includes participants who have an impairment of, or disturbance in, the functioning of the mind or brain that results in incapacity to consent to the research;
- the research proposed is not a clinical trial covered under the Clinical Trials Regulations.

12.11   If the above circumstances apply, the Act and the Code of Practice set out certain duties and responsibilities of the organisations and individuals listed below. There is a different emphasis placed on the responsibilities of each, but overall two broad issues must be considered:

- is the involvement in this research of participants who may lack capacity appropriate or not, as judged by the criteria set out in the Mental Capacity Act, the Code of Practice, and in research guidance?
- Does the research protocol include the necessary procedures and protocols as set out in the Act, the Code of Practice, and in research guidance to ensure compliance with the Mental Capacity Act?

12.12 It is the responsibility of all concerned with research to act ethically and responsibly and in accordance with established practice. However, in the context of this Act, the following organisations and individuals have specific responsibilities:

- the 'Appropriate Authority' as designated by the Secretary of State (normally a properly constituted independent Research Ethics Committee);
- others (referred to as a Third Party) who know the potential participant and who must be consulted about whether it is appropriate to involve him or her in the research (see section 32);
- the Principal Research Investigator with overall responsibility for the research project and the researchers directly undertaking the research (referred to as R in the Mental Capacity Act).

PART 3: REQUIREMENTS FOR APPROVAL

12.13 Section 31 sets out criteria which must be met in order for any proposed research covered by the Mental Capacity Act to be lawful. These are set out in a number of international instruments, such as the World Medical Association's Declaration of Helsinki, and the Council of Europe Convention on Human Rights and Biomedicine. The Act and other guidance place an emphasis on the specific role of the organisations and individuals.

Responsibilities of Principal Investigator and Research Group

12.14 The conditions that apply to research in general also apply to research involving people who may lack capacity. It is the responsibility of the Principal Investigator to ensure that all relevant guidance has been complied with. The main points are summarised below:

- the interests of the patient (participant) always prevail over those of science or society;
- research must be subject to the approval of an appropriately constituted independent Research Ethics Committee;
- research must be carried out in accordance with relevant professional obligations and standards and national guidelines;
- potential participants must be informed of the nature of the research and any potential consequences and risks, and only participate in the research having given informed and voluntary consent if they have the capacity to do so;
- if a participant has the capacity to consent, it is for him/her to choose whether to partake in the research or not, and any decision taken must be voluntary, and any refusal to take part must have no consequences in terms of the care he/she receives;
- information obtained as part of the research is kept confidential and managed in accordance with the appropriate guidance and the Data Protection Act;
- where research includes participants who are found to lack the capacity to consent to the research, additional procedures and safeguards apply as set out below.

Additional Responsibilities When Someone Lacks Capacity

12.15 Where research may involve participants who lack the capacity to consent to the research, a range of additional safeguards (as well as those above) must be considered as set down in the Mental Capacity Act, sections 31, 32 and 33, and in international, national, and professional guidance. It is the responsibility of the Principal Investigator to ensure that all relevant additional guidance has been complied with. This is summarised as follows:

- the research must be concerned with the incapacitating disorder itself and/or its consequences;
- there are reasonable grounds to believe that the outcome of the research is of potential benefit to the person, or others with a similar disorder, and could not be done solely involving those with capacity;
- as part of the consent procedure the capacity of the person is determined according to the criteria set out in the Act and in the Code of Practice and is clearly documented;
- appropriate means are used (such as giving information in a simplified format) to maximise the person's understanding of the research and enabling him/her to be party to the decision-making process;
- an appropriate Third Party associated with the person is identified and consulted and this third party clearly advises that he or she has no objections to the person being involved in this research;
- The person is not involved in the research if he or she is actively dissenting at the time of the research – see Section 33 (2)(a); or if the Third Party advises that in his opinion the person would be likely to decline to take part (or withdraw from) the research if he had capacity to do so.
- any previously expressed wish by the person, either directly or through a legal representative (such as a court appointed deputy), that he/she does not wish to be involved in research is respected – see Section 33 (2)(b);
- If the research does not have the potential to benefit the person, then any additional risk or discomfort should be negligible or nil and should not significantly interfere with the person's freedom or privacy.

Responsibilities of Appropriate Authority (Research Ethics Committees)

12.16 In addition to their general duty to examine research proposals from an ethical perspective, the Committee must consider if the proposed research involves participants who may have an impairment of, or a disturbance in, the functioning of the brain or mind. If it does, then additional safeguards apply as summarised below. Where the Committee does not consider it has the expertise, and the research proposal has not been subject to peer review (such as when applying for a grant), and there are issues of potential concern, the Committee may consider obtaining independent expert advice. The additional considerations include:

- whether the outcome of the research is of potential benefit to the person or others with a similar disorder;
- the justification for including participants who may lack capacity to consent in the research and whether the research could be done solely involving those with capacity;
- the assessment of each participant's capacity as part of the consent procedure and how will that be assessed and documented;
- how does the Research Group propose to identify an appropriate Third Party (such as a carer), seek their agreement to be consulted and then consult about including the person who lacks capacity in the research?

- where identifying such a Third Party, known to the potential participant, has been demonstrated to be not possible, what additional safeguards are proposed? In particular, how then would a person unconnected to the research be identified and nominated to be consulted on the person's best interests?
- Whose responsibility will it be to identify whether the person objects to any part of the research (whether by showing signs of resistance or otherwise) and so should be withdrawn?
- What procedure has been drawn up for identifying emergency situations where consultation with carers on the person's best interests cannot take place and where the agreement of a medical practitioner unconnected to P's care and unconnected to the research is required?
- And what procedures have been identified to recognise the end of the emergency situations where consultation should again be required?
- What procedures have been designed for withdrawing the person from research if any of the requirements for safeguarding his interests have not been met?

Responsibilities of the Third Party

12.17 Section 32 sets out a requirement for those undertaking an approved research project to seek out a Third Party, someone who is interested in the welfare of the person lacking capacity, outside of a professional interest. The person concerned should be acceptable to the person lacking capacity and could, for example, include a family member, advocate, or friend. The Third Party must be provided with information about the proposed research. If such a person cannot be identified, the Principal Research Investigator must nominate (in accordance with guidance issued by the Secretary of State) another person who is prepared to be consulted and who has no connection with the project.

The main responsibilities of the Third Party are as follows:

- to consider the research proposal and to advise whether the person who lacks capacity should be a participant in the research;
- in order to form his/her opinion, to consider what the person's views may have been if he/she had previously been capable and, where possible, to determine what the person might wish to happen.

12.18 If the third party forms the view that the person would not have wished or does not wish to be part of the research, he/she should advise the Principal Research Investigator accordingly. The Third Party has the power to advise against involving the person who lacks capacity in the research. Under such circumstances, the person must not be a participant in the research. If the Principal Research Investigator is of the opinion that the research may be of benefit to the person who lacks capacity, he can apply to the Court of Protection. The Court has the power to make a declaration or order regarding the person's participation in the project.

Exceptional circumstances

12.19 Research without consultation must only take place in exceptional emergency circumstances and with well-documented reasons. Where the research requires action as part of emergency treatment, where there may not be time to consult a Third Party, alternative arrangements must be made and documented, such as consultation with an identified member of staff who is independent of the research. It is the responsibility of the Principal Research Investigator to state the reasons why exemption from Third Party approval is, in his/her view, justified.

12.20 It is the responsibility of the Ethics Committee to consider the circumstances under which such exemption is acceptable and how the person's best interests will continue to be paramount. Two separate situations must be identified. The first is any emergency situation where consultation with a third party has been considered and attempted but rejected as impracticable and therefore the agreement of a medical practitioner unconnected to the research needs to be sought. The second is where the urgency of the situation is such that even this safeguard is not practicable and a procedure agreed with the Committee is followed with no consultation. RECs should consider very carefully whether any research proposal should need to carry out research without any of the above safeguards, such as a second doctor's agreement, and RECs need to document clearly the reasons for any such agreements. The Committee may wish to seek an independent second opinion on such matters.

PART 4: PROCESS

12.21 Part 4 summarises the key issues and the processes necessary for the lawful inclusion in research of those lacking capacity to consent to that research. The Act sets out the principle that capacity is decision-specific and should be assessed 'functionally' for each decision.

For the purpose of this Act a person lacks capacity in relation to a matter if at the material time he is unable to make a decision for himself in relation to the matter because of an impairment of, or a disturbance in the functioning of the mind or brain (see also Chapter 3 of the Code of Practice).

12.22 A key principle of the Mental Capacity Act is that individuals should be presumed to have capacity unless otherwise demonstrated. If a person has a disorder that might give rise to 'an impairment of, or disturbance in, the functioning of the mind or brain', then there is the potential that he/she may lack the capacity to consent. If a research study is to include participants who have an impairment of, or a disturbance of, brain or mind, then the protocol must include details of how capacity is going to be assessed as part of the process of seeking consent.

12.23 As with any decision, if someone is judged to have the capacity to consent, then this Act does not apply and the person's decision to participate or not in the research is the determining factor. If a person is found to have the capacity to consent and does not wish to take part in the proposed research, his/her decision must be respected.

12.24 The Mental Capacity Act provides the means whereby properly regulated research involving participants lacking the capacity to consent can lawfully take place. The additional safeguards required by the Act under such circumstances are at the following three levels:

- the Research Protocol itself must meet the necessary ethical and methodological standards and the research must be justified through the potential for benefit to the person and/or others with similar disorders. There must be reasonable grounds for believing the research would not be as effective if carried out on persons who have capacity. The Protocol must specifically address the consent process and the means used to obtain Third Part agreement, and the level of inconvenience, risk or discomfort that the person is likely to experience, and how that might be minimised.

- The protocol must be approved by an appropriately constituted independent Research Ethics Committee that has considered whether the research group has addressed the above issues. The Committee must arrive at an independent view as to whether the proposed research is ethically justified and meets the requirements set out in the Mental Capacity Act and its accompanying Code of Practice. The research cannot proceed in the absence of the approval of the Ethics Committee.

- Once the Research has been approved by the Ethics Committee and has commenced, the Research Group must comply with the Act and respect the guidance given in the Code of Practice. Where the person is found to lack capacity to consent, unless explicitly agreed to the contrary, the agreement of a Third Party will be obtained. If the Third Party objects, this must be respected. If the person who lacks capacity is clearly dissenting, he/she will not be included in the Research.

12.25   The standards expected of all relevant parties involved in the process of research are set down in the Act, the Code of Practice, and in professional, national, and international guidance. The Act provides the means through statute whereby research can be lawfully undertaken within a framework that balances the benefits of research against the need to provide protection against the potential for exploitative and abusive practices.

CHAPTER 13: DATA PROTECTION AND CONFIDENTIALITY

INTRODUCTION

13.1   When making decisions on behalf of someone who lacks the capacity to make them himself/herself, decision-makers will need to have access to personal information, relating to the person lacking capacity, so that they can act in that person's best interests. They must, therefore, have an understanding of how they can seek to access such information and what they can and cannot do with that information. This Chapter deals with these issues and explains the effect of the law on accessing and handling information relating to a person lacking capacity. Part 1 sets out some general considerations about accessing and using information. Part 2 gives guidance to those most likely to have to handle information about someone lacking capacity.

PART 1: GENERAL CONSIDERATIONS ABOUT ACCESSING AND USING INFORMATION

13.2   The Mental Capacity Act (the Act) establishes a decision-making framework for those who are unable to make decisions for themselves. It deals with decisions made on behalf of a person lacking capacity by those acting formally under an order of the Court of Protection, including as a deputy appointed by the court, and by designated decision makers appointed under a Lasting Power of Attorney. It also deals with decisions and actions taken by people without formal powers in matters of day-to-day care for people lacking capacity.

13.3   The implications of the Act are wide-ranging. In addition to the person who lacks capacity and on whose behalf decisions are to be made, there will be many other people involved. Such people may include family members providing day to day care, doctors providing health care, social workers involved in welfare, solicitors and others providing professional services, people acting under a formal decision making power, the Court and the Public Guardian, organisations involved in the person's financial, personal and other affairs, to name but a few.

13.4   Decisions and actions taken on behalf of a person lacking capacity under the Act cannot be carried out properly without the person making the decision using information about the person lacking capacity. People providing care, managing someone's affairs, or acting as an independent consultee need information in order to be able to assess capacity, determine best interests and make decisions. The Court needs information to make orders. The Public Guardian needs information to be able to register a LPA and to supervise a deputy.

13.5   For some of these purposes, it is clear what information needs to be used, what the source of the information is, and who will have access to it. An example is registration of LPAs by the Public Guardian. An LPA must be in the prescribed form and must include certain prescribed information. The source of authority is the donor of the LPA. Any member of the public can apply to get certain information from the Public Guardian about a registered LPA.

13.6   For other purposes, though, the information required will vary widely according to the circumstances. At one extreme, the daughter providing full-time care for an elderly parent makes day-to-day decisions on the information which she has acquired through years of experience and which she carries in her head. At the other extreme, a deputy faced with making decisions about whether someone needs to move into residential care, or whether the family home should be sold and the proceeds of the sale invested, may need information from family members, from the family doctor, from the person's bank, solicitor, etc to enable them to make a decision that is in the best interests of the person lacking capacity.

13.7   Unrestricted access to information is neither acceptable nor lawful (unless consent has been given to, or authority conferred on, someone to have the information), particularly when the information is personal information. Mostly, the information needed for the purposes of the Act will be personal information relating to the individual who lacks capacity, and much of it will be sensitive and confidential. Access to personal information must only be provided in accordance with the law.

Mr A, a man in his sixties, is in hospital after recently suffering a stroke, which has left him disabled and unable to communicate. Mr A's son, despite being reassured that his father is doing as well as can be expected, thinks his father should be recovering more quickly. Mr A's son asks a neighbour who works at the hospital if she can get a copy of Mr A's record for him. The neighbour refuses, saying that it would be wholly improper for her to access a hospital record for this purpose, indeed, it would probably be a criminal offence. She advises Mr A's son to make his request through the proper channels.

13.8   Access to personal information is regulated under:

■   the Data Protection Act 1998 (the DPA);
■   the common law duty of confidence;
■   professional codes of conduct on confidentiality.

13.9   A key principle of the duty of confidence is that information confided should not be used or disclosed further (in an identifiable form) except as was originally understood by the confider or with his or her subsequent permission. However there are exceptions to the duty of confidence that may make use of the information in question appropriate. Statute law requires or permits disclosure of confidential patient information in certain circumstances. Courts may order disclosure of the information. Case law sets out that confidentiality can be breached where there is an overriding public interest.

PART 2: GUIDANCE TO THOSE HANDLING PERSONAL INFORMATION

13.10 It is important for everyone to understand that data protection is not a barrier to sharing of information, provided that the sharing is undertaken on a strictly need to know basis and is in the best interests of the person concerned. Misunderstanding of data protection is not uncommon, and, too often, organisations processing personal information (or their employees) wrongly hide behind data protection when they are reluctant to disclose data for other reasons. The

Information Commissioner (who supervises the application of the DPA) has expressed disapproval of organisations that 'hide behind data protection as a smokescreen for practices which no reasonable person would find acceptable.'

13.11 A person disclosing information concerning a person lacking capacity must be assured that they are acting lawfully and also that such disclosure is justified, having balanced the public interest in the need to know against the right to privacy of the person who lacks capacity.

13.12 It may be difficult to judge when it is in the public interest to disclose information and each case must be considered on its merits. Professional codes of practice can sometimes help. The NHS Code on confidentiality gives examples of when disclosure is in the public interest: to prevent or aid investigation of serious crimes; and to prevent serious harm, such as spread of an infectious disease. It is then necessary to judge whether the public good that would be achieved by the disclosure outweighs both the obligation of confidentiality to the individual concerned and the broader public interest in the provision of a confidential service.

GUIDANCE TO PEOPLE ACTING WITHOUT FORMAL POWERS

13.13 The provisions in section 5 of the Act give protection from liability, in certain circumstances, to those who have no formal powers but who do acts in relation to the care or treatment of people lacking capacity in the course of providing care or treatment. Many, such actions will be performed informally without any need to refer to information about the person being cared for which is not otherwise in the possession of the carer. In these circumstances, no issues of data protection arise, and there is no need to burden the carer with unnecessary procedures. The carer should remember, though, that the general principle of only acting in the best interests of the person who lacks capacity always applies. The carer would be expected to maintain confidentiality and only reveal personal information about the person lacking capacity to others on a strictly need to know basis.

13.14 The situation may arise, though, where the person making a decision or taking an action on behalf of someone who lacks capacity does need to consult a third party (e.g. a health professional or a social worker) in order to decide what is in the best interests of the person who lacks capacity. The carer can ask the third party to disclose. The third party will need to be satisfied that he can lawfully make the disclosure and that the disclosure is justified.

13.15 **Consent**. In this context, consent means consent by the person to whom the information relates to the use or disclosure of personal information relating to him. Under the common law on confidence and under professional codes of conduct (e.g. *Confidentiality: NHS Code of Practice, Department of Health,* November 2003), consent is needed unless there is an over-riding public interest in disclosure. Under data protection law, consent by the person to whom the information relates is one of the possible grounds for lawful processing of personal information.

13.16 The difficulty in the present context is that it is not likely to be possible to get consent from a person who lacks capacity at the time disclosure of personal information is needed.

13.17 However, it is possible that consent could be obtained at the time of disclosure. A person may be judged to have the capacity to give consent to the release of personal information even though they may not have the capacity to make more complex decisions.

Ms B is a young woman who has been injured in a road accident. The injuries that she received in the accident were serious, but not so serious that she needs full-time care. She does, however, have episodes of making what others, including her partner consider to be irrational decisions. She continues to live with her partner, who looks after her day-to-day needs. Ms B has now told her partner that she wants to have a child, but he is worried as to whether she has the capacity to make that decision and whether it is safe for her to have a child in her physical condition. He consults the family doctor, who at first refuses to discuss the matter with him, saying that he has a duty to respect the confidentiality of his patient and cannot disclose anything from Ms B's health record without her consent. The doctor does, however, judge Ms B as being capable of giving that consent. He agrees to seek her consent, and, after obtaining it, is content to discuss the matter with both Ms B and her partner.

13.18 In many circumstances, though, the third party who holds the information will need to be satisfied that even though there has been no consent, disclosure is both lawful and justified. When doing this, the third party will need to consider whether the disclosure is of information which is regarded as sensitive for the purposes of the DPA. He is likely to be more cautious about disclosure if it is.

13.19 The third party may say that he is bound not to disclose by his duty of confidentiality to the data subject. In this case he needs to be satisfied that there is an overriding public interest in disclosure, and it may fall on the carer to argue that this is a case when it is in the public interest to allow another person to act on behalf of someone who cannot act for himself. The carer can remind the third party that he (the carer) has a duty to act only in the best interests of the data subject and explain that he needs to have the information in order to be able to do so.

13.20 The third party should not disclose any more information than is necessary. Furthermore, the carer should be prepared to give an undertaking to the third party that the information will be treated in confidence, not be disclosed to anyone else and not kept for longer than necessary. In many cases, the need to keep the information will be transient, and the carer should be able to reassure the third party that he will not keep a permanent record of the information. If the carer does intend to keep a permanent record of a decision, he should make it clear for how long he needs to keep the information he has based the decision on. (Such undertakings are often sought as a matter of good practice in data handling – there is no legal requirement for them.)

Guidance to people acting under a LPA or as a deputy appointed by the Court

13.21 The considerations in paragraphs 13.13–13.20 above also apply to these persons. However, a donee under a LPA, or a deputy appointed by the Court is in a better position to get access to personal data than someone acting without formal powers as they can require the information by way of a subject access request rather than merely a non-statutory request.

13.22 **Right of access.** Under section 7 of the DPA, every individual has the right of access to personal information about himself (with some qualifications which are explained in the DPA). This is known as the 'subject access' right. It may be exercised by an agent on behalf of an individual. This means by someone acting under a LPA or as a deputy appointed by the Court (to the extent of their general powers set out in the donee's or deputy's instrument of appointment. For this reason, it is important, where practicable, for the authority granted in a LPA to specifically include consent to processing personal data. Subject access only applies in so far as the information requested is covered by the DPA. Information not covered by the DPA (for example, not all paper records are covered by the DPA, although all information held electronically is) is not accessible under the subject access right.

13.23 Whilst it should not be necessary for every request for information to have to be formulated as a formal subject access request, it is helpful that the subject access mechanism may be used if necessary.

Mr C is an elderly man in the later stages of Alzheimer's. Mr C's son is responsible for his care and welfare under a Lasting Power of Attorney. Mr C has been in residential care for a number of years, but his son is becoming increasingly concerned about the quality of care his father is receiving. He asks to see his father's file, but the manager of the care home refuses, saying that he is prevented from disclosing it because of the Data Protection Act. Mr C's son points out that as a welfare donee under the LPA he is, legally, his father's agent and that the LPA gives him authority to look after his father's welfare. Specifically, the LPA authorises him to make a subject access request on his father's behalf to access personal data he needs in order to ensure proper care is provided to Mr C. Rather than preventing disclosure, the Data Protection Act requires, by way of section 7 of the DPA the care home manager to provide access to any personal data held on Mr C.

Guidance to others involved in care, welfare, etc

13.24 There may be many agencies involved in the care, welfare, property and financial affairs of a person who lacks capacity. They may already be sharing information between themselves, for example, in order to provide the necessary care, in which case, they should have data sharing protocols in place. It is beyond the scope of this Code to incorporate details of such protocols, but those agencies which have adopted data sharing protocols should take steps to review them to make sure that they recognise the provisions of the Act and the need to share data with the Office of the Public Guardian when concerns, in particular, allegations of abuse, by deputies and attorneys are being investigated. Steps should be taken to draw up protocols where none already exist. Organisations should also review their internal data protection policies and procedures to take account of the guidance in this Code.

13.25 Some individuals acting in a professional capacity will be bound by professional codes of conduct. Such codes (for example, the NHS Code of Practice on confidentiality) may include guidance on handling personal information, strictly limiting the circumstances under which information may be disclosed. Usually, though, a professional code will make it clear that disclosure may be justified when it is in the best interests of the person who lacks capacity. For example, the British Medical Association's guidance states: 'without the legal authority to consent to disclosure on behalf of an incapacitated adult, doctors have always had a discretion to release information when it would clearly be in the incapacitated individual's interests to do so and the person has not expressed an objection.'

13.26 As well as sharing information between themselves, organisations and individual practitioners may be asked to disclose information to someone providing care informally or to someone acting under formal powers. In this case they need to take account of the guidance to those people which is given in paragraphs 13.13–13.23.

13.27 If it is someone acting under formal powers (for example a deputy or the donee of an LPA), who is requesting information (as agent of the person who lacks capacity) under the subject access right, they need to be satisfied that he has the authority to do so. If he has, then they should respond as if the request was from the person who lacks capacity himself or herself.

13.28 Organisations and practitioners should be particularly cautious about sharing sensitive information with a person acting without formal powers. They will need to be satisfied that the person is acting in the best interests of the person who lacks capacity and that the information sought is necessary for properly informed decision making. For the disclosure to be lawful both a Schedule 2 and a Schedule 3 provision of the DPA will need to be satisfied. They may wish to get an undertaking constraining the use of the information by the person to whom it is disclosed.

Checklists

13.29 The following two paragraphs set out, in the form of simple checklists, the most important considerations when information is to be requested or disclosed.

13.30 The person requesting information should ask:

- What information do I need?
- Why do I need it?
- Who has the information?
- Can I show that I need the information for me to make a decision that is in the best interests of the person on whose behalf I am acting and that that person lacks the capacity to act for himself?
- Do I need to share the information with anyone else to make a decision that is in P's best interests?
- Should I keep a record of my decision or action?
- How long should I keep the information for?
- Am I acting under a LPA or as a deputy?
- If so, should I request the information under the formal subject access provisions of section 7 of the DPA?

13.31 The person who is asked to disclose information should ask:

- Is the disclosure lawful?
- Is the disclosure justified having balanced public interest in the need to know against P's rights to privacy?

13.32 The following subsidiary questions should help to answer these two key ones:

- Do I (or does my organisation) have the information requested?
- Does the information include sensitive information?
- If so, is there a Schedule 2 and a Schedule 3 condition satisfied?
- Am I satisfied that the person making the request is acting in the best interests of someone who lacks the capacity to act for himself?
- Am I satisfied that he has the formal authority to do so?
- If he has formal authority does that make him the agent of that person?
- If so, is the request a subject access request?
  If not:
- Am I satisfied that he needs the information in order to act properly?
- Am I satisfied that he will respect any confidentiality?
- Am I satisfied that he will keep the information for no longer than necessary?
- Should I seek a formal undertaking as to these matters?

13.33 Further guidance regarding the provisions of the DPA is available from the Information Commissioner's Office (at xxx).

Appendix 4
PRACTICE NOTE (OFFICIAL SOLICITOR: DECLARATORY PROCEEDINGS: MEDICAL AND WELFARE DECISIONS FOR ADULTS WHO LACK CAPACITY)

1.   This practice note supersedes practice notes dated June 1996 (sterilisation: [1996] 2 FLR 111) and July 1996 (vegetative state: [1996] 2 FLR 375). It combines the guidance given in those earlier practice notes, and extends it to a wider range of medical and welfare disputes leading to litigation. This practice note deals only with adults who lack capacity. Medical treatment or welfare disputes about children will be dealt with under the Children Act 1989 or the inherent jurisdiction in relation to children (see practice notes The Official Solicitor: Appointment in Family Proceedings, April [2001] Fam Law 307 and Officers of CAFCASS Legal Services and Special Casework: Appointment in Family Proceedings, April [2001] Fam Law 249).

Jurisdiction

2.   The High Court has jurisdiction to make declarations as to the best interests of an adult who lacks decision-making capacity. The jurisdiction will be exercised when there is a serious justiciable issue requiring a decision by the court. It has been exercised in relation to a range of medical treatment issues, in particular sterilisation operations and the continuance of artificial nutrition and hydration. It has also been exercised in relation to residence and contact issues. The jurisdiction is comprehensively reviewed and analysed in *Re F (Adult: Court's Jurisdiction)* [2000] 2 FLR 512.

The need for court involvement

3.   Case law has established two categories of case that will in virtually all cases require the prior sanction of a High Court judge. The first is sterilisation of a person (whether a child or an adult) who cannot consent to the operation: *Re B (A Minor) (Wardship: Sterilisation)* [1988] AC 199 and *Re F (Mental patient: Sterilisation)* [1990] 2 AC 1. The second is the discontinuance of artificial nutrition and hydration for a patient in a vegetative state: *Airedale NHS Trust v. Bland* [1993] AC 789, 805. Further guidance about sterilisation and vegetative state cases is given below. In all other cases, doctors and carers should seek advice from their own lawyers about the need to apply to the court. In the Official Solicitor's view, applications should be made where there are disputes or difficulties as to either the patient's capacity or the patient's best interests. Guidelines were handed down by the Court of Appeal in *St George's Healthcare NHS Trust v. S; R v. Collins and Others ex parte S* [1998] 2 FLR 728, 758–760. It was stressed in that case that a declaration made without notice would be ineffective and ought not to be made.

The application

4.   Applications should be made to the Family Division of the High Court (principal or district registry). The proceedings are not, however, 'family proceedings' for the purposes of Civil Procedure Rules 1998, r 2.1(2). The Civil Procedure Rules will therefore apply.

The claim

5.   In the Official Solicitor's view, the Part 8 alternative procedure is the more appropriate and a Part 8 claim form should be used. The claimant should file all evidence with the claim form. The Official Solicitor is unlikely to be in a position to file all his evidence with his acknowledgment of service. A directions hearing should therefore be fixed when the claim form is issued.

6.   The relief sought should be declarations that (see appendices below for suggested wording in sterilisation and PVS cases):

1.   [the patient] lacks capacity to make a decision about . . . [specify treatment or welfare decision at issue, eg 'having a kidney transplant' or 'where to live'].

2.   It is [or is not] in the existing circumstances in the best interests of [the patient] for . . . [specify treatment or other issue, eg 'him to undergo below-knee amputation of his left leg' or 'her to have contact with the claimant for at least 2 hours each week'].

The evidence

7.   The claimant must adduce evidence going to both capacity and best interests.

1.   *Capacity* The court has no jurisdiction unless it is established that the patient is incapable of making a decision about the matter in issue. The test of capacity to consent to or refuse treatment is set out in *Re MB (Medical Treatment)* [1997] 2 FLR 426, 437. In the Official Solicitor's view, this test can be used for a wide range of decisions. Evidence from a psychiatrist or psychologist who has assessed the patient applying the *Re MB* test to the particular decision in question is generally required. It follows from the terms of the *Re MB* test that global psychometric test results are unlikely to be relevant. The Official Solicitor's experience is that references to the outdated and discredited concept of 'mental age' are of no assistance at all. It is important for the expert assessing capacity to advise whether the patient is likely to develop capacity to make personal decisions about the matter in issue in the future.

2.   *Best interests* In any medical case, the claimant must adduce evidence from a responsible medical practitioner not only (1) that performing the particular operation would not be negligent but also (2) that it is necessary in the best interests of the patient: *Re A (Male Sterilisation)* [2000] 1 FLR 549, 555. The court's jurisdiction is to declare the best interests of the patient on the application of a welfare test analogous to that applied in wardship: *Re S (Sterilisation: Patient's Best Interests)* [2000] 2 FLR 389, 403. The judicial decision will incorporate broader ethical, social, moral and welfare considerations (ibid, 401). Emotional, psychological and social benefit to the patient will be considered: *Re Y (Mental Patient: Bone Marrow Transplant)* [1997] Fam 110. The court will wish to prepare a balance sheet listing the advantages and disadvantages of the procedure for the patient. If potential advantages and disadvantages are to be relied on then the court will wish to assess in percentage terms the likelihood of them in fact occurring: *Re A (Male Sterilisation)* [2000] 1 FLR 549, 560.

The parties

8.   The claimant should be the NHS Trust or other body responsible for the patient's care, although a claim may also be brought by a family member or other individual closely

connected with the patient. The body with clinical or caring responsibility should in any event be made a party: *Re S (Hospital Patient: Court's Jurisdiction)* [1996] Fam 1.

9.   The person concerned must always be a party and should normally be a defendant, with the Official Solicitor acting as litigation friend. The Official Solicitor has a standard form of medical certificate if there is any question about whether the person concerned is a 'patient' within the meaning of Civil Procedure Rules 1998, r 21. If the Official Solicitor does not act as litigation friend, the court will wish to consider whether he should be joined as an ex officio defendant or invited to act as a friend of the court. The Official Solicitor is invariably asked to be involved in sterilisation and vegetative state cases.

The directions hearing

10.   Unless the matter is urgent, the claimant should fix a directions hearing for no less than 8 weeks after the date of issue, to allow the Official Solicitor to make initial enquiries. The court should, if appropriate, be asked to hold the directions hearing in private to protect the interests of the patient: Civil Procedure Rules 1998, r 39.2(3)(d). The court will use the directions hearing to:

1.   make orders where necessary to preserve the anonymity of the patient, family and other parties;
2.   set a timetable for the Official Solicitor to conduct enquiries, obtain expert evidence and file his statement or report;
3.   fix a further hearing, to serve either as a final hearing if the matter is unopposed or as a final directions hearing to fix a contested hearing.

The Official Solicitor's enquiries

11.   The Official Solicitor's representative will always see the patient, review relevant medical/social work records and interview carers, family members and others close to the patient as appropriate.
12.   The Official Solicitor will consider the patient's wishes and feelings, and will enquire as to any earlier views the patient may have expressed, either in writing or otherwise. The High Court may determine the effect of a purported advance statement as to future medical treatment: *Re T (Adult: Refusal of Medical Treatment)* [1993] Fam 95, *Re C (Adult: Refusal of Medical Treatment)* [1994] 1 WLR 290. A valid and applicable advance refusal of treatment may be determinative. Previously expressed wishes and feelings which do not amount to an effective advance decision will still be an important component in the best interests decision.

The final hearing

13.   Any substantive hearing should be before a High Court judge of the Family Division. Cases proceeding unopposed may be disposed of without oral evidence. The final hearing may be in private if necessary to protect the interests of the patient: Civil Procedure Rules 1998, r 39.2(3)(d). If the hearing is in public, there may be orders that the identities of parties and witnesses (other than expert witnesses) should not be disclosed: Civil Procedure Rules 1998, r 39.2(4). An order restricting publicity will continue to have effect notwithstanding the death of the patient, unless and until an application is made to discharge it: *Re C (Adult Patient: Publicity)* [1996] 2 FLR 251. The Official Solicitor will invite the court to make an appropriate order in relation to his costs.

Consultation with the Official Solicitor

14.   Members of the Official Solicitor's legal staff are prepared to discuss adult medical and welfare cases before proceedings are issued. Enquiries should be addressed to a family litigation lawyer at:

The Official Solicitor
81 Chancery Lane
London WC2A 1DD

Telephone: 020 7911 7127
Fax: 020 7911 7105
e-mail: enquiries@offsol.gsi.gov.uk

Enquiries about **children** medical and welfare cases should be directed to:
CAFCASS Legal Services and Special Casework
Newspaper House
8–16 Great New Street
London EC4A 3BN

Telephone: 020 7904 0867
Fax: 020 7904 0868/9
e-mail: legal@cafcass.gsi.gov.uk Staff of CAFCASS Legal will liaise with the Official
Solicitor where it is unclear which office can best represent a child.

Laurence Oates
Official Solicitor
1 May 2001

APPENDIX 1: STERILISATION CASES

1. If a sterilisation procedure is necessary for therapeutic as opposed to contraceptive
    purposes then there may be no need for an application to court: *Re GF (Medical
    Treatment)* [1992] 1 FLR 293. If, however, any case lies anywhere near the boundary
    line it should be referred to the court: *Re S (Sterilisation)* [2000] 2 FLR 389, 405.

The claim

2. The relief sought in relation to an adult should be declarations that:
    1. [The patient] lacks capacity to consent to an operation of . . . [specify proce-
        dure proposed, eg 'tubal occlusion by Filshie clips', or 'laparoscopic sub-total
        hysterectomy', or 'vasectomy'].
    2. It is in the existing circumstances in the best interests of [the patient] for her/him
        to undergo an operation of . . . [specify procedure as above].

The evidence

3. The court must be satisfied that the patient lacks capacity and that the operation will
    promote the best interests of the patient, rather than the interests or convenience of
    the claimant, carers or public. In sterilisation cases, the best interests tests has at least
    three particular components.
    1. *Likelihood of pregnancy*
        An operation must address a current real need. It must be shown that the patient
        is capable of conception and is having or is likely to have full sexual intercourse.
        In relation to a young woman who has no interest in human relationships with
        any sexual ingredient a high level of supervision is an appropriate protection: *Re
        LC (Medical Treatment)(Sterilisation)* [1997] 2 FLR 258 . Any risk of pregnancy
        should be identifiable rather than speculative: *Re S (Medical Treatment: Adult
        Sterilisation)* [1998] 1 FLR 944.
    2. *Damage deriving from conception and/or menstruation*
        The physical and psychological consequences of pregnancy and childbirth for
        the patient should be analysed by obstetric and psychiatric experts. In the case

of a male, these considerations will be different: *Re A (Male Sterilisation)* [2000] 1 FLR 549, 557. Psychiatric evidence as to the patient's likely ability to care for and/or have a fulfilling relationship with a child should be adduced. Evidence as to any child having a disability is likely to be irrelevant: *Re X (Adult Sterilisation)* [1998] 2 FLR 1124, 1129. If the proposed procedure is intended to affect the patient's menstruation, then evidence about any detriment caused by her current menstrual cycle must also be adduced.

3. *Medical and surgical techniques*
    The court will require a detailed analysis of all available and relevant methods of addressing any problems found to be substantiated under (1) and (2) above. This analysis should be performed by a doctor or doctors with expertise in the full range of available methods. The expert should explain the nature of each relevant method and then list its advantages and disadvantages (in particular, morbidity rates, mortality rates and failure rates) for the individual patient, taking into account any relevant aspects of her physical and psychological health. The Royal College of Obstetrics and Gynaecology has published relevant evidence-based clinical guidelines (No 4: *Male and Female Sterilisation*, April 1999 and No 5: *The Management of Menorrhagia in Secondary Care*, July 1999).

APPENDIX 2: PERMANENT VEGETATIVE STATE CASES

1. It is futile to provide medical treatment, including artificial nutrition and hydration, to a patient with no awareness of self or environment and no prospect of recovery: *Airedale NHS Trust v. Bland* [1993] AC 789, 869. The purpose of the proceedings is to establish whether the patient is in this condition. It is not appropriate to apply to court to discontinue artificial feeding and hydration until the condition is judged to be permanent. Diagnostic guidelines are not statutory provisions and a precise label may not be of importance. The court's concern is whether there is any awareness whatsoever or any possibility of change: *Re D (Medical Treatment)* [1998] 1 FLR 411, 420 and *Re H (A Patient)* [1998] 2 FLR 36. The approach of the court has been reviewed in the light of the Human Rights Act 1998 and held to be compatible with Convention rights: *NHS Trust A v. M: NHS Trust B v. H* [2001] 1 FCR 406. There has as yet been no decided case dealing with the discontinuance of artificial feeding and hydration for an adult patient with any (however minimal) awareness of self or environment.

The claim

2. All claims in these cases should be issued in the Principal Registry and will normally be heard by the President of the Family Division unless she releases the case to another Family Division judge. The relief sought should be declarations that :

    1. [The patient] lacks capacity to consent to continued life-sustaining treatment measures and is in the permanent vegetative state.
    2. It is not in the existing circumstances in the best interests of [the patient] to be given life-sustaining medical treatment measures (including ventilation, nutrition and hydration by artificial means) and such measures may lawfully be discontinued.
    3. It is in [the patient's] best interests to be given such treatment and nursing care whether at hospital or elsewhere under medical supervision as may be appropriate to ensure he/she retains the greatest dignity until such time as his/her life comes to an end.

The medical evidence

3. The diagnosis should be made in accordance with the most up-to-date generally accepted guidelines for the medical profession. A review by a working group of the Royal College of Physicians has been endorsed by the Conference of Medical Royal Colleges (**The Permanent Vegetative State**, Royal College of Physicians Publication Unit, 1996; with addendum published in J R Coll Physns (1997) 31, 260). The review concludes that the diagnosis of permanent vegetative state should not be made until the patient has been in a continuing vegetative state following head injury for 12 months or following other causes of brain damage for 6 months. The addendum to the review emphasises that there is no urgency in making the diagnosis and the assessors should take into account descriptions given by relatives, carers and nursing staff who spend most time with the patient. The **International Working Party Report on the Vegetative State** (1996), produced by the Royal Hospital for Neuro-disability, sets out in an appendix a range of vegetative presentations.

4. The claimant should, as a minimum, adduce evidence from (1) the treating physician and (2) a neurologist or other expert experienced in assessing disturbances of consciousness. Both should deal with the diagnosis and their professional judgment of whether continued treatment would be in the patient's best interests. The duties of doctors making the diagnosis are described in the Royal College of Physicians review.

5. The court will generally wish to see at least two reports from experts, one of whom must be independent of the treating clinical team and claimant. The Official Solicitor will usually commission the second expert report.

Other evidence

6. The claimant should also adduce evidence about the views of family members. The views of family members or others close to the patient cannot act as a veto to an application but they must be taken fully into account by the court: *Re G (Persistent Vegetative State)* [1995] 2 FCR 46, 51.

The final hearing

7. It is usual for the final hearing to be in public, with protection for the identities of parties and witnesses. Even if the matter is unopposed, it may be appropriate for at least one expert to attend to give oral evidence. Family members need not attend if this would cause distress.

Appendix 5
DEPARTMENT OF HEALTH INTERIM GUIDANCE: BOURNEWOOD CASE

10 December 2004

ADVICE ON THE DECISION OF THE EUROPEAN COURT OF HUMAN RIGHTS IN THE CASE OF HL v. UK (THE 'BOURNEWOOD' CASE) [Gateway Reference 4269]

Purpose

1. This note is to provide further information for NHS bodies and local authorities about the implications of the judgment of European Court of Human Rights in the case of HL v. UK (the 'Bournewood' case). It covers:

    ■ a summary of the case and the key points of the judgment (paragraphs 2 – 29)
    ■ steps to be taken by the Department of Health to develop proposals for new procedural safeguards (paragraphs 29 – 30)
    ■ steps that might be taken in the interim by NHS bodies and local authorities pending the development of those new safeguards (paragraphs 32 – 38).

The Case

2. The case concerned a man (Mr L) in his 40s with autism and learning disabilities. He is unable to speak and his level of understanding is limited. He is frequently agitated and has a history of self-harming behaviour. He lacks the capacity to consent or object to medical treatment.

3. For over 30 years Mr L was cared for in Bournewood Hospital ('the hospital'), a National Health Service trust hospital. In March 1994 he was discharged on a trial basis to paid carers with whom he successfully resided until July 1997.

4. In July 1997 Mr L was readmitted to Bournewood Hospital after an incident at a day-care centre when he became particularly agitated, hitting himself on the head with his fists and banging his head against the wall.

5. His consultant at the hospital considered detaining him under the Mental Health Act 1983 ('the 1983 Act') but concluded that that was not necessary as he was compliant and did not resist admission. Mr L was therefore admitted as an 'informal patient', in his own best interests under the common law doctrine of necessity. This was in line with standard practice. The consultant confirmed (in her submissions in the judicial review proceedings referred to below) that if the applicant had resisted admission, she would have detained him compulsorily under the 1983 Act as she was firmly of the view that he required in-patient treatment for his mental disorder. For clinical reasons, the consultant advised Mr L's carers against visiting him initially, it appears on the basis that Mr L would think each time that he could go home with them.

6. Around September 1997, legal action was begun on Mr L's behalf to secure (amongst other things) his discharge from hospital. The action was unsuccessful in the High Court, but in December 1997 the Court of Appeal held that Mr L had been unlawfully detained. It also found that because of the Mental Health Act 1983 the common law

doctrine of necessity could not be used to detain someone for treatment for mental disorder. Following this Mr L was formally detained under the Mental Health Act 1983, but was then discharged about six weeks later.

7.   The Court of Appeal's judgment was subsequently overturned on 25 June 1998 by the House of Lords who found that Mr L had not been detained. The case was then taken to the European Court of Human Rights ('the European Court'). A hearing took place on 27 May 2003, and the Court's judgment was published on 5 October 2004. The Court found that there had been a violation of Articles 5(1) and 5(4) ('Right to liberty and security') of the European Convention on Human Rights. It held that these findings of violation themselves constituted 'just satisfaction' and therefore rejected Mr L's claim for damages. Mr L was awarded costs against the UK Government of around €27,000.

8.   The full text of the judgment can be found on the European Court's website at http://www.echr.coe.int/Eng/Judgments.htm (Application number 45508/99).

The judgment and its implications

9.   The case has important implications for NHS bodies, local authorities and other bodies involved in providing or arranging the care and treatment of people who lack capacity to consent to treatment in hospital and possibly in other residential settings as well. (For convenience such people are referred to in this note as 'incapacitated.')

10.   As public authorities, NHS bodies and local authorities are required by the Human Rights Act 1998 to act in way which is compatible with Convention rights (except to the extent that they are prevented from doing so by primary legislation which cannot be read in a way which is compatible with the Convention).

(a) Deprivation of liberty

11.   The European Court found that Mr L had been deprived of his liberty within the meaning of Article 5(1) of the Convention which, in so far as is relevant, reads as follows:

> '1. Everyone has the right to liberty and security of person. No one shall be deprived of his liberty save in the following cases and in accordance with a procedure prescribed by law: . . .
>
> (e) the lawful detention . . . of persons of unsound mind, . . .;

12.   It is important to note that this judgment does not concern the treatment of incapacitated patients generally. It was concerned only with the question of deprivation of liberty of incapacitated person.

13.   The European Court made clear that the question of whether someone has, in fact, been deprived of liberty depends on the particular circumstances of the case. Specifically the Court said that:

> 'It is not disputed that in order to determine whether there has been a deprivation of liberty, the starting-point must be the specific situation of the individual concerned and account must be taken of a whole range of factors arising in a particular case such as the type, duration, effects and manner of implementation of the measure in question. The distinction between a deprivation of, and restriction upon, liberty is merely one of degree or intensity and not one of nature or substance.' [paragraph 89 of the judgment]

14.   The European Court's judgment does not, therefore, mean that incapacitated patients admitted to hospital or to care homes are automatically deprived of their liberty, even if staff would prevent them leaving unescorted for their own safety.

15. There must be particular factors which provide the 'degree' and 'intensity' to render the situation one of deprivation of liberty. The factors might relate, for example, to the type of care being provided, its duration, its effects and the way in which the admission came about.

16. In this case, the European Court said that

> 'the key factor in the present case [is] that the health care professionals treating and managing the applicant exercised complete and effective control over his care and movements':

and, noting that Mr L had been resident with his carers for over three years, the Court went on to say that

> 'the clear intention of Dr M and the other relevant health care professionals [was] to exercise strict control over his assessment, treatment, contacts and, notably, movement and residence: the applicant would only be released from the hospital to the care of Mr and Mrs E as and when those professionals considered it appropriate.' [paragraph 91]

17. Accordingly, the Court found that 'the concrete situation was that the applicant was under continuous supervision and control and was not free to leave.' [paragraph 91]

18. The Court attached particular importance to the fact that Mr L had a settled home with his paid carers to which he was prevented from returning and that his contact with those carers was (to some extent) restricted by the staff of the hospital. The Court did not consider the issue of whether the ward was 'locked' or 'lockable' to be determinative.

(b) Lack of procedural safeguards

19. Unlike the Court of Appeal, the European Court did not find that Mr L's rights had been breached simply because he was admitted to hospital on the basis of the common law doctrine of necessity (ie in his 'best interests'), rather than under specific statutory provisions (eg the Mental Health Act 1983) .

20. However, the Court did find that the absence of procedural safeguards surrounding his admission failed to protect him against 'arbitrary deprivations of liberty on grounds of necessity and, consequently, [failed] to comply with the essential purpose of Article 5(1) of the Convention.'

21. In this latter respect, the European Court was clearly influenced by the 'lack of any fixed procedural rules by which the admission and detention of compliant incapacitated persons is conducted' when contrasted with 'the extensive network of safeguards applicable to psychiatric committals covered by the [Mental Health Act] 1983'. The Court said,

> 'In particular and most obviously, the Court notes the lack of any formalised admission procedures which indicate who can propose admission, for what reasons and on the basis of what kind of medical and other assessments and conclusions. There is no requirement to fix the exact purpose of admission (for example, for assessment or for treatment) and, consistently, no limits in terms of time, treatment or care attach to that admission. Nor is there any specific provision requiring a continuing clinical assessment of the persistence of a disorder warranting detention.' [paragraph 120]

22. The European Court also said,

'the nomination of a representative of a patient who could make certain objections and applications on his or her behalf is a procedural protection accorded to those committed involuntarily under the 1983 Act and which would be of equal importance for patients who are legally incapacitated and have, as in the present case, extremely limited communication abilities.' [paragraph 120]

by which it presumably had in mind the role of the nearest relative under the Mental Health Act 1983.

23. Above all, although it did not question their good faith, the Court seems to have been concerned that the hospital's health care professionals were able to assume

'full control of the liberty and treatment of a vulnerable incapacitated individual solely on the basis of their own clinical assessments completed as and when they considered fit.' [paragraph 121]

24. The Court did not say that Mr L should have been formally detained under the Mental Health Act 1983. Nor, in the Government's view, does the judgment mean that procedural safeguards for people in Mr L's position must be identical to those for patients detained under the Mental Health Act 1983. Indeed, the Court noted the 'Government's understandable concern . . . to avoid the full, formal and inflexible impact of the 1983 Act.'

25. However, the Government accepts that to avoid further violations of Article 5(1) new procedural safeguards are required for patients who are not formally detained, but who are, in effect, deprived of their liberty in their best interests under the common law doctrine of necessity.

(c) Breach of Article 5(4)

26. The European Court also found a violation of Mr L's rights under Article 5(4) of the Convention, which reads as follows:

'Everyone who is deprived of his liberty by arrest or detention shall be entitled to take proceedings by which the lawfulness of his detention shall be decided speedily by a court and his release ordered if the detention is not lawful.'

27. The European Court said that Article 5(4) gives

'the right to an individual deprived of his liberty to have the lawfulness of that detention reviewed by a court in the light, not only of domestic law requirements, but also of the text of the Convention, the general principles embodied therein and the aim of the restrictions permitted by paragraph 1: the scheme of Article 5 implies that the notion of 'lawfulness' should have the same significance in paragraphs 1 (e) and 4 [of Article 5] in relation to the same deprivation of liberty. This does not guarantee a right to review of such scope as to empower the court on all aspects of the case or to substitute its own discretion for that of the decision-making authority. The review should, however, be wide enough to bear on those conditions which are essential for the lawful detention of a person, in this case, on the ground of unsoundness of mind'

28. The European Court also found that, at the time (in 1997 and 1998), neither judicial review nor any other legal remedy was sufficient to guarantee a review of this nature.

29. The Government's view is that action has already been taken in the Human Rights Act 1998 to prevent further violations of Article 5(4).[1]

Next Steps

(a) Proposals for new procedural safeguards

30. As set out above, the Government accepts that to avoid further violations of Article 5(1) additional procedural safeguards are required for incapacitated patients who are not formally detained, but who are, in effect, deprived of their liberty.

31. It will therefore bring forward proposals for appropriate new safeguards as soon as possible. Before doing so, it will consult with interested parties, including representative groups, the NHS and local authorities. Its aim is to ensure that there are procedural safeguards which are effective, proportionate and deliverable in practice.

(b) Steps that might be taken in the interim by NHS bodies and local authorities

32. Until these safeguards are established in law, the effect of the judgment is that it would be unlawful for an NHS body or a local authority (without the prior authorisation of the High Court) to arrange or provide care or treatment for an incapacitated patient in a way that amounted to deprivation of liberty within the meaning of article 5 of the Convention, unless the patient were detained under the Mental Health Act 1983.

33. Nonetheless, the NHS and local authorities will need to continue to provide care and treatment for incapacitated patients, and it is important that neither the safety of those patients nor the quality of the care they receive is jeopardised during the interim period.

34. Pending the development of new safeguards described above, NHS bodies and local authorities will want to consider what steps they can take in the short-term to protect incapacitated people against the risk of arbitrary deprivation of liberty and minimise the risk of further successful legal challenges.

35. The Government suggests that NHS bodies and local authorities will want to ensure they have systems in place so that when making arrangements to provide care to an incapacitated person which involves a restriction on the liberty of that person consideration is given to whether what they are proposing amounts in practice to a deprivation of that person's liberty within the meaning of article 5 of the Convention, taking into account the range of factors identified by the Court as described in paragraphs 12 to 19 above. The same question will need to be asked when reviewing the circumstances of those people who they have already placed who may, in practice, be deprived of their liberty.

36. If patients are considered to be deprived of their liberty (or at risk of it), consideration should always be given to alternatives to ensure that they get adequate care but which falls short of deprivation of liberty. In particular, authorities will want wherever possible to avoid situations in which professionals may be said to take 'full and effective control' over patients' care and liberty.

37. Elements of good practice which are likely to assist in this, and in avoiding the risk of legal challenge, may include:

　– ensuring that decisions are taken (and reviewed) in a structured way, which includes safeguards against arbitrary deprivation of liberty. There should, for example, be a proper assessment of whether the patient lacks capacity to decide whether or not to accept the care proposed, and that decision should taken on the basis of proper medical advice by a person properly equipped to make the judgment

　– effective, documented care planning (including the Care Programme Approach where relevant) for such patients, including appropriate and documented involve-

---

[1] The Government is considering whether any further action is needed in the light of the Court of Appeal's judgment of 3 December in the case of R (MH) v. Secretary of State for Health, which concerned the Mental Health Act 1983.

ment of family, friends, carers (both paid and unpaid) and others interested in their welfare

–   ensuring that alternatives to admission to hospital or residential care are considered and that any restrictions placed on the patient while in hospital or residential care should be kept to the minimum necessary in all the circumstances of their case

–   ensuring appropriate information is given to patients themselves and to family, friends and carers. This would include information about the purpose and reasons for the patient's admission, proposals to review the care plan and the outcome of such reviews, and the way in which they can challenge decisions (eg through the relevant complaints procedure). The involvement of local advocacy services where these are available could be encouraged to support patients and their families, friends and carers

–   taking proper steps to help patients retain contact with family, friends, carers, with proper consideration given to the views of those people. If, exceptionally, there are good clinical reasons why that is not in the patient's best interests, those reasons should be properly documented and explained to the people they affect

–   ensuring both the assessment of capacity and the care plan are kept under review. It may well be helpful to include an independent element in the review. Depending on the circumstances, this might be achieved by involvement of social work or community health staff, or by seeking a second medical (or other appropriate clinical) opinion either from within the organisation or elsewhere. Such a second opinion will be particularly important where family members, carers or friends do not agree with the authority's decisions. But even where there is no dispute an authority must ensure its decision making stands up to scrutiny;

38. If it is concluded that there is no way of providing appropriate care which does not amount to deprivation of liberty, then consideration will have to be given to using the formal powers of detention in the Mental Health Act 1983. However, it is important to remember that:

■   nothing in the judgment changes the requirements in the Mental Health Act which must be met before patients can be detained. It should not therefore be assumed that all patients who are to be subject to restrictions which may amount to deprivation of liberty can be detained under the Act. (For example, it would be unlawful to detain patients under the Act if their mental disorder does not warrant detention in hospital, although reception into guardianship under the Act might be appropriate in some cases.)

■   there are dangers in using the Act simply to be 'on the safe side'. Although it provides procedural safeguards, the use of the Mental Health Act will not necessarily be welcomed by patients themselves or by their family, friends or carers, given the 'stigma' that is often (wrongly) perceived to attach to it. Moreover, a significant increase in the use of the Mental Health Act will inevitably put considerable further pressure on local authority approved social workers, the availability of second opinion appointed doctors (SOADs) and on the operation of Mental Health Review Tribunals (MHRT).

Further Information

39. For inquiries about this note, please write to the Bournewood Team, Room 315, Department of Health, Wellington House, 133–155 Waterloo Road, London SE1 8UG, or via MBBournewood.Advice@dh.gsi.gov.uk Please note, however, that the Department cannot provide legal advice to individual NHS bodies, local authorities, or independent providers. They must take their own legal advice.

Department of Health
10 December 2004

Appendix 6
RESOURCES

BMA guidance

Advance statements about medical treatment, 1995
The older person: consent and care, 1995
Medical Ethics Today: the BMA's Handbook of Ethics and Law, 2nd Edn, BMJ Books, 2004
Withholding and Withdrawing Life-Prolonging Medical Treatment: Guidance for Decision-Making, 2nd Edn, BMJ Books, 2001

Books

Heywood and Massey Court of Protection Practice, Thomson/Sweet and Maxwell, 2001
Cretney and Lush on Enduring Powers of Attorney, 5th Edn, Jordans, 2001
The Court of Protection Practice, Martin Terrell, Tolleys, 2003
Assessment of Mental Capacity: Guidance for Doctors and Lawyers, 2nd Edn, The Law Society and BMJ, 2002
Mental Health Act Manual, Richard Jones, 9th Edn, Thomson/Sweet and Maxwell, 2004
Principles of Medical Law, ed. Andrew Grubb, 2nd Edn, OUP, 2004
Medical Law (Text with materials), Kennedy and Grubb, 3rd Edn, Butterworths, XXXX

Department of Health guidance

No secrets: guidance on developing and implementing multi-agency policies and procedures to protect vulnerable adults from abuse
Confidentiality: NHS Code of Practice

Law Commission reports

Mentally incapacitated adults and decision-making: an overview, London: HMSO, 1991 (Law Com No 119)
Mentally incapacitated adults and decision-making: a new jurisdiction, London: HMSO, 1993 (Law Com No 128)
Mentally incapacitated adults and decision-making: medical treatment and research, London: HMSO, 1993 (Law Com No 129)
Mentally incapacitated adults and other vulnerable adults: public law protection, London: HMSO, 1993 (Law Com 130)
Mental incapacity, London: HMSO, 1995 (Law Com 231)

Websites

Royal College of Psychiatrists	www.rcpsych.ac.uk
Royal College of Nurses	www.rcn.org.uk
Nursing and Midwifery Council	www.ukcc.org.uk
Disability Rights Commission	www.drc.org.uk
Department of Health	www.dh.gov.uk
Law Society	www.lawsociety.org.uk
BMA	www.bma.org.uk/ethics
Mind	www.mind.org.uk

Convention on the International Protection of Adults	www.hcch.net/e/conventions
Making Decisions Alliance	www.makingdecisions.org.uk
The Public Guardianship Office which includes the Court of Protection	www.guardianship.gov.uk
The Official Solicitor	www.offsol.demon.co.uk

INDEX

Elderly Client Handbook

3rd edition

General Editors:
Caroline Bielanska & Martin Terrell
Consultant Editor:
Gordon R. Ashton

Published in association with
Solicitors for the Elderly

Advising elderly clients requires an
up-to-date knowledge of many varied
areas of law and practice. This book
provides a succinct guide to all the relevant law, together with practical
advice on the running and marketing of an elderly client practice.

It provides clear and up-to-date analysis of:
• British Banking Association's guidelines
• Mental Incapacity Bill
• Financial Services Act 2000
• Reforms to health and social care
• Care Standards Act 2000
• Changes to the Court of Protection and Public Guardianship Office
• Benefits including Pension Credit.

The third edition has been fully revised by a team of new
contributors drawn from the membership of Solicitors for the Elderly
and experts in the fields of mental capacity, mental health law and
employment law.

Available from Marston Book Services:
Tel. 01235 465 656

1 85328 872 1
520 pages
March 2004
£44.95

The Law Society

Will Draftsman's Handbook

8th Edition

Robin Riddett

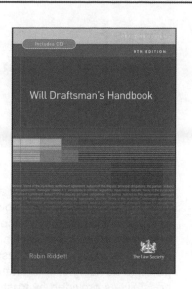

This authoritative reference book provides the will draftsman with the tools needed to prepare wills for the more commonly encountered situations. The text is split into three parts:

- commentary – provides an analysis of the underlying law
- precedent clauses which can be readily assembled to make up wills for most circumstances
- statutory material – extracts from the legislation which informs the law.

Written in plain English, the book takes a practical and up-to-date approach to will drafting which helps make wills comprehensible to clients. As well as commonly used draft wills, over 75 individual clauses are appended on an accompanying CD-ROM for easy word-processing.

Available from Marston Book Services:
Tel. 01235 465 656.

1 85328 826 8
224 pages with CD-ROM
£49.95
Sept. 2004

The Law Society

Trust Practitioner's Handbook

Gill Steel

The creation, administration and taxation of trusts, and the powers and duties of trustees, are now heavily regulated areas. This Handbook provides an accessible guide to advising clients on the possibilities provided by trusts, the tax position, and the administration of trusts.

Busy practitioners will wish to avoid negligence for failing to invest correctly and avoid tax penalties for missing tax deadlines or incorrectly assessing tax bills. Good systems can help and this book addresses how these systems might be used. Delegation of trust management functions like investment advice must comply with the practitioner's regulatory regime and guidance is given on how this should be approached. Making trust administration pay is a challenge and the book also provides ideas to improve profitability.

A 'good practice' guide for all those involved in the administration of trusts, this book makes trusts law accessible with checklists, examples, precedents and case studies.

Available from Marston Book Services:
Tel. 01235 465 656.

1 85328 945 0
432 pages
£49.95
October 2005

The Law Society